fashion today

fashion today
Colin McDowell

Φ

CONTENTS

INTRODUCTION   Dress is servant and messenger to society. Whether speaking in whispers or shouts, it is always heeded because it presages a desire, a need, an imperative of society. Frequently, it articulates that need before other areas of life dare give it voice. The crucial preliminary to an examination of the fashion of the past fifty years must be an acceptance of the social changes which have subverted society; the essential background at the beginning of the period, of how it was organized and for whom. Then, as now, its diversities are essential to its nature. As is to be expected of the art form which, albeit minor, reacts more speedily and completely than any other to the social, political and cultural nuances of its times, fashion in the last fifty years has undergone fundamental changes which reflect society's shifting emphases and altered priorities in a period of unprecedented flux.

Like any other, the twentieth century has known wars, but not all have been military. One could argue that the battles which will have the most far-reaching consequences, stretching well into the next century, have been ideological. Nothing to do with gunfire or trench warfare, they have marked the fight for the freedom of the individual which in its intensity, it is clear with hindsight, marks this century as different from all others.

The century which began as paternalistic ends with every social tenet under constant review. In 1900, kings ruled and aristocratic tastes held sway. Now, the handful of royal families that remain are diminished in power and credibility. The aristocratic ideal has been largely supplanted by middle-class attitudes which, in their turn, are increasingly questioned by working-class cultures based on the emotive power of television, sport and pop music. As ethnic alternatives – religious and philosophical – gain a foothold on a world scale, Western culture, which dominated the world at the turn of the century, no longer seems so all-embracing. The balance between East and West, or rich and poor, which seemed so fixed and firm a hundred years ago, tilts further from its early twentieth-century position with each decade.

Fashion has been at the forefront of the ideological wars, frequently used to clothe radical attitudes and instantly signal a rejection of the past. And, although the first rumblings of social change were apparent even in the last century and gained momentum in the first half of this, it is only in the past fifty years that the

ideological battles and the dress that clothes them have become crucial to the development of society.

The battles for freedoms have been fought on four fronts. Although clearly defined, they also overlap at crucial strategic points. As women have challenged men for the right to stand equal with them, and youth has taken on age in the fight for cultural supremacy, so everyone – young, old, male, female – has fought for the most fundamental of freedoms – the right of the individual to fulfil a personal sexuality without fear of social or cultural reprisals.

After fifty years of open and often intense fighting, there are encouraging signs of a clear victory for the sanctity of the rights of the individual. But there is a bigger and even more crucial battle still being fought. It is the struggle for ethnic equality which, unlike the other three, has really only occurred in the past half century. It is a battle that will bring its benefits – freedom of women, enfranchisement of youth and sexual liberty – to all people, regardless of creed or colour.

It is these battles and their outcomes which have marked the past fifty years most conspicuously: they will decide how life will be lived in the next century, and how it will be clothed. The second half of the twentieth century has witnessed a cultural shift, dramatic in its breadth and intensity. For the first time in history, fashion is now perceived as central to existence by vast numbers of people of all ages and social backgrounds, many of whom have been traditionally excluded from its influence. For some, the young in particular, it has become an obsession. Fashion is now at the heart of global culture, alongside pop music and, increasingly, sport.

Possessions and their acquisition are crucial to democracy. They are not only bonding agents within society, they can also prevent boredom: considered by many to be the greatest cultural danger likely to confront the replete and pampered West in the early twenty-first century. Consumerism – and especially clothes consumerism – is now seen as the tangible proof of individual freedom, and governments acknowledge and accept this. Education may falter and medical services may collapse through under-funding, but no government has the courage to tax its people sufficiently to alleviate the problems. Most governments in the Western world accept that individuals must be allowed to retain enough of their earnings – even at the cost of endangering vital social services – to indulge the desire to possess: a desire which manifests itself most clearly in the changing of wardrobe. It is a defining characteristic of Western society that individuality be allowed to express itself through appearance.

So the century which began with fashion as an elitist pleasure ends with decorative dress as not only a central prop of life, available to all, but also something much deeper than the age-old urge for self-adornment. From the indulgence of turn-of-the-century fashionable life, when clothes were changed several times a day for no reason other than the joy of parading social power through endless display, we now have 'round-the-clock' fashion, acknowledging no change in the time of day or, increasingly, even of season. Furthermore, fashion becomes less sexually specific with each passing decade as men and women assume clothing common to either sex.

The female body, for so long disguised and kept hidden, is trimmed and toned to fit current ideas of fitness and sexuality. Women may now appear in public seminude without fear of social criticism. Whereas traditionally, decisions over female dress have been made by men, women are now, in most societies, finally allowed to make their own choices. Even the age of sexual desirability, divorced from the age-old link with physical maturity and child-bearing ability, is now in flux. Prepubescence has been acknowledged, through fashion, as one of the acceptable notes on the lengthening scale of sexuality.

The male body has traditionally been clothed to display attitudes to the self much more conspicuously than the female. It has also been dressed to present a protective shell contrived to inhibit any questioning of the power which gave men the final say in all things, spiritual and secular. The stringent dress rules necessary to underpin male assumptions of superiority have been fatally undermined in the last fifty years as young men have refused to use their clothing to buy into antiquated and sterile social attitudes. Within the last decade there has been another shift as the male body, increasingly unclothed, has become an icon, part of the intertwined cults of athleticism and narcissism which have spread across class and age barriers as a result of the central cultural position held by sport.

Consumerism, feminism, the new man, black power, gay pride, youth attitudes: all have developed dramatically in the last fifty years, just as they have all been given physical form by fashion. In the most pragmatic century of the millennium, fashion has proved the most volatile and reactive of all the forces forming modern society. In the past twenty years, it has taken a central role not only in the world's economy but also in the development of its creative and artistic movements. Fashion has become important as the catalyst that makes developments in most areas of life possible; it increasingly releases our imaginations and enables us to accept new ideas and concepts. From having been dismissed as trivial and nothing more than a female diversion, fashion has become the single creative force most likely to influence us all.

How such changes have taken place in the last fifty years is as important as looking at what they are. Fashion travels in a continuous line and the present can only be fully illuminated by an understanding of the past. What happened in the Fifties and Sixties, or even earlier, links directly with the preoccupations and interests of fashion in the present. Designers become enmeshed in the glamour of the past, and then reproduce it in a way that both reflects the present and presages the future. We live in an era of revivals. Designers revisit the work of their predecessors, just as Christian Dior did for his New Look and Barbara Hulanicki of Biba did for her pastiche approach to the Thirties.

In fact, as the millennium turns, fashion is more diverse than it was even in the Seventies. Its sources are eclectic and often contradictory. An exercise in intellectual problem-solving in the hands of designers such as Martin Margiela, Ann Demeulemeester and Jil Sander; a potpourri of historic style when seen through the eyes of Alexander McQueen, Dolce & Gabbana or Anna Sui; the city streets writ large in the styles of Marc Jacobs, Calvin Klein and Tom Ford at Gucci, and a circus-master's extravaganza at the crack of a whip in the showings of Christian Lacroix, John Galliano and Jean Paul Gaultier. All things are possible and anything goes in this world where boundaries buckle and fall; parameters are endlessly redrawn and preconceptions are dismissed as so much prejudice. The world of fashion today is as challenging, rewarding and vocal as in any previous period.

This is not a consecutive history of the last fifty years. Each chapter is completely self-contained and should be read separately.

NEW LOOKS

1   (Opener)
     Christian Dior
     woollen dress,
     1948, photo
     Clifford Coffin

2   (Previous page)
     Christian Dior
     'Jungle' dress,
     1947

3   (Previous page)
     Sophia Loren at
     an Yves Saint
     Laurent show,
     1958

4   Christian Dior,
     'Bar' suit, 1947,
     drawing by René
     Gruau

Modern fashion can conveniently be said to start with the New Look, introduced in his first collection by Christian Dior. In fashion terms, it was an act of legerdemain, in that what Dior proposed on the morning of 12 February 1947 was not actually the radical departure from the past suggested by the expression 'New Look' (coined, as far as fashion legend is concerned, by Carmel Snow, editor-in-chief of the American edition of *Harper's Bazaar*). It was a misnomer, but that does not minimize Dior's achievement. As a first collection, it was a *tour de force*, bringing back to fashion a delicacy and femininity not seen in Paris since before the German Occupation in 1940. And, to eyes starved of refinement after the protracted years of war, it certainly gave the illusion of being fresh and different from the clothes that had immediately preceded it. Women who had been used to buying high fashion clothes before the war were overjoyed by the subliminal nostalgia in the collection.

They claimed that Dior made them feel feminine again, to a degree denied them since the Thirties – although what he was proposing had roots going back much further. The constricted, preening figure of the *belle époch* and every variation it produced until the outbreak of World War I was his inspiration. After the years of wartime clothing rations, his designs were extravagant. As *Vogue* wrote in April 1948, 'Dior uses fabric lavishly in skirts – fifteen yards in a woollen day dress, twenty-five in a short taffeta evening dress. He pads these skirts with stiff cambric; builds corsets and busts into the dresses so that they practically stand alone.' Women wishing to return to the delicate femininity of late Thirties' fashion were thrilled.

Others were less easily swayed. World War II had ended in Britain on an idealistic high note. At no previous time in history had the classes identified so closely with each other. On a wave of euphoria and hope for the future, a radical Labour government under Clement Attlee had been given a landslide mandate not only to make postwar Britain great again, but also to bring to British society the sense of fairness and concern for the underdog which produced the Welfare State, with the proper provision of education, social security and health guarantees as the right of all citizens, in what was hoped would be a completely new, classless society. Nothing could have been more out of tune with such thinking than the New Look. It was seen as a symbol of the old luxuries and privileges which many genuinely thought the war had destroyed.

More than that, the New Look was deemed by many as old-fashioned in what it was saying about femininity. World War II, for all its tragedies and privations, had been a liberating experience for many women. Freed from the shackles of domestic service or the difficulties of running a home and bringing up a family, women who had been mobilized in the forces or worked on the war effort in factories, doing jobs previously reserved for men, were not prepared to accept the psychology behind the romantic mood of the New Look.

In America, Dior's collection initially seemed even more remote from the lives of modern women. The war had cut the American fashion trade off from what had previously been considered the wellspring not only of fashion ingenuity but also of taste. Like most countries in the late Thirties, America had seemed, in fashion terms, to suffer from an inferiority complex when faced with the

5

apparent omniscience of Paris fashion. But U-boats and submarines effectively severed the New World from the Old for five years. And, although America joined the war after the bombing of Pearl Harbor in 1941, and its citizens were subjected to a degree of wartime austerities (such as certain restrictions in clothing), the United States was too far removed from the conflict for fashion to come to a five-year halt there, as it did in countries physically closer to the major theatres of war. The result was that Seventh Avenue in New York, then, as now, the heart of the American fashion industry, took courage, had faith in indigenous designers and moved forward in a way far in advance of the proposals that were being made by Christian Dior.

America, the consumer nation *par excellence*, had seen the rise of a new kind of fashion purchaser during the war years, a woman different from her predecessors, who was, in the long run, to have a much greater influence on fashion than Christian Dior and most of the couturiers working in Paris immediately after the war could possibly imagine. The young American woman emerged as a potent commercial force through the bobbysoxer and the teenager – species unknown in Europe at the time, where fashion was still dominated by the mature woman of comfortable means.

Magazines – a sure-fire proof of the power of a new spirit in fashion – sprang up to service her needs. The most influential, because it was most successfully attuned to the new direction, was *Junior Bazaar*, a young version of *Harper's Bazaar* and, like it, published by William Randolph Hearst. Launched in 1945 under the artistic direction of Alexey Brodovitch, whose work on *Harper's Bazaar* (which he joined in 1934) had already broken dramatic new ground in magazine design, *Junior Bazaar* featured the often startling work

of new young photographers such as Richard Avedon and Lillian Bassman. The magazine lasted until 1948, when it was subsumed into *Harper's Bazaar* – in itself a proof of the power of young fashion approaches and their influence on a wider age range – by which time the importance of Junior Miss Fashions (the first clothes ranges designed, sized and priced exclusively for the younger woman) was established in America, although nowhere else for another decade.

Even so, at the time, youth fashion seemed little more than an adjunct to mainstream dress, although, with hindsight, it was clearly the first herald of the future. It is no exaggeration to say that the casual, youth-orientated sportswear that has had so much fashion influence in the last twenty years – and one which seems likely to continue for at least the same number of years again – began in the apparently unpromising soil of small-town and Middle America. Its forcing ground was the college sorority leagues, their fads and crazes which seemed not only unimportant but also foolish compared with the massively funded and heavily advertised mainstream fashion industry of America, the giant and hugely powerful ready-to-wear companies based on New York's Seventh Avenue.

But if *Junior Bazaar* was pedalling an all-American, rather demure image of young womanhood – dominated by deodorants and 'squeaky-clean' hair – the major American magazines of the late Forties and Fifties were firmly behind what was happening in Paris. *Vogue* (still under the indomitable editorship of Edna Woolman Chase, who had held the role – which many thought made her the most important woman in fashion – since 1914), *Harper's Bazaar* (with Carmel Snow as editor-in-chief, Diana Vreeland as fashion editor and Alexey Brodovitch as art editor – to many, the winning hand of

7   Paris collections
     at the Hall
     of Mirrors,
     Versailles, 1952,
     photo Frances
     McLaughlin-Gill

8   Lanvin-Castillo,
     1952, photo
     Frances
     McLaughlin-Gill

9   (Overleaf)
     Christian Dior,
     1960, photo
     Mike De Dulmen

10   (Overleaf)
     Christian Dior,
     1960, photo
     Mike De Dulmen

8

the century) and less specialist magazines such as *Ladies Home Journal*, all backed Paris and the New Look.

America, with its varied climate, diverse culture and huge distances, was unified in the Thirties and Forties by the spoken and written word, through radio and magazines (not by newspapers, which, with only one or two exceptions, saw their remit as serving only localized needs and interests), in a way no other countries were – or needed to be – before television, the global unifier. The effect of magazines on U.S. fashion thinking cannot be over-stressed. Their finest hour was the Fifties, when they became American taste-, opinion- and dream-makers as powerfully as the movies had been earlier.

So, why did the big guns of the American fashion media, although by no means ignoring indigenous designers, back French fashion in the late Forties? As far as the demands of their readers, there was little necessity. A 'Paris gown' or a 'French *chapeau*' were still bywords for luxury and sophistication but, rather like 'French champagne', they were more generic terms for a frame of mind than anything else. With their buying power, middle-class American women in the Fifties were at the centre of a consumer boom impossible for their contemporaries in Europe – still ravaged by the results of war, with dysfunctional cities, armies of dispossessed, shortages and penury – to dream of, let alone comprehend. And they were as happy to be led into buying French clothes – or, at least, good copies of them – as they were into supporting home-grown designers. 'Dollar-minded patriotism', as it has been called, certainly existed. Many Americans, remembering the privations of the

post-Depression Thirties, were unhappy with buying foreign imports, but the vast wealth of the country seemed so omnipotent that most felt there was room for duality in fashion. The consumer boom swallowed up most objections on a wave of buying euphoria that included houses, televisions, cars and clothes. The films *Mr Blandings Builds his Dream House* (1948) and *The Women* (1939), which featured a long fashion sequence, were massive, long-running box-office hits. Europe might be starving, and frequently freezing, in the postwar years, but America appeared to have found its permanent place in the economic sun. The dark undercurrents of the Cold War, McCarthyism and the investigations of the House Committee on Un-American Activities did nothing to dim the sparkling pages of the consumer magazines. The disgrace of the treatment of blacks in the South was, literally, unknown to the majority of female American consumers, cloistered on the East or West Coasts or in one or two prosperous cities in between. The fashion industry was indifferent to social problems, and wished only to serve a burgeoning middle-class need for fashionable clothes. Whereas the defence industry had Franklin Delano Roosevelt's Executive Order 8802 of 1941, forbidding racial discrimination in any firm supplying the government, no such thing existed on Seventh Avenue.

The fashion industry aimed its products, and its advertising, squarely at middle-class white women. In this, editors of the glossy style magazines gave crucial help. As far as they were concerned, the American concept of taste in fashion was based on the matrix proposed in Paris. Ladylike in appearance and manner, the woman of fashion was an easily understood icon in

12

a society more feverishly upwardly mobile than its European counterpart. Whereas in America, 'class' was linked with disposable income which enabled a lifestyle – clothes, home, membership of the social and golf club, transport and travel – to be created and called 'fashion', European class, especially in Britain, was still based on the difficult and amorphous concept of 'breeding'.

Paradoxically, the French ideal of fashion was headlined through a group of American women who, although very rich, owed their position as social and fashionable leaders to the breeding they so successfully married into, becoming more European than American in many cases. That notwithstanding, they were paraded by the fashion magazines as talismans of taste for the American middle-class woman. Beloved of fashion editors, they represented the snobbery inherent in *haute couture* in a form acceptable to readers because they were Americans, and, on the premise that every woman could be like them (with luck), not only their clothes, but also their homes, holidays and social lives were accepted as the standard for which middle-class American women should strive.

As fashion icons, they had a lot going for them. Mona Bismarck, known as the Kentucky Countess because of her upbringing in the Bluegrass State, married Harrison Williams, one of America's richest men, became a close friend of the Duchess of Windsor and was immortalized in a Cole Porter song. On Williams's death in 1953 she married Count Edward Bismarck, grandson of Germany's 'Iron Chancellor', Prince Otto von Bismarck. She had homes in Paris and New York, estates in Palm Beach and on Capri and, at her death in 1983, left a $22 million fortune. She shopped in Paris, almost exclusively at Balenciaga, whose formal evening clothes she often wore for the many portrait photographs taken by her friend Cecil Beaton. She was never out of the society and fashion magazines of America. Always immaculate in her couture clothes, she was perhaps the foremost of a group whose dress was of consuming interest to magazine editors: Elsie de Wolfe, who had backed the American designer Mainbocher when he opened his couture house in Paris in the Thirties; Millicent Rogers, for whom the New York couturier Charles James created some of the most amazingly engineered evening dresses of the century; Pauline de Rothschild, endlessly photographed by Horst P. Horst for *Vogue*, and one of the early supporters of Yves Saint Laurent; 'Babe' Paley, Slim Keith, C.Z. Guest and Gloria Guinness, dubbed the 'swans' by Truman Capote in acknowledgement of their elegance and style. These were the women who gave magazine editors the excuse to turn back to Paris in the

13   Spread from U.S.
      Vogue, 1954

14   Jockey Club
      Race, Paris, 1956,
      photo Jeanloup
      Sieff

late Forties, and to keep returning there throughout the Fifties and Sixties. They were always known by their husband's Christian names rather than their own – Mrs William Paley, Mrs Winston Guest – because, as trophy wives, they were part of the male achievement. Their husbands owned not only millions of dollars' worth of stock; bloodstock aplenty in Wyoming or Kentucky and property in all the places where its value could do nothing but grow, in addition, they had a wife whose fame was based solely on her appearance (for which he paid) – an appearance rarely, if ever, threatened by pregnancies. Such men expected their famous wives to dress with dignity and propriety, and so they did.

These famous wives were a godsend for magazine editors, not only because their clothes, dinner tables and gardens photographed so superbly (representing some of the earliest examples of what the novelist Tom Wolfe was to describe later as 'the graphic depiction of the acts of the rich'), but also because their American roots, and the U.S. money they were so firmly planted in, removed any criticism that might otherwise have been levelled at them for being 'un-American' by shopping exclusively in Europe. The fact is, American magazines needed Paris fashions not only for the clothes but also for the huge advertising budgets that went with them. There was a simple, perfectly understood (but never stated) equation: the editors showed the clothes, the firms placed advertisements, normally for the big money-spinners – perfume, makeup and beauty products bearing the name of a great French fashion house; the readers were given the dream fantasy which magazine coverage of couture always aims at providing but, in this case, in a form acceptable to the United States – on the backs not only of real women, but real American women, who had 'made it' by American standards.

If couture creations from Paris were featured in American magazines as a snob attraction, that was

not their only purpose. As early as the Thirties, it had become apparent that French couture, faced with rising costs, could not rely solely on its traditional market of very rich women as unquestioningly as bespoke tailors could rely on their husbands. As life became less subject to rules, informality crept into the world of women's clothing. It was the beginning of the long, slow decline of couture, which, despite enthusiastic talk of its revitalization, is still continuing today, over seventy years later. As good-quality ready-to-wear clothes became more available, the effort and cost of having everything in one's wardrobe made by hand seemed unnecessary to all but the most fashion-obsessed.

Aware of these problems threatening the continuing excellence of traditional French dressmaking – seen more clearly in the Fifties, when fortunes had been lost and poverty faced those who had previously assumed themselves and their wealth to be untouchable – French couturiers set up a marriage of mutual convenience with some of Seventh Avenue's most successful manufacturers. After Dior's New Look, it was clear that Seventh Avenue still required the stimulus of the French. The old loyalties were put back in place as the American manufacturers paid for the right to copy Paris originals, to sell under their own or, at much greater cost, the original couturier's label – in which case they had to make line-for-line copies, using the same material, buttons and trims as the original garment that had appeared on the couturier's runway.

This was a marvellous way for rich American women to obtain that Parisian look; for magazine editors to fill their publications with glamorous clothes without being accused of elitism (after all, the only thing necessary to wear these clothes, apart from the right figure, was the right bank balance) and for a ready-to-wear industry to be given a creative lead it might otherwise have lacked. And, of course, it gave Paris fashion a huge boost,

keeping it looking healthier than it actually was and bringing in much-needed postwar dollars.

The New Look at the House of Dior stretched beyond the clothes. Christian Dior was the first couturier to grasp fully the importance of capitalizing on his name. Furthermore, he was the first (along with his very shrewd posse of financial advisers) to realize that manufacturing ready-to-wear lines in countries which were strong markets – pre-eminently the United States – meant that the protective tarifs, import restrictions and punitive taxes which governments could levy at any moment could be circumvented. In October 1948, barely eighteen months after his first show, he opened Christian Dior–New York on Fifth Avenue, confident that Harrison Elliot, his PR (another first in fashion), had sufficiently excited the American press and buyers to make it a success. He was, in fact, beating Seventh Avenue at its own game by selling his own line-by-line copies of his couture originals, adapted for American tastes. But, most importantly, they were made in America, as were the clothes of another French couturier, Jacques Fath. Fath's designs, however, were made by an American wholesale manufacturer, Joseph Halpert, while Dior's were produced by his own American company.

If Paris fashions were kept prominent by top wholesale manufacturers in New York through their reproductions of them, they were given even wider exposure through American *Vogue* and, especially, its Vogue Pattern Service. Essentially aimed at readers living outside New York, the service had originally been introduced before World War I because, as Condé Nast, the owner of *Vogue*, made clear at the time, 'It is the avowed mission of *Vogue* to appeal not merely to women of great wealth but, more fundamentally, to women of taste. A certain proportion of these readers will be found, necessarily, among the less well-to-do.'

13

Pinaforte:

VOGUE PATTERN PLAN
FOR A YOUNG
AMERICANA WARDROBE

15 *Vogue* Patterns,
    1954

16 Claire McCardell
    swimsuits, 1945,
    photo Genevieve
    Naylor

17 (Overleaf)
    Claire McCardell
    dresses,
    late 1940s

18 (Overleaf)
    Claire McCardell
    dresses, late
    1940s, photo
    Louise Dahl-Wolfe

MAKE YOUR OWN
PARIS COPIES
via Vogue Patterns

15

'Paris Original' patterns were the glory of the *Vogue* service in the Fifties. Line-by-line copies of originals, they were made up by professionals, photographed to the same high standards as everything else on the editorial pages, and aimed, not at housewives making their own clothes at home, but at trained dressmakers, the 'little women' who made fashionable clothes for clients with more taste than money, who could not afford to go to a couture house or to buy expensive copies in the top stores. Dressmakers have now all but vanished from society, yet until the mid-Sixties they were an essential fashion conduit, bringing smart, well-made clothes to the lives of women at all social levels. Many had worked with top fashion houses and manufacturers and, although standards varied – as one would expect in a corps of craftspeople who were based in small towns as well as major cities – they were responsible for giving fashionable clothing a broadly democratic base that it would otherwise not have obtained. Most importantly of all, they were the people who recreated French glamour for ordinary American women.

Not everyone wanted it, however. Although it sometimes appeared that the entire American fashion industry was in thrall to Paris, there were powerful exceptions. If in the Thirties it had been possible for France to sneer that New York had technical knowledge and manufacturing skills but no creative genius, it was an attitude which simply held no water by the early Fifties. Whereas famous New York fashion entrepreneurs such as Hattie Carnegie and Lilly Daché still turned to Paris for inspiration, the real energy and vigour of American fashion was pulsating in the country itself, under a comparatively new title: 'Sportswear'. Captain of the team was Claire McCardell, and following close behind were other women designers, notably Tina Leser and Clare Potter, alongside Sydney Wragge of B.H. Wragge – all of whom were dedicated to evolving a type of clothing and a stylistic sensibility that was essentially American.

Claire McCardell can rightly be called the founder of modern postwar fashion, even though her name never became world currency, as Dior's did. Unlike him, she was not backed by a billionaire industrialist, lacked the huge advertising budget devoted to spreading the name of her house and, in common with most design houses at the time, had no publicity agent – one of the things which gave Dior a head start on his competitors. She also lacked the glamour of Paris couture; her job was simply described as chief designer for a mass manufacturer, Townley Frocks, Inc. Despite all this she is the Forties' designer whose influence has been more persuasive and persistent than that of any designer

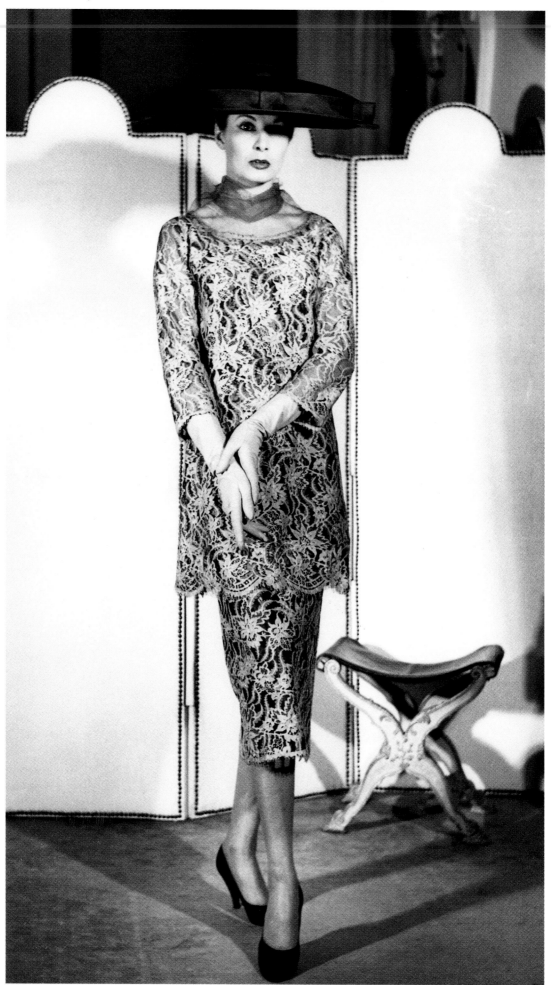

19 Balenciaga, 1955

working in Paris after the war, with the exception of the Spanish couturier Balenciaga. When she first began, her clothes were startling in their almost monastic simplicity. In fact, her most famous creation was called the Monastic: created in 1938, it was revolutionary in that, cut on the bias, with no waistline, it was basically a tent until belted. Although McCardell had originally designed it not as a dress but as a costume for a fancy-dress ball, it went into production and was copied by manufacturers all over America. It is perhaps the only totally timeless, classless and ageless female garment created this century: as right for today as it was sixty years ago. No Chanel design, let alone those of the male couturiers of the Forties, has had such universality.

From such a strong start, McCardell's design philosophy grew to dominate American ready-to-wear in the Forties and continued until her death in 1958. By then, her philosophy of sporting minimalism, based on practicality and ease, had defined dress for the modern woman, who did *not* see herself as a trophy wife and who took pride in choosing clothes to reflect her own sensibilities rather than those of her husband. McCardell's radical approach was responsible for an amazing number of fashion trailblazers. In the days when the rich woman still travelled with steamer trunks, and outfits were packed complete with coordinating hats, gloves, furs and scarves, the McCardell woman took half a dozen separate items which were all compatible and fitted into a small suitcase. McCardell was the inventor of the 'capsule' wardrobe, since claimed by other designers, just as she was the first designer to use double-stitching (previously only seen on jeans), hardware closings such as zips and press studs (subsequently used by Ralph Lauren and Giorgio Armani), and 'spaghetti straps' (a recurring fashion cliché of the last sixty years). Yet Claire McCardell's place in fashion history is assured not for design ideas but for her totally modern assessment of the dress

needs of women and the way in which she fulfilled those needs without any of the atavism which normally bedevils fashion. She was more forward-looking than any couturier in Paris – with one exception.

Cristóbal Balenciaga, a Spaniard, had been a highly successful couturier in his own country, which he left in the wake of the Spanish Civil War (1936–9). Having failed to find work in London, he moved to Paris in 1937 where he made an immediate impact. His clothes had a grandeur, even a stiffness, which was gradually eroded and softened in the Fifties as he addressed the question of what sort of clothes were suitable for modern living. Unlike Dior, who was a romantic, Balenciaga was a realist who was not seduced by the excesses of the New Look. His woman was more svelte and streamlined than Dior's; he did not weigh her down with wide voluminous skirts. Instead, he pared down her dress until it (and she) had the efficiency and elegance of a racehorse. Much has been made of the battle for supremacy between Dior and Balenciaga, but it is a battle only in hindsight. Both men respected each other's work; they acknowledged their similarities and understood their differences.

The fundamental difference between the two men was one of pace. Christian Dior changed his line each season in his determination to garner the publicity necessary for his wide-ranging licensees to make money from his name. Balenciaga believed that each collection should grow from the previous one, developing and refining ideas that would last not just for seasons but for years. When asked by a fashion journalist what changes he would be making for the new season, he was appalled. 'Change?', he replied. 'Why, I never change my clothes.' He was right. His clothes evolved slowly, more like a painter's *oeuvre* than the average fashion designer's frenzied search for novelty. Unfortunately, the Dior approach became the norm. As huge fashion empires flourished (and Dior's *was* huge compared

with other couture establishments in the Fifties), they required not the reasoned honing of ideas but the feverish, publicity-catching novelty of the fashion show which has made the work of top designers increasingly irrelevant to most women, who refuse to join this fashionable dance of death that ends in almost instant obsolescence.

Fashion is not a separate entity. It has always been part of the leisure industry and has, since Dior's day, been largely subsumed into the entertainment business. It was Dior's attention-grabbing fashion changes which first put it there. For all that, the Parisian clothes that really mattered in the Fifties were found on the runway of Cristóbal Balenciaga. That was where he slowly softened the silhouette, loosened the outline and gradually evolved ideas which have become standard elements of modern fashion. It was Balenciaga who perfected the semi-fitted suit, the stand-away collar, the sack, the tunic and the baby doll dress. He was the father of modern French fashion.

It would be tempting to claim that Chanel was its mother. Lured from retirement in 1954 in order to boost sales of Chanel perfumes, which had slumped without the publicity provided by fashion shows, she started badly. Her first postwar collection suffered from the political backlash of the war. Chanel had been a collaborator, living openly with a German officer at the Ritz in Paris. Both the French and the English took their revenge by giving her a tepid reception. The generally voiced opinion was that she had left it too late to return. It was felt that her clothes were sad, the inspiration of an old woman whom time had left behind.

Chanel had one idea which saved her, and that was her modern version of the soft, unstructured suit which had been so successful in the Twenties and Thirties. Its great merit was that it could be copied simply, adapting very easily to mass production. It was her only idea and she traded on it until her death in 1971. In fact, she was

saved from the humiliating rejection for which many
of the French had hoped by the British and American
ready-to-wear manufacturers who realized how easily its
very simplicity could make it what Seventh Avenue called
'A Ford' – a design which would go on and on with only
the slightest variation over the seasons. In Britain, Jeffrey
Wallis 'revolutionized the consumer pattern of the retail
world', according to *Vogue*, by selling line-for-line copies
of Chanel in the Wallis high-street chain. He calculated
that there was a world market of over five million women
eager to buy Paris copies at top ready-to-wear prices.

If he was right, the majority were to be found in
America, and the French designers knew this. They bent
all their efforts to serving American needs, designing
increasingly with U.S. lifestyles in mind, choosing
their advertising campaigns to appeal to transatlantic
women and, above all, fêting the *grandes dames* of
the American fashion press. Although motivated by
commerce, it was based on something more than that.
Not only in France but also throughout Europe, America
was seen as the cynosure of the world, full of goodness.
Hadn't American money, GIs and generals won the war?
Wasn't American money helping to put Europe back on
its feet? Weren't American politicians the guardians of
freedom in the new and sinister Cold War? Although
French designers had no wish to imitate American
clothes, they did everything possible to ensure that
French fashion was what counted with the movers and
shakers of the country that seemed fashion's consumer
paradise compared with Europe.

They were not alone in realizing that the real money
was to be found on the other side of the Atlantic. British
couture, albeit tiny and derivative compared with the
strength and originality of Paris, had finally become a
force which made some small inroads into the American
market. Strongly backed by the British editions of *Vogue*
and *Harper's Bazaar*, the London look gave a slightly
different slant to Paris fashion by concentrating on

tailoring and grand ballgowns – although both were done
better by the great names in Paris.

London fashion was a tangible proof of the adage that
when the English feel confused, uncertain or insecure
they form a committee and immediately feel better. In
the Fifties, they were assailed by all three. Government
regulations, export rules and continuing shortages did
not necessarily make for strength, although the designers
put on a brave front – another English characteristic in
the face of adversity. There were seemingly endless
promotions of British couturiers in North America; there
was also much bombast. John Cavanagh proclaimed
that 'a couturier worth his name must design in the world
stream'. Norman Hartnell talked of 'the dresses worn the
world over and launched here by the lovely women of
London'. Hardy Amies claimed, 'We are closer to Paris
than the very esoteric French would ever admit.' This
confidence was unfounded, however, as Cavanagh and
Hartnell were to close their doors, leaving only Amies,
a shrewd businessman, still trading.

Banding together to give themselves strength, London
fashion did produce a lot of committees and groups,
not all pertaining to the grand world of the couturier.
The Incorporated Society of London Fashion Designers
was the one with the most clout, showing annually to the
Queen Mother and her daughters, but there were others
serving every level of the fashion trade. The Model
House Group, founded in 1947 by London's top fourteen
wholesalers, re-formed as the Fashion House Group of
London, with twenty-eight members, including 'top-end'
firms such as Aquascutum, Spectator Sports, Susan
Small and Dorville, and twenty-four associate members.
There were other groups, but nothing they did could
change the fact that British fashion was outclassed, and
its basic trades – the cotton and woollen industries –
were being squeezed out of an increasingly competitive
international market, based on paying its emergent
workforces a fraction of the standard British wages.

An emerging fashion force which *could* depend on
paying low wages was found in Italy. Before World War II,
the Italian fashion industry had been tiny, with no
pretensions to taking a place on the international stage.
But things changed after the war. An industry previously
based on copying French ideas developed its own
unique approach and very quickly became a world-class
player in the fashion field. Its sights were firmly focused
on America and what at the time was undoubtedly the
'almighty dollar'. Italy was still suffering the effects of
the war, with 400,000 people homeless, 8,000 bridges
throughout the country destroyed, sixty per cent of
its major roads unusable and galloping inflation. It
functioned like a Third World country, but it had two
things which Britain lacked: a huge wellspring of talented
craftsmen and a newly dispossessed aristocracy eager
to use its power to restore the fortunes lost during the
war. It was to prove a potent conjunction. An industry
once dependent on fashion designers who had largely
copied Paris in every detail before the war was about to
discover its own design talents. As the Roman couturier,
Simonetta, said, 'the majority of Italian dressmakers went
to Paris twice a year to buy and copy – and at times to
copy without buying – the ideas of Balenciaga, Fath and
the other heavy hitters'.

All this changed in 1951 when, encouraged by sales
of knitwear to London and America, and the fact that
many Italian-designed and made clothes were selling
internationally under foreign labels, Giovanni Battista
Giorgini, the father of modern Italian fashion, held the
first Italian fashion show for foreign press and buyers
in the Grand Hotel, Florence, immediately after Paris
couture week. With a brilliance and foresight sadly
lacking in London, Giorgini had realized that, in order to
compete with Paris, Italy's fashion industries had to offer
something different. Whereas London's downfall was
inevitable because it was trying to do the same things as
Paris – without the skill, flair or artisanal back-up – Italian

21 'Young American
News', U.S.
Vogue, 1954,
photo Richard
Rutledge

22 Design for Sorelle
Fontana, 1953

22

fashion's strength rested on Giorgini's realization that what Italy could offer America, which France could not, were clothes servicing the U.S. market's demand for ready-to-wear garments, made to the highest creative and manufacturing standards, which married elegance and informality.

What America had which Europe lacked was co-eds and career women. They were becoming tired of the inspiration of Paris – still fixated on complicated and over-designed effects reflecting a formality rapidly disappearing from most lives. They were increasingly attracted to the leisure clothes of American designers but they were also looking for the cachet of a foreign label. Italian fashion provided ease and kudos for this new, high-spending consumer group. But it wasn't just the new American woman who wanted a fresh approach. The U.S. fashion industry – the most sophisticated and advanced clothing manufacturing industry in the world, able to take ideas, and make and sell garments in sufficient quantities to generate considerable profits while servicing the needs of the customer – was ready for a new stimulus.

American women in the early Fifties were the most pampered in the world. Most of the large department stores which were, at that time, central props of the commercial quarter of any American city, provided buyers with a service of considerable sophistication. Whereas in England, women normally had a choice of ten sizes per garment, in America that would stretch to

over thirty. Half sizes, common in America, were virtually unknown in Europe: it was a question of economic viability. America's huge population made such refinements not only possible but also commercially sound in a way they could never be in Europe. That is why American ready-to-wear was more sophisticated, and demanding, than anything on the opposite side of the Atlantic, except for the exclusive and costly couture of Paris.

The U.S. ragtrade was based on the presumption that mass-produced clothing must be easy to make and easy to sell. Seventh Avenue was convinced that it could cherry-pick across Europe without damaging its indigenous industry. It took tweeds and silks from London and design inspiration from Paris, but it needed something to service a wider market. It found it in Italy's first great gifts to the fashion world: separates and sophisticated knitwear, both virtually nonexistent in the French fashion world. But it found something even more important in Italy: an aura with which it could captivate the American buying public.

In brief, Italy was considered colourful, carefree and exotic. Its fashion industry had been given huge media exposure when the American actress Linda Christian had chosen the Roman couture house, Sorelle Fontana, to make her wedding dress. But there was more to it than that: American GIs had discovered that young Italian women were sexy and lighthearted. Early Fifties' travellers, such as Tennessee Williams and Truman

24

Capote, had written glowingly of the easy Italian way of life. The *dolce vita* years of glamour and sophistication were about to begin. Italy's time had come.

Giovanni Battista Giorgini knew and understood the American market. In the Thirties, he had crossed the Atlantic almost monthly. He knew that Italy must attract the buyers who came to Paris and persuade them to extend their European stay sufficiently to view Italian merchandise. In the late Forties and early Fifties, when most buyers travelled from America by boat, this was a tall order. Already away from home longer than they liked, they were reluctant to spend time anywhere but Paris. London's Incorporated Society began leaning on U.S. press and buyers to make England a permanent stopover on their way to the French capital – with some success. How could Italy break in?

The solution that Giorgini found was based on the fashion world's inherent snobbery. He lured the American press and buyers by offering them palaces, princes and Emilio Pucci. He obtained government backing to use the Pitti and Strozzi palaces in Florence for runway presentations and receptions. It was a masterstroke, offering, as it did, a glimpse of prewar luxury and privilege. Madge Garland, fashion editor of British *Vogue* at the time, captured the scene in the Sala Bianca of the Pitti Palace: 'Rarely have clothes been seen in more palatial surroundings than in the vast ballroom … air-conditioned against the summer's heat, its huge chandeliers winking in the lights, white-gloved attendants … the commentary spoken in four different languages, magnificent guards in the full panoply of Renaissance costumes to herald the lovely Italian model girls – this was making the most of Italy's national assets.' The invitations read, 'Mr and Mrs Giorgini will welcome their guests at their home. A ball will follow.' And the designer made sure that the place was full of aristocrats. It wasn't just a winning combination, it was irresistible.

25   Pucci ski clothes,
     1948, photo
     Toni Frissell

26   Pucci designs:
     (left) 1950s cotton
     cocktail dress;
     (top right) printed
     tunic over silk
     trousers, 1962–3;
     (bottom right) silk
     beaded evening
     dress, 1967

25

The aristocrat whom the Americans already knew and loved was Emilio Pucci who, as well as being titled (the Marchese di Barsento), had also been a member of the Olympic ski team and an officer in the Italian air force. He was Italian fashion's dream ticket: tall, aristocratic and heterosexual, he had a great deal of mileage in him. Best of all, he was a highly original and witty designer whose talent had actually been discovered by America. In 1947 he was photographed on the slopes at St Moritz wearing ski clothes he had designed himself. The photographs, by Toni Frissell, appeared in *Harper's Bazaar*, whose editor, Carmel Snow, then continued to give him, his designs and his lifestyle considerable coverage. After being contacted by the prestigious Fifth Avenue store, Lord & Taylor, he became a fully fledged designer. If Pucci's beginning could be called the birth of the 'Made in Italy' miracle that was soon to recast the globe of world fashion, the midwife was the American press.

But again, it must be stressed that Italian fashion benefited from an attitude of mind which affected the way foreigners perceived the country and its people. In England, teenagers – a new and potent class of consumer rapidly catching up with America in spending power – wanted Italian Vespas, Isetta bubble cars, Italian haircuts and shoes (winklepickers and stilettos), espresso coffee bars – in short, Italian style. But it was more than that: what the world was fascinated by was Italian sexiness.

It was that sexiness which conquered the world and made Italian fashion for both sexes irresistible. On a wave of busts and beauty, Italian stars such as Gina Lollobrigida, Claudia Cardinale, Elsa Martinelli and above all Sophia Loren, personified the glamour of Italy. They sold the world the idea of Italian fashion, and made Italy the premier European vacation destination for Americans hoping to find the carefree world captured in Audrey Hepburn's 1953 film, *Roman Holiday*; the poignancy of Katharine Hepburn's *Summer Madness* of 1955 and even Vivien Leigh's desolation in the 1961 film of Tennessee Williams's novel *The Roman Spring of Mrs Stone*.

All three films had American heroines. This was right and proper at a time when American cultural attitudes and values were spreading across the globe and dress designers everywhere were eagerly trying to come to terms with them in order to tap into the wealth they were capable of generating. There were some surprising – and highly successful – new fashion capitals stimulated by the American market. One of the most efficient sprang up in Dublin.

27 Clockwise,
    beginning top left:
    Sophia Loren,
    1958; Gina
    Lollobrigida, 1956;
    Claudia Cardinale,
    1965; Claudia
    Cardinale, 1968;
    Gina Lollobrigida,
    1961; this page:
    Sophia Loren,
    1958

27

In order to benefit from Marshall Aid from the U.S. government (set up to help postwar reconstruction in Europe), countries had to initiate their own export trade and, in the Republic of Ireland, this was spearheaded by fashion, which provided work for the Irish fabric industries, primarily the linen and woollen trades. Dublin fashion found its inspiration and lead in Sybil Connolly, born in Wales in 1921 but resident in Ireland throughout the Forties, where she designed for the firm of Richard Alan. In 1953, she showed her own-name collection to various American stores and, like Emilio Pucci, became a star. Americans responded to the way in which she tailored tweeds and fine wool, used crochet and lace, and made flannel a high-fashion fabric. But it was her use of finely pleated Irish linen which raised the profile of Irish fashion and made it a popular seller throughout America, not just in cities with a preponderance of Irish expatriots. Again like Pucci, Sybil Connolly's skill lay in creating clothes with recognizable ethnic roots that were sophisticated enough to stand alone on the international fashion stage.

It was a scene of increasing complexity and competitiveness as the Fifties began to move towards the watershed of the Sixties, the period described by the novelist Angela Carter as the 'ramshackle yet glorious decade'. The hegemony of Paris had been challenged; the power of couture had been compromised; the growth of ready-to-wear had begun. The stage was set for forty years of explosive, contradictory and often anarchic fashion changes which were to prove that fashion not only illustrates and illuminates history, it also writes it.

YOUTH REVOLUTION

1   (Opener)
Courrèges
miniskirt, 1967,
photo Peter
Knapp

2   (Previous page)
Young men in
denim, *c*.1955

3   (Previous page)
Marilyn Monroe,
1955

4   'Hung on You'
boutique, London,
1966

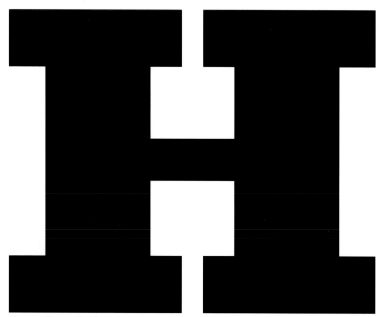

History distorts fashion, as it does most other things. Many popular myths have grown up around the concept of youth fashion. We think of the miniskirt, minimal underwear and the apparent freedom of young women's dress in the late Sixties and early Seventies; we read about 'Swinging London', Woodstock and the 'Youthquake' revolution; Carnaby Street and the King's Road; and we assume that the profound changes which took place in social values, sexual attitudes and the freedoms of women sprang into existence fully formed, the result of some immaculate fashion conception which appeared out of a vacuum. We have a mental picture of corseted dowagers in tightly-constructed couture, complete with hats and gloves who, on seeing the new visions of long-legged youthful freedom, constrained by nothing but the skimpiest underwear, covered by the briefest, least shaped dresses in the history of fashionable female clothing, panicked and ran screaming into fashion's dark night, never to be seen again. All in the twinkling of an eye.

Anachronisms aren't so suddenly made. They are what is left as things slowly evolve. Change is rarely a dramatic rupture with the past, able to be pinpointed to a month or year. The mood that finally became obvious to everyone in the Sixties had been growing for a long time. It could be argued that the power of youth first showed itself as far back as World War I, when alternative female attitudes began to emerge, influenced by the cinema (a new cultural force for a new century), which created heroines younger and less awe-inspiring than the *grandes dames* of the theatre, who had dominated the ideal of female perfection until then. Mary Pickford, simperingly innocent, captured the hearts and

minds of a much wider, and therefore less sophisticated, section of the world's population than Sarah Bernhardt. Irene Castle, the first dancing star and precursor of Ginger Rogers, Cyd Charisse and Liza Minnelli, presented an ideal of woman relaxed, liberated and enjoying herself in a way inconceivable even to Isadora Duncan. But these were merely precursors, pointers to a long-term future.

It is generally considered that power in the fashion world changed hands in the Sixties, when London was 'swinging' and other major fashion centres were trying hard to catch up with its youth-orientated commercial success in fashion, music and lifestyle. In fact, the cult of youth and the power of young fashion were both first seen in Paris. Purists would claim that they were brought to the fore in the early Twenties when Chanel, closely pursued by Jean Patou, conceived not only a new form of dress but, more radically, a new approach to femininity, sexuality and clothing which, in Diana Vreeland's memorably hyperbolic phrase, 'invented the twentieth century for women'.

For the purpose of our survey, however, the roots of the youth revolution are found in a more recent and much greater designer. The true father of the youth revolution was Yves Saint Laurent, the man who took over as design director at Dior, the world's grandest fashion house, in 1957, when he was barely twenty-one. The collection that pointed the way to the future was his fifth at Dior. Inspired by the Beat Generation, it was a couture collection – as couture was what the House of Dior concerned itself with at the time – and was therefore conceived, executed and presented in a way quite alien to the ready-to-wear still to come to

5   Bernadette Lafont,
     1959, photo
     Jeanloup Sieff

6   Juliette Gréco,
     1950, photo
     Studio Harcourt

7   (Overleaf)
     Yves Saint Laurent
     after his first
     collection at Dior,
     1958

6

Paris, although it was already the mainstay of American fashion, the dynamo which generated creativity and sales for the garment district clustered around Seventh Avenue in New York. Saint Laurent was in the tradition of French couture – and yet *not* in the tradition. In common with Schiaparelli, Dior, Balenciaga and all of the great couturiers who had made Paris famous, Yves Saint Laurent created clothes with the instinctive belief that fashion was part of the world of art, albeit minor in the way that the work of a silversmith or a furniture-maker is.

Saint Laurent's revolution was strong and pointed because it had behind it over two hundred years of organized attitudes and beliefs which had informed and illuminated the world of the arts not only in Europe but everywhere that Western standards of civilization and art were seen as an ideal. That is why his 'Beat' collection was considered so revolutionary and received such a bewildered reception from Dior customers and many of the press. It seemed that he was setting out to destroy a culture which had sustained fashion since Charles Frederick Worth in the nineteenth century and even further back. Whereas Chanel had believed that fashion should eventually be seen on the streets, after a decent interval in which she would sell clothes exclusively to her private customers, Saint Laurent's approach was viewed as not only revolutionary but deeply threatening because he wanted to reverse the flow which had for so long been taken for granted, and draw his inspiration from the streets.

Being part of a cultural tradition which had at its roots refinement of thought and artefact, Saint Laurent's bow to the streets in 1960 had nothing in common with the street styles that were to develop later. Unlike them –

and, indeed, anything that happened in 'Swinging London' – his inspiration had an intellectual rather than a visceral basis. The collection that gave the Dior executives the chance to remove him from his post, because they could detect a dangerous undermining radicalism in his attitude, was not about what the kids on the block were wearing but how a group of Left Bank intellectuals, political radicals and philosophers thought and expressed themselves as much as how they dressed. The fact that they had a type of uniform – black berets, polo-neck sweaters and straight black trousers – was incidental. What mattered about the Existentialists for Saint Laurent was the way they thought – not least about femininity. Simone de Beauvoir, Jean-Paul Sartre's partner, wrote *The Second Sex* in 1949, and, of course, like every other artist and intellectual in Paris, Yves Saint Laurent had read it. Like that book, his 1960 collection was subversive – but subversive within a system.

To modern eyes, the Beat collection is striking for its supreme elegance rather than its shocking modernity. To eyes of the time – especially those at Dior – it was considered alarmingly unbalanced because it clearly could only be worn by young women. And they were right. These clothes shocked because of the modernity of the attitude behind them, which was that the young could not only influence but actually lead fashion. This was the Saint Laurent breakthrough. Whereas most fashion since the Twenties had been conceived to be shown and photographed on youngish women – which, by the mores of the times could mean anything from twenty-five to forty – it had always been designed with the clear understanding that it could be adapted to be

8   Mary Quant
    designs, early
    1960s

9   André Courrèges,
    1967, photo
    Peter Knapp

worn with dignity and style by older women, who were – almost by definition – the ones who were most likely to be able to afford it. What frightened the Dior management into sacking its young protégé was the alarm raised by these women: they could not imagine themselves wearing creations which to them were not only *outré* but broke the tenets of couture's *raison d'être*, which was to flatter age so that it felt – and even frequently looked – youthful: a state rarely achieved by dressing in self-consciously youthful styles.

So, as with all successful revolutions, the youth revolution began in the very heartland of the opposition and, again true to form, the subtle efforts of the instigator were swept aside by the more simplistic and direct approaches that followed. But that does not detract from Yves Saint Laurent's position as revolutionary and rebel. In 1960, he was twenty-four, the youngest couturier in the world; but he was not the only young couturier in Paris. Pierre Cardin was only thirty-eight in 1960 and had been head of his own house for seven years. Hubert de Givenchy, five years younger, founded his own house in 1952. André Courrèges, who was to open his own house in 1961, was thirty-seven in 1960. By today's standards, to call such men young would seem slightly perverse, but in the late Fifties and early Sixties they were considered so by the standards – and ages – that ruled Paris couture. In fact, the House of Dior had been condemned as a reckless risk-taker in appointing Yves Saint Laurent, against the wishes of many powerful forces. Their argument was simple: how could a man so young, regardless of his talent (which nobody questioned), understand how to dress

the soignée woman, no longer young. But the dissident voices belonged to people looking backwards, whose belief that couture could continue in the same way forever blinded them to the dramatic changes taking place in society, and whose arrogant assumptions of superiority worked on the principle that any fashion conceived outside the couture system was, by definition, crude, simplistic and vulgar – and, as such, of no interest to the keepers of the flame of couture standards.

French couture had created a cocoon for itself in its pursuit of perfection, and by 1960 this had not produced a glorious butterfly but instead had become a shroud, isolating it from the realities of life and fashion, not just in Paris but across the globe. A strong wind was blowing that would tear away the cobwebs, crack the shell and bring a refreshing gust of air to even the most backward-looking fashion house. It was the backdraft from the youth revolution. And the gauntlet it carried with it, with which to strike the traditional face of fashion, was the miniskirt, revolutionary because of its exclusivity and ageism. For virtually the first time in history, here was a look that could only be worn by young women. The only other fashion trend that could be considered a threat to the hegemony of traditional attitudes had been the flapper's unstructured garments in the Twenties, and even they could be adapted to suit older women. But the miniskirt was grotesquely ageist in that it was not only almost unwearable for anyone over twenty-five, it looked superbly right – and sexy – only on the very young, and even unformed, figure.

The youth movement has been claimed by London as a result of its superior skills in marketing, propaganda and hype, but to believe that youth fashion was led by what happened there is as wrong as assuming that what London produced was the best of the new approach. In fact, Paris and London fashion entered the Sixties on broadly parallel lines. What gave London the edge and convinced history that its fashion was the superior of the two was the power of its newly emerged pop culture. Whereas Paris fashion was still largely working within an elitist cultural frame, London fashion was part of an anti-elitist movement which, able to muster vast numbers, eventually won the day. But it was a Pyrrhic victory. The clothes produced in Paris had an intellectuality and a strong design lineage. They made much of London fashion seem trite, opportunistic and exploitative of the ignorance of its chosen market: the young.

Those who care about such things argue fiercely over where the mini first emerged. Was it a manifestation of the King's Road and Carnaby Street or the effect of St Germain, the Avenue Montaigne and the Place Vendôme? In fact, being first is not the important thing. In fashion, as in most things, the plaudits of history go to those who do new things most memorably and convincingly. The two major contenders as inventors of the mini are Mary Quant in London and André Courrèges in Paris, although in fact, the spirit which made the mini possible – the lowering of the ideal fashion age, beginning with Yves Saint Laurent's collection for the House of Dior – was found in New York and every other place where the young were beginning to take the reins.

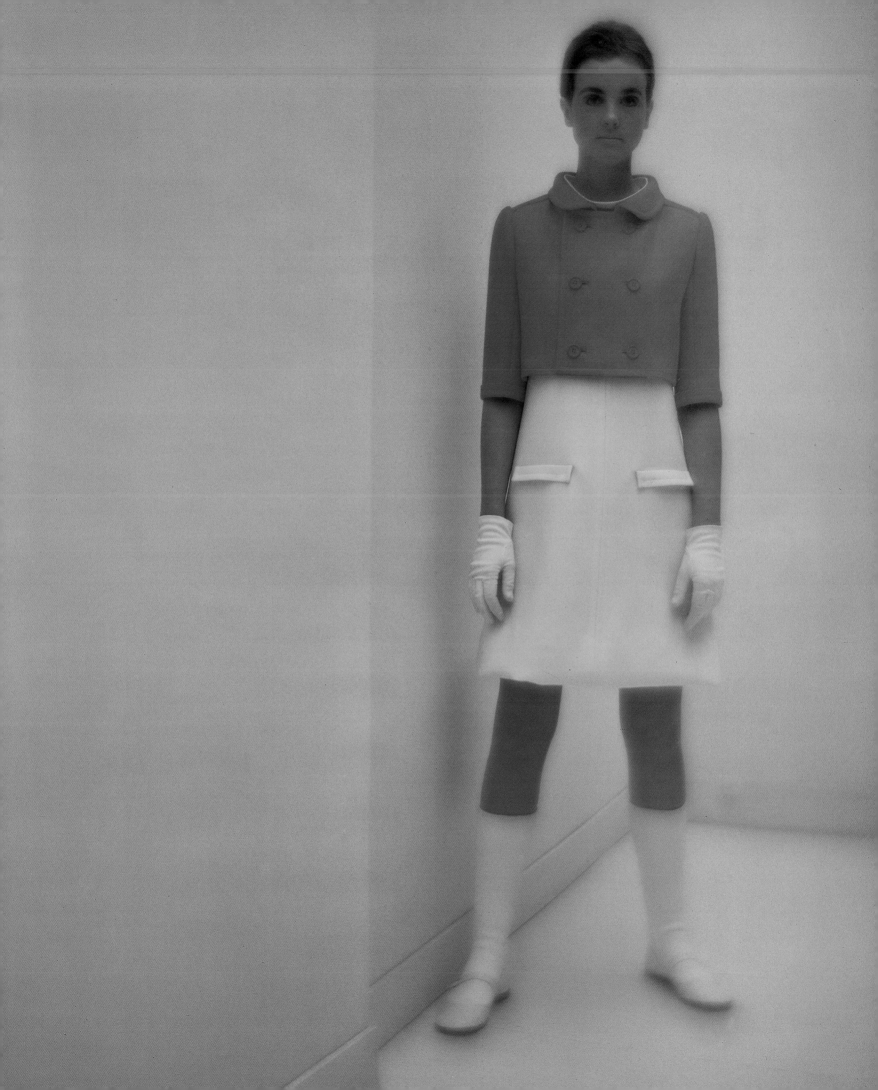

11

12

10

It is possible to make a good case for the youth revolution starting not with women, but with men. Extreme, individualistic fashion, owing nothing to the dictates of couturiers or tailors, was certainly a male prerogative long before it became a female one. Over twenty years before Mary Quant and André Courrèges, the Zazous in Paris, the zoot-suited Hispanics found pre-eminently in Southern California and the Teddy Boys in London – all exclusively male fashion statements – had made it clear that, when it came to fashion radicalism, young men were far in advance of young women. Cynics might say that the reason is that, rather than being led by the nose by couturiers, as women were, men wore clothes which reflected how *they* felt. Mods and rockers, Hell's Angels and punk all began as manifestations of social aggression and the political alienation felt by men.

But women's clothes hadn't been entirely static. The Fifties had seen two events which moved fashion forward to a free and less constricted future which, in itself, meant that the age of fashion power would drop. In 1954, infuriated by the 'idiocies' of what she condemned as 'pederast' designers, Chanel risked coming out of her self-imposed retirement to create a new and entirely modern version of her famously relaxed jersey suits from the Twenties. At about the same time, Balenciaga, in reaction to Dior's strict and constrained line, was beginning to loosen up clothes so that they shaped, rather than accentuated, the contours of the body. Both couturiers were instigating a quiet revolution that would have considerable repercussions for the

15 Balenciaga, 1963,
    photo William
    Klein

16 Chanel, 1963,
    photo William
    Klein

16

young. It is important to note that, of the new wave of youth-driven designers, André Courrèges and Emanuel Ungaro both learned their trade at Balenciaga, while Emmanuelle Khanh had been his house model before beginning to design under her own name. In fact, Balenciaga, considered so extreme, aloof and remote from the streets, was the man whose fundamental searching for modern solutions to the question of female dress broke the barriers of static good taste. He was the first couturier to feature high boots on his catwalk. He created mini-culottes. But his real contribution to the future, which only hindsight reveals, were his tunics and the chemise line of 1957, from which so much of Sixties' youth fashion grew.

What Balenciaga and Chanel achieved for youth fashion was amazing when we realize that they were both old people. He was seventy-three when he retired in 1968; she was seventy-one when she reopened her fashion house. They both proved the lie in believing – as so many do today – that only the young understand how the young wish to dress. Of course, Balenciaga and Chanel created nothing that had a specific appeal to youth. Their contribution was more subtle: they changed the concept of fashion. Previously, it had been based on the rigidly controlled body, 'aided' by corsets, wired bras and foundation garments to help the older figure appear young. Chanel's unstructured jackets and straight skirts, like Balenciaga's 'baby doll' chemises, required a normal and unconstricted figure – a figure which only young women have. It was only a short step from these to the mini.

But it was a step taken at a tangent. One of the greatest influences on Fifties' attitudes, including approaches to dress, was the change in how people approached the newest in postwar social developments. Leisure had previously always been the privilege of the few. As late as the Thirties, long working hours had meant that, for the majority of people, free time was limited and the need for casual wear hardly existed. In contrast to today's patterns of dress, for most working-class people time away from factory or field meant dressing up, not down. Sartorial codes, part of a clearly defined social hierarchy, were rigid. Their purpose was to keep formal occasions formal. Suits, hats, gloves, dark colours: the dress of both sexes was tightly prescribed.

The Fifties permanently changed this situation. Newly liberated from social shibboleths, people wanted to dress for their free time in ways that emphasized their freedom. Church-going declined and with it went formality. Popular box-office successes starring young actresses like Doris Day and Debbie Reynolds reflected

the easygoing dress codes of Southern California; travel opportunities expanded experience – the espadrilles of the Mediterranean made the long trek north, to be followed later by olive oil and garlic, to become part of the newly released lifestyles of ordinary people who had begun to feel, regardless of their class, that they weren't so very ordinary after all.

It was a man who created the look for modern youth and gave the world its first international example of the power of street style – and he had nothing to do with organized fashion. James Dean captured the imagination of the world as the archetype of the young rebel. His image was built on a casual attitude to clothes. Blue jeans, T-shirts and cowboy boots were only part of the charismatic cocktail. He made facial expression, physical stance and demeanour equally as important as clothes in a fashion statement. The first youth icon to display 'attitude', Dean also had the first truly modern face. Like Brigitte Bardot, he had something never seen before, something which predated Twiggy, Jean Shrimpton and the fashion icons soon to come.

It was sex. Not sex appeal, which had been around for a long time, but sex as a raw and compelling emotion. Young women looking at him didn't fantasize about chaste and tender arms gently enfolding them. They weren't interested in Cary Grant-style sophisticated repartee or even Spencer Tracy-type toughness and wisecracks. What they wanted was what in their virginal state they could only imagine was pulsating within his jeans. Thousands of young men around the globe shared their fevered speculations but kept their longings carefully hidden, as the law insisted in most countries.

The rest of them could be more open. For them the sex-kitten, the pouting little girl lover who had all the wiles of a skilled and adult woman, was personified by Brigitte Bardot. Launched by the director Roger Vadim in *And God Created Woman* in 1956, she shocked and excited the world because her appearance heralded a cultural shift. Previous sex goddesses of the screen – from the androgynous appeal of Greta Garbo, Marlene Dietrich and Katharine Hepburn to the clearer commerciality of Jean Harlow, Joan Crawford and Myrna Loy – were idealizations of their type. Perfect, unique and unattainable, they were the stuff of dreams and were not likely to be encountered on the bus or in the village shop. But Bardot's appeal was less exclusive. You just might meet a girl not so different; a girl with a face devoid of breeding but alive with animal vitality. And whereas it was hard to imagine kissing the perfectly painted lips of the screen goddesses – even Grace Kelly's peerless beauty was more calculated to repel the rude advance than succumb to it – Bardot's lips seemed

18   Paul Newman on
     the set of *Pocket
     Money*, 1972,
     photo Terry O'Neill

19   James Dean on
     the set of *Rebel
     Without a Cause*,
     1955

18

to ask to be bruised with the strength of an animal passion which the dreamers assumed would be reciprocated with equal abandon.

Her clothes were modern, young and, to coin a word which was only beginning to become politely acceptable, sexy. Semantics reveal shifts of emphasis almost as quickly as dress does. The introduction of the word 'sexy' into everyday speech – and, especially, into the language of fashion – marked not merely a change but a radical realignment. Although the old attitudes and their language – the belief that elegance, allure and glamour were what women required from their clothes in order to feel confident and sexually appealing – didn't vanish overnight, their relevance to young women was soon to diminish rapidly. Formality was beginning to be seen as stuffy; dresses which made a 'statement' were soon to be relegated to the charnel house of the most old-fashioned couture establishments. Whereas Dietrich wore perfectly-cut suits, elegant hats and slinky, opulent evening dresses, Bardot and her imitators, both in real life and on the screen, including Françoise Hardy and Leslie Caron, wore simple cotton dresses, went hatless and rarely appeared in anything even vaguely like the evening dresses favoured by the fashion establishment. Free and easy, stockingless and wearing sandals (if any footwear), they shared an element of dishabille in their dress. It wasn't just informality and casualness, it was about sexual liberty and social equality. These looks required no personal maid to make them possible. They could be removed easily and even hastily – and just as quickly put on again – without any of the rituals demanded by more traditional, structured clothing. And who needed foundation garments and heavily boned bras when bodies were young, firm and fit? No wonder 'sexy' became a term of approbation and has maintained its lead for the past forty years, still being considered by many to be the highest term of praise, even for things far removed from sex or fashion. It was James Dean and Brigitte Bardot who set it on course to become the universal semantic catch-all that it is today.

If Bardot brought a new vocabulary of dress to young women, the semantics of James Dean's clothing were so strong they leapt across the sexual borders. His jeans, blouson jackets and casual shirts were surely the very beginning of the androgyny which made possible the greatest shift in fashion history of this or any previous century: the acceptance of the fact that women can dress entirely in traditional male clothes without either compromising their femininity or risking accusations of lesbianism. James Dean divided the world into Jocks and Nerds. For women, as much as men, the former were the sartorial leaders; the latter, the stragglers.

But sartorial leadership is like any other: it doesn't take place in a vacuum. James Dean and his looks were not an isolated cultural manifestation. They were part of a sea change taking place in society. Youth had not only found its feet after the sad postwar years; it was beginning to prance and, above all, to dance. After centuries of hierarchical culture during which the rules of taste and style had been conceived and imposed by an upper class which had little, if any, interest in popular culture – and certainly no interest in elevating it to the level of those arts respected, understood and followed only by the educated and refined – the creative underbelly had begun to heave. A birth long delayed, but long awaited, was about to take place.

For years, although popular culture such as music hall and traditional song or folk art and vernacular building had held their place, and frequently influenced the mainstream of the arts, there was virtually no crossover from worker, peasant, street or farm into the world of smart fashion, with the exception of young upper-class males in the late eighteenth and early nineteenth century who enjoyed aping the manners, clothes – and oaths – of coachmen and jockeys. It was a shortlived fad. Lower-class manners, mores and modes traditionally hold no lasting interest for those born into different classes.

The change in this situation had begun in the Twenties with the vogue for black music. Crossing from America – a continent newly revealed by film and freshly opened to European travellers by the transatlantic liners promoted by governments as proof of their modernity and advanced technical status – jazz was taken up with almost fanatical enthusiasm in Paris and, remarkably, even had an impact on London, traditionally more hostile to cultural influence from other societies.

Fashion is wrongly assumed to change quickly. In reality, in its basic premises it moves very slowly, a fact disguised by the quicksilver, surface changes of mood in response to sudden fads. It is possible to say of twentieth-century fashion that there have been only two serious permanent changes: the move from long skirts to short and the adoption of trousers by women. All else has been fashion fadism. The effects of the new cultural force were much more subtle and slow-moving. What it did was to set in motion a movement which, aided by free universal education and the weakening of the power of church and state – both accelerated by the World Wars which sliced across the century like a surgeon's knife – was to break the hierarchical system and assert the power of the culture of the people.

And the catalyst – one could even say the leitmotif – was popular music and the way in which it enfranchised

20 Duke Ellington,
    1967

21 U.S. dancehall,
    1942

22 Bill Haley and
    the Comets, late
    1950s/early 1960s

23 Jitterbugging,
    Detroit, Michigan,
    1942

24 (Overleaf)
    Frank Sinatra,
    1968, photo
    Terry O'Neill

those previously neglected. Above all, it empowered the newest class of all: the young. The big bands of the Thirties and Forties (Duke Ellington and Count Basie), the crooners (pre-eminently Frank Sinatra and Johnnie Ray) and the jazz vocalists Billie Holiday and Ella Fitzgerald increasingly sang about situations or emotions which appealed not merely to general, non-elitist tastes but, increasingly, articulated the needs and longings of the young. By the time that Bill Haley appeared in the early Fifties, jazz, jive, jitterbug and bebop had relegated less energetic dances such as the foxtrot and quickstep to the safe, sound and seemly dancefloors of the old guard – the hunt ball, the golf club dance or the country club social evening. But it was the new beat of the bass that was making the young leap to their feet and throw themselves around in dances that seemed to their elders to be little more than pagan paroxysms. Twist and shout were the clear directive – the new cultural force – and the fact that both music and steps were so plebeian in their lack of grace gave them even more power.

It is easy to look at punk in the Seventies and assume that the lure of supposedly 'subversive' behaviour first caught the young in that decade. In fact, using clothes and music in order to differentiate between the young and old – and not merely to differentiate but to alienate at the same time – really began in the Forties with the dance crazes. It was carried forward by the Mods and Rockers and the Hippies, by which time it – and the youth it had socially enfranchised – had become historical fact.

If the driving force was music and dance, dress codes were cultural adjuncts, albeit important ones. And what the new form of dress – deliberately exclusive and anti-Establishment – did was to ignore all accepted fashion rules in its determination to be different. The concept of personal style, as opposed to fashion, that was eagerly pounced on by a sick and failing fashion industry in the

20

22

21

Eighties, was originally created by the young in their
insistence on not becoming part of the commercial
fashion world which, even as early as the Fifties, was
beginning to be seen as a juggernaut in danger of
crushing young imaginations and idealism. As the late
twentieth-century fashion paradox – is true fashion the
result of the dictates from the designers or the spirit of
the streets? – began to emerge, it became clear that
the more choice apparently offered by the industry, the
less scope there was for individuality. It was the young
who first realized this and reacted against it.

They had good reason to, certainly in France and
England where, despite the attempts of the mass
manufacturers to harness a market which they realized
had considerable commercial potential, there were few
clothes available to young women that were not prissily
pretty or, in most cases, little more than a watered-down
and weakened version of the sort of clothes worn by
their mothers. British *Vogue*'s 'Young Ideas' section
consistently featured young fashions that perpetuated
the class system for which, at that time, the magazine
stood – just as the British edition of *Harper's Bazaar* and
Queen did. Rigid taste lines – formulated on an upper-
class judgement of what was suitable attire for a young
lady – were accentuated by bland photography. It is little
wonder that young women already beginning to respond
to the seductive siren call of the King's Road were ill at
ease with the Establishment approach.

But, in the late Fifties and Sixties, was the King's Road
so very different? Did it play a role that would subvert
the dress codes of the West End? The answer can be
seen in even a cursory glance at the husband-and-wife
team who, for the media of the world, came to personify
'swinging' London fashion. Mary Quant and Alexander
Plunket Greene were lucky to arrive on the social cusp
when credibility was just beginning to turn from the
charmed world of London's upper-class *jeunesse dorée*
– Austin Healey sports cars, weekends in the country,
pubs in Chelsea – to something much grittier which
eventually emerged in the Seventies: regional accents,
council flats and state education. That Mary Quant
had talent is axiomatic. That the class of her social
life – and, especially of her well-educated husband
– opened doors and made things possible is equally
axiomatic. What is interesting to contemplate is what
they would have achieved a decade later, when class
differentiations had become much tougher – forced on,
not, as traditionally, from above, but from below.

The importance of the miniskirt lay in the change in
social attitudes that it revealed: attitudes which affected
not only women, sex and morality but also begged the
question that every generation addresses in its search

for modernity. It isn't simply a question of 'how far can
you go?' or to what limits new ideas can be pushed. It
is also about the redistribution of social power. And, as
with all fashion change, a battle ensued between what
the old guard would accept and what the Young Turks
felt they had the right to demand. Ascot and the Ritz
said 'no' to the mini, although both were to capitulate in
the face of its sheer force; King's Road, Carnaby Street
and the popular press, all working to an agenda quite
different to that of the old guard, said 'yes'. There
wasn't really much of a contest because the mini was
the spearhead of an entrancing new freedom, where
personal choice had nothing to do with the attitudes of
'elders and betters'.

For young women, life changed with the Pill. By putting
them in charge, it also altered things for young men,
who had already seen major changes taking place.
After centuries of deferring to their superiors, they had
wrested the social power from their hands. The great
divide was World War II. Men from backgrounds where
to call the local vicar or doctor 'sir' was considered not
merely desirable but necessary went to war with one
attitude and came back with quite another. Not only
was it that they didn't care what their fathers and
schoolmasters thought, they couldn't have made them
understand the excitement of the new compulsions
pushing them forward, even if they had tried. Sexy, in
the sense of being empowered, was the only word for
how the new movement made them feel.

And it wasn't just a word, it was a literature. The
book which most clearly reflected fashion's shift to
the excitement of youth and the special allure of the
young girl – which was to flare into a major issue in
the Eighties when pre-pubescence became a fashion
obsession – was Vladimir Nabokov's *Lolita*, published
in 1955. After that, the sexual equation was no longer
men/women or even men/men, women/women. With
Lolita, children came into the open arena of sexuality,
although they had been part of the sexual cocktail of
virtually all Western societies for centuries, of course,
accepted but never acknowledged.

Nabokov's *Lolita* was published a year after Françoise
Sagan's stylishly dolorous novel, *Bonjour tristesse*,
which articulated the sadness of the young in love, and
the self-absorption of a woman overwhelmed in a way
not seen since Gustave Flaubert's *Madame Bovary*
(1857). It perfectly reflected the needs and longings of
young women who knew instinctively that their lives
could not, and would not, follow the pattern of their
mother's. Just as J.D. Salinger's 1951 classic *The
Catcher in the Rye* had told a whole generation of boys
what they were, and were not – the boys whose sons

26

27

would carry on the tradition of non-conformity by
becoming the Stüssy-wearing, baseball-capped Beastie
Boys fans – so other politically motivated novels
articulated the behaviour and attitudes of the young
urban working classes. John Braine's *Room at the Top*
(1957) was almost a primer on how to beat the class
system. It wasn't alone. Shelagh Delaney's play *A Taste
of Honey* (1958) addressed the newly emerging social
problems of unwanted babies, racial tensions and
homosexuality.

But much of the old guard attitudes remained, even
with the young Jacqueline Bouvier, who was later
to marry John F. Kennedy. In 1951 (aged twenty-two)
she won American *Vogue*'s Prix de Paris for her literary
essay, *People I Wish I had Known*. She chose a
culturally safe trio – Oscar Wilde, Charles Baudelaire
and Sergei Diaghilev. A symbol of class, Jackie Kennedy
was not a young woman who wore the mini, any more
than the charmingly distant Grace Kelly or the perfectly
boned Audrey Hepburn, whose face was claimed by
Cecil Beaton to embody the spirit of the day. Hepburn's
beauty rested on bone structure – as classic, upper-
class beauty always had. Much more typical of the
Fifties was Marilyn Monroe, who in 1953 posed nude
as a pin-up (predictably denounced as 'filth' in Great
Britain), but by 1955 was delighting the world in *The
Seven Year Itch*. Of her, Beaton wrote 'she is an urchin
pretending to be grown up', adding that her general
appearance had an impromptu look, 'even to the point
of blowsiness'. What Beaton was facing was the New
Woman: young, assured, sexually relaxed and totally
free of the hidebound conventions which caused
debutantes to feel outraged, their class betrayed
when, in 1958, five years after the coronation of
Queen Elizabeth II and the Kennedy wedding, their
annual presentation to the monarch was abandoned.

How could it be otherwise in a decade which saw Elvis
Presley, the archetypal lower-class sex symbol, become
the pop phenomenon of the age with the release of his
first single, 'That's All Right, Mama', in 1954. In 1957,
Bill Haley toured Britain, routing Skiffle, the country's
tame attempt at youth music, with his energetic rock
and roll. His 1956 film *Rock Around the Clock* had
been condemned for encouraging rioting – although,
in fact, the extent of the problem was little more than
some jiving, singing and clapping in the aisles when the

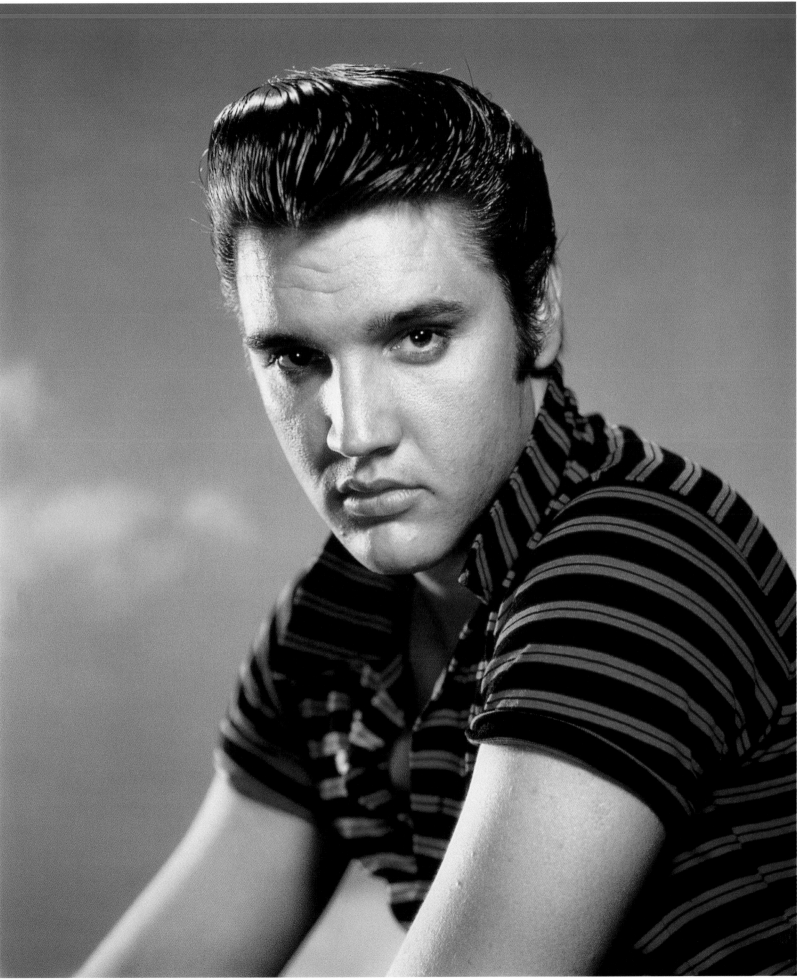

31 Mick Jagger,
c.1965, photo
Terry O'Neill

32 Diana Rigg as
Emma Peel in
The Avengers,
1965–7, photo
Terry O'Neill

film was shown. But even staid middle-aged members of society couldn't resist the way the young turned Haley's 'See You Later, Alligator' into a catchphrase for the hip and cool with its laid-back reply, 'In a while, crocodile.'

And that showed the extent of the change. Youth was now clearly in the lead, culturally, if not politically. In 1957 Jack Kerouac's *On the Road* was published, a year after Allen Ginsberg's *Howl and other Poems* – both were Beat Generation manifestos that were taken up by the hippies. *On the Road* was the story of a journey from Greenwich Village in New York, through the French Quarter of New Orleans via Diversey Avenue, Chicago to Haight-Ashbury, San Francisco. It was a route and a pilgrimage which led to Flower Power and an attempt by much of American youth to distance themselves from what they saw as the false values of their country – just as Salinger's Holden Caulfield in *The Catcher in the Rye* had done, becoming in the process a hero to students for his ability to spot a 'phoney'.

Amid unprecedented clamour and worldwide interest, D.H. Lawrence's *Lady Chatterley's Lover* was finally allowed to be openly published in 1960, after a complex obscenity trial, the transcript of which now seems almost unbelievable in the paternalistic – even primeval – attitudes it reveals. Lawrence's damp squib of a book – which the prosecution felt should not be read by servants or women in case it might undermine the fabric of society – was followed in 1961 by the U.S. publication (the book had been published in France in 1934) of the much more subversive *Tropic of Cancer* by Henry Miller. In this book Miller opened – only by the merest fraction – the door guarding the passage down which fashion was to stride with enthusiasm later, the passage leading to behaviour and attitudes previously labelled perverse. In some quite crucial respects, *Tropic of Cancer* can be seen as the first modern fashion book, detailing the concept of the squalid, sordid and ugly as beautiful, fine and noble that was eventually to lead to Punk, Grunge and the glorification of the visually offensive which has been a constant of much Nineties' fashion. It was followed in 1964 by *Last Exit to Brooklyn* by Hubert Selby Jr, the first book to attempt honestly to portray the tragedies and uncertainties of sexual deviancy, and its dress, in a way that made it comprehensible to a public largely ignorant and unaware of gay attitudes and semiotics. Predictably, it ran into censorship problems around the world.

Twentieth-century history, more than any other, is misshapen and distorted by the media, never so powerful as it is now. With the increase of literacy that characterized the first half of the century, the importance

of newspapers and journals as opinion-formers grew in a way previously unthinkable. New conduits of information – radio and television – became even more powerful. None of them consistently told it like it was, but they all told it memorably. It was the media that nurtured the concept of the Swinging Sixties, but they were ten years too late. The really important postwar decade was the Fifties: when huge psychological and sociological shifts took place that were to make possible much that was 'swinging' in the next decade.

The Beatles and the Rolling Stones, hallucinogenic drugs, Twiggy and Penelope Tree: there are many reasons why the Sixties are considered to be the 'sexy' decade of the postwar period. However, in fashion terms, they were a sterile fag end to the Fifties. That was the time when the really new fashion thinking took place. It was during those years that the attitudes that would change approaches to self, society and sexuality were moulded.

How were such diverse strands of class and culture to be dressed? The answer was different for each sex. For women, the short skirt and simply cut fashions of Mary Quant and David Bond (creator of the costumes for Diana Rigg in *The Avengers*); for men the narcissism of frilled shirt fronts and brightly coloured cummerbunds from John Stephen, who, lured by cheap shop rents, began the Carnaby Street cult when he moved there in 1957. But, for both sexes, the newest, even 'sexiest', development that helped make the new young fashions known worldwide was television. In America, it had been a cultural force since the Forties. In Britain, it only began to take hold in the Fifties with the broadcast of the Queen's coronation in 1953 – although two years before it had been estimated that 35 million U.S. viewers had watched the atomic tests in Nevada on their televisions. No wonder it was developed to become youth's cultural medium, through pop shows like *Ready, Steady, Go*, later to be transformed into the phenomenally successful *Top of the Pops* – the precursor of *MTV*.

Suddenly, or so it seemed to those who had been inattentive during the Fifties, fashion was fighting alongside pop music as the basis of youth culture, each vying for the disposable wealth of an increasingly affluent group. Neither actually stole the lead, and they have walked more or less in step ever since. But fashion showed a powerful face in the Sixties, not least in film, and the media revolution, begun in 1962 when the London *Sunday Times* published its first colour supplement, came to rely heavily on fashion to enliven its pages with a mixture of sex, glamour and sophistication, as, indeed, the media still do today.

32

33 Julie Christie in
    Darling, 1965

34 Anita Ekberg in
    La Dolce Vita,
    1960

33

Christine Keeler's trial in 1963 under the Official Secrets
Act for literally sleeping with the enemy, a Soviet naval
attaché based in London, while the mistress of a cabinet
minister, can be dismissed as an ultimately not very
important manifestation of Cold War paranoia; the 1965
film, *Darling*, starring Julie Christie as an amoral model,
which echoed the Keeler case in many ways, was much
more seminal – as were *Blow-Up*, Michelangelo
Antonioni's 1966 paean to the fashion photographer
as the new sexual stud, and Silvio Narizzano's *Georgy
Girl* (1966) – the proof that girls could have fun, if they
wanted to. All were as much fashion films as Federico
Fellini's *La Dolce Vita* (1960) or, in 1971, Stanley
Kubrick's remarkably prophetic film of Anthony Burgess's
1962 novel, *A Clockwork Orange*, in that the dress of
the actors had an impact as great as, and possibly
longer lasting than, the acting or plot.

In a decade of flux and uncertainty, what stands out
about the Sixties is not just the joy and excitement that
the young derived from their newly enfranchised state
but, much more, their knowledge that, no matter how
their elders might try to obstruct them, they were
unstoppable now. Youth had arrived and would not be
going away again.

In fact, in fashion, as in most aspects of late twentieth-
century life, the young have become the main protagonists
in the majority of the movements, and even fights, for
change. The significance of their contribution must be
acknowledged across a range of the topics in this book,
but it is true to say that they reached their apogee in
the Sixties and Seventies. That was their revolution
– but that does not diminish their post-revolutionary
significance.

DESIGNER AS SUPERSTAR

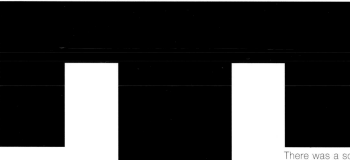

There was a scandal in the 1940s when an American newspaper suggested that Christian Dior was as well known as Sir Winston Churchill or the Pope. Today, it is often assumed that most of the great fashion designers are better known than even the most famous politicians and religious leaders. In the remotest parts of the globe, Calvin Klein's name is familiar to people who might have to pause before naming the President of the United States and would be incapable of naming any European prime minister. John Galliano appears regularly on the cover of magazines from countries as far apart as Korea and Chile, something not achieved by the Prime Minister of England. In fact, in terms of celebrity status, dress designers are in the top echelons of heroes, alongside film, sport and pop stars, eclipsed in world fame only by Margaret Thatcher and Diana, Princess of Wales, whose names, although fading as part of our daily heritage, still resonate with their past power.

The designer as superstar has become a standard part of our culture. We know designers' views on women, we are familiar with their homes, we learn their favourite recipes, we are told which parties they attend: we are aware of everything, no matter how trivial, except, perhaps, their sexuality. That is normally glossed over in the 'in-depth' profiles of top designers which are so rarely probing that they can be considered exercises in hagiography, or even sycophancy, in their lack of critical stance. Heterosexual designers like Ralph Lauren give rise to little interest in their sexual lives and those like Jean Paul Gaultier, honestly homosexual, who proclaim their sexual preferences, tend to leave the information at that. But all other details are freely available, except, of course, hard facts concerning the company finances.

In truth, not many of the readers who devour these personal interviews actually want hard facts. For some of them, merely to say that the designer is rich is sufficient to keep the romance alive. The fact is that we don't want our designers to be poor. Unlike a starving painter, a poor designer has failed us in our expectation of what a designer should be. It is interesting to note how little coverage John Galliano received from the mainstream international press in the mid-Eighties when, for all his talent, he seemed to be permanently teetering on the brink of bankruptcy; and to contrast it with the miles of newsprint and film devoted to him in the Nineties, once he had the glamour and wealth of the House of Dior behind him.

How did the cult of the fashion superstar evolve, and why? Like everything else in fashion, the evolution has been slow but distinct. Halston, the American designer whose minimalist fashion approach had a profound influence on Seventh Avenue in the Seventies, pointed out that designers were only as good as the people they dressed. It was a lesson that hit home. As the importance of individual customers dwindled, something had to be found to fill the gap. The solution was the designer himself. It was a fundamental shift. Designers were no longer to be admired because they had been chosen by women who led rich and glamorous lives. The designers were to be admired because they too lived rich and glamorous lives, often far grander than those of their clients. Valentino entertains his friends, including favoured customers, on his private yacht. Ralph Lauren lives to a level of aristocratic splendour, with a priceless collection of vintage cars and a fine stable of horses. Calvin Klein enjoys the outdoor life in

5   Calvin and Kelly
     Klein at their East
     Hampton home,
     1991, photo
     Lord Snowdon

6   (Overleaf)
     Posthumous
     tribute to Gianni
     Versace in Milan
     Cathedral, 1997

his East Hampton house. Karl Lagerfeld has houses in
Paris, Rome and Monte Carlo, each full of furniture and
museum-standard works of art. When Gianfranco Ferré
worked at Dior, he commuted between Paris and
Milan in his personal jet. Gianni Versace's funeral was
attended by Diana, Princess of Wales, not in an official
capacity, but as a friend.

Fashion designers long no more to dine with princes
or kings. They *are* the princes and kings. There are two
reasons for this, apart from our need to make them so.
First, historically, since the days of Charles Frederick
Worth, the grand couturier has held a social role far
above that of humble dressmaker, although many have
preferred not to assume it; and secondly, as some of
the richest individuals in the world (occasionally with
personal fortunes that exceed the gross national
budget of many Third World countries), the great fashion
designers pinpoint the fundamental change in the mores
of high society, whereby what matters isn't breeding
but the wealth to enjoy a lifestyle that, if opulent and
self-indulgent enough, puts the individual almost
beyond criticism.

We are talking of the cult of personality, probably the
easiest thing of all to manufacture in a vacuum. After all,
if we don't know the people concerned, how can we
disprove things they are reputed to have said or done?
Did Chanel really dismiss Schiaparelli as 'that Italian
artist who has started making clothes', or was it what
someone felt she *might* have said? Who was actually
present when Carmel Snow, editor-in-chief of *Harper's
Bazaar*, reputedly coined the expression 'the New
Look'? As everyone knows, a good saying is better if
there is a personality attached to it. Personalities can be
easily mixed in the bottle of PR chemistry and, with a
press willing to accept at face value everything it is told
– as most of the fashion press has been, for the major
part of this century – designer *bons mots* can, and do,
litter our newspapers and magazines to such an extent
that they annex not only the press but also the reader as
part of the personality-making machine. It is not merely
words that require 'the willing suspension of disbelief',
it is everything to do with fashion – and nowhere is it
more necessary than in the cult of the designer.

Larger-than-life characters are as much a part of the
fashion world as they are of the theatre. Emotional
extravagance is often part of the creative process for
those in both fields. Occasionally, they cross over.
Jean Paul Gaultier is an extrovert: he enjoys talking –
wittily, extravagantly and always intelligently – as much
in English as in French (perhaps even more so; as a
confirmed Anglophile who admits to travelling to London
for inspiration from the streets and clubs and 'to fall in

love'). His humour and theatrical talents were harnessed for the television programme *Eurotrash* (which he presented alongside the equally extrovert Antoine de Caunes), where his personality made him a cult figure whose popularity bore fruit, not in selling his clothes, but in the much more lucrative world of high-fashion fragrance. His scents for both sexes are bestsellers, not because they are necessarily better perfumes than those of other international designers, but because people are buying them in order to become part of the international, showbiz, eccentric personality known as Jean Paul Gaultier.

Seventh Avenue knows more about projection in order to gain sales than most of the rest of the fashion business put together. It is appropriate here to mention Isaac Mizrahi, who is the closest thing America has to rival the omnipresent personality of Gaultier. Mizrahi is, by his own admission, obsessed with show business and the media. Always happy to appear on a television chat show or even to host it, he projects an all-American, down-to-earth directness and ragtrade humour – half hopeful, half hopeless – which makes him much sought-after. His skill is to pretend to take lightly, even dismissively, what he clearly believes in passionately: the world of high-fashion glamour. Renowned for his slick soundbites, he even went so far as to make his own film, *Unzipped* (1995), that went some way towards capturing the frenzied hope and despair which so often characterizes the world of fashion. He continued what has been described as his love–hate relationship with the world of high-profile media fashion coverage in a series of comic strip books,

written by him, called *The Adventures of Cindy the Supermodel*, which makes fun of the extravagance of the international fashion scene and its more bizarre characters. Perhaps he allowed his interests too wide a range. Possibly the public felt uneasy that all his energies were not channelled exclusively into the making of clothes. In 1998, Mizrahi lost his backers after the disastrous failure of the launch of his second line, and was forced to go out of business. Interestingly, he professed himself relieved and talked of following other enterprises which stimulated him much more than fashion.

Why are the world's top designers spending their time on what many would see as ancillary matters? Is something lacking in their creative life? What chimera do they pursue? I believe that the worm in the bud, the fatal canker at the heart of the designer's world, is insubstantiality – and its corollary, evanescence. Fashion, by its nature, is ephemeral, and must be so if it is not to become old-fashioned. That is the problem. All creators wish to leave a mark, to give their existence some sort of permanence. It is the search for the solution to the conundrum – Who needs things so briefly important and so swiftly devalued? Who rates such things when they only affect us for a small fraction of time? – that drives fashion designers to cover their backs and take out as many insurances as they can against the indifference of posterity. They frequently do so by opening their life and soul in the hope that they will emerge as a multifaceted creator, at least some of whose genius will be remembered for posterity.

Dresses fade and decay, reputations become blurred with the dust and cobwebs of the years, but personality survives. A century and a half ago, Charles Frederick Worth understood this. Even earlier, Rose Bertin, overbearing taste-maker to Marie Antoinette, realized that, to rise above the morass of petty milliners thronging Versailles, the one who would reach the top would need to be the one with the strongest personality. Paul Poiret, at the height of his powers in the early years of the century, was the ringmaster – even the spin-doctor – for Parisian high society, despite the double-edged assessment of Edna Woolman Chase (long-term editor-in-chief of British, French and American and, briefly, German *Vogue*) that he was 'as fatuous as he was shrewd'. Although few fashion pundits could identify more than one or two of his creations, the legend of Poiret's arrogance and extravagance has survived.

For the first sixty years of the twentieth century, fashion meant couture – individual clothes made for a specific customer within the matrix of the couturier's projections for each season – the nearest fashion has ever come to being worthy of consideration as one of the arts. In the Twenties and Thirties, it was tacitly accepted that it might have an intellectual, as well as an emotional dimension. Sonia Delaunay, primarily a painter, designed textiles and clothes. For the woman who invented the concept of creative simultaneity, fashion had an immediacy which art rarely obtained. In Russia, Rodchenko, Tatlin and Popova designed clothes, confident in the belief that they were contributing to society. Chanel's work with the impresario Sergei Diaghilev is well known. Elsa Schiaparelli and Salvador

Dalí cooperated on many aspects of the couturier's presentations. Above all, Jean Cocteau, French society's cultural *éminence grise*, was passionately involved in the affairs of the grand couture houses. He regularly sat in the front row of fashion shows, next to writers such as Colette and intellectuals of the calibre of André Gide, as well as being involved in the conception of the clothes, visiting designers in their ateliers and acting as unofficial muse (in a similar way to the artist Christian Bérard, considered by many to be the real creator of the New Look) by suggestion, encouragement and inspiration.

The people who could command such solid intellectual backing were of interest not only to the high society coteries from which they drew their customers, but also on a wider scale: a reader of a good newspaper in France would be as happy with a piece on Chanel as one on Picasso; and would be as open to the opinions of Jean Patou as those of Gertrude Stein. But all the reader was given was opinion: about fashion or the arts, especially theatre, ballet and literature. No one was allowed a glimpse of the private person; dignity kept all intimate doors firmly closed. One searches old copies of *Vogue* or *Femina* in vain for the sort of 'personality' interview found endlessly in their modern equivalents. On their pages, the designer's names were almost exclusively reserved for the attribution of the clothes featured. The clothes were meant to tell you all that you needed to know – just as monographs on artists were, at that time, so impersonal in content and concentrated so much on critical assessment of their work that it required considerable concentration to discover anything about the artists themselves.

Of course, couturiers talked to journalists. Their lives were not lived behind high walls with the drawbridge firmly up. Naturally, they mixed with their customers in the habitats of the wealthy – a right wrested from a reluctant society by Worth in the last century and never

to be surrendered again – but they were part of the closed world of high society where people gossiped endlessly about each other but only the utter cad or gold-digger told it abroad.

Even in the Fifties, when people such as Edna Woolman Chase, Bettina Ballard (editor of American *Vogue*) and Cecil Beaton (whose book *The Glass of Fashion*, 1954 is arguably the best ever written about the fashionable world) published their memoirs and referred to their friendships with the great couturiers, they never gave personal details. They kept sacrosanct the aura of the individual while, of course, enhancing their own through their association with people who were household names – not only in the households of women who actually bought their clothes, but also in any house which took *Le Figaro* or the *Daily Express*. Newspapers in the United States took another path, preferring to inject glamour into their pages with gossip columns devoted to Hollywood or endlessly fascinating speculation over the lives of the stars – their homes, holidays and loves.

The cult of personality journalism, surely the most synthetic, sycophantic and insincere form of writing, started with Hollywood gossip columnists such as Hedda Hopper, whose articles were syndicated nationwide, usually on a daily basis. For the most part, their columns were pure hagiography. They were also almost total fiction. Intelligent readers knew (or suspected) this, but somehow the gods and goddesses of the screen were so much larger than life, so unreal, that stories of their loves and lifestyles were expected to be much the same. Society gossip columnists in Europe, although obsessed by the lives of the upper classes, followed much the same path. But, strangely, the private lives of the great couturiers remained private.

The man who set fashion on the Hollywood path it now enjoys was not a journalist, diarist or social commentator. He was a couturier, and a very good one

at that. Jacques Fath, who entered fashion in 1937 and came to prominence in the Forties as designer and 'social animal', provided the key needed to open the Pandora's box of publicity. He alone in Paris had the youth, good looks and charisma to be made into star material. Dior was pushing fifty; shy and retiring, he loved gardening and making wine. Balenciaga was so hostile to the press that he would barely speak to journalists. Schiaparelli, much quoted in the Thirties and, even before publishing her biography, *Shocking Life*, in 1954, more inclined to reveal her inner world than most, had lost much of her social lustre and artistic position by spending the war years in America, although she was raising money for the war effort by giving talks and making personal appearances at charity functions and major store promotions.

But Jacques Fath had everything required. With good looks, a fashionable actress wife and an outward-looking personality, he was the ideal man. And, to coin a modern phrase, his legendary love of partying would give John Galliano a run for his money. Journalists on both sides of the Atlantic loved him. Through his business connection with Joseph Halpert, he enjoyed a U.S. profile rare in the late Forties and early Fifties. Only Christian Dior had the same transatlantic presence. Fath was invited to all the grandest parties in Paris; French society loved dressing up and playing games after the long austerities of the war. Fath's appearance was welcomed across Europe by aristocratic hosts such as Charles de Beistegui and the Marquis de Cuevas, the super-rich such as Daisy Fellowes and the party-giver to outshine all party-givers, the Duchess of Windsor's friend Elsa Maxwell. It was no surprise to anybody when Rita Hayworth chose him to design her trousseau for her marriage to Prince Aly Khan in 1948. From Fath a whole new world developed for the couturier, a world which has designers such as Valentino, Oscar de la Renta and Donatella Versace popping up all over the globe, as

10 Elton John,
Donatella Versace
and David Furnish,
1995

an essential part of their job, wherever a stiff damask napkin is unfurled and a little quail in aspic offered.

It would be wrong to imagine that while Fath was performing his fancy dress fire dances, other couturiers hid, scowling, under a stone. Christian Dior, fully conversant with the power of the written word, lost no time in capitalizing on his name to make an impact beyond the confines of couture with the publication in 1957 of his memoirs, *Dior by Dior*, which was an international bestseller. In London, Norman Hartnell wrote his memoirs, *Silver and Gold*, in 1955, a year after Hardy Amies' book *Just So Far* and Schiaparelli's *Shocking Life*. But it was probably the American designers Elizabeth Hawes and Claire McCardell whose books had the most influence. In allowing ordinary women to believe that there might be a place for them in the rarified world of fashion, they ensured that their names would be known across the country.

Hawes wrote *Fashion is Spinach* in 1938, a splendidly debunking and down-to-earth commentary, still much referred to but now seldom read. It was the *Gone With the Wind* of fashion books – a must-have, must-read accessory not only in the fashion world but also for the millions of American women who never saw *Vogue* but read *McCalls* and the *Saturday Evening Post*. It gave her a profile as high as any coming out of Paris – and with that, of course, it raised the whole level of North American fashion as something to be taken seriously by those previously inclined to ignore it. It was a breakthrough in the 'designer as someone with something to say' syndrome. Claire McCardell's book, *What Shall I Wear? The What, Where, When and How Much of Fashion*, published in 1956, two years before she died, coming from the designer of clothes as a practical adjunct to modern, busy lives, became a bestseller in North America. Slowly, a new curiosity was forming. People wanted to know about dress designers: not only what they thought but also how they lived.

The designers were more than ready to oblige by spilling the beans on many, if not all, of their interests. American *Good Housekeeping* and *Homes & Gardens* began to produce discreet spreads on designers' homes: usually their summer residences or beach houses – places lived in only sporadically where no telltale personal evidence could build up – but rarely their true homes. Long before fashion people joined the great and the good in the Hamptons and took over Fire Island, it seemed that the most successful way to prise open the keyhole of their private lives was to see the surroundings they chose for relaxing, having fun and 'being themselves'. It was a pure Hollywood, Hedda Hopper approach, but it worked. Designers had finally broken into the celebrity mainstream.

They were about to enjoy the intimacy that being famous brings – the annexation of the grand name by anonymous millions who refer to celebrities as if they were their close friends. Film stars, musicians, politicians – all become part of public life, to have people discussing them, and everything about them, almost as if they were blood relations. As Hollywood columnists have long known, if people are fed enough 'intimate' details, then they really do begin to believe that they know (and love) the person. It is a technique still used today, especially on the sports pages, because it engenders a loyalty which cannot be bought. That loyalty – nothing less than brand-name preference in fashion – was as vital then as now to designers keen to sell increasingly wide ranges of merchandise bearing their names.

As the Fifties slipped into the Sixties, designer interviews – a rarified, kitsch mix of the pretentious and the banal – became commonplace. Pierre Cardin, riding high as the most financially successful designer in the world at that time, expressed his views on design in general, fashion in particular and future dress codes for what he predicted would be a quasi-space age lifestyle.

Mary Quant's opinions on the dress attitudes of the young were eagerly solicited by journalists on both sides of the Atlantic. Zandra Rhodes tried to reveal the spirituality of the creator's role by linking it with the culture of 'uncorrupted' societies such as those of native American or pre-twentieth-century Japan. The presses rolled, the words spewed out and designers inched ever closer to the final nemesis which has made their counterparts today not just celebrities but showbiz personalities.

However, it wasn't all plain sailing, even in the Sixties. The designers as international stars had their rivals and were frequently hard-pushed to keep their heads above water in the personality stakes. The great threat, from which fashion was to learn so much, was posed by the newly emerging pop idols. As the Beatles brought screaming teenage girls all over the world to their knees, and the Rolling Stones – much more androgynous in appeal – were getting the boys so overexcited that one of their fans was actually murdered at a concert in 1969, the designer as international media star lost a considerable amount of his lustre. To begin with, designers often come over badly on television – a proletarian medium wielding ferocious power over the young and impressionable. Their comments seemed affected, their personal style mannered. Effete, epicene and well-spoken as so many of them were, they couldn't compete with the raw, expletive-ridden, raunchy young pop stars. Even working-class fashion heroes such as Ossie Clark or Bill Gibb, ethereal and down-to-earth respectively, or Betsey Johnson, cheerfully feigning madness for publicity purposes, couldn't really compete as entertainment with an East End lad or a West Coast guy, complete with guitar, tumbling curls and a taut body. While largely spitting out dress designers as unpalatable for the general taste, television couldn't get enough of their cool counterparts on the music scene.

11   Yves Saint Laurent,
     1971, photo
     Jeanloup Sieff

12   Yves Saint Laurent
     and his portraits
     by Andy Warhol,
     1972, photo
     Jeanloup Sieff

11

Things could only get worse. If the Sixties had been a troubled decade politically and socially, the Seventies were even more ill at ease. An era of upheaval, it saw four antiwar protestors killed at Kent State University in Ohio (1970); the beginning of the Irish problem; international hijackings and the seizure of hostages; the rise of the Ayatollah Khomeini in Iran and, above all, Richard Nixon's troubles, beginning with the Vietnam War and draft dodgers and ending with Watergate. The winds of change were blowing, and they were affecting not only the profile of fashion but also the profiles of the great designers. Frenzied efforts were made to staunch the flow as it became increasingly difficult to get the life-giving adrenalin shot of personal publicity.

The solution came from the people whom designers court and fear in roughly equal measure. If they were in trouble, the press was even more beleaguered. As colour supplements and weekend 'specials' proliferated, editors began to foresee a time when they wouldn't have enough editorial matter to support the advertising which was becoming an increasingly vital part of a newspaper's revenue. The 'in-depth' designer interview was born. For the cost of two thousand words and a 'mug shot', not only were vital pages filled, but also the interest of the public was regenerated. The world's top dress designers had made the unlikely step towards becoming 'sexy'. They were moving forward to their apogee of the Eighties.

It wasn't just newspapers. Magazines began to spring up in order to fulfil the need for an exotic world as compensation for the dreariness of everyday life. In Italy, especially, there seemed to be a new one every month. *Donna*, *Per Lei*, *Harper's Bazaar*, *Vogue*, *Linea Italiana* – Italian magazines were the best in the world, thick and juicy with advertising carefully aimed at different market levels, from the young (*Per Lei*) to the established (*Donna*). Top designers such as Valentino, Pino Lancetti and Mila Schön would be featured in solid blocks of advertisements, paid for in the main by fabric manufacturers, with anything up to twenty consecutive pages in the peak collections issues in March and October. Licensees using the designer's names advertised in fewer pages but with as much determination. Whereas French fashion houses

made their money through sales of ancillary products such as make-up and perfume, in Italy it was accessories that kept the designer's name current – especially sunglasses, which every self-respecting Italian changes every year. In fact, an Italian fashion insider whom I asked to explain the wealth of his country's designers, replied with only a slight smile, 'Occhiali'.

In troubled times, editors fall back on what Dr Johnson believed was the last refuge of the scoundrel: patriotism. Italian magazines increasingly featured interviews with Italian designers, largely ignoring Paris and New York on their fashion pages, although fully covering French literature or American films on their arts pages. American *Vogue* concentrated on boosting Seventh Avenue. English magazines were partisan about their home-grown product. In the mid-Seventies, when most young women preferred street style and tended to create their own fashion mix out of anything they could afford, from antique nightdresses to workers' dungarees, the designers appeared to be about to join the endangered species list.

It was *Interview* which really saved the designer as personality. Founded in 1969 by Andy Warhol as a film magazine, it soon changed as Warhol's obsession with glamour grew. By the early Seventies, it was devoting more space to fashion personalities and gossip than any other magazine, but it had a different approach to most of its competitors. As its name suggests, this was the first personality-led magazine where talking to people in the fashion world, at every level, was more important than showing clothes. It was a godsend for the designer as superstar. The first of many designer interviews appeared in May 1972, when Halston talked to the actor Pat Ast. It set the tone and style. Virtually every designer with a North American profile appeared in *Interview*, from Yves Saint Laurent, who talked to Bianca Jagger in 1975, to Jean Paul Gaultier ten years later. Diana Vreeland appeared twice, first talking about Chanel, and then talking about herself. The fashion world soon realized how ideal an article in *Interview* was for the making of celebrities. With its soft-edged questions, minimal editing and a readership consisting almost exclusively of fashion insiders, eager to learn and questioning nothing, designers were queuing up.

15

14

If *Interview* was the spearhead, it was swiftly followed by another American fashion publication. *W* was the arrestingly esoteric name for the social magazine published as an offshoot of the specialist trade newspaper, *Women's Wear Daily*. Initially broadsheet size, unbound and with advertising heavily outweighing editorial, it has since grown into a perfect-bound magazine, still very much larger than any others, but with much more emphasis on editorial content. Since its inception in 1972, *W* has concentrated on designer interviews – but just when people were beginning to become satiated with the predictability and clichés which are endemic to the genre, it took an encouraging new turn. In the mid-Eighties, it augmented its interviews with photographic essays, in the *House & Garden* tradition, of the designers in their habitat, always suitably glamorous. *W* featured Yves Saint Laurent in his Marrakesh hideaway, Valentino at Gstaad or on his yacht, Ralph Lauren at his Colorado ranch or Karl Lagerfeld in his Paris *pied-à-terre* with his outstanding Louis XV furniture. The designers were portrayed as superstars living rarified lives in superlative surroundings.

Designers *were* superstars and the whole world knew it. Allowing us carefully edited glimpses into their private worlds did the trick – and why should they do otherwise? Even superstars are allowed some privacy and, as we've all known since childhood, an unrevealed mystery intrigues much more than throwing wide all the windows and doors. Wise designers keep some details of their gilded lives to themselves in order to hold our attention that bit longer.

The Eighties will surely be seen in retrospect as the most decadent and dubious decade of the twentieth century. Driven by greed, fuelled by envy and powered by indifference to everything but personal ambitions, it worshipped success and all but deified the super-rich. Such a single-minded era had the courage of its convictions. It enabled the lucky ones to achieve what they longed for. Perhaps a coup in the City of London or a windfall on Wall Street wouldn't enable a complete lifestyle change and couldn't buy them an island retreat such as Giorgio Armani's on the Mediterranean island of Pantelleria, or an eighteenth-century country hideaway like Stone House in New England where Bill Blass lived the life of an English country squire. But, as the Eighties built up to their climax, and more and more people found themselves in a financial position to buy their dream house (at whatever level), it could be predicted that the glitter of the great would come to be seen as merely tinsely or even tawdry by sophisticated readers of glossy magazines.

16

Greatness surrounds itself with greatness. Throughout history, the rich and the powerful have been attracted to each other. It is a question of reflected glory. And it was that which gave a new twist to the designer as superstar in the second half of the Eighties. In a way, the wheel had come full circle. In the past, as Halston had said, designers gained their kudos from the grandeur of their customers. Even as late as the early Sixties, couture customers, treated by couturiers as surrogate trophy wives, were proudly displayed and neurotically guarded. No fashion house is happy about divulging the names of private customers – now, as then, they are the subject of infinite tact and, like the cost of the creations they buy, kept as secret as possible. But they were – and are – proudly displayed in subtle, indirect ways.

In the past, a top Paris fashion house might have over two thousand customers. It was a point of honour not to lose one. The person responsible for keeping the customer happy, giving her the illusion that she was making entirely her own decision and making sure that her appearance in public would reflect well on the house and its standards, was the vendeuse. Half saleswoman, half confidante and friend, the vendeuse needed to know her customer very well. It was her job to ensure that the house kept its identity in the clothes a customer wore but provided her with fashions suited to her life and her figure. Couturiers hated promiscuous customers: they expected to dress all but their grandest clients exclusively. Diana Vreeland once asked Balenciaga for his reaction to a woman who would buy from several houses. He shrugged. 'I wouldn't dress her because it shows she is merely interested in clothes and doesn't understand fashion.' Old-fashioned and untenable as such a position appears today, the thinking still remains, at least residually. No modern couturier will appear on high-profile occasions with even the richest of women if they aren't at least seventy-five per cent

loyal – a loyalty rewarded with price reductions and even some free clothes.

Designers have always been happy to act as 'walkers' to the richer women on their client list. In the Seventies and early Eighties, the American designer Bill Blass almost made a second career out of it. But the Eighties saw the supermodels oust the superclients. More newsworthy, sexier and usually much more fun to be with than the average customer, they appeared to have been sent from heaven for the designer wishing to attain an international high profile. As the supermodels grew as a phenomenon, so did the desirability of being seen by their side. The paparazzi loved them and so did editors. For the first time in history, models appeared on the front page of quality broadsheets like the London and New York *Times*. The designer's chief rivals in the supermodel walker league were photographers. The designers usually won. Kate, Naomi, Cindy et al. were happiest on the arm of one of the top designers who, with the possible exception of Helmut Newton, Irving Penn and Richard Avedon, had more 'profile' – and much more money. And to keep in their favour, designers would usually present the model with the dress she had worn at the event. This pattern has modified slightly in the Nineties with sexy actresses nudging models aside as people to be 'walked' – not only were they often as beautiful in face and figure, someone of the stature of Gwyneth Paltrow, Demi Moore or Nicole Kidman had her own very considerable profile to bring to the coupling.

By the late Eighties, the axis had changed, in any case. Rather than gaining kudos by association, designers were in a position to confer it with an authority previously lacking. The turning point had come with Christian Lacroix, whose debut was greeted with such a blaze of publicity that, in less than six months, he was famous on both sides of the Atlantic. What Lacroix

20

brought to fashion was a theatricality and extravagance
which made for such marvellous photographs that,
singlehandedly, he made couture newsworthy to an
extent not seen since the New Look. But this was a
new couture. Glamorous, opulent and exciting as it was,
it wasn't aimed primarily at private customers: it was
created for the media.

Other designers lost no time in jumping on the new
bandwagon. Gianfranco Ferré produced a series of
clothes so convincing in their decorative authority that
he was chosen to be the artistic director at Christian
Dior in 1989. Versace began showing couture.
Valentino's shrewd commercial sense and many years
of experience meant that a high proportion of the few
remaining private customers patronized him, or Oscar
de la Renta, who was creating couture at Pierre Balmain
from 1993. As with most European high fashion, the
men who appealed most to private customers were
those who had worked at couture level for over thirty
years. Karl Lagerfeld at Chanel and Yves Saint Laurent
created some of the most memorable collections in the
Eighties and continued to do so in the following decade.

The new couture can be seen as an extension of the
art of dressmaking or merely another facet to the
personality cult which kept the superstar designer high
in the firmament. Those who were up there – their
names in lights – knew it, not only by their swelling bank
balances but also by how the press and the public
addressed them. Like heads of state and major political
figures, they could measure their status by the fact
that they were referred to by surname alone – the most
flattering shorthand of all – unless, of course, they were

23 Vivienne
    Westwood
    wearing a dress
    from the 'Five
    Centuries Ago'
    collection, 1997,
    photo Gian Paolo
    Barbieri

24 Vivienne
    Westwood, 1996,
    photo Platon

24

women. No modern female designer has reached the deified state of Chanel.

However, one has managed to get close. Vivienne Westwood, the greatest exponent of self-promotion her country has produced in fashion, has grown in stature over the past fifteen years to become a world-class name. Always contentious, with the brilliant knack of knowing how to *épater le bourgeois*, to quote André Breton, her personality, simultaneously vulnerable and vainglorious, has been as important in making her a star as her clothes have – perhaps even more so. Whereas success enabled a designer like Ralph Lauren to step out of the public eye, allowing his clothes, and how they are marketed, to say all he wishes to say, Westwood, as tender as she is tendentious, is in love with the ex cathedra remark and can never resist the temptation to be outrageous. The Westwood appearance has been transformed many times and, in its current manifestation, is inclined towards grandeur, but it is a grandeur as confused as many of her utterances. She appears to be transforming herself, for official 'portraits' at least, into a facsimile of Elizabeth I but, in fact, it is Good Queen Bess as she might have been played by a Restoration fop: rather too highly coloured and extreme to have any verisimilitude. But, by her appearance, utterances and clothes together, Westwood has become a frontline superstar – the first British designer to do so.

25 Alexander
    McQueen, 1997,
    photo Sean Ellis

26 (Overleaf)
    Alexander
    McQueen for
    Givenchy
    haute couture,
    1997–8

She has been followed by others to such an extent that it is hard not to imagine that all young British designers leave college with the belief that relying on the clothes to speak for themselves is far too slow a process, and that a little chutzpah in the self-publicity department is the key to quick fame. Is that the secret of Alexander McQueen's success? Certainly, his personality has been marketed quite as actively as his design skills. Interviewers have delighted in giving him the opportunity to prove that he is not in the mould of the traditional English gentleman so beloved by the rest of the world. His anarchic views, coarse language and apparent contempt for the press cannot be disguised. If Vivienne Westwood has proved that outrageous behaviour (wearing no underwear or appearing in a body stocking with nothing but a fig leaf to cover her nakedness) is newsworthy, McQueen has learned the lesson. The superstar designer as *enfant terrible* has been the marketing ploy of Jean Paul Gaultier for twenty years, but most of the outrage appeared on the catwalk and the shock was always tempered with wit. McQueen seems to need to go further. Apparently totally devoid

of humour, his clothes and his personality spit angrily at what he sees as the contemptible world of conventional fashion. And it is that personality as much as his radical fashion approach which has made him a superstar.

Although it would be wrong to suggest that the man overshadows the work, it can confidently be assumed that when he was hired by Bernard Arnault to take over the design role at Givenchy after Galliano had accepted the post of design director at Dior in 1997, the decision was made in light of the fact that McQueen himself would be as newsworthy as anything he placed on the runway. In fact, McQueen at Givenchy presented a fashion profile tamed and refined, although his personality, encouraged by success, became less tractable and more outspoken. His criticisms of Paris fashion and Givenchy himself made him unpopular in France, but he rewarded Arnault's faith by creating clothes of a traditional beauty and accomplishment that were featured in the world's media almost as frequently as those of Galliano at Dior. Such a man has no need to 'walk' anyone in order to stay in the limelight. McQueen feels no compulsion to let a glossy magazine into his

private life, and yet he has achieved more publicity than many who have. Does he herald a new era where, instead of playing the social games of the wealthy, the designer has merely to outrage in order to be kept in the public eye?

Outrage, personal or public, is only one aspect of superstardom for the new-guard Nineties' designers. It is part of fashion's love of the excessive, which has grown from the extravagance of the Eighties' fashion scene. Then, it was Christian Lacroix and his revival of couture which caught the world's imagination. Subsequently, it has been John Galliano who has fascinated both fashion commentators and the general public. He has become a superstar because of the overall package he presents. Many see his approach to fashion as fantastic, highly decorative and difficult to relate to the tenor of the times. Whether working under his own label or at the House of Dior, Galliano's clothes are rich with references to the past. But in fact they are not the flight from reality which many erroneously judge them to be. Neither are they a pastiche of the past, in the way that Vivienne Westwood's are. Indeed, they lack the sense

27   John Galliano,
      1996, photo
      Paolo Roversi

28   John Galliano
      ready-to-wear
      collection, 1997–8

of humour which is her saving grace. What they are is a modern reworking of past obsessions, entirely practical in a way that many of her most brilliant ideas are not. And so is Galliano's own appearance. He loves dressing up and literally transforming himself from season to season, usually to reflect the mood of his new collection. Rarely seen in public, he is, nevertheless, keen to have his different fancy dress appearances recorded, and has posed for many of the great fashion photographers in various guises and with different gender emphasis.

But it is neither the clothes nor his appearance which have made him the fashion superstar of the late Nineties. It is the extravagance of his fashion shows. Funded by budgets few designers are able to command, Galliano has staged his fashion shows with all the showbiz razzmatazz of Barnum and Bailey, the Ziegfeld Follies, Diaghilev's Ballets Russes or the Folies-Bergère – and to the same ecstatic approval. The designer as superstar stands transformed into the designer as showman, ringmaster to a hectic, eclectic mix of period inspirations and styles, shaken up by the designer's imagination and spilled out as a kaleidoscopic cornucopia of ideas in which the setting is equally as important as the fashions being shown. Galliano has given us the ethereal, with a haunting fashion show in an empty and deserted house. He has transformed sterile show spaces into New York rooftops. He has reanimated a seventeenth-century château, peopling it with models and 'props' to bring it alive. He has recaptured the glory of the Paris Opéra in its heyday and has even recreated a transvestite bar from the Twenties – all in order to make clear that he is not merely showing clothes but is also using them to recreate a total fashion aura which reflects his personal interests and obsessions.

And it is that which has made him the superstar of the moment. At the beginning of the twenty-first century it is clear that, to keep the interest of the world, a designer must do much more than merely create fashion. They must create themselves, in a form which people can understand, accept and be excited by. The fashionable world – which includes most of us now – clamours for gossip, as it always has. But what excites us is not merely learning how designers live, who their friends are, or even their sexual predilections. What we are all saying now is what Diaghilev said almost a century ago: 'Astonish me'. It is the skill to do that which has captured the imaginations even of people for whom fashion and the glamorous life are not of compelling interest. We are talking of personality, something surprisingly rare in fashion. But not just personality. What the world demands from its superstar designers is the Poiret option – behaviour so extravagant and outrageous that it amuses and entertains at all levels. For the last years of the twentieth century, the personalities *par excellence* have been people of the calibre of Westwood, Gaultier and Mizrahi. For the twenty-first century we will admire only those designers who, like McQueen and Galliano, appear to stand outside the system and show us that fact not only by the extravagance of their personal worlds and fashion presentations but also by their ability to use both to say something new. Glossy poolside photographs and carefully styled studies of designer drawing rooms no longer satisfy. The New York writer Fran Leibovitz's comment that 'Polite conversation is no conversation' couldn't be more true than in the fashion world. To satisfy in the future, we need the expletives – literally and metaphorically.

With the directness on which a good part of her myth
rests, Coco Chanel summed up the role of the fashion
model when she told Marcel Vertès, the artist and
fashion illustrator, 'I pay them to make women envious.'
She knew that envy was the first step on the path
to sales, just as, hard-headed businesswoman that
she was, she realized that future sales – and the
continuance of business – depended on designing
clothes that kept women envious. Her contemporary and
competitor, Jean Patou, shared her view. His decision in
1925 to use American women as his models, claiming
that their healthy, sporty looks were more in tune with
the times than the refinement of French models, created
a sensation and made his European customers envy
their fresh new looks. More importantly, it acknowledged
the strength of American influence during the twentieth
century, in fashion, as in every other cultural area.

By its choice of fashion models, Europe recognized the
importance of the American market at an early stage. In
the Twenties, Edward Steichen – considered by many to
be the doyen of fashion photographers – chose as his
model the American, Marion Morehouse, because of her
figure (long and sporty), her assured and relaxed stance
but, above all, for her essentially transatlantic modernity.
Since then, models have been fashion's storm troopers,
introducing looks which shock at first but then produce
lookalike copies in every section of society. Although
many of the most influential have been Europeans, the
majority have been Americans. In the elegant Fifties,
they ruled entirely. The sisters Dorian Leigh and Suzy
Parker, Dovima, Sunny Harnett and Anne Saint Marie
were the editorial and advertising queens, photographed
by Horst P. Horst, Richard Avedon and Irving Penn,

6

7

whose wife Lisa Fonssagrives was considered by many
to be the greatest of her generation. They all had wit,
style and confidence in front of the camera. They knew
how to look elegant, even ethereal, without looking stiff,
artificial or pompous. In this respect, they had the edge
over their European counterparts, especially British
models, such as Barbara Goalen, whose icy perfection
must surely have frightened away more women than it
attracted. If Chanel's dictum is true, its corollary is that
envy leads to emulation, but it is hard to imagine most
women having the temerity to imitate such polar
remoteness.

   However, things were to change. American
egalitarianism was nudged aside – although not
destroyed – by European singularity as the model-
as-character evolved. Almost entirely European, these
women were loved by photographers for their unusual
looks. By no means always beautiful and often with an
aura of sexual and social ambiguity, they especially
appealed to the new young photographers who were
part of the Swinging London fashion revolution, most of
whom were very different from the established British
fashion photographers such as Cecil Beaton and John
French. The photographers David Bailey and Terence
Donovan, although trained by such men, came from a
different class and culture; they rejected the upper-class
ideals that obsessed Beaton in particular for his entire
life. Above all, they were heterosexual and what they
wished to capture on film was not elegance, grandeur or
finesse, which they considered old-fashioned and elitist,
but the healthy sexuality of the young, fit woman who
saw herself as an individual. It was at this point that the
concept of allure was dropped from the fashion lexicon
for good in the twentieth century, as the tweed and tulle
models suddenly found themselves replaced by those
they regarded as urchins of the streets – and not the
streets of Mayfair, either. Ingrid Boulting, Penelope Tree,
Veruschka and Twiggy were all unique and even Jean
Shrimpton, conventionally the most beautiful of them all,
had a quality that other models attempted to copy but
never captured.

Being unique is one thing. Selling clothes is another. As Chanel knew, if fashion is about anything, it is about persuasion: the ability to convince people that altered states are not only possible but desirable, so that they have to purchase items neither necessary nor useful. For that to happen, a model has to have her look interpreted by a photographer who fully understands it, finds it exciting or needs to exploit it. With models like Twiggy, whose skinniness could have made her appear androgynous or grotesque, the right photographer was crucial. It took a great photographer to make her look so right for the times that no other look mattered. David Bailey did for her what he had already done for Shrimpton. He made both women icons for fashion followers on both sides of the Atlantic. More importantly, he made them news, convinced the public that their humdrum job was exotic and glamorous and placed them on a pedestal with other larger-than-life people whom ordinary morals are meant to watch, envy and even, perhaps, emulate – according to the media. In fact, both women were a gift to newspapers, magazines and television programmes: Twiggy's bizarre voice, figure and movements, once described in *Newsweek* as 'four straight limbs in search of a woman's body', made her an international 'personality', with store mannequins designed in her image, while Shrimpton's beauty was regarded by the world as the personification of refined British 'class'. The impact of the new British models was so great that, for the first time, even people with only a marginal interest in fashion became aware of them.

It was a watershed. No women whose stock in trade was beauty had previously enjoyed such universality,

except the great turn-of-the-century actresses such as Eleonora Duse and Lillie Langtrey, a handful of pre-World War I beauties, and the great film stars of the Twenties and Thirties such as Gloria Swanson, Greta Garbo and Katharine Hepburn. But now Twiggy was treated as if she were a film star – a role she eventually adopted, although with considerably less success than she had achieved in her modelling career. In fact, the importance of Twiggy as a model, and a fashion figurehead, would be hard to overestimate. Not only did she start a mini-cult of 'model turned actress' transformations in the Sixties and Seventies, as women such as Charlotte Rampling, Jacqueline Bisset and Capucine followed the earlier example of Lauren Bacall and Grace Kelly, but Twiggy also gave the model a financial status that forced the world to take her seriously as details of her annual earnings were revealed in newspapers. Although Twiggy was not the first fashion model to become well known – Barbara Goalen's name was familiar not only to readers of the glossy magazines but also in the popular press, and Suzy Parker was for many the face of American sophistication that rivalled and even outshone the European version – her universal appeal was something entirely new. Crowds gathered wherever she appeared, in the same way as they did for stars like the Beatles and the Rolling Stones; although not in such numbers. The model had now acquired a previously unknown status.

Modelling was about to become part of the entertainment business, to enter a world of gossip and speculation, where details of the personal lives of the few who become household names make them seem

as familiar as the girl next door. Star quality is about image dissemination; superstar quality is about image saturation. Twiggy was not the greatest model of the first twenty years of the postwar period, but she was certainly the most famous. It was inevitable that she would move into film and television at a time when mass-culture heroines had to be accessible, even ordinary, as the success of Mary Tyler Moore and Goldie Hawn have demonstrated.

Twiggy pointed the way for what came later – the cult of the supermodel – but, before that, other developments had to take place; most importantly, the distinction between photographic and runway models which had grown up in the late Forties, had to disappear. In earlier years, all types of model had normally remained anonymous to the general public, although fashion insiders knew the women who showed the collections of the couturiers, many of whom were named and had their contribution to the success of a fashion house acknowledged. In his biography, *Dior by Dior* of 1957, Christian Dior devoted a chapter to the importance of his house models in helping him form his overall mood each season. In fact, house models were chosen by couturiers because they felt that their looks and aura would not only be an inspiration but also be understandable to customers. Models were an ideal to which it was hoped those customers would aspire. Dior had nine house models, each meant to personify an aspect of his fashion approach, and customers had their favourites. Choosing a model to wear a particular dress was a crucial decision: would it look better on Victoire and inspire the customers who identified with her to buy

11   12   13   14

15

16

15 (Previous page)
    Yves Saint Laurent
    and house models
    in the 'Trapeze'
    collection, 1958

16 (Previous page)
    Still from
    William Klein's
    film *Qui êtes-vous,
    Polly Magoo?*,
    1966

17 Walter Albini
    catwalk show,
    1971

it, or would more of Lucky's fans see themselves in it? The house model was normally employed by a couturier on an exclusive basis; the photographic model, who was freelance, worked directly for a magazine. With the growth of ready-to-wear, runway models appeared. They were rarely photographed by the magazines and were never under contract to the designer. By the early Eighties, runway and photographic models had merged into one and house models had become anonymous, used for fittings but rarely seen by the public and never used in shows.

When a couture house produced little ready-to-wear clothing – which was never shown on the runway and only appeared on hangers in the couturier's boutique – in-house models were sufficient. However, by the beginning of the Seventies, ready-to-wear had become the driving force behind all fashion houses. Even Yves Saint Laurent, the greatest couturier of the second half of the century, declared couture dead when he stopped producing it in 1971, although he soon realized its importance in creating the image necessary to sell the vital licensed goods, and quietly reinstated it less than two years later.

If the *raison d'être* of Paris couture was an elegance attainable by only a handful of women, demanding, as it did, a sophisticated way of life, ready-to-wear was fashion of the people, for the people. The heightened elegance that couture models had portrayed, taking it to almost grotesque limits, the statuesque gravitas and the affected body language had all been satirized by William Klein, the disenchanted American fashion photographer, with whose genius *Vogue* never quite came to terms, in his 1966 film, *Qui êtes-vous, Polly Magoo?*, a sharp attack on an industry he felt had betrayed him and a damning commentary on fashion models.

Although the film had little impact on women outside the fashion world due to its limited distribution, it had a profound effect on the industry itself in emphasizing the

democratization of fashion inherent in the concept of ready-to-wear. The change in attitude to models and their role was dramatic. No longer selling a fantasy, their job was to sell clothes. Looking extraordinary was considered hostile to sales. For the mall-shopping suburbans at whom much of ready-to-wear was aimed, normality of a kind which still had enough gloss to be aspirational but not so much as to be frightening was the norm. Models now had to look as American and everyday as Jane Fonda or Sharon Tate.

Although the product had changed, modelling was still a desirable and well-paid job in the Seventies, but the power of the house model had gone. Whereas couture presentations had needed no more than eight to ten models, working at a pace that by modern standards would be considered stately, if not funereal, ready-to-wear shows were vaudeville by comparison. In a short space of years, gilt chairs in heavily perfumed salons had been declared dead, and spaces that could seat a thousand people – on plastic stackable chairs chosen for their practicality rather than aesthetic or symbolic reasons – were necessary to accommodate the increasing numbers of buyers, journalists, well-wishers and hangers-on who were attracted to this glamorous and sexy form of showbusiness as fashion began to take a central role in cultural life, a position it has maintained ever since. House models had seen it as part of their duty – indeed, their real job – to stand for long boring hours of fittings, not daring to move until they fainted from fatigue, a common occurrence in any grand couture house as single-minded maestros pursued a dream of elegance so compulsive that they were totally unaware of anything or anyone around them. The show was the model's perk and moment of glory for enduring such privations. Such an attitude was out of kilter with the new ideas of fashion presentation evolving in the city that soon challenged the hegemony of Paris as the fashion capital of the world.

Italian fashion, which started in Rome, base of its couture industry, and flirted with Florence, centre of its vitally important postwar knitting and leather industries, was entrenched in Milan by the mid-Seventies. Its eyes were firmly fixed on America as the market to annex. The Italian designers were about to change a fifty-year-old pattern of trade between France and America and recast it in their own favour. For years, Paris had provided the ideas, America the technical know-how of mass production. American manufacturers paid high prices for the right to reproduce Paris fashion which they then had made up in their own factories in the United States. It worked for Paris because French fashion was, in industrial terms, a cottage industry based on couture houses, many of which were small enterprises, although with enough ideas to support the entire American fashion industry.

The Italians spotted the gap in the market. They realized they had the manufacturing skills lacking in France as well as a much higher level of craftsmanship than that found in America. To exploit both, they invented the 'Made in Italy' label, which provided such snob appeal in foreign markets that it soon overwhelmed the rather tired 'Paris Original' label which had been the mainstay of French design for over fifty years. Like Patou before them, Italian designers – foremost among them Walter Albini working with Mariuccia Mandelli, whose house, Krizia, founded in 1954, became a driving force in late Seventies' and early Eighties' fashion – turned to America for its runway models, creating a totally new sub-genre.

House models lost their status, and they never recovered it. Photographic models continued to work in their highly paid field, but the Italians had pointed the way to the future. The new runway models soon achieved a stature that threatened the power of the photographic model and, as *Newsweek* tacitly acknowledged when it hailed Jean Shrimpton as

18 Lauren Hutton
    for 'Ultima' II
    by Revlon,
    c.1973, photo
    Richard Avedon

19 Isabella Rossellini,
    1984, photo
    Terry O'Neill

'the template from which the face of Western beauty will
be cast until further notice', it was a considerable power
as theirs were the only faces of models that the public
normally saw because runway pictures of fashion shows
had not become an integral part of newspapers as they
were in the late Eighties and the Nineties.

Just as the broad new market created by ready-to-wear
stimulated a new, less elitist approach to fashion, so the
photographic models in demand were increasingly
required to have an all-American look: perfect teeth,
bright eyes and squeaky-clean hair. Indeed, the
airbrushed faces on the covers of American fashion
magazines from the late Seventies or early Eighties now
look sterile, interchangeable and saccharine. It seemed
as if America could no longer produce women like
Wilhemina, the highest paid model of the Sixties, raised
in Chicago but with the added international cachet of
having spent her childhood in Holland and Germany.
Non-threatening to other women and just exotic enough
to stand out, she had the same calm dignity as Grace
Kelly and her face was as finely chiselled as Audrey
Hepburn's. In fact, she was the face of fashion's halfway
house as it exchanged the exotic for the accessible.

Accessibility came with Lauren Hutton, whose appeal
was summed up in Richard Avedon's comment that
she represented 'the link between the dream and the
drugstore'. Gap-toothed and radiant with health, she
personified not only the woman whom Middle-American
women wanted to be, but also the confident, reliable
and good-looking woman whom Middle-American men
desired as mother to their children. She represented the
triumph of normality and the sexiness of the everyday –
the reason why she was chosen as the 'face' of Revlon's
Ultima make-up range in 1973, the first of the big-money
exclusive contracts that would lead to make-up and
perfume houses signing stars like Isabella Rossellini,
international figures such as Liz Hurley and models
like Karen Elson – for considerably more than
Hutton's $400,000. At the time, however, that figure
was considered a mind-boggling and even morally
reprehensible sum to be paid for something as transitory
as being the face to which dreams could be attached –
the impermanence of which is shown by the dropping
of Rossellini when she reached the age of forty.

Hutton's face, like those of all models whose
photographs appeared publicly in the Sixties, was
Caucasian. The fashion industry has a murky history of
bigotry in its dealings with black women. In the Sixties
and early Seventies, top New York model agencies such
as the Eileen Ford agency were reluctant to take them
on, not because of racial prejudice but for commercial
expediency. They were given few photographic

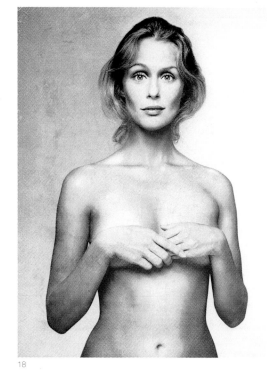

18

21

22

assignments and it was not until 1974 that Beverly Johnson became the first black American woman to appear on the cover of *Vogue*, albeit in August, a 'dead' month when any adverse reactions would be least likely to affect sales that were already lower than those for other months. It was a landmark moment, but black models were still largely confined to working for magazines and advertising campaigns aimed solely at black women. Other ethnic groups were less likely to be kept out in the cold, especially if they had an exotic background. The Eurasian model China Machado had worked as a house model for Hubert de Givenchy as early as 1956; Tina Chow, an Asian–American, had been a successful model from the late Sixties; and Marie Helvin, a Hawaiian–American, was an established international figure. Even so, the world of the photographic model was still predominantly the domain of white women.

It was catwalk modelling that destroyed this stranglehold, and the breakthrough was spearheaded by one woman, whose looks, skill and style opened the floodgates for black models. Pat Cleveland is one of fashion's prodigy figures. Part of the powerful entourage of the fashion illustrator Antonio Lopez, who was responsible for introducing her and Jerry Hall to Europe, she outshone all the other models in a show. She had the authority of a prima ballerina, which relegated the rest to the corps de ballet.

Italian designers loved her and realized that her theatricality – raucous or refined, according to mood – was what they needed on their runways. Black girls poured into Europe for their shows. Many, like Billie Blair, were almost of the same stature as Cleveland, but Cleveland had the edge on them because of her histrionic flair. All were tall, beautiful and exotic. In a feeding frenzy for the new look, Milanese designers booked them in preference to traditional white models; indeed, many of Milan's most important runway shows in the last years of the Seventies contained no white models at all, as they were considered vapid, stilted and too ladylike. By contrast, the confident black models exuded a powerful sexuality as they strode down the runway, laughing, joking, dancing and singing, often in groups of as many as twenty at a time, to the sound of the enthusiastic applause of thousands in the audience.

Black models were regarded by the Italians as the vital missing link in fashion. The French, however, used black models with greater circumspection, never allowing them to destroy their client base. Though black models appeared in Paris, they never swamped a presentation. French fashion attitudes have always been conformist and bourgeois even when they have produced forward-thinking and radical designers. It is one of the industry's paradoxes. In the Seventies, most Parisian fashion houses used black models cautiously because they were afraid of alienating their major customer, the great American fashion stores. The French designer Jean Paul Gaultier tells a salutary tale of his early years working for Patou. His suggestion that the firm should use a beautiful black woman he knew as a model was instantly rejected because of her colour, on the basis that American clients would not be happy with the choice.

23   Jerry Hall, 1971,
     photo Terry O'Neill

And that was in the Seventies, when black models had
already made their presence felt in Italy.

Nevertheless, black runway models not only made the
job of showing clothes as glamorous and prestigious as
photographic modelling, they also changed – or, at least,
helped to modify – design attitudes by their presence,
their colour and their larger-than-life catwalk style. In
fact, the only person with enough 'showbiz' charisma
to challenge the supremacy of Pat Cleveland was Jerry
Hall, a tall Texan, as languid as Cleveland was energetic.
Able to exude a heavy, musky sexuality allied with a
laconic self-mockery, she became the favourite of
such designers as Thierry Mugler and Claude Montana,
whose kitsch, high-camp creations she wore with total
conviction because she understood the ironic comment
on femininity that these clothes were making.

'Larger-than-life' women required clothes with the same
characteristics. New York designers such as Bill Blass,
Halston and Oscar de la Renta joined Italian designers in
creating what, in the Eighties, became the Power Look
that spawned a thousand exaggerated silhouettes:
military shoulders, wide and heavily buckled belts and
figure-hugging skirts and trousers. It seemed as though
the whole fashion world was under Mugler's influence,
but designers were really only responding to what was
for many of them the alien but exciting power and
confidence of black models.

In fashion, nothing lasts for long and the days of the
over-all pre-eminence of black models were numbered
even before the Japanese arrived in Paris en masse
in the early Eighties and completely swept away their
runway presence, though not their influence, which
resurfaced in the late Eighties, with the rise of the
supermodel. The Japanese put models firmly back in their
place, relegating stars such as Jerry Hall and Iman, who
had made almost as great a media impact as the clothes
they were paid to show, to a back seat. The Japanese
designers Rei Kawakubo of Commes des Garçons,
who arrived in Paris in 1980, and Yohji Yamamoto,
who opened his boutique there in 1981, brought with
them an aesthetic entirely free of vulgarity, cheap show
tricks or traditional fantasy. Their highly original clothes
were designed with the realities of the last quarter of
the twentieth century in mind. Totally rejecting all the
model archetypes that had gone before, they proposed a
solution never previously seen on the catwalks of Europe
and, by doing so, they raised important questions.

Fashion – especially in its highest form – has
traditionally been about sexuality and the power it
bestows on women. Over the centuries, it has renewed
that power whenever it has shown signs of flagging
through overfamiliarity by changing its emphasis and

23

highlighting what the fashion historian James Laver called the 'shifting erogenous zone'. Breasts, waists, legs, ankles, necks and even wrists have been pinpointed at various times. The desired effect was always to create sexual excitement in the male onlooker – and, maybe, occasionally, in the female. No matter how trite such devices were, fashion played an adult game and it was played by adult women.

What the Japanese proposed by their choice of model was something much more complex, and very much more ambivalent. Their first shows, alarming enough to those used to Western fashion and traditions, with which the new Japanese movement seemed to have nothing in common except fabric, were made even more puzzling by their austere presentation. The early Japanese shows in Paris were as sombre in mood and atmosphere as the clothes being displayed. Models walked out one at a time with their heads slightly lowered, their eyes looking straight ahead and their arms held stiffly by their sides in a decorous manner. Nothing they did suggested any attempt to ingratiate themselves with the audience. Everything about their demeanour seemed judged to intimidate the onlookers. It was as far as anything could be from the Seventies clap-and-shout, 'Come on! Let's party!' approach of the presentations featuring black models. Even the least perceptive member of the audience knew that a gauntlet had been thrown down. There were to be no stars in this situation. The audience were assumed to be adults capable of concentrating on the clothes without the aid of nursery antics.

It was an unsettling moment. The Seventies had seen fashion – and pre-eminently fashion shows – become part of the entertainment business. The Japanese put a stop to that immediately and made even the good fashion that had been produced in the previous decade seem self-indulgent and superficial. In this respect they were wrong, but their clothing was so uncompromising in its approach that, within one season, they gave French

fashion an inferiority complex verging on a communal nervous breakdown; excited hopes and dreams in young British designers and students; panicked the Italians and totally bewildered the Americans.

They also set the modelling world in a different direction. The girl–woman was born. Adolescent in shape, ethereal in face, but rarely traditionally beautiful, and unsettlingly short after tall models such as Jerry Hall – a lack of height deliberately emphasized by flat heels – she was entirely subservient to the clothes. Above all, she was very young, and made to look even younger by the garments she wore. There were no erogenous zones in Japanese fashion, any more than there were in traditional menswear, with which the new wave seemed to have more in common than with the historic attitudes of French high fashion.

What the Japanese designers were doing was not only subversive by accepted Western standards, it also fundamentally redefined the concept of femininity. Their clothes were created not to produce an exaggerated sexuality aimed at exciting men and, by doing so, reducing women to sex objects for male gratification. This had been a strong element in late Seventies' fashion, soon to be taken to grotesquely pantomimic excess by Jean Paul Gaultier's fetishistic clothing which, despite its raunchiness, paradoxically rejected stereotypes of sexiness as thoroughly as the Japanese. The clothes of Kawakubo and Yamamoto, looking inward, warming and rewarding the wearer's inner femininity for her own self-esteem, not that of male onlookers, introduced a startlingly new and modern element to Paris fashion.

As a result of the Japanese invasion, the fashion silhouette changed. Models now had to be slightly built, with figures as straight and thin as boys in their early teens, their hair short or exuberantly out of control in a parody of a Pre-Raphaelite beauty, and their walk – a crucial element in the presentation of any model and one

that reflects the mood of fashion at a given time with uncanny accuracy – had to eschew all theatricality and histrionics. It was, in every sense, a sobering moment for fashion and one of such importance that the early Eighties' Japanese archetype has become a permanent part of the vocabulary of modelling, no matter what the mainstream look might be.

Suddenly, the plainest, gawkiest youngster, the school's ugly duckling whom traditional modelling would have rejected, could become a model. Hundreds of them did. However, it was not true to say that the woman with the traditional attributes had been replaced by the girl with none. Clothes are sold by models, as Chanel said. Japanese clothes only appealed to the youngest women. Traditional designers still held the field as far as sales were concerned and they could see no mileage in the sexless androgyny of the Japanese approach.

However, others found the new wave exciting. The debate as to whether fashion influences or merely reflects social change is a long-running one. Clothes in themselves can provide various messages, specific or not. What concentrates the message is how they are worn. On the catwalk, any sexuality they may possess is imparted by the person who is wearing them. Many commentators accuse the Japanese designers of causing the apparent upsurge in paedophilia which has become one of the distinguishing features of fashion at the end of the twentieth century, just as it was at the end of the nineteenth.

Photographers certainly saw the potential of underage models and in the early and mid-Eighties schoolgirls were pictured as adult women – a trend that continues intermittently today so that a sixteen-year-old wearing a $100,000 couture dress for a fashion shoot is not an extraordinary occurrence. In the Eighties there was such a strong tendency in this direction that the editor of British *Elle* felt it necessary to instruct her fashion team not to use models under the age of fourteen.

25 Sarah
   Stockbridge,
   1987, photo
   Nick Knight

For modelling, the Japanese approach resulted in a brief eclipse of the Hall–Cleveland type of superstar on the runways. Plain or ethereal, pre- or post-teenage, there was little mileage (or money) to be made out of the new-style models as individuals. Many of those involved in the business found the lack of variety – or, even, of distinguishing features – in rows of unformed figures and inexperienced faces made fashion deficient in the essential elements that gave it its vitality. Dissatisfaction showed itself most strongly in London, where a new breed of young, wild and iconoclastic designers appeared in the early Eighties. They shared much of the Japanese view that traditional fashion found in Paris and Milan was irrelevant, although for different reasons: for the Japanese, it seemed pointless to those with a sophisticated fashion intelligence; for the British, it had nothing to say to the young in their search for novelty.

Many British fashion designers, including Katharine Hamnett, Vivienne Westwood and the short-lived but temporarily influential Body Map, brainchild of Stevie Stewart and David Holah, adopted the thinking of Issey Miyake and decided to make their runways a multicultural and non-ageist forum, as Kenzo and Jean Paul Gaultier were doing in Paris. The middle-aged and the old mingled with the young. Babies and toddlers were carried on to the runway. Fat and ugly people, antisocial, even criminal, looks – all took part in fashion shows as patronizing as they were exploitative. In most cases, such models were used for totally different reasons from the original Japanese intention. All too often it seemed that, instead of nullifying the personality of the model in order to allow the clothes to speak, London's designers used grotesque models to take attention away from the clothes – which were always inferior to the Japanese garments in technique and finish, quite apart from rigour of thought – in order to make a fashion show a visual, emotional and cross-cultural 'happening' type of experience.

Everyone involved was having fun playing with the concept that the extraordinary (and many of the early Eighties clothes shown in London *were* extraordinary in their invention), the disregard for tradition and the ruthless challenging of the status quo in everything from the tenets of taste to the stereotypes of sexuality – the bizarre and the mundane – could be mixed and misappropriated at the whim of a designer and the newly empowered breed of stylists. Anything was acceptable provided it seemed different and shocking. Everything else was dismissed as boring, the most derogatory of all fashion's critical words in the Eighties.

London was rarely described in that way; but a gap was growing between designers and their customers.

Were clothes to be regarded as a showbiz diversion or a serious suggestion as to how people might wish to dress? British designers seemed incapable of realizing that those who buy designer clothes might well be amused by runway antics that have a scantily dressed fifty-year-old woman apparently re-creating the role of the Madwoman of Chaillot or a teenager who gives every impression of being insane, but they rarely identify with them. And it is that identification that makes for sales on the scale that has made American designers such as Calvin Klein and Ralph Lauren so economically powerful. Even a designer of the calibre of Vivienne Westwood had difficulty in translating her world profile as a fashion entrepreneur into business profits until her fashion house began to benefit from Italian economic knowledge, which brought the realization that originality and commerce need not be mutually exclusive. However, in London in the early Eighties, it seemed that the show was all-important. There was an arrogant assumption that those who failed to understand London's special contribution to fashion were the inadequate ones, rather than the designers, so many of whom, despite their undoubted talents, were bankrupt and forgotten before the end of the decade. Scenes reminiscent of the theatre of the absurd – or even cruelty – do not sit well on glossy pages. Most importantly, they do not please the powerful advertisers who make those glossy pages possible. London avant-garde fashion in the Eighties, rather like the Japanese version, received much less coverage in traditional glossy magazines than mainstream designs from Paris, Milan and even New York. It was left to the 'upstart' publications such as *The Face* and *i-D* to champion the new, the original and, sometimes, the ludicrous.

The models they used were pretty, pert and lively. One of the most popular, Sarah Stockbridge, Vivienne Westwood's favourite, summed up the new mood with an appearance that was cheeky, jokey and deliberately projected as 'common'. It was the new fashion's way of thumbing its nose at the craze for designer clothes, which, having started in Milan, fanned out across the Western world in a decade dominated by money and the determination to flaunt it by buying expensive international labels. The high-gloss professionalism – at all levels, including promotion and marketing – of the large designer conglomerates such as Giorgio Armani, Ralph Lauren and Calvin Klein was anathema in London design circles. British designers were still fatally split between a longing to preserve handwork, craft skills and the individuality that can only be maintained by remaining small, and the financial imperative to survive, which normally precluded such approaches.

26 Gianni Versace
    and Kate Moss at
    the *haute couture*
    1995–6 collection

27 (Overleaf)
    Versace 1994–5
    collection, photo
    D. Ordway

Despite its energy and originality, London fashion was eventually swamped and almost sunk by the economic power of Milan and New York. Those who survived – designers such as Jasper Conran and Bruce Oldfield – realized that the only way to be taken seriously on the international stage was to use international models who could give enough gloss and sophistication to make London clothes accessible, especially to the American press and buyers catering for a market much more demanding and knowledgeable than its British counterpart. In fact, it was a strategy that failed. Nervous backers pulled out when it became apparent that, no matter how glamorous London runways could be made – and, it has to be accepted, they never quite reached the level of presentation of the shows put on in other fashion capitals – the British fashion industry simply lacked the necessary infrastructure and investment to become a real contender in the international Big League. Even so, for a brief time, London fashion certainly benefited from its influx of world-class models, many of whom, it was rumoured, worked without pay as they found the London scene so exciting.

Despite London, sex, power and status returned as the most important aspects of fashion and, to show them to maximum advantage, models, of the kind not seen since the Seventies, were rediscovered. Glamour models reinstated the concept of bodily perfection. High fashion, which, in presentation, at least, allows for no blemishes, was fashionable again. In the hands of designers such as Thierry Mugler, Claude Montana and Donna Karan who, after many years working for the Anne Klein label, founded her own business in 1985, it had never gone away. The designers who brought back sex and glamour were Gianni Versace and Azzedine Alaïa, a Tunisian who, for years, had worked semi-anonymously in Paris (including five days at Dior and a longer period with Mugler) before coming to prominence with his first ready-to-wear collection in 1980. Both had an obsession with the flawless female body, an ideal which, if not actually fascist was certainly totalitarian, rejecting all but the most perfect specimens in a ruthless determination to create a master-race of models.

Models became more glamorous – and infinitely more exciting – than any of the clothes they showed. Just as Christian Lacroix, for all his genius, turned couture into a form of pantomime where Cinderella *always* went to the ball (frequently dressed in the same poor taste as the ugly sisters), so Alaïa and Versace made sure that every model had the extraordinarily long legs, sexy bottoms and perfectly formed breasts as her fellows. Those who were not naturally endowed had to look elsewhere in order to make up for their deficiencies. With implants, injections, nips and tucks, many of the top models who strode confidently down the catwalk of those couturiers wealthy enough to afford them had been under the knife. The supermodel was created. She was so perfect and perceived as being so essential to fashion that she finally broke down the last barriers between runway and photographic models. The new breed were so hip that they had to be seen in front of the cameras, whether in a show or doing a shoot for a glossy magazine. The top models knew no lines of demarcation. They were omnipotent and omnipresent, despite the fact that their perfection was out of touch with reality and so-called 'ordinary' women found it difficult to identify with them or with the clothes they wore.

Working with bodies like theirs, many designers forgot what their *raison d'être* was. It was hard for them to waste the opportunities the supermodels offered. A show became less a prediction of what the designer intended for the following season and more an entity in itself – part cabaret, part strip show, part vaudeville. Perfect breasts, whether silicone-aided or not, and beautifully formed buttocks had to be highlighted and exposed. Whole areas of clothing disappeared from many of the top runways: suits, day dresses and winter coats. It is easy to see why. If a designer is working with, and paying handsomely for, some of the most perfect bodies the world has ever seen, it requires a will of iron to waste the opportunity – not to mention the money – by covering them up in real fashion. Some designers were so obsessed with supermodels and their perfect figures that they sent out more clinging, diaphanous evening dresses than any other item of clothing, and even turned daywear into, if not eveningwear, then boudoir styles with slip dresses, bias-cut, in satin: anything, provided it was revealing.

Gianni Versace is the designer some consider to have made the supermodels into international cult figures in the Eighties, while others claim that Thierry Mugler brought together the top few on his runway, along with remarkable survivors like Jerry Hall and Marie Helvin. Mugler's obsession with 'drop-dead' glamour led him in the late Nineties to use Cyd Charisse, Ivana Trump and Carmen Dell'Orefice, who had been photographed for *Vogue* by Beaton as long ago as 1945. All three had very good legs, though it was breasts that most mattered in the supermodel class. They were *the* obsession in the obsessive world of perfectly toned and fit bodies which were now *de rigueur* in fashion. From Jane Fonda, whose fitness videos made sweating fashionable, through the body builder Lisa Lyon, whose feminine but extremely well-muscled body so fascinated Robert Mapplethorpe that in 1996 he published a book of his photographs of her, to the example set by Madonna's tough, resilient, super-fit body in all its different manifestations, female physical power was an essential attribute of the new sexiness and the status it conferred on women. The six-foot-tall Australian Elle MacPherson, who was, along with the voluptuously breasted Christie Brinkley, one of the first of the new Amazons, apparently found nothing demeaning in being nicknamed 'The Body', as if a decade of feminist campaigning had never taken place.

28   Linda Evangelista,
      1993, photo
      Nick Knight

29   Naomi Campbell,
      1999, photo
      Bettina Rheims

30   (Overleaf)
      Cindy Crawford,
      mid-1980s, photo
      Terry O'Neill

31   (Overleaf)
      Linda Evangelista,
      1993, photo
      David Sims

28

Fashion gets the fashion models it deserves. The Eighties were a time of brashness and lack of subtlety in most areas of life, but nowhere more so than in fashion. Supermodels evolved because their image reflected the times more fully than any other section of society, even the money-grubbing Young Turks of Wall Street and the City of London. Cindy Crawford, Claudia Schiffer, Christy Turlington, Linda Evangelista and Naomi Campbell were the glamour quintet who seemed to embody the fantasy of fashion in the public mind as they appeared on the top runways, in the most glamorous magazines and – for the hugely lucrative advertising work for which they were in great demand – on the prime-site billboards in cities all over the world. There was nothing they couldn't sell. Whatever they did was instant news. They guaranteed worldwide publicity by even a five-minute appearance at an event. Their sex lives were ruthlessly exposed. Indeed, it seemed that the balloon would never burst. They were a winning combination of Hollywood glamour and pop music accessibility. In the famous George Michael 'Freedom 90' video, which featured the stars of the modelling world, there was no doubt that they were adding kudos to his name, not the other way around. Fashion shows became celebrity rites, with obligatory appearances in the front row by pop stars, actresses and international personalities. The supermodels were the dream ticket for the media, having cameo roles in films, becoming standard fixtures on chat shows and, as in the case of Cindy Crawford, even hosting their own shows, appearing on calendars, being used for a new range of Barbie Dolls and, in a final, but short-lived apotheosis, opening their own theme restaurant, The Fashion Café, in New York in 1995.

However, they are now best remembered, not for any of these achievements, but for the money they earned. In a hyperbolic industry, where true costs are never admitted, claims of their earnings are probably exaggerated, though the fact that they are believed is proof that they are not so wide of the mark. Linda Evangelista gave the breed a bad name when she claimed that she wouldn't get out of bed for less than $10,000 and it was generally accepted that Gianni Versace, who was convinced that only supermodels could show his clothes properly, put them in a new financial league because he was prepared to spend up to $30,000 each to secure them. Naomi Campbell was given in excess of $500,000 for *Swan*, her ghost-written novel which appeared in 1994. Christy Turlington signed a $3 million contract with Calvin Klein, and Claudia Schiffer's income at the height of her fame as Karl Lagerfeld's favourite model for Chanel was estimated to be well over $15 million per year. For a remarkably long time the supermodels were bigger than the fashion industry that employed them.

Eventually the supermodel phenomenon burnt itself out. It simply could not continue with the full blaze of publicity for everything a supermodel did, said or even thought without boredom setting in, for the public, if not necessarily for the media. Supermodels continued to be a force in the fashion world until almost the last three years of the millennium. In a sense, it was the murder of Gianni Versace in 1997 that finally destroyed their power base. However, modelling continued to capture the public imagination as more normal and natural-looking women began to command the catwalks and the column inches. No longer flawless beauties, with disconcertingly perfect bodies, they brought to fashion the variety of character: something missing during the supermodel era. Models with bizarre and unconventional looks or irregular features walked side by side with more traditional beauties. Helena Christensen and Shalom Harlow belonged to the long tradition of beauty that stretched back to Suzy Parker. Stella Tennant, Honor Fraser, Erin O'Connor and Jodie Kidd were marketed as bringing 'English class' back into fashion. Kristen McMenamy's unsubtle, eccentric looks provided the model equivalent of a song sung by Ethel Merman – belting, obvious but with infinite variety – while women like Eve Salvail, Guinevere van Seenus, Karen Elson and Jenni Shimizu brought an idiosyncratic quality to traditional fashion glamour by breaking the stereotype created by the supermodels and forging a closer link between high fashion and ordinary women.

The fashion industry often finds itself out of fashion, if not actually old-fashioned and, in the case of models,

33

34

37

38

many designers trail behind public attitudes. For every
model of the calibre of Amber Valletta or Galliano-
favourite Nadja Auermann parading the runways,
there is only one Sophie Dahl. This is the legacy of the
supermodels. Antony Price, London fashion's only 'glam'
designer worthy to be mentioned in the same breath as
Mugler and Montana, points out the basic problem that
still creates a credibility gap between models and real
women: many of the most glamorous models have
totally different measurements from ordinary women. A
model, he maintains, will often have size 12 shoulders,
size 10 bust and size 8 hips, whereas real women have
size 8 shoulders, size 12 bust and size 10 hips.

At the end of the twentieth century, statuesque, six-foot
tall models are no longer right for the mood of the times;
their looks would seem unnatural and artificial. Fashion
models reflect the attitudes of the their moment just as
actresses do. Stars like Cameron Diaz, Nicole Kidman,
Drew Barrymore or Minnie Driver have an unthreatening
element to their sexuality. Although they are beautiful,
their faces have an accidental, girl-next-door look to
them. They could quite easily have been plain. Although
they have temporarily pushed models aside as the faces
that sell fashion magazines, especially in the fiercely
competitive American market, it is the models inside the
magazines who excite our interest not, as in the case
of the actresses, because of the people with whom
they are starring, but because their unusual and often
challenging forms of beauty intrigue us. In fact, a good
late Nineties' model must have the chameleon-like
quality found in Madonna. Her ability to change her
appearance and to predict a mood are well documented
and she is probably the woman who has had more
influence on the way women look – or wish to look
– than *any* model in the last fifteen years.

A model who shares this quality is Kate Moss. The
Obsession campaigns photographed for Calvin Klein by
Steven Meisel, in which she features, contain everything
we need to understand about the attitudes, aspirations

40

and obsessions of young women at the end of the
twentieth century. In these advertisements, Kate Moss
has looked poised, beautiful, sordid and washed-out by
turns, but she has always been entirely contemporary.
There are other models who share some of her qualities.
Maggie Rizer and Audrey Marnay bring an extraordinary
presence to their work on the runway or before the
camera, but they also have the ability to change their
mood as well as their appearance – an attribute
increasingly important for models and one that brings
them closer to the world of acting than they have been
for many years. Those who regret the end of the
supermodel era might find that the new breed lacks
drama, though they are not mundane. Working with
the new wave of fashion photographers such as Terry
Richardson, David LaChapelle, Craig McDean or Inez
van Lamsweerde, the model no longer has to make
women envious about individual items of dress, as in
the Chanel days, but to create a mood that excites,
intrigues and sometimes unsettles or repulses but
always compels. Although the mainstream fashion of
the long-established glossy magazines and the famous
runways has yet to acknowledge that fashion is now
frequently driven by perversity, alternative magazines
and the fashion shows of young designers are clear that
the concept of the model looking glamorous, clean and
middle class in order to sell middle-of-the-road clothes
is seriously behind the times. Today, it is the strangeness
of models like Devon, the strength of Erin O'Connor, the
unambiguous sexuality of Jacquetta Wheeler, whose
Gucci advertisements have led to her being hailed as the
new Twiggy, as much as the traditional beauty of Carmen
Kass which appeals to designers, photographers and the
magazine-reading public.

THE MEDIUM AND THE MESSAGE

1   (Opener)
     Inez van
     Lamsweerde and
     Vinoodh Matadin
     for Yohji
     Yamamoto, 1998

2   (Previous page)
     Craig McDean
     for Helmut Lang,
     1998

3   (Previous page)
     Mario Testino,
     *Arena Homme
     Plus*, 1999

4   George
     Hoyningen-Huene,
     Harper's Bazaar,
     1939, clothes
     by Mainbocher

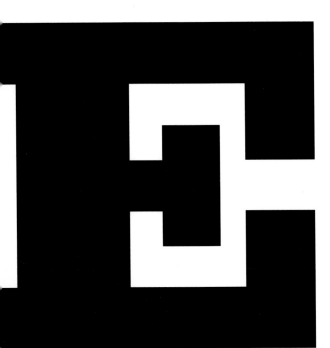

Edna Woolman Chase, editor-in-chief of all editions of *Vogue* from the Twenties to the Fifties, the single most influential individual in the fashion media of this century, was the last person to be faced with the dilemma which, during her tenure, had increasingly arisen in magazines over how best to illustrate fashion. Christian Dior's New Look was first shown in 1947. Mrs Chase recognized its importance but was undecided how to present the new line on the cover of the collections edition of *Vogue*. Should she commission a drawing or a photograph? She chose a drawing, by Dagmar, and followed it up with illustrations by Eric, *Vogue*'s star illustrator, although Bar, a beige silk jacket with a black wool skirt, now considered the most important and directional of Dior's new looks, was shown in a photograph, by Balkin.

It was the last time any editor would have to make such a serious choice. Although drawn covers on fashion magazines occasionally appeared well into the Fifties, they were believed to lack impact, especially in the face of the new advances in printing and photographic technology, which gave colour photography a vibrancy previously unknown. By the end of the Fifties, drawing had been almost totally banished from advertising pages and relegated to illustrating 'difficult' items such as undergarments, cheaper fashions and clothes for the older and fuller figure – all of which presented problems when photographed – on the editorial pages of the world's great fashion magazines. Since then, fashion drawing as a way of illustrating current styles has almost disappeared, and seems unlikely to resurface as a vital contribution to a magazine's character. Even though it occasionally

appears on editorial pages devoted to cheaper lines of merchandise, it is only very rarely used to illustrate important fashion statements, which are almost invariably given to the magazine's top photographers to interpret. Paradoxically, as the prices paid for old fashion magazines, especially *Vogue*, climb it is the editions with drawn covers and a high proportion of fashion illustration on the editorial pages that command the highest prices, not only because they are the oldest but also because to modern eyes they have a charm lacking in magazines exclusively using photographs. A Thirties' photograph by George Hoyningen-Huene or Martin Munkacsi has a period quality that today gives it considerable cachet, but a drawing by Beaton in the Twenties, a Thirties' illustration by Eric or one by the Fifties' illustrator, René Bouché, is still seen by collectors as a more direct and complete evocation of its time.

It isn't just charm or evocative mood that was lost with the suppression of fashion illustration. In the hands of a maestro such as René Bouët-Willaumez or Christian Bérard, a fashion drawing invariably pleased a couturier more than a photograph – even when it was by a doyen of the genre such as Horst P. Horst or George Platt Lynes – because the artist's craft involved a combination of the hand and eye, much as the original creation had. Skilled artists – and only those of the highest quality were allowed a full page in *Vogue*, *Harper's Bazaar*, *Le Figaro* or *L'Officiel* – never attempted to draw with an Ingres-like precision. They were not interested in delineating every pleat or reproducing every button. Instead, they saw their job as being to capture the original spirit of the couturier's

5   René Bouché,
U.S. *Vogue*, 1945

creation. Indeed, they felt a strong affinity with the couturier, whom they regarded as a fellow 'hands-on' creator. The choice of brush thickness, the medium – ink, paint or Conté-crayon – the type of paper, the amount of colour applied, the degree of shading, even the pose of the model were all calculated not only to make a minor work of art but also to emphasize the beauty, skill and originality of the couturier's carefully conceived garment.

By no means were all fashion illustrators trained. Fashion drawing is often an instinctive gift. Even those who had not studied at art school knew how to respond to fabric, feathers and fur and the way in which they fell and draped themselves around the body. They were working at the same coalface as the couturier. Their sensibilities – and sensitivities – were aroused by the plastic possibilities of fabric moulded on, stretched over and hung from the human form. Whereas photographers had a barrier of essential technology between them and their goal – not to mention frequently a small army of technicians and helpers – artists could make direct contact with the object. All they needed was a tool, a surface and a sympathetic eye.

Fashion illustration gradually fell out of favour for a variety of reasons. The Fifties were an exciting period of discovering new horizons and possibilities, in fashion magazines as in most areas of life. They were a particularly buoyant time in American consumer markets. Many more people had well-paid, secure jobs than ever before. In particular, women – young, professional, single – had good prospects and high expectations. They were, indeed, the first modern women and they were a rich and exciting consumer market for all the durables American manufacturers had convinced them were essential to living a modern life. American women were bombarded with advertising not only for clothes, perfumes and beauty products but also for refrigerators, television sets, telephones and even cars, at a time

when only a fraction of their European counterparts had any of these consumer goods.

Fashion was used to sell them all. Detroit and Seventh Avenue combined forces to produce the right fashion colours for the gleaming new cars rolling off assembly lines that were cleverly marketed as part of an overall fashion story aimed at women. High-powered conferences deliberated over upholstery – tweed? stripes? plaid? – or studied the small details considered important to women. Where does a woman put her handbag while driving? How does she touch up her lipstick before parking and meeting that special date? Household items such as kitchen equipment and bathroom accessories were given the same coordinated treatment – colours, shapes and textures were changed regularly to fit altered fashion moods – with a view to increasing sales.

It was a decade which saw American female consumers as a major untapped growth area. European women who visited major American cities were agog at the possibilities still denied them. They regarded their own shops, still hit by rationing and austerity, as dull and lacking the necessities a modern woman had the right to demand. The glossy consumer life could not be delayed for long in Europe. The waters slowly rose and then, with remarkably little warning, became an all-engulfing flood in the early Sixties as British youth – and later, French and German – became financially, sexually and socially empowered. The arrival of the Pill opened the way for personal choice in many areas of women's lives.

Advertising is the vital chain linking product and consumer. If, in the Fifties, it had become such a crucial part of women's magazines that many readers preferred the advertisements to the editorial pages, by the Sixties, its role in fashion magazines was central across the entire Western world. Its effect was to relegate fashion drawing for ever. Advertisers wanted an object's material

qualities to be reproduced so exactly that potential purchasers, having seen the advertisement, could go out, identify it and, they hoped, buy it. That meant using a photograph, no matter how unoriginal, over a drawing, no matter how expressive. Frequently there was a compromise, with the object – usually a vehicle or a refrigerator – being depicted by a photograph with a group of admiring women, who it was feared might alienate less perfect women if they were photographed, being drawn around it.

What happened on the advertising pages inevitably had an effect on the editorial section of fashion magazines. Eyes used to Cinemascope and Technicolor at the cinema needed something much more direct than an artist's impression, not only for the fashion section of a magazine but also for other exciting editorial areas that were opening up. Travel, long the privilege of the rich and leisured, gradually became a possibility for office workers and minor civil servants in the late Fifties as flights became less expensive. For encouraging people to buy a holiday, a drawing of an exotic beach was not in the same league as a glossy colour photograph, any more than a drawing would suffice on the sophisticated cookery pages today. Only photography would do. For the advertisers who increasingly influenced the contents of a fashion magazine as well as the customers, drawing began to seem too lacklustre to attract, let alone hold, the attention.

Fashion drawing should have died completely by the end of the Sixties, it appeared so rarely in magazines. Yet it hung on through the Seventies and into the Eighties, often by a thread but sometimes with remarkable success. One of the talented fashion illustrators who survived was René Gruau, born in Rimini in 1909, who began working in Paris in the late Thirties, later drawing for *Le Figaro* during World War II and illustrating for French *Vogue*. His work was strongly

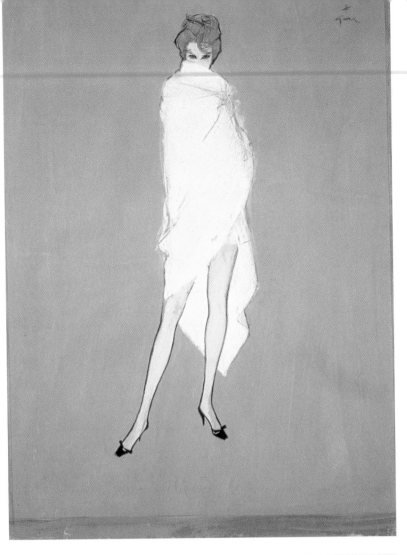

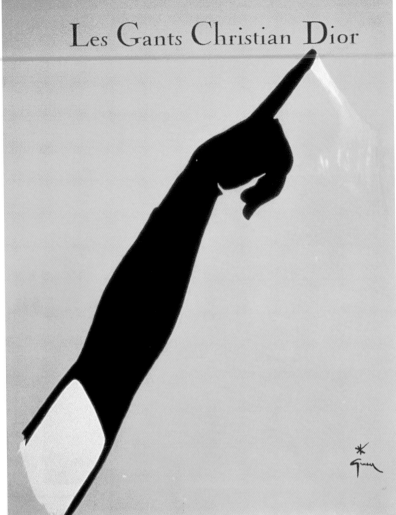

Les Gants Christian Dior

lingerie

Christian Dior

6   René Gruau for
    Christian Dior,
    1947–60

7   Tony Viramontes
    for Valentino
    Couture, 1984

8   (Overleaf)
    Mats Gustafson,
    Gianfranco Ferré
    for Dior *haute
    couture*, 1989

9   (Overleaf)
    Gladys Perint
    Palmer for Jean
    Paul Gaultier,
    1991

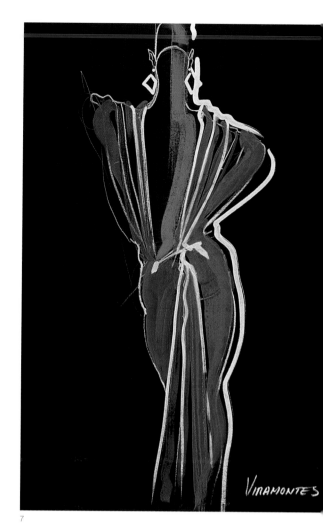

7

formalized, his trademark being a thick black line that enclosed and delineated the figure. What his illustrations lacked in subtlety they made up for in drama. His highly lucrative career in advertising began in the late Forties with work for Christian Dior – whose perfumes, aftershaves, stockings and scarves he illustrated in striking images – and continued into the Nineties.

If Gruau managed to survive by tapping into large advertising budgets, other illustrators kept in work by diversifying. The American Joe Eula began his career in the Fifties working for the New York *Herald Tribune* and the London *Sunday Times*. As that source of income dwindled, he found an outlet for his quick impressionistic line and instant splashes of colour in creating eye-catching posters for Broadway shows, as well as drawing famous theatrical personalities. In the Sixties, he designed costumes and sets for Broadway productions, particularly George Balanchine's New York City Ballet. He returned to the fashion fold in the Seventies, drawing for the American designer Halston, and then began work with the Italian and French editions of *Harper's Bazaar*. His fashion sketches – energetic, with little specific detail – showed his marvellously free hand to its best advantage, a point noted by the Italian couturier, Valentino, who used his work to create the mood of his fashion in his advertising campaigns in the late Seventies.

Fashion illustration only survived in Europe in the Seventies. British and American magazines dropped it almost completely from its pages and even *Women's Wear Daily* (*WWD*), which had always used illustrations for most of its major high-fashion coverage, changed course when its owner and publisher, John Fairchild,

decided that photographs would please the designers more – and ensure more advertising. In the mid-Eighties the world was – almost overnight it seemed – robbed of the highly sophisticated and uniquely *WWD* line of top-class fashion illustrators such as Steven Stipelman and Kenneth Paul Block whose work for various advertisers had brought them to the attention of a much wider public.

If their line looked back to a pre-Sixties concept of elegance, other *WWD* illustrators produced a more contemporary image by elimination and exaggeration. Pedro Barrios, in particular, created a style based on large, expressive hands displayed with all the drama of Gloria Swanson at her high-camp full register, dramatic eyes swirling sideways. Kitsch glamour at its best, it influenced many illustrators, including the Californian artist Viramontes, whose bold, simplified line and thick impasto created some of the most sensuous and aggressive fashion imagery of the Eighties. His world-weary wit made his drawings infinitely more sophisticated than those of his many imitators. His death in the late Eighties, when he was just twenty-eight, marked the end of an era when, despite the odds, fashion illustration had come to life again. With the exception of the Swedish illustrator Gustafson (whose controlled way of floating colour across paper to create a non-specific impression is almost ethereal in its subtlety) illustration as a vibrant force in fashion ended there, although the late Nineties saw a resurgence in the witty, stylized observation of Ruben Toledo and Gladys Perint Palmer.

Fashion illustration fell into decline as much because of the artists themselves as because of the indifference of

10 Antonio Lopez,
    Paloma Picasso,
    1984

11 Antonio Lopez,
    Krizia editorial for
    Vanity magazine,
    1981

12 Antonio Lopez,
    designs by
    Emmanuelle
    Khanh, *Elle*, 1967

10

the media and public. Few illustrators were able to give their drawings a contemporary feel. Most of them turned to a derivative and sterile attempt to reproduce past glamour. Their drawings instantly looked old-fashioned as they insisted upon adding a stylish hat to help the illusion of elegance in their illustrations of contemporary fashion, apparently indifferent to the fact that fashion for the most part had turned its back on veiled millinery, elbow-length gloves and the appurtenances of extreme and mannered elegance long before. But there was one notable and marvellous exception.

The art of fashion illustration was kept alive – artificially, in the opinion of some – during much of the Eighties by two European magazines dedicated to revealing fashion through the eyes of artists. *La Mode en Peinture*, edited by Prosper Assouline in Paris; and *Vanity*, edited in Milan by Anna Piaggi, one-time muse to Karl Lagerfeld. In the case of *Vanity*, Antonio Lopez, known as Antonio, established himself as the most important fashion illustrator of the last forty years. From the Sixties to his death in 1987, Antonio was at the creative centre of fashion. His friends read like a roll call of talents: Anna Piaggi; Paloma Picasso; Hélène Gordon-Lazareff, founder of French *Elle*, generally considered the first modern, democratic fashion magazine, who brought him to Europe in 1967, having seen his work in *WWD* and *The New York Times Magazine*; models such as Jerry Hall; and everyone who was anyone in the international fashion world. Habitué of Studio 54 in New York and Club 7 in Paris, Antonio and his friend and collaborator, Juan Ramos, literally lived the life they drew, admired and respected for their energy and drive as much as for their ability to have fun: early in his career Antonio worked with the legendary couturier Charles James in New York, capturing the designer's creations on paper. This work gave his drawings their authenticity in years to come.

Antonio has earned a place in fashion history because he managed to establish his formal fashion illustration as a valid form of art in magazines even in the photography-dominated Seventies and Eighties. His versatility and flair excited fashion followers everywhere, not least students determined to copy the essence of his art. None succeeded. Antonio had a unique way of drawing that made fashion illustration cutting-edge reportage in a way it had not been since the early Fifties. Drawing on a wide range of art-historical sources for inspiration, including the painters Balthus, De Chirico and Delacroix, Antonio created, by the force of his personality, work that is instantly recognizable, despite his frequent changes of stylistic spirit. Commenting on his importance for the European mood in his heyday of

11

13   Erwin Blumenfeld
for Dayton's
department store,
Ohio, 1961

the late Seventies, Anna Piaggi has described fashion as a sandwich, 'One layer, Antonio, hot and spicy; one layer Karl Lagerfeld … a pinch of Andy Warhol, indispensable chemical sealer of the period, a dose of Café Flore and Hotel Crystal.' He was more than a fashion artist, he was a creative catalyst.

No movement or individual, no matter how strong, could fight for long the power of photography in the face of the demands of advertisers. Starting with the advantage of being more directly understandable than fashion illustration, fashion photography had, even in the first half of the twentieth century, produced images of such strength, subtlety and sophistication that they have become classics of their genre, defining and illuminating the moods and aspirations of their times. In the Thirties and Forties – even the Fifties – fashion photography, as Beaton's diaries make clear, was a gentlemanly, even leisurely occupation. There was little sense of pressure. Despite being the magazine's leading photographer, he frequently had to fill no more than one or two pages for *Vogue* per month. By contrast, today photographers of the calibre of Steven Meisel or Bruce Weber might be expected to produce stories running to many pages – for Italian *Vogue* possibly numbering over twenty – for

one edition of the magazine and then work at the same speed for the next edition.

Erwin Blumenfeld adapted Man Ray's explorations to meet the modern challenges of postwar fashion, photography and art and, in doing so, created some of the most striking images of fashion this century. Two photographers dominated the Fifties: Irving Penn at *Vogue*, working with Alexander Liberman; and Richard Avedon, who was hired by Alexey Brodovitch, the art director at *Harper's Bazaar*, to be staff photographer. Together they embodied the last days of the high style of *haute couture*. Penn's approach was the more painterly of the two. In the Forties he had produced still lifes with all the precision and intensity that characterize a Vermeer or a Chardin. As in their work, a silvery light plays over the spaces between objects in a Penn composition – a quality he brought to his fashion work. In any Penn fashion shot it is what that light is doing in the spaces around the figures that gives it a unique quality.

Penn, again like Vermeer, was able to give the small and insignificant detail a monumental quality that never became pompous. Like Goya, his humour emerged in portraits – and, for Penn, in fashion shots. Happiest

when photographing clothes with an architectural quality, he was at his best when bringing out the form and mass of garments by Balenciaga – whose clothes, influenced by the Spanish painters Goya and Zurbarán, were never photographed better than by Penn – and the fluid monumentality of Issey Miyake's powerful, individual experiments in controlled liquefaction. He produced amazing still lifes of lipstick chunks and blocks of frozen vegetables and gave them the strength of an Anthony Caro sculpture. His fashion work was intimate but distant, a mixture of grandeur and emotion.

If Penn showed the dignity of postwar fashion grandeur, the impudence was surely provided by Richard Avedon, whose portfolios of Paris high fashion captured the spirit as well as the reality of the fashionable woman. Full of movement, life and vitality, his models became real people, captured in real situations by a photographer who was technically unbeatable and was able to reveal the essence of any garment he showed, from the grandest evening dress to the simplest summer dress. Above all, this mastery of movement has proved one of Avedon's greatest legacies, affecting contemporaries such as Norman Parkinson and Antony Armstrong-Jones (Lord Snowdon)

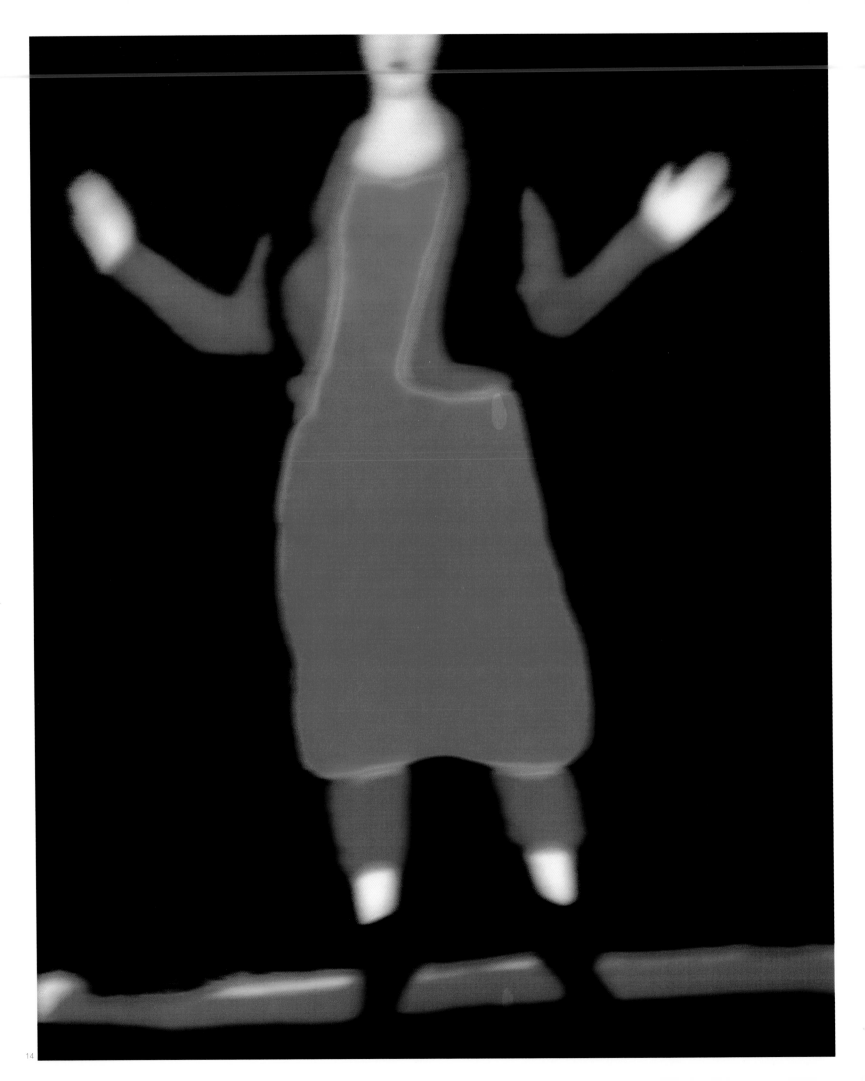

14

16

15

and later photographers such as Steven Meisel. Avedon has, like Penn, been interested in portraiture all his life but, whereas Penn worked mainly with the famous, Avedon was more often attracted to the anonymous faces of those on the margins or even the breadline of society. Avedon's clarity of vision recalls Ansel Adams and, in a long career, his sense of fun, his vigour and his strength of personality reflect a remarkable fashion intelligence.

The list of highly competent – and even inspired – photographers working in the Fifties and Sixties includes many names almost forgotten by the general public. Clifford Coffin, Henry Clarke, Bert Stern and Hiro – who is still working today – deserve to be remembered more than they are but it is in the nature of such a proliferating profession that only those who have really exerted an influence – on the way we see society as much as the manner in which fashion perceives itself – can be considered in such a crowded field. Bob Richardson, Art Kane and Duane Michals in the Sixties; Sarah Moon, Deborah Turbeville and Guy Bourdin in the Seventies; Arthur Elgort, Peter Lindbergh and Gian Paolo Barbieri in the Eighties; Paolo Roversi, Jean-Baptiste Mondino, Chris von Wangenheim … even a random list of photographers who have produced memorable images of their times is long, and growing. New approaches in the Nineties and the photographers who wished to break away from the mainstream must be examined more closely.

In the last twenty-five years, only two unquestionably great photographers have emerged: the German Helmut Newton and the American Bruce Weber. Both have exerted enormous influence, although in different spheres. Helmut Newton has often enough been accused of photographing his private obsessions and fantasies, but what is less frequently acknowledged is that they are the obsessions and fantasies of so many people that his work can almost be read as socio-sexual documentary, charting landmark shifts of attitude concerning the barriers between the sexes. Newton is never interested merely in the clothes. What he does is imagine how they will affect a certain type of woman – and those around her – if they are worn in a particular way. In a long career of memorable, shocking and disquieting fashion pictures and portraits, he surely had his most productive year in 1975, when he created two

seminal images of our time, one for the May edition of American *Vogue* and the other for the September edition of French *Vogue*.

The American *Vogue* picture depicted the empowered late-twentieth-century woman, in the shape of model Lisa Taylor sitting on a sofa in a demure navy and white Calvin Klein skirt and top, with the drawstring neck left untied. Typical of many fashion pieces photographed not to fulfil fantasies but to sell clothes in a clear and understandable way, it is accessible, easy fashion of the sort the editor Grace Mirabella felt her readers required after many years of high fashion fantasy, which was the approach of her predecessor, Diana Vreeland. Seen through any other lens, the outfit would have been a very acceptable, even charming picture of fashion. Instead, Newton made it into an iconic image of altered sexual attitudes and one that is still arresting years later.

Newton arranged his picture so that a male figure was half seen on the right-hand side of the shot. Photographed with his back half turned to the camera, the man wears immaculate white trousers but no shirt. His well-muscled back and its shadow cast on the wall behind the seated woman frame and enclose the model. She sits, legs spread apart, one hand on her hip, the other teasing out a lock of hair, facing the man, with her eyes on his torso. The expression in her eyes asks, 'Is he worth it? Can I be bothered?' It is the insolently predatory look that many men sitting in exactly the same way give to women as they pass by, undressing them with their eyes. Newton has completely reversed the convention – the cliché, even – of centuries of male woman-watching in order to make a comment on changed roles and the newly empowered sexuality of women, except that we know that Newton is merely bringing out into the open the obvious fact that women also speculate and even fantasize about male sex appeal. The picture is saying that post-Pill women now share the sexual power of men. Or is it? By his brilliant use of shadows to box the woman in, he seems to be taking the argument a stage further to suggest that, although women think that things have changed and that they can be in charge as much as men, the man is still the one who makes the decision and the woman is still the caged object of his desire. It is a powerful and even disturbing image, revealing that a good fashion photograph must capture a social mood and a sexual attitude as well as revealing the qualities of the clothes.

Newton's second seminal image appeared in French *Vogue*'s *haute couture* coverage for 1975–6. A woman appears in a street at night, wearing an Yves Saint Laurent 'smoking' (a tuxedo). Everyone understands its cross-dressing and androgynous overtones, but what few realize is that the same woman appears in the magazine on the left-hand page and on the right-hand page, where her short hair and cigarette are still visible, though she now wears a low-cut crepe evening dress with a diaphanous jacket. The juxtaposition of the two pictures has the effect of altering our perception of the left-hand picture. Seen alone, it seems to acknowledge the sexual ambiguity in a woman wearing clothes that are basically masculine. Seen together, the pictures declare that there is no ambiguity in the sexuality of the woman. Her gamine look has not changed. Her dress does not make her look more feminine. The silhouette and shape in both photographs is almost identical. Newton seems to be asking us to consider if and how the woman's allure and sexuality are different in each picture and, if they are not, maybe he wants us to consider the possibility that androgyny is in our minds, not merely in clothes.

In the Seventies Newton played many games of this kind with our sexual sensibilities and went on in the Eighties to examine the nature of seduction: who is predator and who is victim – if either exists in his sophisticated scenarios – in a series of complex and enclosed tableaux, often involving three people and shot in surroundings that, for most readers, suggest decadence. In the Nineties, after a gap of some years, Newton used fashion photography in order to continue his examination of wealth, power and exhibitionism through fashion. The pictures that are the most disturbing – and certainly the most exciting – have been the ones he has made for American *Vogue* featuring

glamorous, iconic women in obligatory high heels but with limbs shackled with the paraphernalia of paraplegia: splints, crutches, callipers and wheelchairs. The frisson of shock suffered by readers at the juxtaposition of beauty and pain, elegance and ugliness makes them question their attitudes (and those of society) to disability. Why, Newton asks, do we assume that a disabled person cannot be beautiful and desirable like other women? Alexander McQueen asked the same question in 1998 when he used Aimée Mullins, born with no fibular bones in her legs, as a model in his London fashion show, arguing that her physical disability in no way disadvantaged her in the company of the other beautiful women modelling his clothes. Newton's unique image had paved the way for McQueen's shock tactics by doing what his photographs have always done: suggest an alternative way of seeing.

Newton's disturbing approach continues his lifetime work of destroying the concept that high fashion is the province of the refined and ladylike. He has created shock waves with his photography by taking fashion, seen by many as frivolously peripheral to the serious issues of our times, and making it central to our deepest psychological concerns. His *oeuvre* may be about obsessions but Newton's photography – radical, questioning and frequently uncomfortable – speaks powerfully to us of both fashion and reality.

Bruce Weber, the other great force in modern fashion photography, dominated the Eighties. His work continues to be highly influential in the Nineties, just as Newton's is. The man who has claimed that *National Geographic* magazine has some of the best fashion he has ever seen is not likely to take a well-trodden path in his approach to fashion pictures and, in fact, Weber brings to his task a totally original eye. Like Newton, he takes a highly selective approach to sexuality, finding men if anything more erotically challenging than women, and, just as Newton made us adapt the way we view

women – with men, with other women, or alone – so Weber is the man who evolved a totally new, and highly sexual, way of photographing men so that we are forced to look at them in ways we previously had not dared.

To understand Bruce Weber it is necessary to go back into American history, to Thoreau and Twain and pre-Twenties' college boys in their racoon coats; to the small-town lads horsing around at the drugstore, tinkering with ancient Model T Fords; to Margaret Bourke-White's photographs for *You Have Seen Their Faces*, her investigation with the novelist Erskine Caldwell of the Depression on American sharecroppers; above all, it is essential to know the masterpiece of that genre *Let Us Now Praise Famous Men*, published in 1939 with text by James Agee and photographs by Walker Evans, a twentieth-century American classic which illuminates the lives and attitudes that Weber's photographs have translated for the modern world.

Every photograph Bruce Weber takes is a photograph by an American. His unique sensibility could come from nowhere else. His attitudes and imperatives are far removed from those of most fashion photographers. In fact, it is hard to imagine that he even considers himself a fashion photographer. A gifted storyteller, Weber does not set out just to tell the story of a dress at the moment the camera clicks. His main interest lies in the stories of lives, and the clothes in his photographs are only part of a complex picture. Episodic, random and many-sided, as most lives are, his best work is found in the photo-essay, a genre that gives his imagination freedom to wander. The most convincing cover many pages and create a world apparently so real that it is sometimes hard to believe that the pictures aren't snapshots – albeit, technically perfect ones – of actual people, optimistic and happy, in empathy with their possessions and surroundings. In fact, one of Weber's most important influences on the Eighties was through the type of model he used. Far from being abstract

20 Nick Knight for
    Yohji Yamamoto,
    1987

21 Nick Knight,
    Skinheads, 1982

visions of impossible perfection, his subjects not only
looked like real people, not models, they frequently
were. He started a vogue for models of character with
highly individual faces, expressions and bodies. Male
bodies had to be toned and fit from hard physical work,
but not grotesquely musclebound from pumping iron in
a gym.

Starting as a photographer on the American edition
of *GQ* in the late Seventies, Weber made his mark by
frequently using groups of men in his pictures, whereas
other photographers normally used only one model per
shot. Taken on by British *Vogue*, he worked with stylists
Liz Tilberis and Grace Coddington to create fashion
stories that were often extended metaphors on the work
of important American novelists such as Willa Cather or
Eudora Welty. Like much of his work, they also drew
on the themes of great American film classics – the
integrity, innocence and strength of the rural or small-
town community with its church meetings, state fairs,
pool rooms, hard physical work and permanent shortage
of money. It's easy to imagine Weber enjoying *Shane*
and *Our Town*.

Bruce Weber's influence stretched beyond the pages
of fashion magazines in the Eighties with his work on
advertising campaigns for Ralph Lauren and Calvin Klein.
Totally at one with Lauren's view that he was interested
not in fashion but style, Weber created images
reminiscent of the film world based around Edna Ferber
novels acted by Rock Hudson, Paul Newman and James
Dean; the world of *Giant*, broad acres and the old-rich
life of Texas; the lives of rich sophisticates whose wealth
derived from the steers roaming their vast lands. For
Klein, Weber produced something harsher, more
contemporary and urban, to publicize Klein's underwear
in a remarkable series of photographs of the male as an
erotic icon whose imagery appealed equally to gay men
and heterosexual women.

While Weber was perfecting his hymns of praise to
American culture with his advertising and editorial work,
there were other remarkable talents developing in the
Eighties. One of the best – and most influential – was
the English photographer, Nick Knight, whose work for
the British magazines *i-D* and *Arena* was both eclectic
and cutting-edge. A maverick in the fashion world,
Knight trained as a scientist, studying human biology,
before following a photography course. Like Weber, he
is a photographer who ranges far beyond the bounds
normally associated with fashion: his first 'break' came
in 1985 when *i-D* commissioned him to take a series
of one hundred portraits of London's creative, media
and fashion personalities, to celebrate the magazine's
fifth anniversary.

21

22

22 Marc Lebon,
    'Party Up!',
    i-D, 1988

23 Nan Goldin,
    'Vivienne in the
    Green Dress,
    New York', 1980,
    in The Ballad
    of Sexual
    Dependency,
    1986

As a result of this work, he was asked to photograph Yohji Yamamoto's catalogues in the mid-Eighties. His *i-D* sensibility had been metropolitan but, with Yamamoto, Knight showed a pastoral, gentle side. Given the freedom to experiment, he explored at many different levels – technically and creatively – using each catalogue to expose a different facet of his increasingly strong fashion eye. Like Weber, Knight was a fashion outsider – and happy to be so. Like Blumenfeld, he was a technical innovator, using lighting and complex printing for effect. Like Man Ray, he exploited his medium to the full. The result was a sparkling series of photographs that were about, but not of, fashion. Studied, even mannered at times, his photographs are in the tradition of Bill Brandt – and nowhere more so than in his pictures of skinheads, which again link Knight to Weber in that both know precisely how to photograph men in a way that brings out their appeal for both sexes.

In the Eighties, it was magazines like *i-D* and *The Face*, to be followed by *Arena*, which placed men at the centre of fashion. Many of the seminal pictures of the time were taken by Knight, in the initial spirit of *i-D*'s determination to identify style as the ordinary and uncontrived way the young put together their clothes – a ludicrously unconvincing concept in the eyes of high-style fashion glossies but one that had thousands of young urban followers. Their preoccupations and paranoias were photographed by people like Marc Lebon, who worked with British fashion's leading lights in the Eighties, including Katharine Hamnett, Rifat Ozbek and Body Map. He was one of the main protagonists in the movement pushed hard by the style magazines to make fashion a part of an overall approach to lifestyle, inseparable from music, sex and all the other pleasures and preoccupations of the urban young. In 1988, he photographed seventeen pages, styled by Judy Blame and published in *i-D*, which were in the inventive spirit of *Nova* fashion stories in the Seventies, though they went much further. Called 'Party Up!', the shoot was a triumph of styling as much as photography, mixing fashion shots, children's drawings, found objects and even postage stamps to great effect. Most importantly, it made clear that the centre of London fashion, which had been sliding east from

Sloane Square for over a decade, had finally landed in Hackney.

It was in the Nineties that the attitudes held by Knight and Lebon really began to bear fruit in a series of challenging and uncompromising pictures that emphasized the enormous gap between designer-led fashion, promoted in the world's great fashion magazines and bolstered by huge advertising budgets, and fashion encouraging individuality, which carried as much kudos in certain circles as the grandest designer label did in others. In fact, the catalyst for what might be called the Dirty Realist school of fashion photography was almost certainly the exhibition, 'American Images', at the Barbican in 1985. Covering the period from 1945 to 1980, it was an important show, bringing to London the work of photographers previously known to only the photography specialist or those interested in the sociology of the disadvantaged classes of contemporary American life.

The photographs had an enormous impact not only on the numerous art students who came to view them, but also on Nineties' fashion photographers. The powerful images deliberately deglamorized America and took a humanist approach, looking at the tackiness and banality of ordinary life: such as Danny Lyon's pictures of bikers; Larry Clark's images of teenage sex and drugs; the domestic interiors of Bill Owen; the surrealist sequential images of Duane Michals; Weegee's unabashed shots of suicide and murder victims juxtaposed with tender explorations of poor black and Irish New Yorkers celebrating or mourning; William Klein's hugely influential street pictures of New York; and the work of Diane Arbus, whose eye for what Susan Sontag called 'assorted monsters and borderline cases', resulted in a creepily compulsive effect. All had more influence on Nineties' fashion photography than anything seen in the glossy magazines.

The work of Nan Goldin, whose *Ballad of Sexual Dependency* of 1986 consisted of 700 pictures of the subcultural life of New York, shows the influence of 'American Images'. As a piece concerning life and death – of the spirit as much as the body – it perfectly suited the mood of the times in London. A deep pessimism hung over metropolitan life for many of the young, which photographers who were working at the unglamorous

24

end of the fashion business wanted to communicate
in their pictures. They were, in fact, carrying on the
war against the Establishment values that began with
Baudelaire and Rimbaud and continued with subversive
writers like Jean Genet and film makers like Pier Paolo
Pasolini. They wanted their pictures to raise questions
by juxtaposing the positive and the negative, pushing
everything to its limits until freedom became excess,
and independence became disorientation. Eschewing
professional models, they photographed their families
and friends in unsophisticated places or situations:
council flats in Brixton, tenements in the Bowery, low-
cost hotel rooms, kitchens piled with unwashed dishes.
Dralon curtains with cigarette burns and stained nylon
carpet in Seventies' shades of orange and brown were
all considered to add the correct social undercurrents.

Out of these unpromising surroundings have come
some of the most powerful style photographs of the
past fifty years. Taking tangential viewpoints designed to
deglamorize, fashion photographers set out to reveal the
darkly troubled beauty of daily life; the dangers of city
streets; and, often, the black humour diffusing it all, as
in Terry Richardson's feature 'Repulsion' in *The Face*,
which showed a model shaving off her eyebrows and
putting her head in the gas oven. It was a time when
the ordinary became the extraordinary in the pictures
of Pamela Hanson, Ellen von Unwerth, Cindy Sherman
and, above all, Corinne Day's shots of Kate Moss which
British *Vogue* had the courage to publish although it
unleashed a storm of criticism from the media and howls
of dismay from advertisers who couldn't understand
why an Establishment magazine would wish to feature
pictures that so clearly threatened the status quo. It
was a bold acknowledgement of how London fashion
was moving, but *Vogue* did not repeat the experiment.

It really didn't need to. Glossy fashion magazines
worked to one agenda, style magazines to another.
Photographers of the calibre of Stephen Callaghan,
Glen Luchford and Mark Borthwick were, like Terry
Richardson, perfectly at home with the latter, although
Nick Knight, towering above them all, made the move
to luxury magazines with no problem in the Nineties:

29

his seminal 'Chaos Couture' of 1990, in which he
presented a glamorized, glossy version of inner-city
toughness, appeared in *i-D* but could have sat as easily
on the pages of *L'Uomo Vogue* or *Vogue Hommes*. In
fact, it was in European magazines – often dedicated to
menswear – that the crossover between fashion and
style seemed to happen most naturally, as a school
which might be called the Luxury Realists began to
develop with Mario Testino, Steven Meisel, Craig
McDean and David Sims increasingly asked to re-create
the subversive quality of style magazines for the
mainstream market. Meisel, in particular, captured the
waif-like character of young male models for his *L'Uomo
Vogue* swimwear shoot in 1995, with the boys looking
like hustlers picked up in the street, a strange mixture
of the brutalized and the vulnerable, the innocent and
the aware.

Much of the photographic work of the Nineties was,
like the art of the period, about rebellion and rejection.
British artists such as Lucian Freud – especially in his
portraits of Leigh Bowery – and Francis Bacon, whose
technique was used in Mario Sorrenti's Keren series of
photographs in 1995, influenced photographers already
working on methods capitalizing on – and transforming
– home movies and Polaroids, often using computer-
generated images. Photographs by Juergen Teller
and Wolfgang Tillmans frequently look like amateur
snapshots in a perverse denial of the skill that actually
goes into their creation: Juergen Teller's pictures of
Kristen McMenamy in the nude are an example of a
photographer not being overawed by the glamour of
fashion but showing that beauty is not synonymous
with physical perfections with a pose which sends up
glamour shots of the Fifties and Sixties. McMenamy
proudly displays her scar and bruises and smokes
a cigarette in defiance of the rules of glamour. The
'I love Versace' sign drawn on her breast in lipstick
and eyeliner is a sharp reminder, as she is naked, of the
emperor's new clothes syndrome which haunts everyone
in fashion.

Much of this work is exploratory, created because the
photographer finds it an interesting line of investigation.
It is often too avant-garde to be commissioned by
fashion or style magazines. But there are photographers
who are able to inject humour into their work even in
the mainstream magazines, most of which make no
pretence that high fashion is about anything other than
competition and sales. Fashion photography even has
its satirists. One of the most imaginative and original
is Jean-Paul Goude, who began work as an illustrator
and was art editor of *Esquire* in the early Seventies. He
became Grace Jones's manager and art editor in 1976

32 Paolo Roversi for
    Yohji Yamamoto,
    1997–8

33 Paolo Roversi for
    Yohji Yamamoto,
    1997

32

and was responsible for many extraordinary and
memorable images of her, most notably as a caged
wild animal. He reached a world market in 1989 as the
director of La Marseillaise, the bicentennial celebrations
of the French Revolution, in which he directed 8,000
performers, including Jessye Norman, but it is as a
photographer that he will be best remembered. During
the Eighties his pictures of his close friend and designer
Azzedine Alaïa, his work for continental fashion
magazines and his record sleeves all show a well-
balanced sense of humour, a particularly welcome
attribute in the fashion world. It is a quality Goude
shares with his compatriot Jean-Baptiste Mondino,
who, as well as directing music videos for David Bowie,
Sting, Prince and Madonna, has worked with Jean Paul
Gaultier on the couturier's stylishly irreverent publicity
campaigns, bringing his own unique view to the world
of fashion photography in what are best described as
a series of hoaxes for the eye.

  Newer talents continued the traditions of fantasy for
the Nineties, none more flamboyantly than David
LaChapelle, whose witty tableaux, glittering and
sparkling with highly coloured images, appear regularly
in Stern and French Vogue. Always arresting, they
have the same effect as the photographs of Inez van
Lamsweerde and Vinoodh Matadin, whose brilliant
colour and perfected airbrushed figures are the epitome
of camp glossiness, reminiscent of the sun-filled world
of Mitzi Gaynor movies in the Fifties and the barley-
sugar bright icons of Eighties' and Nineties' kitsch
in the photographs of Pierre and Gilles. Colour of a
more subtle kind is found in the photographs of Paolo
Roversi, where the image seems to have been gently
bleached and stained to create effects that can only
really be described as ethereal. The same technical

34

brilliance is found in the photography of Stéphane Sednaoui, once a runway model but now one of the most accomplished colourists in fashion photography. Like the American David Seidner, who died in 1999, he manages to marry in his work elegance and spirituality with modern techniques.

Whether the result of fantasy, good technique or the use of colour or black and white, the photographs of style and fashion in the Nineties consistently produced memorable images. Some of these photographs will last long after the names of designers and even, perhaps, many of the magazines that commissioned them are forgotten. They transcend mere image-making and present a visual checklist of much that has been found moving, exciting and compulsive in fashion and its attitudes over the last fifty years. In fact, they go much further. At their best, they vividly reflect the changes in society that are so often first seen in fashion. Even more, as portrait photography has moved away from the hagiography it inherited from painted portraiture, it is the human figure in its ambience that attracts photographers. The same is true of the approach of style photographers: they show us the true fashion in which people live by placing them and their clothes in their surroundings. Glossy pictures of expensive clothes on perfect model bodies taken on tropical beaches may well feed our dreams, but it is the kitchen in the neglected low-rent apartment, with sauce bottles on the table and the woman painting her nails while the man combs his hair in a cracked mirror above the sink ready for a night out, which will tell future generations how fashion was *actually* lived by many in our time.

SELLING THE DREAM

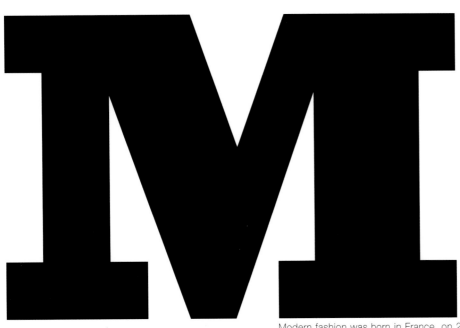

Modern fashion was born in France, on 21 November 1945, when, at a newsstand cost of fifteen francs, *Elle* magazine first went on sale. The brainchild of Hélène Gordon-Lazareff, the magazine was a declaration of faith in a new order, proclaiming that a different kind of woman had emerged from the privations of World War II: a woman stronger and more motivated than her sex previously had dared to be. *Elle* was predicated on the principle that elitism and class privilege would no longer dominate either fashion or life as they had in the past. The magazine was an instant commercial success.

In a world of fashion ruled by *Vogue*, *L'Officiel* and *Le Figaro*, all of which, in order to fill both their advertising and editorial pages, turned exclusively to the couturiers, fabric houses, perfumiers, milliners and make-up companies that hovered around the Place Vendôme, *Elle* was initially viewed as an upstart, the first women's magazine to set out to create a quality product of interest predominantly to young women, most of whom were far removed from the privileged world of Paris *haute couture*.

Hélène Gordon-Lazareff was a Chanel-suited visionary. From the *Elle* that she edited so well sprang a host of modern magazines for educated, intelligent women, eager to be informed. From the beginning, the magazine faced up to the challenge of representing the fears and worries that had plagued ordinary women for generations. In its first year, the magazine published an article entitled 'I Don't Have Enough Time'. It addressed the problem of being a working woman expected to juggle domestic and work responsibilities. The article was a declaration that *Elle* readers were radically different from the women targeted by the traditional glossy magazines, whose lives involved nothing more taxing than a morning spent at the hairdresser, lunch at the Ritz and an afternoon of bridge.

In 1951, *Elle* carried an article on plastic surgery. In 1952, turning its back on the coldness of the traditional high fashion model, it used its new young discovery, Brigitte Bardot, to model young fashions. It employed writers of the calibre of Colette, Simone de Beauvoir, Françoise Sagan and Marguerite Duras. By 1961, years before the top glossies would dare to address such a subject, *Elle* examined the problem of unwanted pregnancies in an interview with a 32-year-old married woman who was desperate because she was expecting her sixth child. A few years later, it was pinpointing the disgrace of the annual 800,000 backstreet abortions that took place in France.

Elle romped through the Sixties and into the Seventies, publishing highly political photographs by Henri Cartier-Bresson, addressing issues raised by feminism and featuring France's most directional fashion: from Dorothée Bis and Kenzo to Jean Paul Gaultier and Issey Miyake. The magazine virtually launched the career of André Courrèges. Its great fashion strength was the way in which it kept pace with emergent talents, featuring young French designers such as Emmanuelle Khanh, Sonia Rykiel and Guy Paulin and their opposite numbers in London (Mary Quant, Zandra Rhodes and Ossie Clark), often well before they appeared in the upmarket French magazines. Above all, *Elle*'s fashion philosophy – eclectic, adventurous and totally committed to ready-to-wear at all levels, while still featuring couture – meant that, for the first time in a 'quality' magazine, its stylists could make strong fashion statements, using

Retour à la terre du marron des villes : ça fait bien sur le hâlé... et sur l'herbe ! Ici, c'est en gabardine de coton Sanfor, un costume « costaud » de petit paysan : gilet à poches plaquées resserré dans le dos et pantalon droit (Cacharel. Gilet, 45 F ; pantalon, 49 F, chez Belù). Pour lui garder son charme champêtre : chemisier en Dacron à fleurs naïves (Arrow. 64 F, chez Conniel). Pour courir toutes les vacances : bottillons en toile.

Là, c'est en toile fibranne, une formule un peu plus classique : la veste-chemise assez longue pour camoufler des hanches rondes est boutonnée sur une patte surpiquée, le pantalon est fermé devant (Tiktiner. 219 F, chez Amie). Foulard en soie beige et brun (Boutique de l'Inde). Bracelets Casty.

PAGE 153 : OÙ TROUVER NOS MODÈLES

131

5

UNE LIGNE JUNIOR A GRANDES ENJAMBEES. Jupe portefeuille à taille élastique, col roulé long à écharpe attenante et cardigan coordonné (Kenzo pour Jap, 165 F, 270 F, 365 F). Carré en étamine (Issey Miyaké). Accessoires (Jap). Chaussures (Maud Frizon).

50 cm de jupe

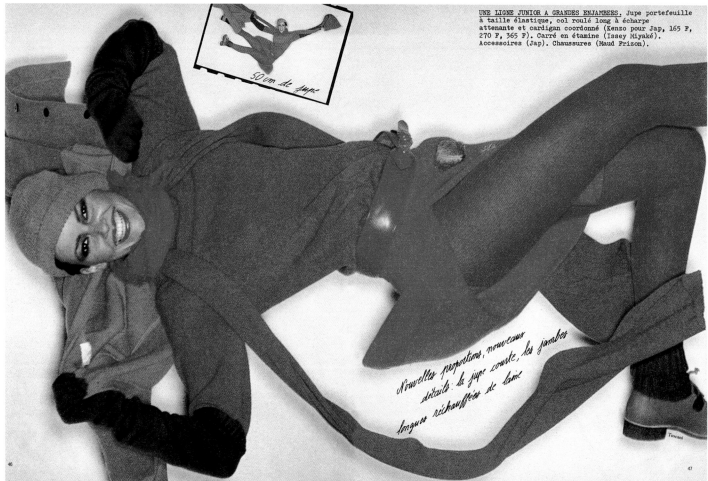

Nouvelles proportions, nouveaux détails : la jupe courte, les jambes longues réchauffées de laine

46

47

6

5   Spread from *Elle*,
    1964, photos
    Ronald Traeger

6   Spread from *Elle*,
    1976, photo
    Oliviero Toscani

7   *Elle* cover, 1971

clothes accessible to all women, from 'les grands magasins' of France, such as Galeries Lafayette and Printemps, as well as the small boutiques which began to spring up across the country in the Sixties.

But it was the typography and layout that made *Elle* such a trailblazer. Although nothing that its editor, Hélène Gordon-Lazareff, did was entirely new, the mixture she created for *Elle* seemed fresh, exciting and challenging. Print was ribboned across photographs that were used large and often placed on their side across a spread. Artwork and photography were superimposed together on the page to give a lively, young graphic movement. *Elle*'s photographers were allowed a high degree of artistic license. As early as the Sixties, an *Elle* story could be instantly identified through its individual and often quirky pictures. Even though art editors came and went, the spirit of *Elle* remained, whether in Bill King's running, jumping and dancing fashion stories, shot against crisp white backgrounds – copied everywhere, including British *Elle* when it was launched in the mid-Eighties – or the balancing charm of Oliviero Toscani's pastoral idylls and Jean-Baptiste Mondino's powerful colour statements. Antonio Lopez was drawing the prêt-à-porter collections for the magazine as early as 1967, and Jeanloup Sieff became one of the magazine's photographers in 1955. Loulou de la Falaise and Catherine Deneuve modelled for the magazine.

Elle enjoyed a phenomenal success – it went from an initial readership of 100,000 to over a million in the Sixties. Like many great enterprises, it was the brainchild and obsession of one woman who was aware of journalistic developments not only in France but also in America. Hélène Gordon-Lazareff spent World War II in America and knew the work of Carmel Snow, Diana Vreeland and Alexey Brodovitch on *Harper's Bazaar*. She was also conscious of the success of the French magazine, *Marie Claire*, founded in 1937: a fortnightly publication aimed at modern women. It was very much in reaction to, and in the spirit of, *Marie Claire* that Lazareff founded her magazine. *Elle* was also a fortnightly magazine, a formula to which the French edition has remained faithful, although *Marie Claire* went monthly in 1954 (many believe this was the result of pressure on advertising revenues as *Elle* became such a successful competitor). For Lazareff, the fortnightly format was sacrosanct. She believed that the pace of life for young professional women was too fast for them to be satisfied with a monthly magazine. She was convinced that the reader loyalty she needed was a result of a continued involvement with the issues raised in the magazine. For her, a month was too long a gap to keep that involvement fresh.

Her will prevailed. She succeeded in giving *Elle* not only a chic but also a political profile. For example, *Elle*'s positive approach to Chanel's emergence from retirement in 1954 was a political act. Chanel had spent most of the war living in the Ritz with a German lover, escaping to Switzerland when Paris was liberated. She was an unpopular figure in many sectors of French life, not least the fashion world, and the media took its revenge, dubbing her comeback collection boring, dreary and the work of an old woman who had lost her touch. However, Lazareff refused to let her opinion be clouded by prejudice, and judged Chanel's clothes solely on their merit and relevance for the modern woman. *Elle* championed the new Chanel and, by doing so, had a definite – and, most would say, benign – effect on the future of fashion.

Lazareff was an innovator. In 1948, she introduced a regular article called 'Le Bon Magique', which featured cheap and readily available fashionable items, ranging from Pyrex cooking dishes to clothes specially created for *Elle* by many of France's top ready-to-wear designers. In 1969, cookery cards appeared in the magazine, followed in 1975 by knitting patterns. Such additions exemplified Lazareff's belief that, to be useful, a fashion magazine had to be practical. Such thinking was also behind her most overtly political move when, in 1970, *Elle* sponsored the États Généraux de la Femme, a conference named deliberately to echo the Estates General, the national assembly whose collapse precipitated the French Revolution. Photographed for the magazine by Cartier-Bresson, 325 delegates discussed conditions for women in France and what reforms were needed to give them parity with men. So that nobody would miss the revolutionary connotations or fail to link them with history, the conference was held at Versailles. It was the first time that a woman's magazine had been able to raise a collective consciousness, quite apart from how powerfully it did so. It is, perhaps, not surprising that Hélène Gordon-Lazareff's *Elle* has, to date, spawned over twenty *Elle* magazines worldwide.

But it was French *Elle*'s effect on magazine publishing that was immense. If Lazareff broke down barriers in her views of what women needed in a magazine, her art editor, the Swiss photographer Peter Knapp (who joined the magazine in 1959) was responsible for giving it such a powerful and forward-looking design that its influence was felt worldwide and for at least two decades. He had previously been artistic director of *Nouveau Femina* while also working for Galeries Lafayette, but it was Lazareff who gave Knapp the creative freedom to take decisions which reflected his originality.

7

THE CONSENSUS OF OPINION

9

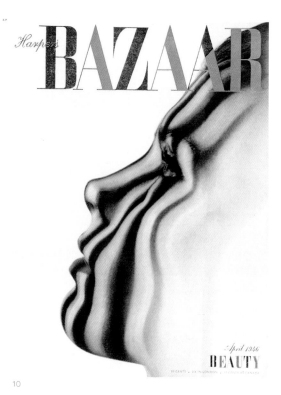

Art editors are the power behind the throne in magazine publishing. Their input is vital as they are the people who interpret the editor's ideas, hire and brief the photographers and stylists and conceive a layout and typographical pattern which makes their magazine instantly recognizable, and distinguishable, from all the others. It isn't surprising, therefore, that there have been instances of art editors actually being paid more than editors. Quite simply, they create the visual character of a magazine from which its overall character flows.

The most famous and admired of art editors is Alexey Brodovitch, who worked on the American edition of *Harper's Bazaar* with Carmel Snow in the Thirties, Forties and Fifties. In a very true sense, he can be seen as the father of modern magazine layout. His elegant use of space and sparkling typography influenced many more art directors than merely Peter Knapp at *Elle*: Brodovitch's attitude and sensibility was seen in the Sixties in the London men's magazine, *Man About Town*, Jocelyn Stevens's *Queen* and the *Sunday Times Magazine*. It should be noted that American *Vogue* also benefited from inspired art direction: Dr Mehemet Agha with Edna Woolman Chase and, from 1943, Alexander Liberman, who made *Vogue* visually strong by directing and suggesting to young men such as Irving Penn roads they had not yet considered. For example, he encouraged Penn to use the special knowledge and colour awareness that he had gained while spending a year in Mexico in 1942, trying to be a painter, which led not only to the elegant stillness of his fashion work, but his famous portraits of sitters in enclosed spaces and, in 1974, his book *Worlds in a Small Room*, in which he collected his portraits of people from around the world. Due to him, American *Vogue* was one of the leading world titles in visual sophistication from the Forties to the Sixties – a period in which editor Diana Vreeland set standards that are still emulated today.

What was happening in American magazines in the Sixties was exciting, with Brodovitch's influence having a profound effect and the battle for excellence fought by *Vogue* and *Harper's Bazaar* increasingly reliant not only on the high quality of the photographs but also the skill with which they were placed on the page. It was the era of white space, when a magazine spread could be devoted to one elegantly positioned line of copy against

10

8

a plain background. It was also the era of intense movement, where the images made the eye dance across the pages with the energy associated with *Elle* but also with an essentially American elegance. The natural successor to French *Elle* was in fact the London magazine, *Nova*, published between 1965 and 1975, when it was unceremoniously killed by a management made increasingly nervous by its relentless iconoclasm. By then, it had created its own legend, which is still potent today. It set out to achieve things not previously attempted by a British magazine. The founding art director was Harri Peccinotti, with Penny Vincenzi as his fashion editor. Peccinotti was to stay only until 1966. David Hillman took over as art director in 1969 – a post he remained in until the magazine closed – but Vincenzi left after eight issues and was replaced by Molly Parkin. In October 1967, when Caroline Baker began her period as *Nova*'s fashion editor, her brief was simple: to be as different as possible from *Vogue*. She fulfilled it with such flair and originality that *Nova*, already being watched by other magazines around the world for the strength of its art direction, became compulsive reading for every fashion editor.

Although Peccinotti's stint as art director of *Nova* was brief, his influence was immense. He continued his association with the magazine, working with layouts and photographing much of the fashion. In Baker, he had a willing, and worthy, accomplice. Collaborating with a succession of avant-garde photographers: Jeanloup Sieff, Hans Feurer, Helmut Newton, Terence Donovan, Bob Richardson, Guy Bourdin, Sarah Moon and Deborah Turbeville, a roll call of Seventies' talent, nothing was too risky for Baker and they were all given free rein to produce pictures that would almost certainly not have been accepted by other glossy publications at the time. In March 1972, Sieff photographed a model, scantily clad, sitting on the lavatory, with her tights rolled

down. Baker's fashion shoot of December 1971, 'Every Hobo Should Have One', used inner-city dereliction as the background for a story featuring a model posing as a tramp – but wearing the most glamorous of furs. It was an approach which lit a slow-burning but remarkably powerful fuse in fashion magazines that smouldered away until *i-D* and *The Face* took up the concept of accepting urban dereliction and the attitudes it engenders as part of their style equation, and was then taken on by Nineties' magazines such as *Dazed and Confused*, *Wallpaper* and even mainstream publications such as Italian *Vogue* and *L'Uomo Vogue*.

Another way in which *Nova* presaged the future was that it never saw itself as being exclusively, or even primarily, a fashion magazine. Like the *Sunday Times Magazine*, it was aimed at the new first generation art school and university graduates and all of their interests, of which fashion was merely one. It was the earliest of the style magazines in that it brought to its readers very particular attitudes and expected them to reach out to *Nova* in order to discover that their own style attitudes could be articulated. The synthesis of the two created a constantly changing and frequently adjusted composite of the emergent 'new woman'. It goes without saying that the attitudes found in *Nova* were cutting-edge feminist, but Peccinotti and Baker never forgot that, not only because of the raunchy fashion spreads but also for its persistent iconoclasm, the magazine was also read (if not bought) by men. The *Nova* woman was a high achiever, in charge of her life and her sexuality. She leapt across the fashion spreads and stared uncompromisingly from the beauty pages with a confidence and vitality that, for most of the magazine's readers, was as much a fantasy as the ideal woman depicted in other magazines. But, somehow, with *Nova*, women felt that there might just be a chance of harnessing some of the energy for their own lives.

A testimony to Caroline Baker's zany genius, it was high fashion, outrageous fashion, and even when it became kitsch fashion it still managed to keep a foothold in reality and have some sort of common touch.

Above all, what *Nova* brought to its readers was a monthly injection of adrenaline, a challenge to conventional attitudes and a determination to present its credos so aggressively that they could not be ducked. Its cover lines offended as much as they pleased: a picture of two young men with the caption, 'They Consent in Private'; a little black girl, beautifully dressed and 'You May Think I Look Cute: But Would You Live Next Door to my Mummy and Daddy?'; a naked man fresh from the shower and 'Lucky You – Now You Can Ogle Me. That's what I call liberation … do you?'; and the classic line emblazoned across a heavily made-up pair of eyes: 'What a Hint of Mascara Could Do For Harold Wilson' (the British prime minister at the time).

Despite its sparkle and glamour, *Nova* subconsciously had a deathwish. It couldn't continue to be that provocative without the risk of offending backers. It couldn't show fashion and style with such an obvious indifference to market forces without alarming advertisers. When it was closed down, many claimed that it marked the end of an era. In a sense it did. *Nova*'s role had been innovatory. Its shock tactics had taken effect, making art directors, publishers and fashion editors think again. However, by the mid-Seventies, other more commercially minded magazines had taken on the message and there was a need for a completely new way of shocking the fashion world out of its complacency.

It came with double force in 1980, the year in which Nick Logan founded *The Face* and Terry Jones began *i-D*. Of the two, *i-D* has proved the most influential, although throughout the Eighties *The Face* was seen

14

NOVA

MAY 1971 20 PENCE

How to
undress in front of
your husband
*and a flick-book
to amuse him while he waits*

**POLANSKI
HIGH ON
POLANSKI
MOROCCAN
FASHION
GARDEN STATUES
COME INDOORS
IS YOUR CHILD
INHERITING
YOUR
HANG-UPS?
FIRST LOVE
REMEMBERED**

NOVA

MARCH 1971 4/ 20 NP

**DARKLY, DEEPLY,
BEAUTIFULLY BLUE**
Good on you

**IS OLD AGE
A PUNISHABLE
OFFENCE?**

**CAN A WOMAN
LOVE TWO
MEN AT ONCE?**

**THE GOSPEL
ACCORDING TO
A HOMOSEXUAL
PRIEST**

NOVA

OCTOBER 1975
25p

**LUCKY
YOU—
NOW
YOU CAN
OGLE ME**
That's
what I
call
liberation...
...do you?

HOW TO
KEEP YOUR
COOL
WHEN YOU
LOSE IT
**BARBARA
WINDSOR'S,
AHEM,
ASSETS**
AROMATIC
FACTS ABOUT
HERBAL
REMEDIES

**COMPLETE
SIX-MONTH
BEAUTY
COURSE**

15

NOVA

JULY 1971 **20p**

**IT'S AN UGLY
BUSINESS BEING
BEAUTIFUL**

**A FATHER'S RIGHT
TO BE LEFT
HOLDING THE BABY**

16   *i-D*, 1989, photo
Nick Knight

17   Spreads from the
first issue of *i-D*,
1980

16

by many, including those in New York, Paris and Milan, as most accurately reflecting London's unique mix of music and fashion. Both magazines were committed to acknowledging popular music not only as a cultural force but also as the driving energy behind much that was happening in fashion. Logan, who had edited the music publications *NME* and *Smash Hits*, emblazoned early editions of *The Face* with the slogan, 'Rock's Final Frontier'. Jones deliberately modelled *i-D* on the cheap, instant and accessible fanzines which, in the late Seventies and early Eighties, had appeared so frequently, staffed by dedicated students, out of work advertising graduates and devoted groupies all working hard for little, if any, money.

It was precisely this energy and commitment that the new style magazines were to harness. *The Face* and *i-D* were essentially London phenomena, picking up and exploiting a unique chemical mix which saw music and fashion, art school students, clubbers and young design hopefuls come together to produce a creative charge new to both music and fashion. Both magazines were quick to realize the unique quality of London's creative life in the early Eighties, becoming sound and shrewd reflectors of the moods, manners, movements and modes of the young and hip, chronicling the powerful club scene, noting art school attitudes – especially those at St Martin's School of Art, creative powerhouse for the decade – and keeping up with every fad and fancy that caught hold of the fashionable coteries.

In fact, it is probably true to say that the fashion attitudes found not only in London but also in New York and most of Europe's major cities in the early Eighties were formed by a hardcore of a thousand dedicated London clubbers, stylists, design students and fashion movers and shakers who endlessly reinvented themselves and constantly changed the goalposts as far as style, cool and commitment were concerned. The art schools were the crucible in which new ideas were created, not only by fashion students but also by those studying graphics, illustration and fine arts. John Galliano's degree show at St Martin's attracted them all, eager to help and be part of his intensely creative world, as last-minute sewers, models or merely as members of the audience and, therefore, part of the scene.

Students have frequently received bad press in Britain, and it would have been easy to condemn what was happening in British art schools as shallow, flippant and self-regarding. It was magazines such as *i-D* and *The Face* which first realized the enormity of the revolution that was taking place. They caught the speed and energy of student fashion and gave it coherence on their pages. By visually articulating what in many cases was

narcissistic, amateur and crudely executed, they gave it a voice that removed it from the level of student posing and beamed it out to an eagerly waiting world as London's style attitudes achieved a universality they had not enjoyed since the Sixties.

In an era when style was beginning to make serious inroads into traditional designer fashion and its attitudes, Logan and Jones realized that visual presentation was crucial. Terry Jones, who had worked on British *Vogue*, was determined to make *i-D* the champion of the 'ordinary', but he knew how to present it with a deft touch. The first issue of *i-D* had as its lead story 'Wild!', which consisted of twenty-nine shots of people photographed on the street. Chosen for the originality of their appearance, details of their clothes – whether second-hand, thrift shop or homemade – were given in a pastiche of glossy magazines and their all-important details of the price and availability of featured merchandise. To give *i-D* its quality of immediacy and street credibility, the print style of the magazine had a battered, 'old Olivetti' typed quality. On the back cover Terry Jones threw down his gauntlet to a generation. '*i-D* is a fashion/style magazine', he declared, adding, 'Style isn't what, but how, you wear your clothes. Fashion is the way you walk, talk, dance and prance. Through *i-D* ideas travel fast and free of the mainstream – so join us on the run!' It was a clarion call to all those tired of the manipulation of the glossies and the highly-priced designer labels that were their stock in trade but, by the mid-Eighties, when he commissioned Nick Knight to photograph London's style gurus, Jones' magazine, which had begun as a stapled-together affair with a print run of two thousand copies per month, had all the visual panache of the glossiest of glossies. The choice of people to be photographed and the fact that they were asked to name their favourite club and top record shows how strongly the magazine was influenced by the music scene. The club entrepreneur, Steve Strange, the DJ John Peel and the model, Scarlett (known as the Blitz girl after the club of that name) were there along with John Galliano, John Richmond and Maria Cornejo, and the stylists Simon Foxton and Ray Petri – a perennial poser but London's most powerful style influence, who had begun working with *i-D* on issue sixteen. There were those who wondered if the knowing wink which became a feature of the magazine's covers from issue five was symptomatic of a different kind of exploitation from that so clearly seen in the more blatant glossy magazines.

i-D's readers loved the ad hoc immediacy of the early issues. They had a sense of looking at something happening now, hot off the streets and fresh from the

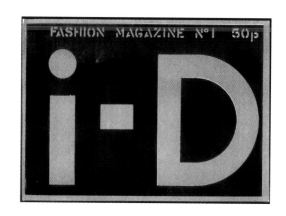

FASHION MAGAZINE N°1 50p

i-D

ETTER BADGES

NEW BADGES!

BADGET - RICKY'S HAND
ONSIBLES
B

HOGS
OLE TUDOR
ON SILVERBLADES
IX NOUVEAUX
INVASION 80
NLY ONES

DOCTOR
ASSES
NT 5
NO ROOM
BOYS
AT THE CONTROL
T

A.
I ANGELES)
LODO
DOVE
HY AND PEACE
WAR NOT WARS
HEART
RED
REY

A plus 10p POST
ETTER BADGES
TORELLO RD LONDON W10

3

WiLD!

STRAIGHT UP

Photographed by Steve Johnston

COLIN: Mode - Colin is wearing black pleated trousers which he made himself. The cardigan is from Marks and Spencers, £9.99 and the shoes from Axiom in the Kings Road, £5.99. Fave music - Siousxie and the Banshees and David Bowie.

Anonymous girl with spiky hair-do.

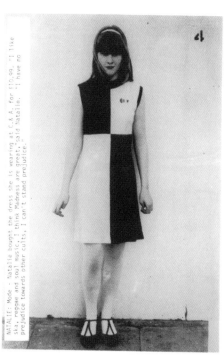

4

NATALIE: Mode - Natalie bought the dress she is wearing at C.&A. for £10.99. "I like ska, reggae and soul music. I think Madness are great," said Natalie. "I have no prejudice towards other cults, I can't stand prejudice."

5

PATRICIA: Mode - Sunglasses from Harrods, shirt from Paris for just 20p, shorts bought from John Lewis Boys' Sportswear Dept. and the rollerskates cost £7 at a sports shop. Fave music? Patricia, a model, likes disco. "I also like Cat Stevens and Elton John, but can't stand David Soul. Generally though I have no prejudices and I have no time for people who have," she added.

CLINT: Mode - Clint, who works in a Pizza Hut sports a shirt by Paul Smith from Stanley Adams. "I paid £18 for it," said Clint. The trousers are from the Seditionaries, 27 quid, and the Johnsons shoes set me back 20t. Clint listens to Jazz, the Specials, Madness and Abba. "I don't like the Wurzels or Western soundtrack but my taste at all" he added.

17

cover star: **shalom** photographed by **carter smith** october 1998

i-D

£2.50 US$6.75

fast forward

18

Left: Knitted skirt, sweater and hat, all by Yohji Yamamoto. **Right:** Cellophane covered feathered head dress from the Amazon; cellophane covered sweater by Martin Margiela.

KOYAANISQATSI
A state of life that calls for another way of living

Photography by Carter Smith
Styling and concept by Jane How

Photographic assistance by Greg Sorrensen and Tesh
Styling and production assistance by Rebecca Owen
Make-up by Virginia Young at Streeters
Hair by Neil Moodie at Premier for Aveda
Model: Shalom Harlow
Special thanks to Simon Webb at English Nature:
Abbey Scar Limestone Pavements National Park,
Lake District, Cumbria; Francesca
and Maria at Katy Barker Agency

19

i-D THE FORWARD ISSUE 267

clubs. Above all, they felt they were a part of the excitement. *The Face* took a more controlled approach. And, if *i-D* quickly annexed the power of Nick Knight, whom Juergen Teller dubbed 'The Hero', *The Face*, which by now was calling itself 'Best Dressed Magazine', also had its strong man. Neville Brody had studied at Hornsey College of Arts and Crafts and the London College of Printing – the right credentials in early Eighties' London. They could have been clouded by the fact that he had worked briefly for *Tatler*, but his dismissal of the society magazine as an intolerable 'self-indulgent in-joke' cleared up that problem. Brody's work with the record companies *Stiff* and *Fetish* reasserted his street credibility, but what mattered for *The Face* – and, indeed, a generation of graphic designers – was the fact that he was a total original. His artistic influences – Dada, Constructivism, Moholy-Nagy, Malevich and Rodchenko – affected the pages of *The Face* and made them unique. Their effect on other graphic designers was immense.

Brody's powerful design, based largely on his belief in the strength of original typography, most of which he designed himself, challenged the 'flick-through-and-forget' approach adopted by most magazines. He set out to make *The Face* deliberately challenging, with a layout that was often difficult to decipher. If a reader had to puzzle over a page for several minutes before understanding its message, that was all to the good in Brody's mind because it inevitably made for an involvement which, in his view, was missing from the pages of other magazines. When Logan had first conceived *The Face*, his major influence was news magazines, especially *Paris Match*, and when, in 1986, he created the men's magazine *Arena*, 'for *Face* readers ready to move on', he ironically used the titles of other publications for its regular features, including Spectator, People, Avanti and Vanity. *Arena* was a much more commercially conscious venture than *The Face* had ever been. When he started *The Face*, Logan didn't particularly care about attracting advertisers, and the magazine was in its fourth year before it had anything approaching a fully functioning advertising department. But, as Terry Jones also learned, dress codes and social documentation are like anything else in the magazine world. Even at the risk of compromising editorial freedom, revenue beyond that produced by newsstand sales is essential if standards of production are to be maintained. Logan, Brody, Jones and Knight exerted a worldwide influence through the titles with which they were variously involved. Their magazines were entirely metropolitan. One could tell at a glance that the type of clothes featured were chosen to appeal to a specific

22

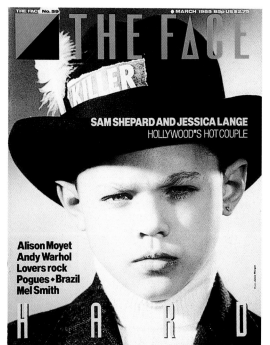

23

urban readership, but their approach to dress was as close to classlessness as anything to do with the parade of fashion can be. Like *Nova* before them, their strength rested on the stylists and photographers they employed and the design risks they were prepared to take with their work.

Caroline Baker's unique 'mix-and-jumble' approach was moved forward under their guidance, and behind all their fashion stories was an implicit rejection of the role of the supermodel – although in 1993 Linda Evangelista appeared on the cover of *i-D* – and, even more importantly, a questioning of the role and relevance of the superhero fashion photographer, a figure of dominant power in the Nineties. Baker and Peccinotti had pioneered a satirical attitude in their fashion stories and they had delighted in displaying cheap clothes, including army surplus wear, which many consider to have been invented as an alternative fashion approach by Baker but, like much else in modern fashion, was first presaged by Yves Saint Laurent in the Sixties. *The Face*, *i-D* and *Arena* took on board not only the intense physical energy of Baker's pages but also her belief that fashion as lifestyle and dress as identity were what ultimately mattered – much more than flaunting designer labels.

If Nick Knight straddled London's photographic scene like a colossus, gaining fans and emulators each time his work was published, his equivalent in the world of styling was Ray Petri who, until his death in 1989, dominated *The Face*, *Arena* and *i-D*. In fact, he did much more: his visual approach defined the Eighties in London. Sole begetter of *Buffalo* – as much a stance and an attitude of mind as a style – his menswear pictures summed up his own definition: 'tougher than the rest', which he first coined when describing the boys of Paris. His best work was done with the photographer Jaimie Morgan and includes the classic 'Killer' cover of *The Face* from March 1985, featuring the scowling face of the young model Felix, repeated inside opposite the words, 'Hard is the graft when money is scarce. Hard are the looks from every corner. Hard is what you will turn out to be. Look out, here comes a Buffalo! "The Harder they come, the better." (Buffalo Bill).'

It was music to the ears of no-hopers as much as to achievers, and it defined masculine style, in all its ramifications, not just for the Eighties but for the Nineties as well. 'NYC', a story for *Arena*'s fifth issue in autumn 1987, set the tone with classic black-and-white Brody layout, photographs by Norman Watson and Petri's choice of overtly masculine fashion from Jean Paul Gaultier's zipped vest to cowboy hats and a domino-based neck decoration designed by Judy Blame for the

cult boutique House of Beauty and Culture. Petri's approach to masculinity was copied throughout the media, notably in advertising: it was his bold approach to styling that helped make the young male body – hard and toned – acceptable to advertisers, from Marky Mark modelling for Calvin Klein to all the pumped-up California dreamboys in Gianni Versace's campaigns. Petri has many memorials but perhaps the most erotic thing he did for young men was to make the MA-1 flight jacket almost ubiquitous, either on the backs of skinheads or clubbers. It was the archetypal Buffalo garment – dripping with street cred, whether in olive or black or with a fur-lined hood (but always with its bright orange lining). Bought at army surplus stores and customized with badges, emblems and slogans, it was the jacket that nobody ever removed in a club.

Petri was a hard act to keep up with, let alone follow, but Judy Blame shared his cult status as one of the stylists that everybody was watching. A powerful figure in the Eighties, he worked with Rifat Ozbek and John Galliano, as well as creating stories for *i-D* and *The Face*, and was one of the earliest examples of a stylist playing a vital role in projecting a designer's message – a role that was to grow enormously in the Nineties. Blame has styled the pop singers Neneh Cherry and Björk, and works with London's fantasy milliner, Philip Treacy, on his fashion presentations, seen by many as the highlight of London Fashion Week. He shares his status with *i-D*'s Simon Foxton, whose story 'Strictly', photographed by Travis (Jason Evans's pseudonym) for *i-D*, was important for the early Nineties in the way that Blame's 'Party Up', photographed by Marc Lebon for *i-D* in 1988, had been at the end of that decade. Given their heads, stylists and photographers captured the mood of contemporary London while using the urban scene as a powerful background to their comments on race, gender and social mores. In fact, 'Strictly' was set in leafy suburban streets, with three black male models standing four-square and uncompromising against garden gates and pebble-dashed walls. The clothes Travis had chosen made the point: shoes by Polo, Ralph Lauren and Kickers, plus-fours or riding trousers from the upmarket leather specialist Swaine and Adeney and a Chanel monocle were teamed with sportswear and inexpensive department store accessories in photographs which shattered virtually every stereotype.

Fashion stereotypes have been banished by style magazines in the Nineties. Fashion stories have been superseded by 'people' stories where photographers and stylists attempt to create scenes which could be taken for real life, using both models and clothes as accessories to make a social point. Elaine Constantine's

strictly

24

27 *i-D*, 1998, photo
Marcus Tomlinson

28 (Left to right)
British *Vogue*,
1980, styled
by Grace
Coddington;
portrait of Grace
Coddington,
1970; British
Vogue, 1981,
styled by Grace
Coddington.
Photos Barry
Lategan

work for *The Face* is a good example of the genre. In 'Sarf Coastin'', published in *The Face* in November 1997, she featured a group of teenage girls having a rave at the seaside. An amusing exercise, it lacked the authenticity of its true inspiration which was the genuine photo-reportage of Grace Robertson in the Fifties; in particular, her photo essays 'Mothers' Pub Outing' for *Picture Post*, which followed a group of Battersea housewives on a 'ladies only' pub crawl and, for *Life* magazine, a similar exercise following a group of Clapham women on a coach tour, taking in visits to a fairground and pub. And whereas Robertson's photographs – using only real people – never became stale or stereotyped, the 'real life' urban underbelly pictures in most magazines have already become as sterile and formulaic as the earlier fashion pictures against which they rebelled.

But the past twenty years have neither been totally dominated by working-class images nor by the style magazines. Some of the most amusing and intelligent fashion coverage in the Eighties appeared in *Tatler*; the work of Michael Roberts, style maverick, who subsequently moved to American *Vogue* and now works for the *New Yorker*. A writer, illustrator and photographer, he approaches his subject with sardonic detachment. His work for *Tatler* revealed a love–hate relationship with the English class system and the aristocratic way of life, hiding behind a satirical lens. He is responsible for some of fashion's most telling images, which reveal much of the mood of the times. Amanda Grieve (later Harlech) also carved a niche for herself early in the Eighties with an eye for upper-class eccentricity. Having worked as a stylist on *Harper's and Queen*, she 'discovered' John Galliano after seeing examples of his work in Browns of South Molton Street in London. Recognizing that his was a sensibility of a unique order, she tracked him down and thus began a close creative cooperation which

lasted until 1997 when Galliano became design director at Christian Dior and she joined Karl Lagerfeld at Chanel. Her styling for Galliano opened the door to an artistic eclecticism which owed its charm to its utter illogicality and yet seeming inevitability. Harlech's imagination, wide-ranging cultural background and fastidious style revealed a highly sophisticated mind and a uniquely sensitive eye. Twigs and clocks in powdered hair; broken spectacles, held together with sticking plaster; women with clay pipes, like nineteenth-century fishwives; walking sticks and quizzing glasses with labels still attached as though fresh from a country house sale: everything Amanda Harlech styled in the Eighties revealed a deeply pastoral English quality, uniting the decade with medieval courtly manners and eighteenth-century country life, while taking in Shakespearean and Romantic characters in a vision of compelling power. For many, her work with Galliano defined a new, uniquely British approach to fashion.

At British *Vogue*, under the editorship of Beatrice Miller, Grace Coddington and Liz Tilberis were taking an equally romantic view of styling, as they had since the mid-Seventies. But their worlds of the imagination stretched beyond the poetry and culture of England to America, India and the desert. Punk might have been dominating London's streets but *Vogue*'s fastidious eye looked elsewhere, to the multicoloured layers of a romanticized mittel-European fantasy world; to Bruce Weber's brilliantly evocative recreations of nineteenth-century America and even to Helmut Newton's hard-edged pictures of sophisticated decadence: a necessary antidote to the many fey stories shot in knee-high meadows and featuring the clothes of quintessentially English designers such as Gina Fratini and Laura Ashley. In the early Eighties, British *Vogue* fell in love with the wide open spaces: the Australian outback, the Adirondack Mountains, the fashions of

29

Santa Fe and Nebraska, Navaho blankets and Andrew Wyeth's vision of rural New England, and talked of 'thinking and dreaming about things in the past and the future' and presenting a spirit 'of practicality, rectitude, charm and, first up, best-dressed'. Tousled but clean hair, scrubbed freckled faces, the freshness of natural looks: Tilberis and Coddington made English *Vogue* in the first half of the Eighties the most beautiful fashion magazine in the world. Grace Coddington in particular stands out as possessing one of English fashion's most imaginative outlooks. Her stories – in-depth, saturated studies of the time and place she wishes to evoke – are the result of a serious commitment to fashion, and are far removed from the average shoot, being more akin to painting a picture or, perhaps, casting and creating a film or play. The words of Ralph Lauren, explaining his fashion approach, sum up her attitudes succinctly: 'I paint dreams. These clothes have a heritage; they're not frivolous, but things to cherish, even when they get old.'

Sensibilities like Grace Coddington's were much in demand in the Eighties. She was employed by Calvin Klein as a style guru because she had such a good eye. At the same time, ex-fashion editor Ann Boyd was putting her British taste at the disposal of Ralph Lauren, although he might well have considered Polly Mellen, one of America's most consistent stylists who learned her trade with Diana Vreeland and worked for many years on American *Vogue* before moving to *Allure*. Boyd's cool, even distant, elegance of eye was perfectly attuned to Lauren's approach, but Mellen's broad fashion knowledge and enthusiasms might have seemed too wide-ranging for his vision. One of the great survivors, she has few favourites, no specializations and clearly considered that all fashion is a God-given gift. In an industry often cynical and frequently too tightly focused, she is a Pollyanna, always positive and eager to be shown something new.

Boyd perfectly captured the mood of Lauren's clothes and was instrumental in creating a new development as, impressed with Lauren's publicity, designers increasingly used the best stylists and the top photographers to produce advertising campaigns which they could personally control and that truly expressed what they were attempting to achieve. Whether inspired by disappointment at the way their clothes were usually photographed for magazines or whether the designers were making so much money that spending a million dollars on a publicity campaign seemed money well spent, this development lead to something entirely benign for fashion: the designer-inspired, designer-controlled glossy catalogue. For photographers it was heaven after the constraints of working for a magazine.

There was no question of censorship of their work; no need to kowtow to publishers, advertising managers or even timorous editors; no serious budget constraints and total artistic carte blanche: all that was required was to produce stunning photographs of the highest artistry, which could be beautiful, arresting or even shocking. The only proviso was that whatever was done required the approval of the designer before it could be published.

Designer catalogues were the great hidden glory of the Eighties because, although some of the pictures would be used for publicity campaigns, the majority of them were limited edition publications, sent out only to favoured friends and key journalists. Most of them became collector's items almost as soon as they were published and few reached the general public. The absolute antithesis of the hard sell, some were so oblique in their approach, so subtle in atmosphere and so frequently removed from fashion that they often caused confusion. The cleverest by far were the Comme des Garçons limited edition magazines, *Six*, published from 1988 to 1992. The imaginative range displayed in them was stunning. Far from concentrating solely on Rei Kawakubo's clothes, they featured anything from historic pictures such as Madame Yevonde's 1935 photographic portraits of society women dressed as mythical figures to Dennis Hopper's photograph of Andy Warhol or Alessandro Mendini's *Interior of an Interior* – and even several pages printed solely in black. When the clothes did appear, they were stunningly photographed by such talents as Peter Lindbergh, Steven Meisel, David Seidner and Javier Vallhonrat. Supplements to *Six*, number 5, in 1990 were entirely devoted to Enzo Cucchi's pencil, chalk and charcoal drawings and the bronze jewellery, buttons and 'witch' mirrors of the Fifties' designer line Vautrin. *Six* was published twice yearly and there were eight issues in all but, even before it appeared, Kawakubo's fellow countryman in Paris, Yohji Yamamoto, had begun producing catalogues in order to encapsulate the spirit of his fashion moods.

Published twice a year since 1984, to coincide with the fashion seasons, they used a variety of formats. Some were oversize; others were smaller than a fashion magazine; some were bound in plastic. But all were visually memorable. They were all photographed by great photographers – Paolo Roversi, Nick Knight, David Sims, Max Vadukul, Inez van Lamsweerde and Vinoodh Matadin – and designed by some of the most creative art directors in the world, including Marc Ascoli, the M/M (Paris) studio, Peter Saville and Pentagram. The choice of models was equally strong: Stella Tennant, Kirsten Owen and Maggie Rizer were favourites. It was the

34

Ascoli–Knight collaboration on the 1986–7 catalogue
which produced the most famous picture of Yamamoto's
work: a girl in a coat and baseball cap, silhouetted like
a Victorian figure, but with a glorious billowing red tail
– set against a white background. The year before,
Roversi had produced arresting images using the
extraordinary face of Sascha Robertson in a 3D-
Whistler's Mother conceit of ruby red, green and blue
colour saturations. It was followed by Max Vadukul's
homage to New York and the photographs of Weegee
and William Klein, the men who best captured the spirit
and speed of the city.

There were strange and unsettling images in some
of Yamamoto's catalogues, especially the two
photographed in 1998 by Inez van Lamsweerde and
Vinoodh Matadin. Using the model Maggie Rizer,
they had a perverse fairy tale quality, with out-of-scale
furniture and menacing landscapes which brought an
air of *Grimm's Fairy Tales* to the images. David Sims's
pictures were similarly strange and compulsive,
frequently featuring stuffed animals in a petrified
forest setting.

There were other designers happy to have their image
memorialized by pictures far removed from normal
publicity shots. Among the most extraordinary were
styled by Marc Ascoli and shot by Craig McDean for
Martine Sitbon for her Winter 1997–8 collection. Using
Stella Tennant in a deliberately unreal woodland setting
with stuffed foxes, squirrels, rabbits and a baby deer,
they were part pantomime, part nineteenth-century fairy
tale and totally unlike anything else. The catalogue is
now an eagerly sought-after collector's item.

Not all catalogues and publicity campaigns were so
esoteric. Franco Moschino's in the Eighties aimed at
nothing more menacing than recreating the wit and
mayhem of his runway. Like his shows, they were
brightly coloured, lively and, beneath the fun, packed a
serious moral punch, as is to be expected from the man
who made 'Smash the Fashion System' his motto. Slick
and sharp, Moschino's catalogues were essentially
Italian in their glossy professionalism, as were those
of Gianni Versace. Versace used a roll call of honour
including some of the greatest photographers of the last
two decades: men such as Newton, Ritts, Weber and
Meisel. But it is Richard Avedon's name which is most
closely associated with the Italian fashion house, not
least because his work appears more frequently than
any other photographer's in the books published by
Versace, including the infamous *Rock and Royalty* and
Do Not Disturb volumes.

The images – many of them showing nude or seminude
models – had energy, wit and, occasionally, passion,

37   Mario Testino for
      Gucci, 1997

38   Inez van
      Lamsweerde and
      Vinoodh Matadin
      for Calvin Klein,
      1996

something which dominates Mario Testino's work for
Gucci. His pictures perfectly encapsulate the hard-
edged, high-profile sexuality of Tom Ford's clothes. The
shots for the perfume Envy were considered by many to
verge on the obscene – a criticism constantly levelled at
the advertising campaigns of Calvin Klein who has used
homoeroticism, Grunge, heroin chic and even, in the
eyes of some, paedophilia, in order to sell perfumes,
using models from Marky Mark and Kate Moss (Klein's
all-time favourite) to line-ups of young kids, tattooed and
looking very ordinary, sharing the fragrance CK One with
each other, a reference with obvious drug undertones,
and kids in basements looking 'grungy'. He has recently
moved forward from such realism by using Inez van
Lamsweerde and Vinoodh Matadin to photograph an
oiled and pumped-up super-stud in Calvin Klein
underpants with distinct references to *The Rocky Horror
Picture Show*; a considerable departure from Klein's
down-to-earth, realistic, publicity photographed by
Steven Meisel as a celebration of the sexiness of the
young adolescent figure.

  Klein flirts with story-telling but his compatriot,
Ralph Lauren, has always used it as his means of
communicating his message in order to create an
atmosphere (even a world) into which his clothes fit
perfectly. Affluent, patrician and timeless, contemporary
yet nostalgic, it involves large social groups from
children to grandparents. The pictures, taken by Bruce
Weber, are classic images of the good life, with models
looking as gracious as Katharine Hepburn and as real
as Spencer Tracy. It is not by accident that many of the
images are in black and white and give the impression
of just having been removed from a family album or even
taken from a Thirties' film. They are brilliant examples of

37

40

manipulation. Very few people would not wish to buy into and become part of such privileged groups, if they felt they could live up to the honour.

Slightly different stories are told by Dolce & Gabbana. Like Gucci, their advertising campaigns deal with the joys of sex rather than the pleasures of class. But, unlike Testino's shots, which are full of overwhelming sexual passion (with heavy hints of fetishism and perversion) D&G view sex more directly as power. Their best campaigns have been shot in the hothouse atmosphere of Sicily – part of their cultural heritage; Domenico Dolce is from Palermo – and are as intensely passionate as Anna Magnani in the film of Tennessee Williams' *The Rose Tattoo* (1955). That atmosphere was brilliantly captured by Steven Meisel using Linda Evangelista (looking remarkably like Sophia Loren in the Fifties) and Isabella Rossellini oozing star quality, but the most powerful images were the campaigns 'Il Gattopardo' – its name a homage to the 1958 novel by Sicily's greatest literary figure, Giuseppe Tomasi di Lampedusa, and 'La Sicilia' – a homage not just to the island, its attitude and way of life but also an acknowledgement of its unique cultural background, different and separate from the rest of Italy – photographed by Ferdinando Scianna, with Marpessa as the model.

Even commercial catalogues like those produced by the German sports and ski wear firm Willy Bognor are photographed and art directed to the highest standards. Bognor's 'Fire and Ice' publications, styled by i-D's Terry Jones in the Nineties and photographed by Stefan Ruiz, were a brilliant fusion of landscape, light, bodies and movement as, in the Lauren manner, 'families' of young, fit and sporting people created their own world for the lens, from Australia to Alaska. Glen Luchford for Prada, Craig McDean for Jil Sander, Herb Ritts for Donna Karan, the list of cooperations grows and now includes mid-price, mass-market labels – British firm Jigsaw used Juergen Teller for its menswear campaign in 1998.

One of the most interesting developments of the Eighties and Nineties was that, no longer merely content to control their own image, designers not only conceived but also executed their own advertising campaigns. Thierry Mugler, who has been interested in photography since he was a ballet dancer in Strasbourg, took an amazingly powerful set of photographs of his clothes in the Eighties that were published as a book. They showed models interacting with the grandeur of Thirties' buildings in locations such as Paris, Rome and New York, or in wild and open spaces. The images were strong and highly professional, leading some years later to Mugler being commissioned to photograph a selection of his clothes for a feature on 'Erotic Chic'

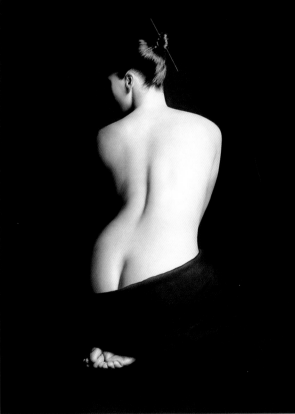

41

44

for *Playboy* magazine's fiftieth anniversary issue in January 1999.

Mugler was not the only couturier in Paris who was interested in photography. Karl Lagerfeld, probably the nearest thing to a polymath that fashion has produced in the past fifty years, has photographed his own clothes, those of Galliano (worn by Nicole Kidman) and his muse, Amanda Harlech, during the Nineties, just as he compulsively drew Anna Piaggi, his previous muse, in the Eighties, not for publicity but merely because they were there, a challenge that his febrile imagination could not resist.

Piaggi is one of the most intelligent and informed figures in international fashion. Her knowledge of European costume is considerable, that of twentieth century fashion almost unrivalled. She has used both to inspire and encourage designers, stylists, photographers and journalists for over thirty years. Her appearance is eclectic but informed by an assured and educated taste. A deft cocktail of historic dress, vintage clothing and contemporary design, it is an animated version of her famous Doppie Pagine (Double Pages) which have been a feature of Italian *Vogue* for over ten years. They demonstrate not only how wide-ranging and all-encompassing Piaggi's vision is, but are also a testimony to the far-sighted approach of Franca Sozzani, Italian *Vogue*'s editor, which has made the magazine as essential to fashion followers as Piaggi's magazine *Vanity* was in the early Eighties.

Isabella Blow, considered by some to be Piaggi's natural successor, does not attempt to mix periods and moods in her dress but prefers to show her convictions by wearing a designer *in toto*, to leave no doubt of her support. The first to spot the talent of Stella Tennant, she will be remembered as a great judge of originality. She bought Alexander McQueen's entire degree collection – although it took a year to pay for it – and then vigorously promoted his career, as she already had (with phenomenal success) the career of Philip Treacy. She was one of the first to champion the esoteric attitude of Jeremy Scott and to take an interest in the arcane approach to couture of Viktor & Rolf. Isabella Blow's ability to spot the value of the new and even bizarre talents in design, styling, modelling or photography had considerable influence on certain areas of fashion in the Nineties.

Fashion photography has become increasingly an end product in itself. No longer the handmaiden of the designer's creations, many photographers use clothes merely as props which show sexual personality by what is chosen and how it is worn. In fact, in their attempt to create pictures which they hope will have an artistic

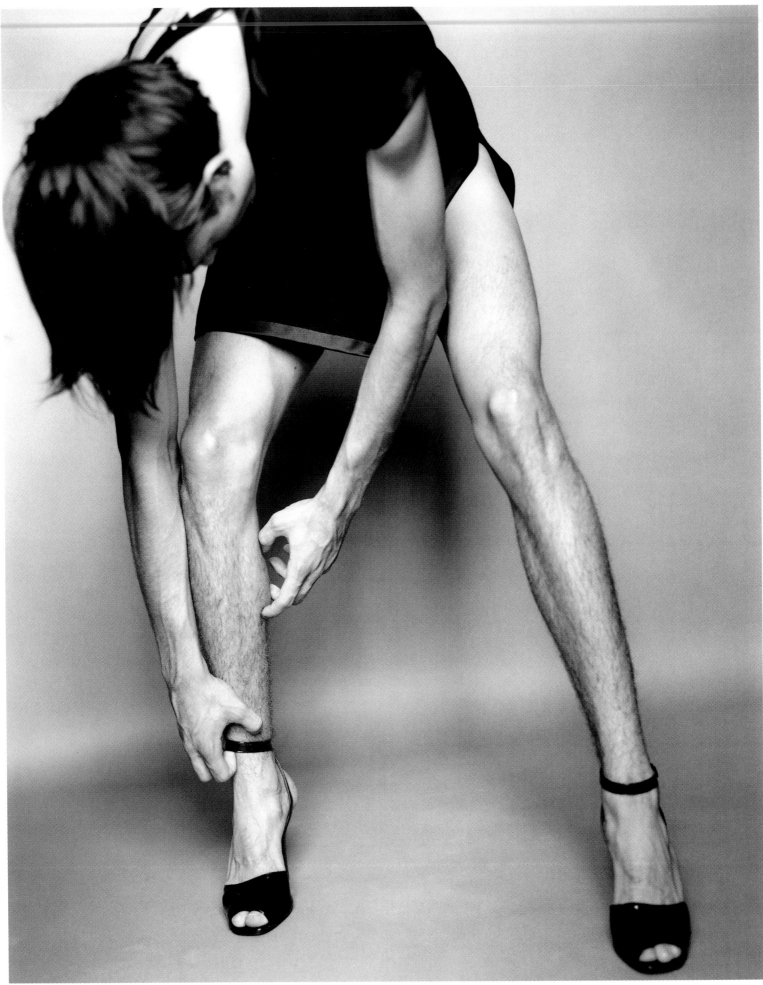

48

47 Mario Testino for
    Visionaire no.18,
    'The Fashion
    Issue', 1996,
    clothes by Yves
    Saint Laurent

48 Marcus Tomlinson
    for *Visionaire*
    no.27, 1999,
    clothes by
    Hussein Chalayan

49 (Overleaf)
    Jerome Esch for
    Visionaire '2001'
    issue, 1999,
    clothes by Saskia
    van Drimmelen

credibility, they increasingly photograph sexual personality, the biggest growth area in the human psyche in the last thirty years. Such photography is rapidly becoming not only independent of the fashion it depicts, but is assuming the status of a new art form. And it has its showcases beyond the pages of the magazines. Chief among them is the prestigious New York quarterly, *Visionaire*, brainchild of ex-photographer Stephen Gan. Tellingly described as a 'fashion and art portfolio', it relies heavily on photography but is far removed from the normal fashion publication. If anything, it has more in common with the contemporary art magazine *Artforum* than with *Vogue* or *Harper's Bazaar*. It has no overall formula: each issue is edited by a guest editor – a photographer such as Mario Testino or designers as different as Rei Kawakubo and Tom Ford – who will be given carte blanche, not only in the choice of images but also in their packaging. *Visionaire* has ranged from a Louis Vuitton bag full of photographs to a wooden box and even a circular one reminiscent of an old-fashioned chocolate box. Although not cheap, retailing at around £120 ($300) per issue, *Visionaire* sells out quickly and, as it is a limited edition, rises rapidly in price in the collector's market, even before the next edition is issued.

Fashion photography is not alone in being treated as art. Fashion itself has been moving closer to art in the previous decade, with august dealers or famous auction houses not only selling *haute couture* but also producing prestigious and costly catalogues. In 1997, Sotheby's New York held a sale of clothes owned by the Duke and Duchess of Windsor that was accompanied by a two-volume scholarly catalogue. In the same year Christie's New York sold a collection of dresses owned by Diana, Princess of Wales, and it ended the century with a sale of Marilyn Monroe's personal effects. Throughout the Eighties, Issey Miyake's clothes were exhibited in museums and art galleries, including London's Victoria & Albert Museum, and appeared on the cover of *Artforum*.

Designers have sponsored their own films: Isaac Mizrahi's *Unzipped* (1995), Wim Wenders's *Notebook on Cities and Clothes* (1989) for Yohji Yamamoto, Martin Scorcese's *Made in Milan* (1990) for Giorgio Armani – all tried to unravel the mystery of the true nature of fashion as it increasingly seemed that clothes and the traditions of the catwalks and magazines were no longer enough to explain a subject which bewildered as much as it fascinated a public eager, even desperate, to know more. It was only a question of time before art would join the fray.

In 1996, an extraordinary event took place in Italy with the staging of the Florence Biennale of Fashion and Art. It was an apotheosis, of a sort. The aim behind the Biennale, as explained in the thick, fully illustrated catalogue entitled *Looking at Fashion* (and produced, significantly, not by a fashion magazine publisher but by the distinguished art publisher Skira) was 'to explore a number of the central issues of contemporary experience'. The exhibition, called 'Of Time and Fashion', consisted of seven autonomous exhibitions: Art/Fashion; New Persona/New Universe; Visitors; Habitus, Abito, Abitare; Elton John Metamorphosis; Emilio Pucci and Bruce Weber Secret Love. The Art/Fashion exhibition was subsequently shown in New York, at the Guggenheim Museum. It looked at the dress ideas propounded by the Italian Futurists, the photography of Man Ray and the fashion of Elsa Schiaparelli. Seven architectural structures designed by Arata Isozaki, and aimed at 'bringing art and fashion together in one same energy field', were home to 'pairings' such as the sculptor Tony Cragg and Karl Lagerfeld, Roy Lichtenstein and Gianni Versace or Damien Hirst and Miuccia Prada, in the hope of establishing a common linguistic thread between fashion, art and architecture. Other sections of the exhibition were devoted to most of the major fashion designers working in the Nineties, from Rifat Ozbek to Anna Sui, Donna Karan to Manolo Blahnik, although

50 Marcus Tomlinson
    for *Visionaire*
    no.25, 1998, hat
    by Philip Treacy

51 Martina Hoogland
    Ivanow for *Dazed
    & Confused,*
    1998, clothes by
    Olivier Theyskens

50

Geoffrey Beene and Ralph Lauren were conspicuously absent.

The Biennale was judged a commercial and artistic success. It was generally felt that its explorations had gone some way towards solving the art/fashion conundrum. However, it was noteworthy that, two years later, in the catalogue of the Metropolitan Museum of Art (New York) exhibition *Cubism and Fashion* – a follow-up to the 1987 *Fashion and Surrealism* exhibition – the curator, Richard Martin, wrote: 'One is right to be sceptical of the supposition that art and fashion are made of, animated by, or heading toward the same aims and criteria. Fashion is irrevocably commercial; its system is somewhat different from the system and culture of art.' It was a salutary caution after half a century of confused thinking about both disciplines.

Hard commerce now drives fashion magazines, but the right editor can ensure good sales, and the advertising revenue they engender, without totally compromising on artistic and creative matters. Liz Tilberis made *Harper's Bazaar* a magazine which captured the beauty and elegance for which it was famed in the Fifties; Anna Wintour, her counterpart at American *Vogue*, has consistently featured avant-garde fashion and encouraged her photographers to take risks, rightly judging that fashion followers have a sophisticated visual approach and demand imagery of the highest calibre. In her decade long tenure, *Vogue* has outstripped all its rivals in the American market and is generally considered the 'Bible', to be read by all in the fashion business at any level.

Aptly enough, the most influential style magazine of the Nineties on either side of the Atlantic was the British publication *Dazed & Confused*. Far from seeing its brief as helping designers, photographers and stylists to sell the dream, for many readers it seemed, at times, to be closer to pedalling a nightmare. Its creative director, Rankin, who refuses to allow its pages to be devoted to traditional, narrow and commercially constrained fashion, pushes forward the concept of fashion as something more than the sum of its parts – of which clothes are not even necessarily a major component. Since its first issue in 1992, *Dazed & Confused* has confounded, questioned and concentrated fashion attitudes with its relentlessly confrontational and provocative non-conformity. Its persistent querying of the status quo has already become a form of status quo in itself, as the world awaits a new approach for the next millennium.

REDISCOVERING ELEGANCE

1   (Opener)
     Krizia, 1995,
     photo Patrick
     Demarchelier

2   (Previous page)
     Club Monaco,
     *Arena Homme
     Plus*, 1998,
     photo Nathaniel
     Goldberg

3   (Previous page)
     Christian Dior
     haute couture,
     1999, photo
     Jerome Esch

4   Givenchy, British
     Vogue, 1995,
     photo Nick Knight

When two or three fashion people are gathered together, the conversation eventually turns to the question of icons. In a game of 'Mirror, mirror on the wall', certain key figures are sure to be paraded. All will come from the twentieth century – or at least the last years of the nineteenth – and it will be found that the link which joins people from different periods and places is elegance.

Elegance is an essentially modern concept. It is not a word found in descriptions of Queen Elizabeth I or Marie Antoinette. In Jane Austen's novels it is a term more likely to be used to describe men than women. It is a state of mind, a physical manner of presentation that only really came into existence when women took on the silhouettes and shapes of male fashion, which aim at elongating and narrowing the body, rather than the traditional bulk of female fashion, which filled space and constrained movement.

Sleek, svelte and stripped of unnecessary ornament, elegance became a manifestation of the machine age, which came into its own in the twentieth century when functionally efficient design was achieved by removing all references to the past in order to facilitate as well as reveal an object's purpose. The architect Mies van der Rohe was not interested in recreating Edwardian opulence for people living in the streamlined Twenties. Charles and Ray Eames created chairs for life in the Forties and Fifties that were as far removed from their Georgian predecessors as possible. Architects and industrial designers have long realized that there is no logic to finding design solutions to modern problems by looking back. They know that only by assessing the mood of the present can answers by found which might stand comparison with the great designs of the past.

And, by being totally different, the solutions become the same: answers so right for their moment in time that they keep their significance for years, even centuries, ahead.

Fashion has never held to such a rigorous approach. Modern designers have cherry-picked their way across the centuries with little regard for stylistic integrity. At no period has this tendency been stronger than in the last forty years. But, in fashion, every trend has a countertrend, usually working simultaneously. For a Vivienne Westwood, we have the countercheck of a Giorgio Armani. John Galliano's exuberant historicism is balanced by Donna Karan's cool minimalism. Those gathered-together fashion folk could argue for hours over which side most fully reflects the spirit of the age but, in truth, only time will tell.

Certainly, both sides seem strong as the new century begins, but it is arguable that those who prefer to pare down rather than pile on have been more true to the late twentieth century and what it stands for. However, it must be accepted that the 'elegance of refusal' minimalist designers have plundered the past just as enthusiastically as their decorative counterparts in the last thirty years. But they plunder from a past much more recent and considerably less diffused. They rarely go back beyond the turn of the century, and the matrix in which they work is almost entirely Western. They often share the same sources as the extravagants, but they read them with different eyes. A case in point is the Marchesa Luisa Casati, turn-of-the-century socialite, whose elegantly narrow silhouette, as painted by Giovanni Boldini in 1914, has exerted considerable influence on John Galliano but, stripped of her outrageous make-up, extravagant hats and accessories

5   Greta Garbo,
     1931

6   Katharine
     Hepburn,
     late 1930s

7   Marlene Dietrich,
     1942

5

6

– including her tame monkeys, parakeets, snakes and her favourite pet leopard – she would look perfectly at home on the runway at a Donna Karan show.

Elegance has traditionally been the province of the male, certainly since the early years of the nineteenth century, when masculine dress became sober and simple, relying for its effects not on decoration but on perfection of cut and quality of material. Beau Brummell was the icon of the new approach, leading men's fashion away from Regency foppery to the more sober approach to dress that is exemplified by Savile Row tailors. The male silhouette was honed and perfected during the nineteenth century when women's fashion – in strong and sociologically interesting contrast – ran the gamut of decorative idiocies, from the crinoline to the bustle. In fact, it can be argued convincingly that modern fashion for women only began when they adopted the male silhouette in the early years of this century.

It began as a high-fashion look with Chanel but soon broadened under the influence of film. By the mid-Thirties, the elegant woman of power played by Joan Crawford, the sexually mysterious woman portrayed by Marlene Dietrich and the androgynous woman of mystery, personified by Greta Garbo all dressed in the way that Patou called 'the American silhouette': long and slender. It is these women, their appearance and aura, who inspire modern designers in their search for elegance – plus the tomboyish independence of Katharine Hepburn, the archetypal all-American woman, whose dress sense was as sharp as her wisecracks. When modern designers look back to the elegance of the past they almost always look to the powerful

personae of the screen goddesses of prewar Hollywood, or the international fashionable women who took their dress cues from them, rather than the creations of earlier couturiers.

What made Garbo and her contemporaries fascinating and lasting icons – as opposed to the myriad of pretty, lesser stars that Hollywood swallowed up and threw away with alarming rapidity – was the fact that, in different ways, they all appeared on the screen as strong, complex characters, able to hold their own in any situation and having many characteristics which in real life would be considered masculine. They looked their best in tailored suits and the simplest narrow evening dresses that eschewed fluffy femininity for direct and uncompromising female power. The adrenaline-shot of perversity that the film world knew how to exploit was carried into real life as the stars began to appear off, as well as on, the screen in trouser suits. Marlene Dietrich was once ordered off the streets of Paris and warned by the mayor for wearing trousers. It was probably a carefully contrived publicity stunt, but the fact that the incident gained attention shows what a dangerous thing it was considered for a woman to wear trousers in public, as if, by adopting an item of male dress, she somehow annexed some of his power.

It was this danger inherent in men's clothing worn by women that was exploited by Yves Saint Laurent in 1967 when he introduced his first 'smoking'. He was not attracted to the style merely for its elegance. It was its association with the Parisian nightclubs and dance halls which catered to lesbians and homosexuals that he was keen to recreate. It was clothing on the edge as far as Saint Laurent was concerned, and he wished it to be

8

9

projected with the full force of its political, sexual and social associations. It was given exactly the mood he required when Helmut Newton photographed it for French *Vogue* in 1975. In a deserted street in Paris at night, a woman stands. Aware of being watched, waiting tensely for something or someone, everything about her is a question mark. Her suit is cut to the most stringent levels of male tailoring, her soft blouse with its falling jabot has more of the authority of the huntsman's stock than anything gently feminized. She holds a lighted cigarette. Her hair, short and plastered down, is like a gigolo's. Her make-up is subtly neutral. Everything about her is equivocal.

Both suit and photograph caused a sensation: nothing so bold had appeared before. Newton had created a seminal image, not just for the moment, but for the century. The fashion world loved it; the rest of the world was scandalized by its echoes of louche bars, the novelist Radclyffe Hall and even Gertrude Stein – although she had never appeared in such an overtly masculine garment. In 1967, normal, nice women might well wear trousers to relax in the privacy of their homes; they might wear trouser suits in public. But they did not wear the ambiguous smokings of Yves Saint Laurent: those would take another ten years to gain acceptance. And yet, both suit and image were a homage to the new female elegance – years before their time – which, as with so much that Saint Laurent created, would become the banner behind which many future couturiers would muster.

It was in America that his lead was most eagerly taken up. Manhattan in the late Sixties and early Seventies was the only place on earth that fully comprehended what Yves Saint Laurent was saying about women. The most liberal and confident women in the world, New

York's high flyers (many of whom played powerful roles in fashion and the media), were saying 'Why not?', while others were mouthing 'Definitely not'. There was a need, after all the muddled thinking of hippie fashion and thrift shop promiscuity, for something clean, clear and precise – even 'directional'. As always, the designers to serve the need were right there, only a heartbeat behind the longing.

It wasn't only because he was so in tune with the times that Halston emerged as *the* New York designer in the Seventies. It wasn't even that vast amounts of money were spent to give his name kudos and authority. The reason Halston was adored was that he was a media person – in fact, almost a media creation – at a time when the media (dominated by his friend Andy Warhol) ruled fashion as ruthlessly as they promulgated its attitudes. Everyone 'adored' Halston, from Diana Vreeland to Liza Minnelli. Like his clothes, he was cool, understated and almost too elegant. A New Yorker once said that the expression 'piss elegant', that double-edged sword encompassing both contempt and praise, could have been coined to describe Halston, and he was right – about the man and his fashion. Halston used ultrasuede and jersey to create clothes that were almost totally devoid of extraneous decoration. To modern eyes, they seem simplistic, but their elegance is undeniable. Columns of crepe and slivers of silk jersey in tightly controlled colour ranges, his clothes were devoid of ideas because everything was subservient to one ideal: to give women of any age and figure type elegant clothes that, as Halston would have said, made them look 'a million bucks'.

Halston wasn't the only one in New York treading the minimalist path to slimline elegance. Although less consistently part of the social circles that made Halston

12

successful – the Vreeland/Warhol/Steve Rubell of Studio
54 axis – Zoran had an original voice, too strong to be
relegated to the dustbin of fashion history, which seems
to be a current danger. He arrived in the United States
in 1971, having studied architecture in his native
Yugoslavia. Like many immigrants, despite his
education, Zoran had to work his way up from the
bottom to find his place in New York fashion, and it
wasn't until 1977 that he showed his first collection
under his own name. From the beginning, his design
approach was fabric-led. He used cashmere, velvet and
silk in understated colours. White, beige, grey and faded
pastels created a mood of elegance that was essentially
complex in what it rejected from the brightly-coloured,
busily-patterned eclecticism of much Seventies' fashion
while looking effortlessly casual. His *dégagé* approach
was not easily understood by Seventh Avenue. His
shapes were, like Halston's, accommodating, and they
barely changed over the seasons. One of the earliest
exponents of the minimal wardrobe, which gave flexibility
by the fact that its items were multi-functional and able
to be combined to create a variety of different results.
Zoran believed, as Claire McCardell had before him, that
a few silk T-shirts, some cashmere sweaters and fine
woollen trousers were all that a sophisticated woman
required. Assured women, such as Lauren Hutton and
Isabella Rossellini, are attracted to a concept which is
essentially flattering to the individual because it puts her
in charge of her clothes, rather than the reverse, which
is often found in more decorative design approaches.

While Halston and Zoran were raising the flag for
elegant understatement in New York, a designer much
greater than either was beginning to make his mark in
Milan. Walter Albini's name has been almost forgotten,
but he was the true father of Italian ready-to-wear. He
died in 1983, aged forty-two. Had he lived longer, he
would have been recognized as one of the world's great
fashion designers. Eclectic and wide-ranging as his
imagination was – he produced several different
collections for a variety of fashion houses each season
– he returned constantly to the Twenties and Thirties in
his search for past elegance which could be recreated
to serve the needs of the Seventies, the decade when
he was at his strongest. Obsessed by Chanel – as
designer and individual – and deeply impressed by the
graphic work of Sonia Delaunay, his heroines were the
great stars of the Thirties, especially Katharine Hepburn
and Marlene Dietrich. Although Italian, he understood
both the French and the American design sensibilities.
His forte was understated, sports-inspired elegance
and, with hindsight, he stands out clearly as the
precursor of both Giorgio Armani and Gianni Versace,

16

the lodestars of the two sides of Italian fashion in the
Eighties and Nineties.

Giorgio Armani, the greatest exponent of elegant
minimalism of the late twentieth century, showed his first
menswear collection in 1974. A year later, he introduced
his women's range. Both were predicated on the
assumption that clothes which allow people to function
unhindered are the basis and the epitome of elegance.
Armani's ethos was once summed up by an American
journalist as 'Quality costs' and, certainly, his clothes
have always been expensive. It isn't just that Armani
uses the finest materials – cashmere, alpaca, silk and
wool of a refinement rarely found elsewhere – it is the
fact that he is a fashion elitist who believes that good
clothes must be expensive to maintain their integrity.
Therefore all of the Armani labels are exceedingly costly,
no matter what their level. But he has exerted huge
influence because women understood what he was
doing for them and found the results so flattering that
they were eager to buy into his world. The thing that
Armani had in the Seventies and early Eighties, when it
was rare indeed, was an unshakeable belief that clothes
should never patronize. No flouncy flamenco skirts or
garishly coloured flower prints were allowed to sully his
runway. Instead, taking advantage of the experience
gained working in a textile factory while he was
menswear designer for Nino Cerruti in the Sixties, Armani
concentrated on purity of cut and perfection of fabric.

18

Having begun his design life in menswear, Armani, perhaps predictably, developed his womenswear on masculine tailoring principles. But, as would be expected from the fashion radical responsible for deconstructing the male suit, he was too sensitive to the needs of women to create for them anything overtly male. Building on Saint Laurent's 'smokings', he made a statement of his female suits, but it was quite unlike the Frenchman's. For Saint Laurent, the *frisson* of excitement was provided by the feeling of ambiguity inherent in his use of menswear. His early smokings were straightforward examples of women wearing masculine-cut clothing. Armani moved in a different direction and made his suits a feminine statement – one which could be understood by the mainstream fashion world. The result was that the Armani trouser suit exerted more influence at every level of fashion in the Eighties than any item created by other designers in the fashion capitals of the world. Its universality was based on a formula that was so totally thought-out that the Armani suit looked perfect on virtually every figure type. It had a structure and precision that gave control and formality, and yet there was a softness which imparted total femininity. With its collarless rounded neckline and beautifully contrived shoulders, it was an instant classic. The effortless elegance was enhanced by Armani's choice of colour for his soft woollen tweeds: beige, grey, taupe and stone perfectly matched the masterful simplicity of cut. It is not surprising that it was copied at all price levels. In fact, an Armani-inspired suit became as essential as a briefcase for millions of upwardly mobile businesswomen in the Eighties and Nineties because it gave them credibility in a masculine world, without sacrificing their femininity.

Armani's clothes have been seen as the epitome of Italian fashion's tasteful elegance for over twenty years. He judged the spirit of his country and the needs of the world so perfectly that it is his suit which comes to mind when the 'Made in Italy' label is mentioned. That is the degree of dominance achieved by his slim, 'masculine' elegance. But he is not alone. Many Italian designers take a purist view of modern fashion,

including Mariuccia Mandelli, founder and chief designer of Krizia, and Miuccia Prada. Mandelli, who had employed Walter Albini in the Sixties, learned much from his amalgam of glamour and elegant tailoring. She added her own spice of wit, while retaining a total modernity of line. Sharp, even acerbic, her humour never becomes whimsy, even in her animal prints. Her success lies in her ability to absorb the American style ethos without losing her Italian individuality. Her modern equivalent, Miuccia Prada, also retains an Italian sensibility in her design while exhibiting a non-conformist attitude to both dress and sex which has a great appeal for younger women. Both bring a strong personal attitude to their work which includes a view of femininity and the morals involved in high fashion clothing, an area largely skated over by male designers. Neither understands the love of retro which affects so much of current fashion. As Prada has said, 'In the end, fabric is fabric. What is really new is the way you treat it.' It is an attitude shared by other female designers, including Ann Demeulemeester, Jil Sander and Gabriele Strehle of Strenesse.

The name of Gianni Versace is not instantly associated with the idea of elegance based on a masculine outline. He was known for the sexually explicit femininity of his line. But, in fact, in silhouette, he was essentially a design classicist, exactly like Armani. Versace understood elegance just as well as his great rival. He never fell into the trap of creating an ultra-feminine style based on volume. No flounces or wide sweeping skirts will be found in his *oeuvre*. Although his idea of sexiness was very different from Armani's, they both had the confidence to create simple clothes which allowed the sexually confident woman to project herself as she wished. Furthermore, although Versace's taste struck many as vulgar, he could also produce a masculine tailored suit to rival anything from Yves Saint Laurent's atelier. His work of the late Seventies and early Eighties showed real elegance. It is, perhaps, a pity that, as his success grew, Versace preferred to follow the path of showbiz glamour – something easier, but much less lasting, than elegance.

21 Gucci, 1998,
photo Luis
Sanchis

22 Tom Ford, 1999,
photo Hasue

23 Gucci, 1998,
photo Cometti

24 (Overleaf)
Gucci, 1996–7,
photo Mario
Testino

22

But it is when Italian design instincts and New York commercial nous come together that the synergy to which Versace came close actually happens. Tom Ford, Seventh Avenue-trained and imbued with Garment District commercial instincts, has achieved the apotheosis of Italo–American stylistic completeness with his work at Gucci, one of the oldest names in Italian retailing but one that fell into decline in the late Seventies. After several rescue attempts, the company turned its fortunes around in 1994 by appointing Ford as its design director. Since then, it has become fashionable to denigrate his achievements by suggesting that he is not a designer but a stylist. It is a more telling comment on his critics than on him. What Ford has achieved at Gucci is the amalgam of elegance and sexiness for which Versace strove and occasionally achieved. In Ford's case, it happens almost continually. Just like Armani and Versace, he realizes that the narrow, controlled masculine shape is what creates elegance. He also knows, at the end of the century just as at the beginning, that tapering is the secret to sexuality. He avoids all fussiness of shape and detail in order to achieve that end. Tom Ford may have his excesses and occasional vulgarities – always tongue-in-cheek, controlled and never inadvertent – but decorative overkill is certainly not one of them.

That is what makes him a true son of Manhattan. New York is the home of efficiency in clothing. At least two generations of its designers have been imbued with the absolute necessity for clothes that work and fulfil their purpose, and that do nothing to prevent the wearer doing the same. It is a design approach which, in less than skilled hands, can produce banal, uninspired looks, predictable and safe along the lines of Henry Ford's comment: 'Any colour so long as it's black.' American stores are full of the results of such an unimaginative approach. But, in the hands of an inspired designer, the search for efficiency can lead to clothes that not only work but also do so beautifully.

Like the Italians, New York designers believe that the notion of chic is to do with cut. Their most successful looks are tailored and, in this, they are part of a continuing fashion tradition. Immaculate cut, to rival any to be found in Paris, was the trademark of Charles James and Norman Norell in the Fifties. The copies of Chanel and other top French designers that were sold at Ohrbach's department store were in no sense inferior to the Paris originals in quality of tailoring. So, it is not surprising that the three top international names in New York fashion – Ralph Lauren, Donna Karan and Calvin Klein – have achieved, and maintained, their pre-eminence by eschewing prettiness, opulence and daring

23

25 Ralph Lauren,
    1985, photo
    Bruce Weber

26 Donna Karan,
    1999, photos
    Peter Lindbergh

originality and adopting the masculine efficiency of the elegant line.

Ralph Lauren's inspiration for his womenswear as much as his menswear comes from the great sartorial figures of the Thirties: Cary Grant, Fred Astaire and, above all, the Duke of Windsor, alongside Katharine Hepburn and Myrna Loy. They were all renowned for their elegant appearance, which has proved to be remarkably timeless and is now seen to be totally classic. Perfectly cut flannel trousers, cotton shirts and well-tailored jackets are totally contemporary in Lauren's hands and yet they live up to his belief that clothes – in his eyes, not necessarily the same thing as the fashion world's – must not only last for more than one season but should also really come into their own when they have been worn for several seasons. This is, after all, the man who has frequently expressed his impatience with fashion's insistence on the new – and even with fashion, per se.

Lauren's fellow New Yorker, Calvin Klein, shares many of his attitudes. Like the older man, he has a genius for marketing himself and his fashion in a way that is understood, and acted upon, around the globe. He could only have been produced by Seventh Avenue. There are times when Klein's design input is so understated that you have to look hard to find it, but, no matter how underplayed the creativity, his clothes – sporty, practical and realistic – are never less than accessible. He designs for women who like the traditional luxuries – cashmere, silk and suede – and want the silhouette of their clothes to be as sleek, toned and efficient as they themselves usually are. Klein may be a minimalist but his clothes are some of the most elegant and sophisticated to come out of New York. Their spirit is summed up by his 1987 comment in the *New York Times* that he admired the work of the painter Georgia O'Keeffe because 'she has pared down, simplified, gotten to the essence'.

It is an approach which is fully understood by Donna Karan, who made an instant impact with her first collection under her own name in 1985. She had learned the aesthetic of sportswear in her years working for Anne Klein: her clothes skimmed and clung to the body; they were draped and tied to give a narrow, streamlined fit which eschewed all detailing that didn't reflect how the fabrics – luxurious cashmere and silk

29

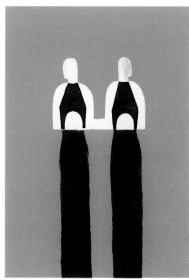

28

crepe – naturally behaved. The result was a firm
statement, both elegant and sexy, which has been the
basis of everything Karan has done since.

Paradoxically, the most successful New York minimalist,
whose clothes are insouciantly elegant, full of painterly
references and sculptural nuances, is barely known
outside America. Geoffrey Beene has been following
his own path, with no interest or concern for what
other designers are doing, since 1963. A total original,
incapable of compromise, he takes a ruthlessly logical
approach to design. Paris-trained, he was described in
1993 by Carrie Donovan in the *New York Times* as 'an
artist who chooses to work in cloth', and his sensuously
fluid clothes are both elegant and understated. Not a
designer for the hoi polloi, Beene is accepted almost
without demur as the greatest living American fashion
designer: an accolade well deserved but of no concern
to the man whose only interest is in creating clothes
for real women, not the pages of glossy magazines
– clothes which continue the traditions of elegance,
created within the tenets of good taste.

Good taste is almost axiomatic in elegant dress, which
may well be why elegance is found less frequently in
London fashion than anywhere else. London is, perhaps,
too earthy, too rumbustious and exuberant for elegance
to be a consideration for many of its young designers.
Certainly, as a philosophy of design, in the manner of
many of the designers working in Milan and New York, it
is a rarity. Although there are designers who understand
that elegance is lasting whereas excitement quickly
fades, decorative excess was the leitmotiv of London
in the Eighties and Nineties. Jasper Conran consistently

30

understates, as his mentor, Jean Muir, used to, but his
fashion approach is swamped by the eye-catching –
and attention-grabbing – fashion tricks for which London
is famed. Nevertheless, Conran has remained his own
man, refusing to deviate from his belief, more American
than English, that elegant clothes require little external
decorative detail. It has to be remembered that Conran,
known to many Americans as 'the Calvin Klein of
London' spent two years studying fashion in New York.
Eschewing fireworks, he gives his clients consistency,
simplicity and continuity. But his elegant understatement
is found increasingly rarely in London, the fashion capital
that feeds the rest of the world not only with challenging
ideas but also with equally challenging designers.

London fashion at the end of the century is about role
play, with identity hidden behind a hundred disguises.
It is a fashion approach which puts visual impact before
the individual who wears it. Although a perfectly valid
approach, it is antithetical to the search for elegance,
which is the art of enhancing the individual. Fashion in
London is totally youth-fixated and the last thing which
interests the young is elegance. Young fashion followers
crave excitement, not understatement. The history of
fashion movements in London – clearly, by no means
synonymous with designer-led fashion – shows a
distinct corporate personality. A love of outrage, a desire
to shock and a determination to smash all conceived
notions of good taste may, for some people, put London
fashion on the level of using naughty words in the
nursery, but it must be accepted that such attitudes
have produced amazing results despite serious
deficiencies. *British* fashion barely exists, because there
is no real British fashion industry. London as a fashion

34 Jil Sander,
    1997–8, photo
    David Sims

35 Jil Sander, 1991,
    photo Barry
    Lategan

35

capital is all head – there is no indigenous body to support it. And yet, British design is considered to lead the world
for originality and flair. But there is no fashion capital so vulnerable. The world looks to London as the new century
begins but, if it refocuses, then British fashion leadership, bereft of an industry, will disappear. Nevertheless, at
this moment the fantasy and hysteria of London fashion is responsible for some of the world's most inventive and
original design attitudes – a fact made clear by the number of young British designers who are invited to design for
established companies in Paris, where they can take advantage of the broad-based fashion industry they cannot
find at home. Histrionics, historicism and hype are what feed much of current fashion. But this does not mean that
elegance is a barren area, washed clean of visual excitement and sterilized into perfection. In fact, some of the most
exciting designers to emerge in the last twenty years have made elegance their *raison d'être* but have pursued it
without nostalgia, finding their own matrix to fit the mood of the times. If most of the designers mentioned thus far
have taken from the past to create a valid present, other designers have proved that more radical approaches,
with no echoes or whispers, can lead to a fashion vocabulary which trails few former glories. For example, Martin
Margiela's work for Hermès and Nicolas Ghesquiere's for Balenciaga have brought a new sensibility to the normally
over-decorative world of French fashion, while the success of Helmut Lang and Hervé Léger have shown that
for many women glamorous fashion is about modernity of shape, fabric and cut rather than a pastiche of past
elegances. They want tailoring that exploits the qualities inherent in the fabric, whether linen, sheepskin or Spandex.
And it is fabric which excites many of the younger designers such as Jeremy Scott, Kostas Murkudis and Andrew
Groves as the new millennium commences.

　Pre-eminent among the designers who achieve elegance through an architectural minimalism is Jil Sander, a
German designer whose clothes are manufactured and shown in Milan. Because she has annexed much of the
thinking behind traditional menswear and has eliminated all unnecessary 'extras', she is frequently compared to
Armani. It is an apt comparison – there are clear similarities in their approach – and yet it is inept because it suggests

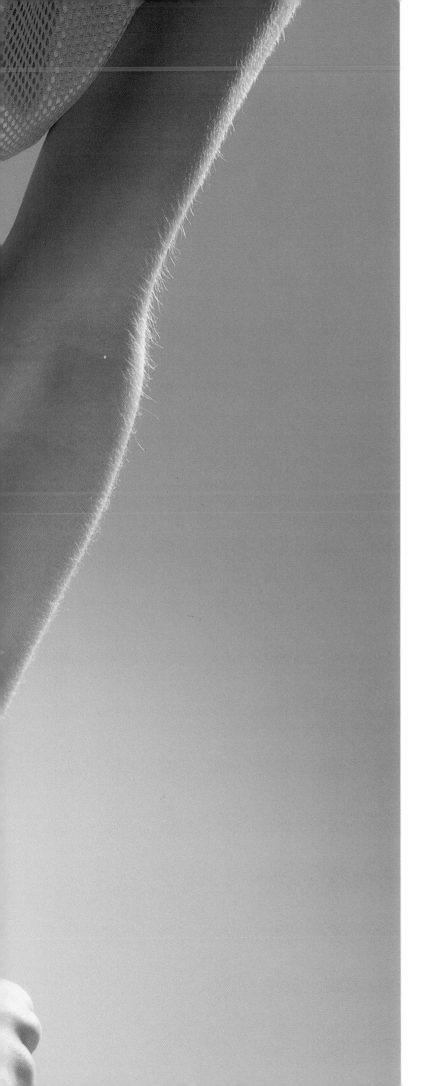

36 Jil Sander, 1999,
    photo David Sims

37 Jil Sander, 1999,
    photo David Sims

37

that she has been influenced by him. In fact, her
approach is more severely cerebral than his, lacking as
it does the voluptuousness found in all Italian design, no
matter how minimalist. There is a softness and femininity
in Armani which is not found in the austerity of Sander's
line. Where the designers are entirely similar is in their
elegance of mind. Her palette, like his, is neutral,
underplayed and pale. Her fabrics are luxurious, as
are his. Her aim, amply achieved, is to bring a modern
elegance to the dress of women who have confidence
enough to stand alone, which is something Armani has
been doing for over twenty years.

   Fashion at the end of the twentieth century is a broad
parish. Many at its centre believe that the way forward is
through extravagant ideas, barely edited, outrageously
executed and crudely marketed. Shock tactics have
become the norm. We lurch closer to fancy dress with
every season. As designers become famous ever
younger, the level of maturity continually drops.
Eccentrics and enthusiasts are successfully 'dumbing
down' fashion on every level, eagerly aided by the
media. Reputations are blown up to ludicrous
proportions, and then dropped and forgotten. When
late twentieth-century fashion is assessed, with the
necessary perspective of time, at some point in this
century, at least seventy per cent of current fashion
could come to be seen as a sort of lunatic fringe coda
to the millennium and totally irrelevant to the future.
The names that will survive will belong to the diminishing
band of designers, exemplified by Hussein Chalayan,
who are able to temper their originality with elegance,
the ones who realize that, as the working lives of both
sexes become increasingly similar, the only practical way
for women to dress for efficiency is by assuming much
from the male matrix of dress. Only the most foolish of
fashion fantasts would imagine that this leads to a
diminution of female sexuality.

THE LURE OF RETRO

1   (Opener)
Pierre Cardin,
1967, photo Peter
Knapp

2   (Previous page)
Paco Rabanne,
1966, photo David
Montgomery

3   (Previous page)
André Courrèges,
1965, photo
Peter Knapp

4   Pierre Cardin and
Raquel Welch,
late 1960s,
photo Terry O'Neill

G

George Canning, British Foreign Secretary and Prime Minister, could well have been speaking for modern fashion designers when he declared in 1824, 'I called the New World into existence to redress the balance of the Old.' In their constant search for ways of moving fashion forward in a manner which will excite but not alienate the public, designers must always be aware of new worlds developing across a wide spectrum, including altered social attitudes, cultural realignments and changing moral preoccupations. It is a crucial element of their job to understand the tempo of the times. Although their forward vision seems a short one, limited to one season ahead, it requires much more than a projection for a brief six months.

The ability to produce new ideas is crucial. Originality is the Calvary of the couturier. If he loses his flair, he is crucified. In the Sixties, the way to fashion originality seemed clearly enough signposted. Pierre Cardin, Paco Rabanne and André Courrèges, all excited by the race for space which had become the obsession of the superpowers, felt sure that the exploits of Yuri Gagarin and John Glenn, watched on television by millions, would swing the public behind Space Age fashion. And, to a degree, their hunch was right. But their canvas was too small to hold the attention they captured. Fashion based on the assumption that clothes can satisfy when pared down to a functional minimalism turns its back on the basic human hunger for decorative devices. They are not just optional extras in fashion but, for most people, actually keep it alive. Clothes which are meant to behave with the efficiency of a spacesuit – or even a worker's overall – allow no room for fantasy or the spirit of imagination that we all crave.

Pierre Cardin's Sixties' experiments, exciting and newsworthy at the time, led nowhere. Nor could they ever. The streamlined efficiency of the machine is not easily translated into fashion – a medium in which novelty overrides most practical needs. Le Corbusier's comment that a house is a machine to live in is clearly incapable of being adapted to the exigencies of fashionable dress. Simple, functional fashion, unlike the streamlined efficiency of a Porsche or the minimalism of a building by Tadao Ando, doesn't satisfy the craving for decorative excess which characterizes fashion. The only way for a fashion designer to look forward is by taking the past and realigning it so that it can serve the purposes of the future. That is why retro fashion has been not only the obsession of the last fifty years, but also, in the opinion of many, the source of virtually everything new.

Many words have been devoted to the question of whether retro is healthy or unhealthy for fashion. Designers have been criticized for their reliance on the past. Many critics feel that originality is being swamped by a tidal wave of restatements of fashion's past glories. And yet some of the most admired designers of the past twenty years – Lagerfeld, Westwood, Lauren and Galliano among them – have constantly reworked the past to make a statement which they feel is appropriate to the present.

They are in good company. Looking back is nothing new in twentieth-century fashion. Indeed, Christian Dior based the New Look on his idealized remembrances of how women looked when his mother was young, in the early years of the century. But the important word here is 'based'. Christian Dior recreated the spirit of the past,

6

yet he was far above the level of mere pastiche. His clothes, for all their opulence and extravagance, could never be confused with costume. Even at his first collection – when the shock of what he proposed was at its most intense – nobody was in the slightest doubt of that.

Dior was moving fashion forward with the biggest jolt it had ever known – by looking over his shoulder. The New Look was a retrospective look, but it was a measure of Dior's ability that it nevertheless perfectly fitted the mood of its time. Yves Saint Laurent, Dior's successor, was not so lucky when, in 1971, he attempted to revive the wartime fashion that was the immediate precursor of the New Look. His 'Forties' collection marked the first full-scale fashion retrospective of a precise historic period. It flopped for political reasons, which should not have surprised anyone. At any level, clothes don't merely convey a simple visual message; they are highly political in their social impact. Although World War II could be assumed to have been forgotten twenty-six years after it ended, political tensions still simmered beneath the surface in France. For many people the period between the collapse of Paris in 1940 and its liberation in 1944 was a shameful time because the Vichy government had willingly collaborated with the Germans during their occupation of the country. To revive such memories by showing the clothes worn at the time seemed tactless to many commentators, especially in the French media.

For all that, Saint Laurent's Forties collection was a seminal moment in fashion history. It was to have a much more durable effect on fashion than the New Look. Saint Laurent didn't merely use clothes from a historic period as the basis for the mood of a collection. He actually recreated the type of clothes worn in wartime France, although his genius meant that they were not mere copies, but bore the stamp of his own personality. Dior's New Look was about changing a moment in fashion; Yves Saint Laurent did something much more profound. He changed fashion's attitude to the past, opening up history as a happy and apparently inexhaustible quarrying ground for ideas. He is the father of all the retro and revival looks which have grown like a tidal wave over the past thirty years. Assessing the results which followed Saint Laurent's show, many might feel that his influence in this respect has been baleful as, almost with each season, modern fashion inches closer to fancy dress. But taking styles from the past as a basis for the present is a perfectly legitimate artistic approach, as other arts show. Did anyone object to Robert Adam's use of Greek decorative motifs in his architecture? Was Rachmaninoff wrong to base a set of musical variations on a theme created by Paganini?

7

No one suggests that each creative period must be kept hermetically sealed, a quarantined historic unit not to be used or adapted in later periods.

The danger with revivalism, in fashion as in any other field, is that it can become pastiche (a straight copy of another period or the work of another creator) or caricature (a version exaggerating its strongest points and weakening both the original and the copy). In the last thirty years, fashion has been bedevilled by the inability to see the difference between the two. But that was the last thing worrying designers in the Seventies as they plundered the past in their desperation to capitalize on nostalgia as a driving fashion force. From Biba to Chloé, remembrance of times past was the characteristic of the most eclectic fashion decade in the twentieth century. Barbara Hulanicki's original concept when she began Biba as a mail-order fashion business in 1963 was to create simple styles that would sell quickly because they were cheap. When her department store in Kensington closed twelve years later, the concept had changed and the Biba look had become a powerful presence on the retro scene. The shop and the clothes had a decadent quality reflecting the world-weary, even cynical, mood of the times. Based on the *femme fatale* glitter of the Thirties' screen goddesses, Biba fashion, for all its strengths (the sombre colours, the originality of the make-up range, which included black lipstick) was too derivative to be considered good fashion. In retrospect, its glamour was spurious, its excitement too perverse. There was not enough design originality to lift it above pastiche, the copyist's art.

Laura Ashley's approach to history went back much further than Barbara Hulanicki's, and it exerted a much

8

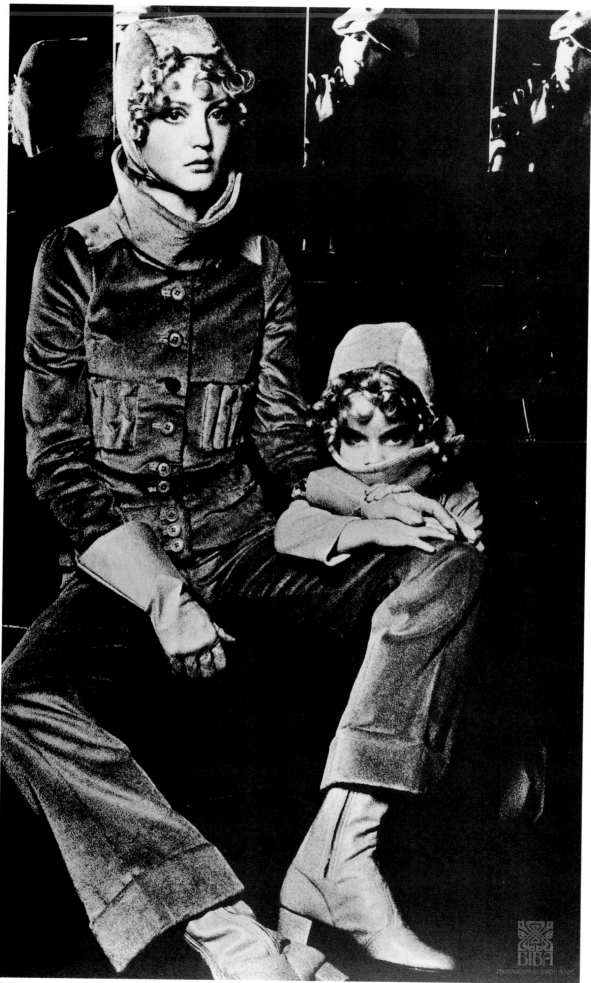

10   Laura Ashley,
      early 1970s

11   Bellville Sassoon,
      1971, photo Clive
      Arrowsmith

12   (Overleaf)
      Pattie Boyd
      wearing Ossie
      Clark, 1973

13   (Overleaf)
      Marsha Hunt
      wearing Ossie
      Clark, 1968,
      photo Harri
      Peccinotti

10

greater influence, not only on how women wanted to
dress but also on how British designers wished to
design. Her skill in updating the past was responsible
for the world craze for British Romanticism in the
Seventies. History has not been kind to Laura Ashley.
She has been criticized for being more a stylist than a
designer, but her originality, and influence, sprang from
her unique vision. Unlike most fashion creators who are
attracted to historic dress, Ashley was not interested
in recreating the grandeur of Versailles, or even of
Hampton Court. Her inspiration came from the lives
of ordinary folk: Victorian schoolrooms and vicarages;
the dress of countrywomen – neat, decent and seemly;
dresses with sprigged patterns and soft shapes of
the sort that would have equally delighted the village
Sunday school teacher and the daughter of the manse.

  She had hit a rich vein, open to endless mining, as
wholesome as an Edwardian album of pressed flowers.
It had little to do with fashion as Paris, Milan or New
York understood it. It was about clothing an attitude of
mind that was as peculiar to Britain as Shaker furniture
is to America. The British have always dreamed of the
pastoral idyll: the thatched cottage at the end of an
overgrown lane, wet dogs and high winds, strawberries
and cream in the rosy bower of a perfect English
garden. British fashion in the Seventies clothed this
atavism so convincingly that the dream became reality
– at least, on women's backs. Floral smocks, 'easy'
shapes and simple fabrics appeared everywhere. It was
more fancy dress than pastiche but it gave credibility to
English designers in a way that the Biba look had not.

  Ashley and Hulanicki were basically retailers with a
clever idea, but British Romanticism threw up two real
designers of undoubted talent. Pre-eminent was Ossie
Clark, who managed to straddle both sides of British
fashion. His *femme fatale* crepe and jersey dresses
were balanced by his innocent printed chiffons, often
with patterns designed by his wife, Celia Birtwell. One of
London's best designers, he was able to take from the
past and still produce something not only essentially his
own but also totally modern. Bill Gibb was less assured

14 Karl Lagerfeld
    for Chloé, 1973,
    photo David
    Montgomery

15 Ralph Lauren,
    1981, photo
    Bruce Weber

and leaned more heavily on the past. His historicism swept back across the ages, using motifs ranging from the early eighteenth century to the years immediately before World War I, but the way he mixed colours and patterns to produce a look as innocent as a Victorian nursery was entirely unique. It is a measure of the success of both men that their clothes, although using the past, were so right for the moment that, to modern eyes, they perfectly exemplify their time – in just the way that Dior's New Look now does.

The most successful pillager of the past during this period was Karl Lagerfeld, working for the Chloé label. The reason why his revivalism has such authority is that, like his near contemporary, Yves Saint Laurent, he can call on a wider range of cultural references than are available to any other designer. With a library reputedly containing a copy of every book on costume and fashion ever written, and an educated mind which roams freely across the disciplines, he has unrivalled resources for recreating the past. In the Seventies, he looked back to the seventeenth century to give us clothes based on the swashbuckling heroes of an Alexandre Dumas novel, the roisterous days of Cyrano de Bergerac, with more than a hint on one hand of the sensuality of Daniel Defoe's Moll Flanders and, on the other, the innocence of Sophia Weston, the squire's daughter in Henry Fielding's *Tom Jones*. But that wasn't what gave his clothes the edge and made them more interesting than anything being produced in London. It was that they were much less ageist, as one would expect from a designer trained in the traditions of French couture.

That being said, on reviewing the Seventies, it is now apparent that, more subtly but just as clearly as in the Sixties, designers *were* taking an ageist stance. Most of the romantic revivals in London and Paris were aimed very specifically at young women. They also leaned heavily on fantasy and the unreality of fairy stories. It was the first inkling of what was to come in the Nineties, when designers such as Galliano were happy to create collections based entirely on dream worlds.

But there was one revivalist who was using the past differently. Whereas Paris and London have a high level of decorative deliciousness – or decadence, according to your point of view – and produce clothes which often look more desirable on editorial pages than on a customer's back, New York fashion is less indulgent. In and around Seventh Avenue, creativity is the servant of practicality and, if this approach leads to banality and sterility in all but the greatest designers, nevertheless, when the two perfectly come together the result is fashion of a sublime purity and sense of purpose.

In the Seventies, the man who most successfully captured the past – and a uniquely North American one at that – was Ralph Lauren.

Ignoring European cultural traditions, Lauren eschewed the magnificence of the French court and the panoply of English social history which were frequently the inspiration of other designers. For his retrospective inspiration, he looked in his own back yard. Not just his, but every American's back yard. What he saw was sufficient to found an empire. Although earlier designers such as Claire McCardell and Bonnie Cashin had used sport and workwear as a basis for much that they designed, in order to create clothes uniquely North American, Ralph Lauren was the first designer to base a fashion philosophy on American history. He took the Wild West of cowboys and homesteaders, the native Americans and their traditional craft skills, the Long Island Edwardian country life of the Vanderbilts and the Whitneys, the American dream of Thirties' movies – and added the ice-cool sophistication of Manhattan in the Fifties and Sixties. Then, with a sure hand and a controlled imagination, he melded them into the Ralph Lauren version of revivalism, a thing entirely his own.

This was different from previous retro looks. Ralph Lauren was not using the past for just one collection. He was taking American history and reinventing it for a vision which, with variations, would permeate not only all his collections but also how he publicized them and sold them for years to come. No other designer had that commitment to the past and such confidence in his own beliefs. He literally took the history of a nation and re-presented it to itself through his clothes. The formula was multifaceted: it mixed Seventh Avenue slickness with the traditional country values of L.L. Bean – the mail order clothing firm, founded in 1912 to provide clothing and kit for hunters, trappers and fishermen which, in the Eighties, became part of mainstream American fashion – brought together Manhattan and Yosemite and found links across the centuries and decades of America's past.

Ralph Lauren has never had any doubt that American culture, even in the early years of the nation's history, when it was largely dominated by Britain, is strong because of the qualities of the people. He knows that is the reason why, since the early nineteenth century, it has grown – independently of what has happened across the Atlantic – to become the most powerful culture in the world. He also believes that, as part of that culture, American fashion is strong and able to stand independent of Europe. He considers that only American designers understand the essence of the United States and, therefore, that only they know how

15

to dress American women and the American way of life. He has done this so successfully that the rest of the world has recognized it and flocked to buy into a concept which has taken historic elements, made them contemporary and then given them classic status. As he has said, 'There's no point in copying things which the French and Italians do better.'

It seems an easy formula, but skill is required to avoid simplification degenerating into banality. The man who likened his fashion approach to making a salad – mixing disparate ingredients to produce something palatable to everyone – claims that his interest is not in high fashion but in style. Lauren is a movie-maker *manqué*. His 'movies', including his Westerns, and his sophisticated New York–Grace Kelly comedies, come down his runway every season. And they always have total authority. He has made quilted patchwork skirts and the frontier scene into high fashion. He has turned prairie denim and leather into sophisticated city wear. Everything he creates is resonant of previous times, and yet is totally modern. Clothes bought from Lauren's Polo label ten years ago can still be worn in fashionable circles today. There are very few designers of whom that can be said.

The Great Gatsby–Annie Hall world of fashion (Lauren made the costumes for both films) required its own approach to retailing, which it obtained in 1986 when Lauren converted the old Rhinelander Mansion on Madison Avenue, New York, into something much more than just a shop. An experience, a happening, a hallucination, its spirit was half up-market Edwardian store, half traditional country estate and, in order to show clearly how his clothes were part of a tradition, it was decorated with items such as old family portraits, scrapbooks and ornaments. This approach was copied in 1998 by Paul Smith when he converted an Edwardian house in Notting Hill into a shop, again containing many collectors' items to be admired but not purchased. Smith's skill, like that of Lauren, is not limited to merchandising. Both men know that the clothes which sell are the ones that are understated but contain an element which raises them above the norm. Suits by Paul Smith have been staples of the normally conservative 'City Boys of London' since the Eighties, and his casual clothes have made him a cult figure in Japan. Fashion's equivalent to Michael Palin, Smith's strong but quirky eye picks up design inspiration from the most unexpected of sources, ensuring a look unlike that of anyone else.

The Ralph Lauren influence has been huge. It proves that looking back can be the most satisfying way to answer the fashion needs of the moment. But it requires a committed vision to sustain it and a strong creative sense in order to enable a designer to use the past without abusing it. Like Christian Dior, Lauren has taken the historic spirit and used it to inform what he does, with no slavish copies and no sacrifice of modernity to historicism.

It is the hallmark of a great contemporary designer that he can use the past without allowing it to overwhelm him. Whereas Lauren has wholeheartedly annexed the past to make his statement, other designers use it with more, or less, intensity depending on their mood and how they judge the spirit of the times. The man who best exemplifies this is also the greatest couturier of our times: Yves Saint Laurent. Throughout his career he has made no secret of his inspirations and obligations, and they stretch far beyond the narrow world of high fashion. Wasn't he the first designer to react directly and immediately to what was happening politically on the streets? His cultural range is vast, taking in the history of art, music (from nineteenth-century opera to the avant-garde), literature and, above all, the ethnic cultures which he adapts with subtlety and sensibility – it should not be forgotten that he introduced the pointed bra into fashion, seventeen years before Jean Paul Gaultier's revisiting of the idea made a *succès de scandale*.

The real forcing ground for creative ideas has traditionally been couture and, in this, Yves Saint Laurent has been very traditional. In the late Seventies, he created some of the most beautiful and influential couture collections in the history of twentieth-century fashion. Two stand out above the others: his 1976–7 Russian collection and his Chinese collection of the following year (both of which are discussed in more detail in Chapter 9). Both were precisely judged exercises in atavistic alchemy. Richly opulent, they were examples of retro at its most romantic, based respectively on nineteenth-century Russian peasant dress and classic Chinese court dress. Neither inspiration nor collections had any connection with Russia or China in the Seventies, and can be read as Yves Saint Laurent's appeal to both drab totalitarian regimes to recall the richness and variety of their cultural past and reinstate them before it was too late. Both collections were highly political in motivation and effect.

They fitted well into a decade when fashion had become diffused and eclectic; when the world was plundered for inspiration; when antique and second-hand clothing was mixed and matched – or frequently mismatched – as people tried to reflect their search for individuality in their clothes, and used their dress as a

16

20 Zandra Rhodes,
    1977, photo
    Lothar Schmidt

21 Gina Fratini, 1971,
    photo Clive
    Arrowsmith

22 (Overleaf)
    Christian
    Lacroix, *haute
    couture*,1999,
    photo Jerome
    Esch

20

way of giving themselves an identity. It was a decade
when London clubbers were proving that, like the
Sixties, the Seventies accepted no preordained dress
codes. Zandra Rhodes and Gina Fratini in London were
concerned with fantasy while Zoran and Halston in New
York were becoming increasingly minimalist. It was the
decade which seemed to have finally killed the concept
of fashion consensus. It was the decade which made
revivalism seem not only acceptable, but inevitable.

The Eighties saw fashion take a pluralist approach,
with the increasing power of Milan and New York as
fashion centres. Dedicated to efficiency in dress, both
cities produced designers who, by the logicality of their
fashion credo, seemed to have finally solved the future
of fashion. To many, they were nearer to Pierre Cardin's
earlier experiments in minimalist dress than any
designers had been since his time. But in Paris and
London, fantasts waited, ready to turn fashion back
to retro with such a force that their beliefs would
have a permanent effect. The two approaches were
ideologically different, and it was couture that made
for the great divide. It had been the backbone of Paris
fashion for the entire century, but it had played only a
minor role in New York. Although America had had its
couturiers – many of them (including Norman Norell, ·
Mainbocher and Pauline Trigere) as good as those
working in Paris – it was ready-to-wear which energized
that country's fashion. Traditionally, Italian fashion had
been centred on the couture houses of Rome, but
when Milan wrested the fashion lead, they dwindled
in importance and Italian fashion became known, as
American fashion was, as a ready-to-wear industry.
London's couture businesses had virtually all collapsed
in the Sixties, becoming a city dominated by the youth
scene. Art students and clubbers in London had more
vibrancy and originality than their counterparts in other
world cities. Outrage and fantasy seemed to come
naturally to them, and the overall sense of being
creatively powerful attracted their counterparts from all
over the world. Leigh Bowery – style guru, nightclub
host and artist's model for Lucian Freud – came from
Australia in 1980 to study design in London, and he
was by no means untypical. Also, by the middle of that
decade London had the two most powerful fashion lures
in the world: Vivienne Westwood and John Galliano,
both seminal figures in retro fashion and both fixated
on the dress of previous centuries.

Their equivalent in Paris, Christian Lacroix, initially
didn't look back so far. His sparkling collections for
Patou, where he became design director in 1981, were
witty commentary on Fifties' high fashion, affectionately
satirizing the fashion attitudes of the grand couturiers of

the time, especially Balmain, Fath and Dior, although
it is provincial French life – and decoration – of the
nineteenth century which exerts the greatest influence
on his work. Born in Arles, Christian Lacroix regularly
revisits the bullring, folk embroidery and, rather
surprisingly, the English country house life between the
wars in his colourfully eclectic collections. Lacroix and
Westwood have had an enormous influence. Their
historicism has made looking back so popular in their
respective fashion capitals that it is often believed that
fantasy and fancy dress are now the only forms that
creative fashion can take.

Although Westwood and Lacroix are, it is to be hoped,
too experienced to fall into that fallacy, their decoratively
exuberant fashion shows have entirely changed the
manner and the matter of how fashion is shown in Paris
and London. Along with John Galliano and Jean Paul
Gaultier, they have made the fashion show perform
something very different from its traditional role, that
was to sell clothes by showing them directly to the
potential customer. In the mid-Eighties, the formula
changed in London and Paris, and the fashion show
became a means of exciting the imagination of press
and buyers by blatantly overstating the designer's
case. There was nothing wrong in doing so. After
the confusion of the Seventies and the bewilderment
caused by the Japanese in the early Eighties, fashion
needed to go to extremes – in presentation as well as
in fact – in order to recapture the fading public interest.

What happened was that the fashion show became
much less fashion and very much more show, as
presentational extravagance took hold. Fashion as worn
in reality in the Eighties was exactly as it has always
been: driven by the needs of the customer. By
definition, something which is so wearable as to be
unexceptional – which is how most women wish their
clothes to be – is unlikely to have the excitement that
makes it memorable on the catwalk. Contemporary
wearable fashion lacks the decorative extravagance
that is needed in order to impress under the lights of
the show. It was in the Eighties that a fundamental split
– theatricality for the show and practicality for the retail
outlet – became the norm. This meant that the fashion
show increasingly became an end in itself, making little
effort or pretence to exhibit the clothes that the
designer was actually hoping to sell.

In fact, all designers continued to make clothes so
unexceptional and so understated in their wearability
that they bore only the most tenuous link to what had
been seen on the catwalk. It was – and in many cases,
still is – possible to walk past the boutiques of the
top designers and see nothing in the windows which

23 Vivienne
    Westwood, 1994,
    photo Paolo
    Roversi

24 Vivienne
    Westwood on
    the catwalk with
    models, 1997–8

suggests the label or season. Confusion and the breakdown of reality was furthered by the fact that nothing to be seen in the shops bore any relationship to the pictures published in newspapers and magazines. Was it to cover this awkward fact that retail outlets became so minimalist in the Eighties that they often showed no clothes at all in their windows?

The public felt confused, and not a little betrayed, as the media began to play the extravagance game. At the time of the collections, the intensity of cover was greater than ever before, but it gave women little guidance as to what might appear in the shops. Geared entirely to 'newsworthiness', front pages featured the most extreme fashions they could find. Designers, no slouches when publicity is required, gave them outrageously sexy or eccentric clothes to answer the need. They were not meant to be put into production, they were meant exclusively for the photographer's lens and the newspaper's front page.

There was a further effect. In order to create clothes with the right dramatic impact, the decorative – and some might say, decadent – designers as opposed to the commercial ones, were, increasingly, forced to look backwards for inspiration. As they had learned, there are limits to the fireworks that can be produced with a tailored trouser suit.

Newsworthy fashion came to rely on an amalgam of sexiness and magpie historicism. The Nineties dawned in the same way as the Eighties had dwindled: on a high note of historical hysteria where already extreme fashion statements were made more so by stylists and accessorizers, people whose profile had traditionally been low. Now make-up, hair and millinery became crucial elements of the projected look, helping to ensure that, whatever it happened to be, it would be made as

fantastical as possible. Shows became wonderfully exuberant affairs, flashing with light and colour and ablaze with outrageously eccentric ideas. Whereas Lacroix had settled for a general re-creation of the *belle époch*, Vivienne Westwood moved towards the eighteenth, and then the sixteenth century, with many other period references to the side, resulting in shows which were, alongside Gaultier's, the most exciting and visually challenging ever seen. For Westwood, outrage consisted of breaking every sexual taboo she could find, challenging moral and social attitudes and smashing all the rules of good taste. Gaultier was doing the same, but his retro approach was tempered – many would say dominated – by a sharp wit and sophistication largely lacking in Westwood's approach. Whereas she was increasingly fond of making 'philosophical' remarks, Gaultier was never happier than when he could prick the bubble of pretentiousness. And the difference showed on their runways.

Possibly the only other talent as rich as Gaultier, Vivienne Westwood's approach has been less ethnic and more historic than his. Since her punk days with Malcolm McLaren, a time when she seemed eager to undermine the structure of British culture with a 'destroy and desecrate' approach as essentially negative as the punk movement in general, she has found her happy hunting ground in the pages of an English history book. Her ability to capitalize on the past is perhaps the result of a simplistic approach to history. She has roamed through the eighteenth century on a Fielding-esque romp of dishevelled sexuality, trailing memories of Fanny Hill and a hundred literary whores; she has revisited the Victorian world of bustles and child prostitution with an attitude which just avoids prurience; she has recreated princesses Elizabeth and Margaret in the Forties,

dressed in sensible tweed suits. Is this continued subversion, or has the renegade designer finally joined the Establishment and come home?

There is no easy answer, but history might well consider that the best of Vivienne Westwood occurred in a small window in her endeavours, in the early Eighties. The childish need to shock, the desperate desire for publicity which had characterized her time with McLaren, had briefly ended. In short, sharp succession she made three brilliant fashion statements, so powerful that they formed London fashion for the Eighties and continued to influence the Nineties. If ever people were doubtful whether Vivienne Westwood could achieve fashion greatness, their answer, ringing triumphantly, was found in 'Savages', her collection for Spring/Summer 1982, 'Buffalo Girls' from the following season and 'Hobos' from Spring/Summer 1983. All three followed on from the considerable impact of her first catwalk show, the 'Pirates' collection of 1981, which had an enormous influence on the emerging New Romantic clubbers. However, for all its exuberance, it was nothing more than a brilliantly decorative and highly inventive form of fancy dress. Her later collections showed a darker and tougher side of Westwood, one which, although embodying the romance which is at the root of the woman and the designer, challenged what one interviewer described as the 'neat Hollywood-amended, Eurocentric categories of taste, seemliness and suitability'.

The 'Savages' collection took the thinking further as Westwood – in many respects in line with the Japanese approach that had recently appeared in Paris – began to undermine preconceptions of scale and fit in a collection which, in its anthropological eclecticism, bowed towards the Third World, while mixing Victorian

24

25 Jean Paul Gaultier,
    haute couture,
    1999, photo
    Jerome Esch

26 Jean Paul Gaultier,
    'French Can Can',
    1991–2, photo
    Paolo Roversi

'Artful Dodger' frockcoats, Aztec patterns, Peruvian and American Indian motifs and 'bag lady' dishcloth tops fastened with huge buttons made from the tops of cleaning containers. It was a subversive mix which excited and puzzled. Many found it impossible to imagine any commercial application for what was shown on the runway. Looking back after twenty years, Westwood's approach now seems less esoteric. Poverty on the streets of London was common enough, with beggars, bag ladies, derelicts and winos shuffling through the affluent crowds, their lives in a handful of plastic bags, their clothes layered for warmth. Artistically, Westwood's dress approach has a striking similarity with the late works of the American artist Philip Guston. An exponent of 'clumsy figuration' and 'bad' painting, his work had the same awkwardness and tension as Westwood's fashion attitude at this time, except it lacked the kitsch quality of her runway presentations.

'Buffalo Girls' was probably Westwood's greatest aesthetic triumph. Continuing many of the themes of 'Savages', it had the same ad hoc, improvisational feel to it. The clothes were oversized and kept slipping off the models' shoulders; damaged knives and forks were used as fasteners, and the whole effect was of a drab, colourless dowdiness, except for one idea that was to have an influence on fashion for the next twenty years. In homage to the black women of the South African townships who were so proud of their Western underwear that they wore it as outerwear, Westwood put a 1950s satin bra over a tunic. No one will ever know whether her decision was part of a coherent fashion statement or a last-minute styling gimmick but it stole the show. The effect was tacky – as intended – but it caught the imagination of the moment.

'Punkatura' (1982) was an amalgam of all the radical thinking which had gone before, and it summed up the looks that would dominate London fashion for many seasons to come. Layered, distressed 'poor' fabrics were mixed with a pantomimic disregard for probability and a determination to destroy previously sacred ideas of taste. At the time, Westwood said, 'I just want to fuck everything up.' She succeeded beyond even her own grandiose dreams. Ethnic and historic borrowings, romanticism of poverty and an increasingly specific sexual stance made Vivienne Westwood the queen of the art colleges and the source book consulted by many more designers in Paris and Milan than would be prepared to admit. Her influence on Galliano was considerable. Her attitudes were an encouragement to his already subversive fashion ideas and her anti-bourgeois, confrontational – and, many would say, basically anti-fashion – stance gave substance to

what he and many students were already thinking. Westwood's approach was highly politicized, but she still did not escape the tendency seen in other designers to capitalize on ethnic approaches by forcing powerful cultures and tribal grandeurs into the constricting world of Western taste. Inevitably, Westwood exploited her sources to a certain extent but, by comparison with many designers, she can be seen to have allowed cultures to speak for themselves, with the minimum of adulteration, although Westwood allowed herself to rely so heavily on the past that her shows became an end in themselves, with no real crossover to what people might actually want.

However, Gaultier kept that vital connection with the streets which is part of the successful designer equation, no matter how extravagant things might seem in the show. It was not a consideration that stopped him having fun. His collection 'French Can Can' of 1991–2 recreated the world of Toulouse-Lautrec. In 1995, he revisited all the styles of the twentieth century in his Spring/Summer 'Fin de Siècle' collection, two of which – Punk and Flower Power – he used as the basis of later collections. All Gaultier's shows, for all their apparent spontaneity, are an exercise in selection and presentation of ideas which fit into a tight intellectual approach and, no matter how exuberant they are, the intellectual control never slips. There is nothing self-indulgent in Gaultier's approach, even when the results are so ebullient that the audience laughs with delight. Like Lacroix, he frequently returns to retro themes but, unlike him, he never fails to make a statement that is not only modern but even prophetic. It is important to remember that the whole underwear as outerwear, boudoir look which was a feature of the Nineties was first introduced by Gaultier in 1983. Shocking in impact then, he revisited the theme many times, refining and restating his position, as he does with all his themes. No matter how extravagantly he presents his ideas, Gaultier is adamant on one point: 'I don't make works of art,' he insists, 'I am not an artist. I am an artisan. I simply have fun with clothes.'

His approach to retro is wide-ranging, proving that he has a cultural depth and artistic knowledge which, although never overtly paraded, inform all that he does. His inspirations range from the life, work and character of Frida Kahlo to French music hall entertainers such as Yvette Horner; the sex shows of Pigalle to the dignity of Hasidic Jews – an inspiration which was highly criticized; Tom of Finland homosexual fantasy figures to Rasputin. He put women in conical bras and men in skirts. His influence is universal and continuing. His work shows that even the most overt retro inspiration

25

29

28

can be modern in the hands of a man working within his own cultural agenda.

New York designers, hard pushed to keep their share of market and coverage, came up with their own version of retro when Marc Jacobs and Anna Sui took an American vernacular style which had as its *raison d'être* ugliness and the reflected Hell's Angels and hippie dress codes of the late Sixties, to produce Grunge – a look which appealed less to the public than to fashion photographers. Based on a pop music subculture which sprang up in Seattle around the group Nirvana, the fashion was like the music: rough, unkempt and deliberately raw at the edges. Just as Grunge music contained echoes of punk and heavy metal and had a comparatively limited appeal, the fashion statement it spawned exhibited a meanness of spirit and a poverty of imagination which largely failed to capture the interest of the fashion world.

Current fashion is increasingly based on looking back at the past, and any period will do. Hollywood in the Forties, American high society in the Twenties, the eighteenth century seen through the eyes of *les liaisons dangereuses*, the ruffs of the seventeenth century, the crinoline of the nineteenth century – all have been used as the basis of modern collections by designers as diverse as Vivienne Westwood, Romeo Gigli, Alexander McQueen and Jean Paul Gaultier. Revivalism is surely the main source of fashion originality at the end of the twentieth century.

No designer has used the past as powerfully as John Galliano. His first collection, presented in 1984 as part of his degree course at St Martin's School of Art, was based entirely on his reworking of the dress of the French Revolution. It was called 'Les Incroyables', and the name was apt. By student standards the show was extraordinary; by commercial standards it was so

forward-looking that many didn't understand it. Galliano had used the clothes of the revolutionaries to create a cut and balance which were entirely new to twentieth-century fashion. In one show he proved that historicism does not need to lead to costume. This was a revival but it did what good revivals should do: it created something new. Galliano's career had started on a high point rarely reached.

During the Eighties, it sometimes seemed that Galliano was in danger of allowing his ability for adapting the past to the present to dissipate under commercial pressures. But his cut remained extraordinary; his shapes continued to be unlike those of anyone else. He maintained the ethereal quality which made his clothes so moving, but his historic references seemed muted – although they were undoubtedly still there and remained the basis for everything he did. It was mainly a question of expediency, not change of heart, which kept some of his preoccupations *sotto voce*. Like the princess in *Sleeping Beauty*, Galliano was waiting for a kiss to revitalize him – the kiss of real financial backing that would allow him to fully exploit his fantasies of the past.

It came in 1996 when, after a year as design director at the House of Givenchy, Galliano was made creative director of Dior, with a flexible budget and a simple brief. His job was to make Dior newsworthy. This he did with a series of retro collections which redefined the rules. Any mix was possible, provided there was a prevailing genius which unified elements that, in one show alone, could be as disparate as the Orient Express in the Twenties, Pocahontas and Native American culture, and sixteenth-century court dress in England and Spain. All of these were skilfully intertwined in Galliano's Winter 1998–9 *haute couture* collection for Christian Dior, which was shown in one of the main railway terminals in Paris. It was the sort of

32

brilliant mix of retro, revival and historicism which Galliano has made his own during his tenure at Dior and, in fact, reveals itself even more strongly in the parallel collections that he shows under his own name.

Galliano's commitment to the past is stronger than that of any other designer, but he maintains that his fashion is entirely modern and even forward-looking. In a strange reversal of George Canning's comment on the Old and New Worlds, he is probably right. He and the other historicist designers have called the old world into existence to redress the balance of the new, and the results have been powerful and prophetic. In fact, it is possible to make out a case that a considerable number of designers are looking back for their inspiration as the twenty-first century begins. If they have a true historic perspective as Lacroix, Gaultier and Galliano do, their search goes beyond the last ten decades, into the nineteenth century and beyond. But most are content to revisit the great moments of the twentieth century's artistic past. The Ballets Russes, the Bauhaus, Thirties' Hollywood, the Grace Kelly era: all have been reworked many times. Even so, there are still some surprises: Anna Sui has gone back to Fifties' Scandinavian fabrics of the sort associated with the Marimekko design studio; Katharine Hamnett has recreated the Forties' fashion look, based on narrow tweed suits and boxed pleats; Julien Macdonald, whose first collection, 'Mermaids', looked back to tourist Capri a decade ago, has plundered Welsh culture and given it a *Casino* gloss; but it is Miuccia Prada who has most boldly annexed the past by taking the late Sixties, generally considered a bad time for fashion with its man-made fabrics, awkward colour combinations, skimpy coats and flared trousers, to create a cult look – although it must be admitted that, like Grunge, it found no answering chord in the public consciousness.

It is in their couture ranges that modern designers find the most difficulty in breaking free of the past. It is not surprising that, as Savile Row, by maintaining the strict standards of tailoring which made it a Mecca for well-dressed men, can modernize only at the expense of what attracts men in the first place, so couture must always remain formal. Casual couture, speaking with a streetwise accent, would clearly be nonsense. Even a questioning young designer like Josephus Thimister cannot break away from the shapes and structures of couture dressmaking, and is forced to attempt to destabilize it by using unexpected, even 'found' materials or painting, or even defacing fabric in order to destroy the old-fashioned, 'old lady' effect which traditional *haute couture* has. His shows have demonstrably been examples of 'work in progress'

34 Viktor & Rolf,
Liberty print
dress, 1998,
photo Lee Jenkins

as he moves forward towards his own solution to the
conundrum. As a Belgian, he joins a loosely woven
'school' of problem-solving designers, led by Martin
Margiela, whose radical independent stance he appears
to share, whereas the Dutch designers Viktor Horsting
and Rolf Snoeren, whose label is Viktor & Rolf, take a
more direct and traditional approach. Like the young
American Jeremy Scott, they subvert much of the
pomposity of couture retro by their ironic and anti-ironic
attitudes. But the compulsion to plunder the back
catalogue of dress, which is such a characteristic
of high fashion at the end of the twentieth century,
persists, raising questions about the nature of fashion
now that we have moved into a new century.

Why do so many designers, in Europe at least, feel
the need to look backwards for ideas? Are they trying
to recapture a soul which they no longer find in their
own times, or are they searching for some form of
sophistication which can raise fashion above the level
of the banal? It is certainly true that the clamour for
decorative excess cannot be silenced in fashion any
more than in other areas of life. We have enjoyed almost
twenty years of minimalism, led by Giorgio Armani in Italy
and Geoffrey Beene in America. We have Donna Karan
and Calvin Klein. It is a fashion approach which appeals
widely, and yet it is apparently not enough. But perhaps
it *is* enough for most of us when we consider how we
wish to dress, rather than how we wish to dream.

And that, surely, is the situation at the beginning of the
twenty-first century. In some fashion houses it would
seem that the ability to dream is all that is required of
a designer. Considerable amounts of money, time and
effort are given to make the dreams concrete – dreams
which, without exception, look back. But the fashion
houses which address the present are the winners in
the end, as anyone who has seen a cheap, mass-
produced line bearing the name of a great designer
knows. When they are asked to create clothes which
sell, rather than make a splash, then even the most
colourful and wide-ranging imaginations are brought to
heel. It is then that the most extravagant designer has to
face the fact of his calling: which is that, although some
of his magnificent imaginings will undoubtedly inform
future fashion, what is needed in commercial terms is
ordinary, unexciting and unexceptional clothes which,
although they may incorporate the ghosts of past
designers' extravagances, are so normal that women of
all age groups and walks of life feel safe to wear them
without the risk of attracting ridicule. How to reconcile
this basic demand with fashion's obsession with retro is
the dilemma of our times.

1   (Opener)
    Christian Dior
    haute couture,
    1998, photo
    Miles Aldridge

2   (Previous page)
    Christian Lacroix
    haute couture,
    1998, photo
    Satoshi Saikusa

3   (Previous page)
    John Galliano for
    Dior *haute
    couture*,
    1998, photo
    David Bailey

4   Hippie clothes,
    1969, photo
    Peter Knapp

5   Italian *Vogue*,
    1971, photo
    Barry Lategan

6   (Overleaf)
    Italian *Vogue*,
    1971, photo
    Barry Lategan

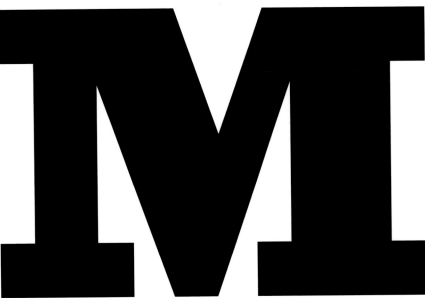

Marco Polo, Christopher Columbus, Sir Walter Raleigh – Western civilization has drawn comfort and strength from its explorers for at least the last five hundred years, as they have journeyed to remote and far-flung kingdoms to discover rare outposts at the furthest reaches of the known world. And when they returned, often after years of danger and hardship, eager with tales to tell and bearing artefacts and even people as proof of the wonders they had witnessed, even the humblest of them was fêted. Kings prized the booty and the trade agreements they brought back with them. Scholars and wise men eagerly read their journals and diaries. Learned societies were set up to promulgate the new information their travels had uncovered. But, until the end of the nineteenth century, nobody in the West ever thought of the civilizations that the travellers discovered as anything other than savage, heathen and primitive, despite irrefutable evidence of strong, intellectually and socially sound cultures that were often more advanced than those found in many Western countries. Had they done so, much warring, cruelty and even destruction of those cultures and civilizations might have been avoided.

But, in all the excitement of the unfolding world, spreading forth with each generation like a vast magic carpet, it was always the collections hauled home across the high seas which caused the greatest excitement. Rich fabrics, strange dyes, exotic stones and craftwork, unknown flora and fauna, ceremonial robes, the panoply of the great: vast numbers of people from every walk of life found the evidence of different worlds exciting in their exoticism.

The rich were determined to enjoy the greatest spoils. Seventeenth-century grandees beggared their estates and mortgaged their patrimony merely to possess a pineapple or a tulip. Their eighteenth-century equivalent took the Grand Tour in order to see the world for themselves, although they tended to confine their cultural excursions to France, Italy and Greece. In the nineteenth century, people went further afield, venturing into Africa, Asia and even South America.

The lure of the exotic is a powerful influence on the Western psyche. That is why continents have been explored, countries annexed, tribes exploited and taboos broken, as entrepreneurs and the military have followed in the footsteps of scientists and anthropologists in their determination to bring it all to the rich and eager West. The exoticism of the Middle and Far East, the wonders of chinoiserie, the beauties of Japonisme: from the end of the eighteenth century to the beginning of the twentieth, no corner of the globe failed to produce a cultural movement in the West, whether in short, recurring bursts, such as the craze of Egyptomania, begun with Napoleon's campaign, which brought us Cleopatra's Needles, Verdi's opera *Aïda* and a thousand decorative devices still current today, or long-term, like our continuing love affair with Classical Greece.

Fashion has defined the fads, and dress has eagerly followed, grasping at the exotic and ethnic to create new moods and attitudes, many of which started international crazes, such as the obsession with the patterns of Kashmir that swept Europe in the late eighteenth century. The cashmere shawl was probably the first 'to die for' fashion item – exceedingly expensive and hard to come by, it was highly prized as a status symbol signifying wealth and taste. We see it

4

8

proclaiming both in Ingres's portraits of fashionable and aristocratic women, with the precious cloth wrapped loosely around their shoulders or allowed to fall casually at their side. Women of all classes longed for cashmere shawls, and those who could afford to were happy to spend a small fortune on them. It was the longest running and most powerful craze ever to hit fashion. It marked a seminal development, because it finally laid to rest the old idea that ethnic, tribal or peasant dress was rude and unlettered. It was the beginning of the West's acceptance of cultures different from its own. British weavers adapted cashmere patterns to their own styles, renamed the product 'Paisley' and made a statement which still flourishes today. But the importance of cashmere is that, unlike previous adaptations of dress items from afar, it retained its own artistic credibility – a 'first' in ethnic dress – and was worn not as costume but as Western fashion, without affecting its integrity.

Since then, the exotic and ethnic have, with varying degrees of intensity, become a permanent element in the structure of fashion, generally popping up on at least one designer's runway each season. Sometimes they play a major part, more often their role is in accessories, patterns and colour combinations rather than in line and shape. In the twentieth century we have seen Poiret borrowing from Russia, Chanel adapting the working clothes of peasants and Schiaparelli introducing knitwear based on traditional Armenian designs. In the last fifty years, the tendency has intensified. Aran sweaters, Spanish lace, Tyrolean leather, the coloured silks of Romanian gypsies, even Amish and Quaker dress codes have inspired designers – and the rest of us, too. Although we have now all become travellers, and quite a few of us could even be called explorers, able to witness the ethnic and exotic at first hand, our appetite for both on the catwalks continues undimmed.

Fashion follows art, sometimes closely, sometimes after many years have passed. The ethnic looks that appeal to designers, and eventually to the public, are normally exotic ones which trail clouds of imagined glories from the past. Designers bring an eye that is calculating as well as plundering to the magnificence of past periods, great civilizations and remote kingdoms. What they do with cultural heritages is clean them up, dust them down, give them a bit of a polish and then wait for the creative genie to appear, extravagantly clad and bearing promises of even greater extravagance. Designers share Hollywood's view of history and geography. Just as in a biblical epic starring Victor Mature and Gina Lollobrigida, we know that every toga will hang perfectly, no golden wristband will be tarnished and the skies will always be alarmingly blue, so, when a designer goes ethnic, we do

not expect anything that reflects reality: the sartorial efforts of poor and displaced peasants are not required. We want the voluptuous luxury of the Russian court at the time of Catherine the Great. Recreating the ragged clothes worn by ordinary Ethiopians at the time of Haile Selassie would be pointless in the eyes of most fashion followers. What we respond to is the magnificence of the emperor himself. Ethnic looks work only if seen with a selective eye, focusing on exotic fantasies rather than mundane realities.

It is also a suspect eye that can be seen as patronizing in the way that it either adopts or rejects elements of a nation's culture or a civilization's heritage. Almost invariably, the woman who stimulates the designer in whatever culture he is dabbling is the courtesan. All too often it is the pomp and circumstance of the palace, not the realities of the plains and paddy fields, that he is trying to recreate, although it must be said that the military and ideological uniforms worn by ordinary people also attract. This approach can be tactless and inadvertently insulting to the contemporary inhabitants of the country who do not want to be reminded of their opulent and often corrupt and repressive imperial pasts. They have chosen to look to the future with a more egalitarian attitude. Some designers respect this and are able to produce decorative magic from the most utilitarian of dress codes. John Galliano's ready-to-wear collection for Spring/Summer 1999 at Dior took the jackets, caps and regalia of revolutionary China and, with remarkably few decorative additions, gave them a contemporary feel that was both chic and relevant.

Galliano has made other attempts to recreate and romanticize the less glorious moments of the past. For example his Spring/Summer 1985 collection, 'Afghanistan Repudiates Western Ideals', was based on a period of the country's history between 1919 and 1929 when its ruler Amanullah Khan instituted modernizing reforms. These included abolishing the traditional veil worn by Afghan women and encouraging officials to adopt Western dress. The fight to preserve indigenous cultural dress led to his deposition in 1929. Galliano created a look which reflected some of the turmoil: a mixture of Western bureaucratic dress and the loose light clothing necessary in hot climates, with hints at the violence that the edicts caused: one of the stylistic accessories was broken spectacles held together with Elastoplast.

The 'Afghanistan Repudiates' collection saw romance in a less obvious sort of ethnicity but, for most designers, allowing their imaginations to board a phantom Orient Express to faraway places, the search is for the rich and rare, the sumptuous and the voluptuous. The banalities

9   Design for Krizia
     Knitwear, 1983

10   Missoni, British
     Vogue, 1971,
     photo Barry
     Lategan

9

of the real world are not allowed to surface, even the peasants are permanently envisioned in festive or ceremonial dress. The great couturiers view the world through romantic eyes. They are excited by the mysterious aura of the nomads who traverse the Steppes; they thrill to the idea of scimitared tribesmen on richly caparisoned Arab stallions; they imagine silk tents gently rippling in the desert breeze while exotically dressed women idly recline on tasselled cushions as slaves proffer sweetmeats and sherbets.

It is an inspiration both unreal and theatrical, but it has a potent effect on their imaginations. In their search for the wilder shores of love, couturiers almost invariably seek their stimulus not at first hand but through the eyes of nineteenth-century painters – the world of Géricault and Delacroix: violent, passionate and thrilling; the mood of Sir Lawrence Alma-Tadema, Lord Leighton and Gustave Moreau: heated, perverse and obsessive – in a creative equivalent of Hollywood, colourful and stirring but totally unreal. From Yves Saint Laurent to Christian Lacroix and Romeo Gigli, the atmosphere of luxurious exoticism has constantly beckoned to the great couturiers, offering them irresistible opportunities to recreate the mood and excitement of the paintings. Reality has never been part of the equation.

That was left to the hippies, who spent much of the Seventies digging below the surface, in touch with the reality of peasant dress codes and unearthing many things which mainstream fashion would later eagerly take up. They played a valuable role in the fashion development of the decade. Whereas couturiers and dress designers were only interested in working on a grand and luxurious level, the hippies were as happy in the confusion of Middle Eastern souks as they were in the calm of Tibetan temples. They were like entrepreneurs of Seventies' fashion, a tribe carrying on its back the craftwork of every known culture: Mongolian lambswool coats, woven Moroccan bags, Peruvian knitwear, hand-printed Indian cotton, mirror glass, tooled leather, devoré velvets – all shaken up, like yak's milk and rancid butter, to make a rich but rather queasy dress cocktail which the fashion capitals of the world

borrowed and re-formed to create the 'rich hippie' look on their runways.

There have been many designers who have found their stimulation by looking internationally. One of the earliest was Kenzo, who has been described as fashion's most prominent traveller. His imagination has crisscrossed the globe, from Egypt to Mexico, Eastern Europe to China, Scandinavia to Oceania. What attracts him is the strong colour and lively patterns of native dress. His skill lies in the uninhibited way in which he mixes examples from several cultures, not just in one show but even in one garment, often with the kind of wit and humour normally associated with Jean Paul Gaultier, who, following many of the same roads, has been equally eclectic.

Kenzo is not alone in hearing tribal voices and using their design vocabularies to create a style. Just as he has frequently dipped into African civilizations, so has Missoni, the Italian knitwear firm, which uses the colours and geometric patterns of the continent to produce clothes that are uniquely timeless, whether they are early pieces designed by founders Ottavio and Rosita Missoni, or by their daughter Angela, who took over the company in 1997. Mariuccia Mandelli created a range of knitwear for Krizia in the Eighties which featured tigers, leopards and all the most dramatic species from the world of desert, savannah and jungle, inspired by a series of animal silk screens by Andy Warhol, owned by the designer. Ralph Lauren's upmarket dress for the highly sophisticated has also ranged across the African plains, with echoes of Twenties' safaris and railroad millionaires in the Thirties, as well as the ethnic world of early Americana: quilted patchwork skirts, jumpers based on the settler's wife's sampler, denim, leather and good honest cotton. His English equivalent for a brief period in the early Eighties was Bill Gibb who, along with the American Kaffe Fassett, created prints of many stylistic strands for his romantically ethnic fashion that fed on his Celtic roots and grew through the strength of his adaptations of folk costume from Europe, South America, the Middle East and the American West.

Equally as eclectic, the Italian designer Romeo Gigli is attracted by opulent fabrics, intricately embroidered,

12

13

which, he claims, are inspired by memories of the pictures in fifteenth- and sixteenth-century books shown to him when he was young by his father, an antiquarian bookseller. Often described as rich hippie, his clothes have reflected the ceremonial costumes of Middle Europe as well as the festive and religious dress of Spain and Southern Italy – which has frequently provided the stimulus for his fellow Italians, Dolce & Gabbana. The British designers, Alan Cleaver and Keith Varty, who designed for Byblos in Milan during the Eighties, were even more eclectic in their tastes. Each collection was a riot of hot colour, strong pattern and good humour as they allowed their imaginations to swoop across the world, snatching at whatever took their fancy in Marrakesh, Hawaii, India or Havana. In 1988, they chose Tsarist Russia as the inspiration for a collection called 'Anna Karenina comes to Milan'. It was, at best, a jokey homage to a noble culture and, like their skirts printed with postcards and maps of the Bahamas, ended up as fancy dress costume, with little thought of how far even the young will go in wearing a joke.

This is one of the great problems with ethnic inspiration. It requires a tight controlling hand if it is not to result in a theatricality which reduces it to the histrionic level of a Ruritanian romance. When a good designer gives his imagination full rein on the catwalk, the results can be inspiring in the breadth of their cultural and ethnic references, but if you are not convinced that beneath all the originality and beauty lies the idea for clothing which can be worn on the streets, it has failed. That failure is not always a result of extravagance or exuberance, as the folkloric path pursued by the Turkish-born designer, Rifat Ozbek, shows. His imaginative use of ethnic codes produced some of the most interesting clothes of the Eighties and early Nineties, often from ancient as well as native sources but always with a modern feeling. His eye for rich decorative stimuli has enabled him to take inspiration from the Ottoman empire, Afghanistan, Senegal and Tibet and even cowboys and Native American colours, patterns and decoration, using imitation bones and elk's teeth on coats and vests based on the uniforms of Confederate soldiers.

16

In the Nineties, the role has been taken by the Belgian romanticist, Dries Van Noten, whose Tibetan-inspired clothes have a gently elegiac and rhapsodic quality entirely in keeping with the mood of the country that inspires them. His subtle use of gold, silver and bronze embroidery, along with the shot fabrics he favours, present a look of delicacy and refinement which manages to stay clear of costume most of the time. But, like much ethnic-inspired fashion, his is not a robust, 'mean-streets' look: rather, the refined and sumptuous reward for the self-aware and rich appreciator of the beauty and finesse of a certain approach to fashion, where rich fabrics, textures and surfaces are considered more exciting than cut or line.

But there are other problems. A great deal of fun can be had with ethnic themes. Strong pattern, bold colour and traditional shapes can make a powerful impression. However, the great lure of the ethnic and folkloric tradition is the same as that which makes people into travellers: the excitement and stimulation of far-flung cultures. Above all, the appeal is based on the romance of the costume of peoples whose way of life and social attitudes are different to those in mainstream fashion-consuming countries. Unfortunately, the attitudes which made them different and exotic for the West are rapidly succumbing to the global homogenization of dress. There are few places left in the world where indigenous dress patterns still persist on any major scale as an everyday aspect of life. Too often, such attire is worn only on special occasions or, worse, to please the tourists. Even the traditional clothes of India and Asia seem doomed to disappear. It is quite possible that we will then be grateful for the multi-tongued ethnicity of international designers who can save the spirit of folklore fashion, even if they adapt its actuality by investing it with imaginative development.

Of the many designers who find other cultures a stimulus, the master of ethnic eclecticism is Yves Saint Laurent. Born in Algeria and always with at least one home in Morocco, he has allowed the glamour of non-European worlds to feed his imagination from very early days. The rich colours and exotic materials of the East were the catalyst for some of his greatest and most influential collections. Like virtually every other designer in the past fifty years, Saint Laurent responded to the influence of African masks, patterns and colour combinations as seen through the eyes of the Cubists. But, being Saint Laurent, he took note of how the artists had created one of the century's great artistic

19

movements from the artefacts of a primitive world, then looked for himself and found his own excitement. As early as 1967, for the 'African' collection, he was using ebony and ivory jewellery, raffia and flax, along with wooden and glass beads, to create looks never before seen in such uncompromising commitment on the catwalks of Paris.

Harper's Bazaar called the collection a 'fantasy of primitive genius', but what made it exciting was not merely that, in one sweep, Saint Laurent had broadened the scope of materials considered suitable for high fashion dress – an achievement not to be underestimated at a time when ropes of pearls and chains of diamanté were still the norm – but also that he had introduced an angular, pointed bra, taken from stylized African drawings. Made of black silk organza, the dress was embroidered in black beads of wood and jet, with appliquéd plastic geometric shapes. Two eight-inch pointed bra cups completed the picture. Made of plastic and decorated with beads, they bemused the fashion audience. They appeared to be in the worst possible taste, but this was Yves Saint Laurent, fashion genius of the age. Not knowing whether to smile or ignore, the fashion cognoscenti were ill at ease. In fact, these prophetic breast coverings were quietly overlooked in most reports of the show, forgotten about until the idea was recreated by Jean Paul Gaultier in the Eighties, to great acclaim by people who had forgotten or never known Saint Laurent's pioneering work.

Yves Saint Laurent's African dresses had little immediate effect as they were too far in advance of their time, but they were a revolutionary statement in that they took native dress and, instead of smothering it with the Western fashion ethos, allowed it to stand in all its glory. Saint Laurent, unlike so many to follow, had the ability of the great artist to borrow from an alien culture and produce an artefact for his own culture, without being patronizing or condescending to the original, just as Picasso and the Cubists had done. What makes Yves Saint Laurent's African dresses important is their integrity. It is possible to see this as a reflection of the designer's North African youth, steeped as it was in multicultural references, but only a great creator could have made the leap from one culture to another with such assurance. The African dresses were the most complete of Yves Saint Laurent's borrowings at that time, although he did make many brief or oblique references to the Arab decorative tradition that he knew so well, especially in his embroidery, which he often based on the traditional North African string embroidery that for centuries had decorated jellabas.

It was nine years later that Yves Saint Laurent created what many consider not just his greatest collection, but the greatest collection of the century. For this, he turned to Russia and produced a show which the *International Herald Tribune* hailed as a 'revolution'. It was, but not the Russian Revolution. Saint Laurent had gone further back in history, to the glories of the Cossacks, in order to create the richest, most exotic and certainly most costly collection in his career. Tired, he claims, of press criticism that couture was antiquated, he decided to give his answer. His Winter 1976 collection was a sensation, so much so that it finally put the seal of approval on ethnic borrowing, and triggered off the folkloric approach which still forms a major part of fashion today. The press dubbed it a homage to the

Ballets Russes and Léon Bakst, but it was much more
encompassing than that. Using gold lamé, rich silks and
black sable, Saint Laurent created babushka dresses,
gold-trimmed 'gypsy' skirts, richly coloured Boyar vests,
high Russian boots of gold leather, trimmed with wild
mink and turbans of gold and jewel-bright colours. It
was done with such confidence and conviction because
Saint Laurent had brought to his concept of Russia a
mind educated by the country's literature; from Gogol
and Tolstoy to the memoirs of the Grand Duke Alexander
Mikhailovich and the Marquis de Custine's *Letters from
Russia*, as well as an eye that had looked at Slavonic
works of art. It was that education which raised Saint
Laurent above the level of ethnic dabbling and enabled
him to make a valid and influential cultural statement with
his Russian show.

Was it to prove that such magnificence was not a fluke
that Yves Saint Laurent went immediately to Imperial
China for the inspiration of his next winter collection; or
was it to set the tone for the launch of his new perfume
'Opium', that was about to conquer the world? The
motivation scarcely matters. The result was a collection
equally as strong as the Russian one – and one which
also eschewed the artefacts of contemporary China for
the exotic and romantic past. This was the ancient China
of the Imperial Court, Mongolian tribesmen and the
sumptuous richness of the Mandarin: in fact, the mythic
glories of far Cathay. The clothes were as romantic as
the vision: brocade, lamé, satin, velvet and damask
in brown, black, lacquer red and gold, trimmed with
rich furs, were used to create outfits of a dazzling
theatricality. It set the tone for future exotic ethnic
collections. The everyday and the humdrum were out,
the superlative was in. If China was the source, it was
the China of Old Shanghai, of actresses such as Anna
May Wong, Louise Brooks and Marlene Dietrich; of
opium trails and the Shanghai Express. Mysterious,
intriguing and dangerous, this China came to most
designers via film, a medium which has taken the
place of literary sources as the major stimulant for
most younger designers.

The other stimulant is sex. The women that designers
re-created in their exotic fashion exercises were always
slave girls, concubines and houris, if they weren't
princesses or contessas. This is fairytale fashion and
has to be peopled accordingly. There is barely a
designer in Paris who has not followed the road first
taken so wholeheartedly by Saint Laurent. Lacroix and
Galliano have been influenced by chinoiserie; Gaultier
has bowed to Russia. Japonisme, the craze that swept
through Europe and America at the end of the nineteenth
century, influencing painters and poets and leaving a

22

26 Christian Lacroix,
    1987–99

27 Christian Lacroix,
    1997, photo
    Perry Ogden

mark on fashion, furniture, china and fabrics, has rarely been absent from the runways. But to recreate ideas from the past so that they do not merely become a pastiche of history demands skill and knowledge.

Christian Lacroix is, like Yves Saint Laurent, the product of a cultural background which provides both. He may lack the depth that constant re-reading of Proust has given Saint Laurent, but he is *au fait* with the great literature of France – especially nineteenth-century novelists such as Flaubert, Balzac and Zola – and the cultural history of his past. He knows of Versailles and its glories but, as a man with an essentially nineteenth-century spirit, it is the flash and sparkle of the Second Empire (1852–70) that inspires him. He fully understands the bourgeois prides that grew up under Napoleon III and found their outlet in a riot of ornamentation. It is this decorative fecundity that informs his clothes. A Lacroix collection can be inspired by many things, including ethnic stimuli. Like Saint Laurent, he has looked to Persia and then beyond, towards an Africa where the savagery of the fauna is matched by the nobility of the primitive tribes and their ornate dress. Lacroix uses the patterns and colours of Africa for rich embroidery and passimenterie which translates them into modern European times and gives them his own essentially French, *haut bourgeois* quality.

Lacroix's historicism stretches wide to take in the fur trappers and Sioux Indians of North America, the heavy exoticism of Creole culture and the same ornate Russia visited by Saint Laurent. But his real ethnic influences come from nearer home. In fact, his strongest statements are the ones linked with his childhood in Arles in the South of France. The hot, spicy colours of Provence constantly reappear in Lacroix's clothes as he recreates the dress of the nomads and gypsies that he knew when he was young. But, like Saint Laurent, he gives it all a richness and sonority by using the most luxurious of fabrics – embroidered, fur-decked,

re-embroidered and heavily jewelled – in many of the same hot colours: pinks and peppery reds, fuchsias and purples, with black and gold to bring it all to life. The effect is operatic, but the wellsprings are the bullfights, especially the paseo, the toreador's triumphant march into the bullring; the farandole, the dance of Provence; the wide, empty spaces of the Camargue and the cowboys (*gardiens*) who tend its cattle and the triumphant costume of the area with its floral prints, lace bonnets, shawls and aprons. On this ethnic base, Lacroix plays endless decorative variations inspired by interests as disparate as Charles Trenet, the popular French singer of the Thirties and Forties, the circus drawings of Christian Bérard, or even the English upper-class life personified by Cecil Beaton's photographs of Lady Diana Cooper.

The third great ethnic fantast of French high fashion is Jean Paul Gaultier, possibly the most complex couturier in Paris. Unlike Saint Laurent and Lacroix, Gaultier boasts that he missed school as much as he could, cared nothing for education and never reads books: claims that are hard to believe when you analyse the cultural breadth of his work. Probably more than any other designer, Gaultier preserves the integrity of whatever culture or country he uses for his fashion direction. His references never patronize or exploit as he ranges eclectically across civilizations at every level, from the ingenuity of the street scene and the serendipity of the flea market to tribal grandeur and magnificence. He has a rare two-way skill, informed by humour that is both iconoclastic and anti-bourgeois: no one can take the refined and sophisticated down a peg quite like Gaultier. His fashion shows have the energy and drive of Offenbach's *La Vie Parisienne*, with the models informed by the insouciance of his confidence.

Gaultier's eye roams across the world more consistently than most other designers'. He has used the inspiration of ethnic dress – and attitudes

29

– constantly in his determination to sweep away preconceived ideas, destroy sexual and social prejudice and teach us that fashion can be a weapon for social good. He has given us tribal tattoos, body painting and piercing; Russian peasant costume; the ceremonial dress of marriage and mourning; the bravura of Latin costume from Cuba to Colombia; Scottish tartan; Mongolian leatherwork; the handwork of the Inuits and the camp theatricality of the gold-spangled cowboy. Gaultier admits that his clothes are 'very exhibitionist', but they are also full of the spirit of one of the great stylists of ethnic and exotic worlds, made real for current thinking. In 1998, his Winter ready-to-wear show amalgamated two cultures, ancient Greece and Japan, and did so with such skill that the result, which could have seemed like a shotgun wedding, exploited both cultures sympathetically, to produce clothes entirely of their moment. In fact, Gaultier is so brilliantly skilled at such sleight of hand that only once has he caused offence: with his elegant homage to the dress of Hasidic Jews, which he featured in 1993 in a show called 'Chic Rabbis'. Although his handling of the dress codes was both sensitive and honest, the concept offended the public and it was one of his few unsuccessful collections.

One of the great attractions of the ethnic approach is the sexuality of the 'noble savage'. Clearly, much tribal dress is more revealing than Western fashion felt able to be in the early Eighties. Coupled with a growing boldness in borrowing from the boudoir and the bordello, its adoption in the West signified a dramatic change in what would be accepted on future runways. It is hard to realize just how great a change has been

30

33

31   32

seen in the attitudes to sex assumed by designers in the last two decades. Seminudity – for men as well as women – is now an accepted norm on many fashion runways. Diaphanous materials are not just used for shows, they often go into production and are sold in the shops; leather, latex and the belts and buckles of bondage are a commonplace of fashion presentations and are, with only a degree of 'toning down', sold for everyday wear.

Fur and feathers have held a potent sexual charge for mankind for many centuries, and the fashion world is still obsessed with them. In the twentieth century, they were used to symbolize a highly sophisticated sexual approach of the kind suggested by the outfits worn by the *femmes fatales* in films from the Thirties and Forties. Feathers have a particularly ambivalent message. On the one hand, the fluffy softness of marabou or swan's-down suggests feminine compliancy and even vulnerability. Furthermore, it suggests availability. On the other hand, other types of feathers – cockerel's or peacock's tails – have a much more positive sexual quality and give the woman wearing them the appearance of being in control, of making the sexual decisions and playing the dominant role. Both aspects have had a potent appeal for designers who have used them as sexual shorthand in day and evening wear, for men and women, *au naturel* or dyed every conceivable colour. In the Nineties, Galliano, Mugler and Gaultier created multicoloured capes, trains and boleros of brightly dyed feathers which gave women an expressionist quality seen in the works of René Magritte – and, even more directly, the strangely menacing half-woman, half-bird creations found in the paintings of Max Ernst. The fact that many people are repulsed by the feel of feathers and find birds psychologically unsettling, adds to the disquieting effect that feathers have, whether used to create an entire garment, as Yves Saint Laurent frequently does,

or as a trim in the way that Tom Ford at Gucci employed them to decorate his hippie jean statement for Winter 1998–9.

The sexuality of feathers is always present, but it is often overshadowed by the more powerful message of menace – look no further than Alfred Hitchcock's 1963 film *The Birds*, which became a world blockbuster by uncovering fears found in many psyches. However, the feathered shoe – whether a marabou mule with a satin heel, a Roger Vivier stiletto covered entirely in tiny, jewel-bright feathers or a Manolo Blahnik tall boot bursting out into cockerel feathers at the top – has a sexuality that will not to be overshadowed and is totally unequivocal. In this, it is like the feathered hat that was a standard feature of the seductive female's wardrobe for centuries. This footwear means business, its complex message beckoning to fetishists of both sexes and all orientations.

In the eyes of many male designers, it is fur which confers true sexual power on a woman today. No longer mink or sable – the staples of rich women's wardrobes and a sign of pampered pleasures and indolent luxuries – the kind of fur that is now fashionable is much tougher and more aggressive. The fur of the noble big cats is more appealing and evocative than that of small animals which can be farmed. At the turn of the century, the high point of fur in fashion, queens and empresses wore mink and sable to proclaim their position and their acquiesence to a certain social attitude. At the same time, the *grandes dames* of the theatre and their close social relatives, the *grandes horizontales*, were showing the fact that they stood outside any such system by reclining on wolf, wrapping themselves in leopard, silver fox and even giraffe skin in a hothouse scenario of sexuality which is still powerful today.

Wild animals are finally protected so that creatures are not slaughtered purely for vanity and show. But the lure of the feline wild has hardly diminished at all. Women

36 Dolce & Gabbana,
    Wildness, 1997,
    photo Michel
    Comte

37 Philip Treacy,
    London Fashion
    Week, 1999–2000,
    photo Jean-
    François Carly

37

respond to the power of the big cats and designers also love wild beasts for what they represent as much as for their colours and patterns. Fake fur, especially the sort used at designer level, is now a highly sophisticated facsimile of the real thing, apeing its touch and accurately reproducing its markings and gradations. Printed fabrics, from the sheer to the solid, show the same attention to detail in copying the fur of the great cats: the tiger, the leopard and the cheetah. Stylized giraffe and zebra skins are commonplace. Less common, but frequently used, are the real skins of non-protected species – or the hides of cattle and ponies which have been treated to look like them. Wolf and fox are farmed, like mink, and are regularly featured on the major catwalks.

It isn't only the customers and designers who like fur; photographers also love it. In 1997, Dolce & Gabbana produced a book of photographs of women wearing fake fur and fur prints, taken by a number of famous photographers, including Helmut Newton, Steven Meisel and Ellen von Unwerth. Entitled *Wildness*, it was, for many, a sheer voyeur's delight, taking them, in their imagination at least, down forbidden paths. The proceeds from the sales of the book went to an international charity responsible for the preservation of the world's wildlife. At this moment, when mink, chinchilla and fox are becoming fashionable again, what most excites designers are the pelts of wild, rather than farmed, animals, even though they must make do with imitations. It is a lure that pinpoints the industry's love of the romantic and the exotic at the end of the twentieth century. Conjuring up the days when Queen Elizabeth II, Jackie Onassis and Maria Callas wore full-length wild mink is not of interest to them. It seems far too safe and bourgeois. When a designer starts toying with the idea of fur, he will more likely have leopardskin on his mind and a subliminal picture of Carole Lombard or Jean Harlow cocooned from head to toe in its spotted glamour along with memories of *Out of Africa*, *White Mischief* and the decadent pleasures of the white women on the dark continent in echoes of the novels of Somerset Maugham and Ernest Hemingway.

If fur can stimulate a designer's imagination, along with the women who wore it, there are other women who, at the end of the twentieth century, exert enormous influence on the mood of fashion, as designers turn and return to them as muse, focus and personification of all they believe is worthwhile in femininity. Artists such as Frida Kahlo have provided inspiration for many designers, but it is more common for them to turn to the model rather than the artist. John Galliano is obsessed with the paintings of Giovanni Boldini and, in particular, his portraits of the international socialite, the Marchese Casati, who, at the turn of the century, scandalized and delighted with her extreme appearance, her outrageous parties and her private menagerie of wild animals. It isn't who she is that excites Galliano's imagination, but what she stands for: the freedom and wilful independence; the untamed determination to live exactly as she wishes, untrammelled by convention. It is an essentially unreal romanticization of the past. The Marchese lived as she did because of her vast wealth. When she lost it, she ceased to be of interest. Designers also find inspiration in the turn-of-the-century female portraits by John Singer Sargent, Augustus John and Kees van Dongen. Their sitters were often Americans who had married British or European aristocrats, whose life stories are frequently as arresting as their portraits, and are not uncommonly characterized by great unhappiness, despite the pomp of their surroundings. Designers are sentimental and, finding it hard to resist this 'bird in a gilded cage' scenario, regularly return to figures such as Consuelo, Duchess of Marlborough, for a little creative prompting.

They often turn to literary figures for a different sort of stimulus. These muses are predominantly Anglo-Saxon and frequently lived their lives with scant interest in fashion, if they showed any at all. Here the designer's imagination is set off by the most powerful and characteristic of all fashion lives: the personal style that makes a woman unique. It can be found in fashionable women, great beauties, who were at the centre of high society, such as Lady Diana Cooper, but it is more likely to be someone like Vita Sackville-West who dèfied society, Virginia Woolf (a recurring influence on fashion through the heroines of her novels) or even Edith Sitwell in her full-blown eccentricity. If they lack glamour and uniqueness in themselves, they can be used as a

personification of the world they lived in and chronicled, along with other writers such as Colette, Jean Rhys and Isak Dinesen, all of whom closely observed the social scene and the fashionable life. They work their magic by bringing to life their own period from modern history – the *fin de siècle*, the Edwardian heyday, Hollywood in the Thirties, even the great days of couture in the Fifties. After that, the magic tends to fade for the romantic couturier, although Maria Callas was recently the inspiration for an Alexander McQueen collection at Givenchy, and Marlene Dietrich perennially pops up in one manifestation or other. For Lacroix, it is the nineteenth century and its opera that excites: Puccini's *Manon Lescaut* and *La Bohème*, or Bizet's *Carmen*; for Lagerfeld there will be subtle, half-cloaked references to Flaubert's *Madame Bovary* and Dumas's *La Dame aux camélias*; for Westwood it can be any woman from Elizabeth I to Thackeray's Becky Sharp from *Vanity Fair*.

It is important to remember that many designers turn their backs on cultural stimuli that they consider to be old-fashioned, elitist and completely empty of meaning for our computer-led civilization. In the long term, they are almost certainly correct. History and past cultures have increasingly less meaning with each new generation. These designers are more inclined to be stimulated by Damien Hirst than Watteau; will find more meaning in a Patti Smith song than in a Gregorian chant. Their preferred artistic medium is photography – the gritty reportage images of Henri Cartier-Bresson or Brassaï. For them the seminal image of the twentieth century is not a costume by Bakst, a sketch by Cocteau, Picasso's *Les Demoiselles d'Avignon* or Warhol's Campbell's soup cans. It is more likely to be a photograph by someone considerably less well known to the general public. Highest contender is probably August Sander's 1914 picture of three German farm workers, photographed on

their way to a dance. It is the spirit of this picture – along with thousands more photographs of ordinary men and women – which today informs much of the thinking of ready-to-wear designers. It can be seen in the suits, for women as well as men, designed by Dirk Bikkembergs, Jil Sander, Ann Demeulemeester and Dolce & Gabbana – and much more that appears on their runways, as old-style cultures are rejected as too elitist for current moods, and the mundane, workmanlike and frequently moving images of ordinary and often underprivileged citizens take their place.

The list goes on, but traditional artistic sources still predominate and the man who most fully understands the arts and the creative figures of the past – who has the knowledge to view them in depth and with breadth – is Yves Saint Laurent. From Goya and Velázquez to Picasso and Braque, Cocteau and Apollinaire, he brings an informed mind to his recreations of the work of the great artists of the past, and manages to preserve their essence while restating it in his own medium. He summed up what many would see as his strength, and others as his dilemma, when he said, in 1977, that his creative tension arises from the fact that he is 'familiar with one world, yet aware of the presence of the other'.

As the new century begins, the romanticism which has so often driven Yves Saint Laurent forward is the force behind much of the most creative work being produced in fashion. The centre of this creativity is Paris, with London following close behind, and Milan and New York taking different, more immediate approaches to fashion. To the untrained eye, Milan and New York seem to be the modern fashion capitals, taking into account the needs and events of our time, while much of London and Paris is perceived as looking backwards, recreating past glories and spending huge budgets on their exercises in historic or ethnic fantasy, which, many feel, have so little application to modern dress needs that they are nothing more than the

38

39

42

42 Alexander
McQueen for
Givenchy *haute
couture*, 1999,
(left to right)
The Maid, The
Ribbon Maker,
The Equestrian,
The Tailor, The
School Mistress

self-indulgence of designers whose firms are kept afloat by sales of things other than elaborate clothes.

It is a view that is likely to be proved wrong because romanticism is in many ways at the root of what we require from modern fashion. Certainly it is what inspires the highly creative couture designers in Paris – men like Gaultier, Galliano and McQueen. All three are turning back to learn from the refinement and perfection of the grand couturiers of the past in order to produce svelte and elegant fashions which, despite many of the decorative additions which cover them, are essentially statements about modern dress – both wearable and adaptable. For his Givenchy *haute couture* Summer 1999 show, Alexander McQueen took as his inspiration the traditional French village and the people who could be found in it, dressing them in his modern version of their eighteenth-century clothing. In its sophisticated melding of the historic and the contemporary, it seemed a portent of what fashion would do in the future: that is, not be afraid of the decorative urge, but know how to use it for essentially modern ends. It seems sound to let McQueen's eighteenth-century romantic gowns, worn with starkly modern leather pants, point to the future of fashion in the early years of the twenty-first century.

The fact is that publicity of the sort that sells perfumes and other licensed products in vast numbers around the world is presently fixated on the richness of the French design approach at its highest decorative level. Gaultier, Galliano and McQueen feed the current need for extravagance and richness, controlled by stylish and remarkably sophisticated design approaches. They are the modern equivalent of the great nineteenth-century opera composers: Puccini, Verdi, Donizetti and Rossini. Their appeal is emotional, their effect frequently sublime. If it were possible to create the tune of a dress, the whole world would be whistling Gaultier, Galliano and McQueen.

FANTASY AND ROLE PLAY

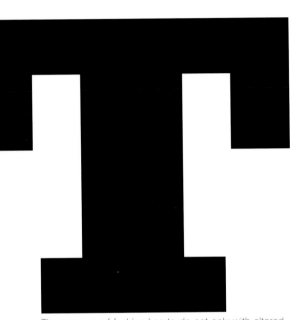

The essence of fashion has to do not only with altered but also with heightened states. The dream of total transformation from ugly duckling to swan, or inadequate to overachiever, has us all buying in, to a degree, every time we pick up a magazine or turn to the style pages of a newspaper. We want to know about the available merchandise and we also need to see what it can do to transform our lives. That is why pictures are so much more important than words in the fashion world. Whereas words can describe a fashion, pictures can demonstrate how it will look – not on our backs, but in its most idealized form. Seeing clothes on an impeccably groomed or perfectly toned young body – and fashion models photographed for magazines are always young – far from inhibiting us, actually inflates our self-hype so that we believe that we could look, if not quite so good, certainly not too bad, in the outfit on the page.

We imagine ourselves in a heightened state of perfection which not only makes us feel superior to our old selves – before the dream began – but also makes us *seem* superior to our fellows. We pay money for new clothing because we believe that it will make us different – and better. That is why fashion is so powerful. Like ancient tribes and their belief in witchcraft, or the alchemists and their experiments, we believe because we wish to believe. At the beginning of the period covered by this book, *haute couture* was a woman's outlet for fantasy. If she were one of the fraction of women in the world who bought couture, even on an occasional basis, her purchases fulfilled a role almost entirely to do with fantasy. If she were one of the vast number of women with no hope of ever wearing a couture garment, looking at couture in the media was

an entirely fantasy experience. And yet it was still considered an important, exciting and rewarding thing to follow the latest developments in the great couture houses as reported in magazines and newspapers, not only because couture was the basis for all fashion development in the high street, but also because women enjoyed the fantasy world they opened to them.

Fantasy and role play have always been a part of high fashion. We have only to go back to Marie Antoinette at Versailles to see it in action. Not only did the queen and her entourage enjoy dressing up and pretending to be milkmaids at Le Petit Trianon, the whole court dressed with a totally theatrical extravagance. It wasn't confined to having one's hair greased and pomaded so that it would stand up like a skyscraper, or to have fantastic head decorations and hats made into any shape under the sun. It was about being so bored that Rose Bertin, dressmaker to the queen and the patrician ladies of the court, could start a fashion in the morning, have everyone frantic to copy it during the day, and kill it with another in the evening – knowing that her edicts, no matter how bizarre, would be followed by people desperate to create a fantasy life for themselves through their clothes.

It can be said that the fantasy side of fashion has never gone away. How else can the extremes of Victorian fashion, from crinoline to bustle, be explained? What other way is there to explain the egrets and swan's-down of all that hugely overscaled Edwardian millinery? Why else did women wear Dior's heavy and cumbersome evening dresses, with trains dragging the ground? It was all to do with fantasies of grandeur, sophistication and role play, just as much of today's fashion is.

The great fantasts of the twentieth century were the young. Barely able to claim a fashion which they could truly call their own until half of the century was over, they made up for lost time by displaying their individuality – and, simultaneously, their membership of a group, clan or clique – by dressing not only in ways which excluded their elders, but also to extremes which they expected would annoy, and even alienate, them. In the Forties, bobbysoxers in America broke all the rules of taste that they dared – rather mildly, in fact, as is to be expected of a small-town, Middle-American, middle-class revolt. It was all considered harmless fun, and parents smiled on indulgently, for the most part, unaware that they were witnessing the first awakening of a youth culture that would eventually destroy much of what they held dear. Considerably more political and menacing was the zoot suit phenomenon. In 1943 in Los Angeles and Chicago protests by young black and Hispanic Americans led to pitched battles with the authorities. It was a genuine political protest, but even so, the long draped jackets, baggy trousers gathered at the bottom, heavy gold watch chains and bootlace ties were a fancy dress for a particular kind of role play. The semiotics of the uniform were, in fact, a pastiche of the standard dress of North American authority, exaggerated to a risible degree. It is almost certain that authority divined that it was being guyed in a way that was not the harmless fun it might have seemed – and quelled it. The excuse given was that to fail to conform in a time of crisis was not only dangerous for the war effort, but also unpatriotic – a tautology for young people who saw conformity and patriotism as a threat to the very individuality they were dressing to preserve.

The movement appeared in France as the Zazous, who were similarly hounded by authority, in the form of the German occupying forces. From there, it travelled to Britain, where it quickly moved from the periphery of 'wide boy' or 'spiv' fashion towards a much less marginalized, if not entirely mainstream, position as the basis for the teddy boy look – arguably the first shot fired in the fight for sartorial leadership between the established fashion élite and the revolutionary outsider. The power of sex was a weapon that had never been used so blatantly as it would be by the young, determined to control their lives and destinies and to prove their new freedom through exclusive dress codes.

Youth culture – via Zazous and teddy boys – was born dissident and it grew, aggressive and confrontational, by actively fighting the rules of society. Paradoxically, street style was initially characterized by much hiding in fantasy and role play, but it was also to become a strong element in salon fashion. The Great Divide in twentieth-century fashion between street and salon has nothing to do with the New Look or the demise (or otherwise) of couture. It has a lot to do with the shift of fashion power, away from Paris, towards London and New York. But it has *everything* to do with pop music. Receiving inspiration and credibility from it, its performers and the attitudes it created, fashion has been influenced by, and developed alongside, every nuance and change in the music business – including, at times when music has become static and unimaginative, taking over from it as the driving cultural force of youth. Both have been used as forms of escapism, something to give meaning and purpose to life. Both have frequently and deliberately taken advantage of uncritical and immature young attitudes in order to make a 'quick buck'. Both accept no yardsticks for excellence except those imposed within their own ranks. Both trade on the desperate need of the young to be insiders. And both have been more vibrant, revolutionary and challenging than virtually all other art forms – most of which have tamely followed their trailblazing lead. And it is no accident that, when the hegemony of Paris first weakened in the Sixties and Seventies, the shift of power followed pop music to the United Kingdom and the United States, where the new popular cultures grew from, and around, the dynamic created by musicians as different as the Beatles and Bob Dylan – who were fashion icons as well as musicians, sanctifying dress approaches totally independent of the diktats of designers.

Highly fashionable dress, stretching across centuries and cultures, can be seen as one long nursery scream for attention, always mouthing 'look at me'. The youth need for fantasy in its fashion has been no different in intent. It also screams for attention, but not in the directly narcissistic way of the past. It doesn't merely say 'look at me', it adds the sociopolitical rider, 'see what I stand for'. Fantasy fashion in such statements is always a form of protest. Often, its protest is banal or easily dismissed for its simplistic attitudes, but it is also sometimes more profound in the comments it makes about society and its accepted values. Either way, its power as utterance comes from the fact that mainstream high fashion speaks to a comparatively limited audience – the majority of people in the world still manage, at the end of a century even more fashion-dominated than the eighteenth, to solve their dress problems more from custom than designer input – while fantasy fashion and its youth corollary, popular music, affects millions. Pop music is the new ideology, the new orthodoxy which makes youth the most homogenous group in the world – and in the *history* of the world. A greater unifier than religious or political beliefs, the garments it clothes itself in are almost equally as powerful. And the fantasy fashion increasingly favoured by the young in the last thirty years makes a comment on society as much as it does on youth per se.

It is pre-eminently as social comment that hippie dress – one of the most enduring of fantasy fashions – has been interpreted. Rightly so. It grew from the disaffection with society that characterized the Beatnik movement. Like it, the hippies were not only anti-Establishment, they were in opposition to the capitalism that was the base and constant preoccupation of Western society. Beatniks, however, showed their indifference to the norms of society by adopting black – the colour of Existentialism – as the basis of their dress code, whereas hippies took a much less rigid approach. Their dress attitudes were neither organized nor controlled by strict ideologies or intellectualities. The only rigid thing which bound them together was their belief that hand-crafted items were always superior to those which were machine-made. Like William Morris, they opposed the sterility of standardization. Like the Luddites, they wished to reinstate the uniqueness of handmade objects.

In fact, most were so steeped in dogma that they were able to extol the virtues even of things crudely and badly done, provided they could be linked with craft skills and unsophisticated thinking. Attracted to Eastern philosophies and artistic tenets they couldn't always understand, they were convinced that such approaches were valid mainly because of their total dissimilarity to Western attitudes. But if the hippie ad hoc approach to many aspects of life irritated, the movement's gypsy dress sense, bringing together brightly coloured and often disparate elements to make statements far more interesting and uniquely individual than the blanket black of the Beat Generation, was life-enhancing even for those with little time for the vague beliefs underpinning them. It is easy to dismiss hippies as spoilt products of the system they professed to despise, bolstered by the very wealth and security which made them turn away from the West: self-regarding, indulgent and partial in their critical stance. There is an element of truth in these allegations, but the hippies and their causes, unrealistic as they seemed at the time, were a springboard to the future, not just for them but for us all.

Their eclectic approach to philosophies, religion and dress codes was often foolish, but it is historically

important because it was a manifestation of the values which mattered for people who were part of the first generation raised on television. Their attitudes marked a seminal moment. No longer able to be relied upon to 'grow up' and conform (in society's mind, one and the same thing), they presaged the instability and unreliability that would characterize Western society as it turned into a nonconformist, disaffected mélange, increasingly hostile to rules and impositions. Brought up on daytime television shows such as *Captain Kangaroo* and *Davy Crockett*, or *I Love Lucy* and *Gunsmoke*, the hippies were used to – and demanded – variety to a degree never known before. The ragbag, cherry-picking cultural approach encouraged by television, where boredom could be alleviated at the press of a button, had an enormous cultural effect on people who in many ways were obtaining their education from the TV screen and nowhere more obviously than in attitudes to dress. Just as young people brought up on Fifties' television required – and received – a hundred different stimuli in a day's viewing, so they created fashion with the same instant and simultaneous effects. The hippie layers and additions, the mixture of colours and patterns, were the sartorial equivalent to channel-hopping, as kaleidoscopic as a rapidly changing television screen.

At the time, the colours and patterns, at their most dazzling in the ubiquitous pop posters found in every student's room, were called psychedelic, after the hallucinatory effects of the popular drug LSD. In hippie dress they were less socket-searing, but colour was an important element of the look – as was non-colour. For every hippie who mixed hot pink, orange and purple, there were at least four more who preferred to use neutrals such as cream, beige and khaki to create a look which to some seemed drab, but to others was subtle and assumed to be ecologically sound: hippies were as keen to preserve nature as to encourage ethnic cultures.

At the base of much hippie thought was a vague pantheism which assumed, in a simplistic equation worthy of George Orwell's *Animal Farm* pigs, that all things wrought by nature and those working closely with it were good, while all wrought by man in industrial nations were bad. It was essentially an antimaterialistic movement, opposed to every tenet upon which generations of Western civilization had been built. Possessions were seen as corrupting elements; the wish to work was a proof of capitalist indoctrination; spirituality was all – but not when found in organized Western religions. For hippies, hope for the future came from turning East.

Hippies were a restless clan, doomed to be perpetually moving, always looking for paradise and always disappointed. Their dependence on drugs and sex, and their total rejection of the norms of society, made them seem dangerous to many people, especially the traditional guardians of public morality and order but, in fact, the hippies were the most peaceful and least threatening of all youth movements. They fought no battles. Ill-focused and fuzzy, their most visible characteristic, and the one which most irritated their elders, was their hair. Long and luxurious for both sexes, it was canonized by the musical *Hair*, a smash hit around the world. Like the hippies themselves, it was cool and, despite the huffing and puffing from authority, posed no real problems for society. The spiritual, gently

8   Janis Joplin,
    1971, photo
    Terry O'Neill

9   Yves Saint Laurent
    and Raquel
    Welch, late 1960s,
    photo Terry O'Neill

10 Tuffin & Foale,
    late 1960s

11 (Overleaf)
    Punks in London,
    1982–4, photos
    Derek Ridgers

'spaced-out' quality of the hippie ethos could only be clothed in dress clearly not mass-produced or industrialized. A large part of the appeal of garments dyed and made by hand in India or Kashmir was the imperfections which made everyone slightly different and thereby unique. The slickness of big corporation clothing, quality controlled so that every deviation was rejected, had none of the romantic associations of an afghan sheepskin coat, dyed by soaking the pelts in urine, nor the practical toughness of peasant dress: you could sleep in your coat without it, or you, being any the worse for it next morning, something which could not be said of a coat bought in a chain store from a rack of its identical fellows, carefully graded according to size.

To the music of Janis Joplin, Bob Dylan and Joan Baez, the hippies drifted up and down California, moved across subcontinents, then returned to Woodstock and the Isle of White in their rough Indian linen shirts, tie-dyed or hand-decorated 'granddad' undershirts, paisley skirts, flared trousers, crushed velvet, headbands, floppy straw hats, patched jeans and patchwork vests, their feet bare or in sandals. Locked in their own little narcissistic microcosm symbolized by their 'Peace' medallions, they were playing a part, half nursery game, half amateur theatricals – and wholly fantasized. It was fancy dress posing as the least aggressive or effective protest in a century of real protests. The rest of the world looked on, bemused, while Establishment fashion in the shape of Zandra Rhodes, Ossie Clark and Yves Saint Laurent produced 'civilized', and commercial, hippie variations of their own. Saint Laurent created the rich hippie look with gypsy skirts and peasant blouses made from the most expensive of fabrics, which had as its only link with its namesake the fact that much of it was handmade. Clark and Rhodes were nearer to being

salon hippies, sharing many attitudes and beliefs – as well as inspirations – with the real thing on the dusty roads to Xanadu.

Beautiful as the clothes created by the salon hippies were, they missed the point. The young wanted fashion to fit the temporary and insubstantial lives they led. No overall head-to-toe designer looks could work for them. In fact, the hippies were much more seminal to modern fashion than they have been given credit for. Their love of the imperfect, the flawed, the oblique and even slightly obtuse in fashion was the visible sign of a completely new attitude to come, where the standardized rules of taste no longer applied and some of the most exciting fashion developments were often the result of deliberate 'bad taste' approaches. The idea that an irregular and eclectic approach to fashion – a million miles from the regimentation of the Chanel suit – was perfectly valid survived because it was part of the young psyche where to be too precise was to be 'heavy' and being cool meant – literally, in much hippie fashion – letting it all hang out. In a direct line from the hippies, it was the thinking which led to the misaligned creations of the Japanese in the early Eighties and the asymmetric, cut-and-slashed approach of Vivienne Westwood and John Galliano. Their 'ragbag' approach was first seen in the hippies who, on their travels, realized that there were other, equally valid, ways of dressing, away from the Western pattern and that the ad hoc combinations of the ethnic poor could produce clothing not only of great beauty but also of great subtlety. The hippies objected to the fact that most people in the West throw away their clothes just when they are becoming interesting and beginning to develop their own personality.

And so did the punks, who so clearly see worn and tattered clothes as part of their antisocial credibility that

12 New Romantics in
    Chelsea, London,
    1981, photo
    Derek Ridgers

13 Bryan Ferry,
    *c.*1975, photo
    Terry O'Neill

they distress and destroy them as much as possible. Although their dress codes seem the antithesis of those of the hippies, most punk dress was as much a part of fantasy and role play as anything worn by the flower people. Deliberately hard and even frightening, punk clothing revealed a compulsion to shock and alienate that can be read as showing how closely they needed to interact with society as part of their being. In this they were unlike the hippies, who genuinely found society and its consumer preoccupations so alien that they needed no interaction with it at all. However, punk was essentially an urban movement. Its scratchy, torn and snarling anarchy needed city streets to bring out its true meaning – which was a cry for help, a need to be noticed and a desperate lunging at a society which had turned its back on that generation. Born angry, it was a movement that became desperate and ended defeated.

Punks were actors who came to believe their lines. Certainly, their attitudes were a howl of rage against the world. Initially, in a classic tit-for-tat scenario, they rejected society – or much that was in it – for rejecting them. But eventually they came to need what they hated and finally sold themselves to it – often literally. Malcolm McLaren annexed punk's incoherent rage and turned it into a commercial movement and, saddest of all, punks themselves were reduced to asking for payment from tourists with expensive cameras wishing to photograph them on the streets of London. There can be no more ignominious end to a revolutionary movement. For many, the lasting image of the end of punkdom – stranded incongruously in the affluent Eighties – was a sad one. Like frost-nipped geraniums at the end of summer, they sagged and wilted, lacking the animation, fire or purpose of their predecessors, not only having nothing to do but, worse, apparently having nothing they wanted to do.

Boredom first became the official religion of the young in the Seventies. After periods of affluence which it was assumed would continue unchecked, the Western world hit a slump. The unskilled, untrained and uneducated were most severely hit as the jobless totals in the advanced countries rose to heights unimaginable since the Great Depression. School leavers – even college graduates – felt that they had come too late to jump on the bandwagon of success and security. With no present prospects, only uncertain futures, they clung together, squatting in empty houses and learning to survive with all the agility and speed of sewer rats. And they made their own world. In defiance of the squalor of their surroundings and the hostility of society, they escaped sordid reality by making their lives into a party. Clubbing became both the *raison d'être* and the escape. It also became the driving force behind what was to be

a powerful and important fashion approach which, in its ecleticism and colour, carried on from where the hippies left off.

New Romanticism may have been born of despair and rejection but, like Ruggiero Leoncavallo's *Pagliacci*, it was a case of 'on with the motley' for London's art school students, wannabe designers and pop star hopefuls. This marvellous mix of disparate talents made an exciting cultural brew which served as the underbelly – and underpinning – of a creativity in the late Seventies and early Eighties, the driving force of which was British, although attracting followers around the world. The disenchanted and disenfranchised dressed up with a dedication and flair not seen in centuries. As fashion, it was entirely alternative – although it would eventually influence mainstream design – but culturally it represented the power that visual and musical styles could wield when brought together.

The tone was set by the music – before the Eighties, undoubtedly the more powerful of the two. In fact, the seminal moment came much earlier, in 1967, with the release of the *Sgt. Pepper's Lonely Hearts Club Band* album, described by George Melly in *Revolt into Style: The Pop Arts* (1989) as 'the Beatles' near flawless *chef d'oeuvre* … proof that pop can be both art and pop, immediate and timeless'. The most complex, original and radical pop/rock album ever released (although, in the minds of many, given a tight run for its title by the group's *Revolver* album), it affected fashion more than anything produced by couturiers – with the exception of the equally complex, original and radical creations of Yves Saint Laurent – giving young people confidence about how they thought of themselves, who they were and where their place was in society. None of the other musical moments which seem more obviously linked with dress – Bryan Ferry and Roxy Music, for example – had the same fundamental long-term effect. It is not surprising when we remember that Roxy Music was an effete and derivative sound with a world-weary quality which appealed only to a certain type of sophistication, whereas the vitality, vigour and sheer *joie de vivre* of the Beatles had a world following.

This is not to say that Roxy Music or the Glam Rock movement were insignificant. In fashion, their influence was considerable because the dress of the concert platform, decadent, overdecorative and theatrical as much of it was, was the first to cross over the footlights and be worn by the audience. New Romantic clubbers frequently upstaged the groups they followed in the extravagance of their dress, although none was as superb as Antony Price's high-camp costumes – a glitter of lamé, a frolic of feathers, a dazzle of sequins – which

13

14 Boy George,
1982, photo
Derek Ridgers

15 (Left to right)
Rod Stewart,
Roger Daltrey,
David Bowie,
Elton John,
Marc Bolan;
photos Dagmar

16 Elton John, photo
Terry O'Neill

14

opened the door for cross-dressing, androgyny and a
great deal of dressing-up fun for young clubbers for
years to come.

Cyndi Lauper, Adam Ant and Boy George followed
David Bowie, Marc Bolan and Gary Glitter as they took
theatrical dress from the Seventies to the Eighties – and
were, in turn, followed by the clubbers who adapted
styles from thrift shops or specialists like Lawrence
Corner in London – still the best place to buy military
paraphernalia and medical dress – or made their own
fashions from any bits and pieces they could find (or
afford) on market stalls.

This was a subversive and subterranean movement
which, as far as possible, kept away from commercial
and mainstream influences. As such, it pinpoints the
developments in youth culture since the Sixties. Then,
the young needed a focal point, a Mecca to attract
them. They found it in Carnaby Street and the King's
Road. They also wanted a ready-made, instant fashion
and they found it in specialist shops such as Biba. The
approaches of the late Seventies and early Eighties were
much more eclectic, ad hoc and self-help, reflecting the
alienation from the commercial world which many young
people – especially those in art schools – felt and
wished to show by their dress. They had no time for
the glamorized punk of Zandra Rhodes. She called her
borrowings 'conceptual chic'; others preferred the word
'cheek', as they felt she had trespassed on sacred
ground in order to make money from a movement which
despised everything it saw high fashion as representing.
They understood much more the comment of Vivienne
Westwood in an interview with *Soho News* in 1981
when she claimed, 'All of my sources, the pirates and
the Indians, are like comic book characters that appeal
to the emotions.' But, above all, they looked to
themselves in order to source their own appearance
and personality.

15

18

In New York, things were more commercial. Stephen Sprouse was designing for Deborah Harry of Blondie, whose clothes were copied by her fans – clothes which, as *The New York Times* pointed out, were the first 'in years to tap into the currents of popular culture and to translate the drive of rock music and MTV videos into retail form'. Betsey Johnson, jumping on the rock and roll bandwagon in much the way that Vivienne Westwood had with punk, pointed out, 'I think designing for rock people is costume designing' and, although she was thinking of groups, it was a remark equally applicable to groupies. Their clothes were costume – and gloriously, life-enhancingly eclectic in the way they pillaged periods and movements in order to create looks uniquely untrammelled by questions of taste or authenticity.

The New Romantics were an élite and inward-looking clique who magnified the importance of appearance to almost fetishistic levels. Certainly, interest in fashion – and self – had rarely been so intense, even in the hothouse atmosphere of Versailles. The early Eighties' London clubs had a narrow clientele when compared, for example, to New York discos and clubs in the late Seventies, which were the playground for off-duty accountants and Wall Street junior executives as much as media tyros, resting actors and hairdressers. If New York's best clubs tended to be basically gay while allowing straight people to join the party, London venues were much more exclusively androgynous – if the clubbers weren't sexually ambivalent, they found it fun to pretend they were. New York clubs were essentially bourgeois, appealing to the 'bridge and tunnel' crowds from New Jersey and Brooklyn as much as to Manhattanites. They also admitted a range of age groups unthinkable in London where youth and the right squat address were *de rigueur*.

Because the London scene was so concentrated, it was so much more powerful. Driven by art schools – especially St Martin's – it was dedicated to sartorial excess, with male peacockry in the lead. Its elements were heavy make-up for both sexes, and platform shoes everywhere. As the Eighties progressed a Glam–Retro look evolved, based on the dress of Seventies' Glam Rock. Centred on Taboo, the club hosted by Leigh

Bowery, with a policy which allowed absolutely everything, where nothing was actually taboo, it was famed for the kitsch outrage of the clubbers. Back came sequins, skin-tight spandex, costume jewellery, fake fur, bell-bottoms, lurex and cheap, slippery, synthetic materials in the gaudiest of colours. The object was no longer sexual outrage. In a sense, sexual battles having been fought and won, sex was not a major issue, although it was obviously still a powerful force. The real issue, for young people alienated by the growing greed and money fixations of 'straight' society, was to express disgust at the standards of the middle-aged middle-classes by elevating bad taste almost to the level of fetish. No dress combinations could be too outrageous, too vulgar or too crude in this visual battle. Boy George and Leigh Bowery were joined by Annie Lennox in cross-dressing semantic games which had a huge influence on the young as nightclubbing became the 'coolest' of all pleasures, and dressing the part was the single most important preliminary to a visual, emotional, musical and drug-fuelled cocktail which became an obsession.

Nightclub mania really got underway in 1978 with the DJ Steve Strange's club, Billy's, which later became Blitz. At the same time, warehouse parties were as much fashion presentations as musical occasions as dance, drugs and dress became the serious preoccupations of the urban young. And there it could have ended, an endogamous tribal meeting with no application beyond its own narrowly prescribed barriers, had it not been that most of the movers and shakers of the club scene weren't just art school students, graduates or dropouts but predominantly fashion students, many of whom went on to hold important posts in the industry and some of whom, such as John Galliano and the milliner Stephen Jones, were to play influential and lasting roles in fashion on a world scale.

The fantasy fashion of the Eighties' club scene was not only important in bringing to the fore clothes that would become standard items of dress – such as the MA-1 flight jacket which, along with Doc Martens and black Levi's, became part of the Buffalo look styled by Ray Petri for *i-D* and *The Face* – it was also significant for the effect it had on London designers, who jumped at

19

20 Body Map, 1984,
photo Albert
Watson

21 Katharine
Hamnett, 1990

22 John Galliano,
'The Ludic Game',
1985–6

23 Vivienne
Westwood,
'Pirates'
collection, 1981,
photo Alex
Chatelain

the no-rules, no-taste ethos it created. Suddenly,
it seemed possible for mainstream fashion to follow
club style and take advantage of the fact that virtually
nothing a designer cared to do was taboo. Body Map,
Richmond-Cornejo, Katharine Hamnett and Pam Hogg
were crucial figures, but the designer who wielded the
greatest influence was Vivienne Westwood. Whereas
the other designers in London were playing with sexual
stereotypes, rubber and fetish themes, she had explored
all those areas in the Seventies.

Her Eighties' preoccupations were different. With
antennae more finely tuned than any other designers' to
'the next big thing', Westwood was uncannily prescient
in anticipating what the young – but not the fashion
industry – would move to next. In 1981, her 'Pirates'
collection was entirely in tune with New Romanticism,
and five years later, her mini-crinis caused considerable
excitement. Most of her collections during the Eighties
relied heavily on fantasy, few of her runway successes
seemed able to be translated into clothing for everyday
life and yet, along with Jean Paul Gaultier – who admits
to the great influence London art school and club
fashion has had on his work – she spawned more ideas
than any other designers; ideas which even now are still
influencing her peers.

But perhaps the most romantic of all the believers in
fantasy fashion who appeared in the Eighties was John
Galliano. Deeply involved with the London club scene
and the 'lords of misrule', such as Strange and Bowery,
who drove it forward; excited by the possibilities
revealed in the iconoclastic approaches of Westwood
and Gaultier, he began working with the stylist Amanda
Grieve almost immediately on leaving college. The first
fashion show that he and Grieve conceived was called
'The Ludic Game' which, the designer explained, was
about 'celtic and runic symbols, while the clothes were
meant to be worn upside down and inside out, by men
or women'.

Right from the beginning, Galliano took fantasy further
than anyone had previously dared. Whereas Westwood
and Gaultier had themed their runway shows so that
they told a stylistic story, usually heavily reliant on fancy
dress and fantasy inspirations such as Good Queen
Bess or Barbarella, Galliano was the first designer to
make the story so fundamentally integral to the fashion
statement that, to a unique degree, the clothes were
used to bolster the tale, rather than the tale being used
to illuminate the clothes. Since moving to Paris in 1990,
the story-telling side of Galliano's approach has become
increasingly dominant. Invitations to his shows set the
tone immediately: a ballet slipper; a heavy, rusted key;
a zebra skin handbag containing pills and used lipsticks;

24 Antonio Berardi,
1998–9

25 Owen Gaster,
cockney funfair
set, 1998–9

26 (Overleaf)
John Galliano
for Dior *haute
couture*,
1997, photo
Terry Richardson

billets-doux and faded, pressed roses; even an old flyer for a boxing match.

From the moment of receiving such invitations, the audience is beckoned into an enchanted world where historic periods – including those of the recent past, such as Fifties' America – are lovingly recreated in sets, surroundings and clothes. These elements are used not only to impose a mood but also to tell the story. And there is, literally, a story which Galliano tells, initially to his collaborators and workforce so that they understand the attitudes that their creations are exemplifying. The story's heroine is usually fleeing from some dark influence towards freedom: a flight which involves many adventures and changes of clothes before it is complete. So totally is Galliano immersed in the fantasy world he builds for himself that he can truly be called the Hans Christian Andersen of modern fashion.

Like a benign Pied Piper, he has such a complete and all-encompassing vision of how fashion should be presented that other designers follow as much as they dare – or are able to afford. Alexander McQueen themes his fashion shows in the same concentrated way but, unlike Galliano, whose purpose is entirely to create a fantasy of beauty and grace, he takes a hard-edged political stance which many people have found offensive. His 'Highland Rape' collection was generally condemned as decadent and degenerate in what it was saying about women and their traditional role as victims of violence. The styling, savage and uncompromising, was considered so powerful that it entirely overwhelmed the clothes, but it was as much about the designer's fantasies as anything produced by Galliano. Other young designers have followed the Galliano/McQueen lead in their own ways. Antonio Berardi creates a set based on downtown New York, and scatters outfits across his shows which are pure sexual fantasy; Owen Gaster does the same with, as background, a full-blown traditional cockney funfair. The element of dressing up – or, more honestly, decking out – a show in the trappings of fantasies with which few women identify and by which few clothes are illuminated or enhanced is the most interesting development in fashion in the last five years. It links some of the best contemporary designers with the hippie and romantic past, while also making it seem to those outside the hothouse inner circle of high fashion that designers are playing self-indulgent games in their own spun-sugar peppermint palaces, far removed from the realities of dress which concern most women.

There is also criticism from within. The work of many London-trained designers – and the fantasy fashion movement is almost entirely centred on London – is

disquieting to many in the fashion world. They detect a misogynist quality in the presentations, and even in the garments. In fact, such accusations – frequently levelled at McQueen, in particular – are an interesting reflection of the pluralism which affects late-Nineties' fashion thinking. Mainstream, commercial big business fashion is still fixated on clothes which make women look attractive to the majority of people. This is as it should be, but most of the creative possibilities of wearable commercial clothing were exhausted a long time ago. Current commercial fashion is essentially a recycling industry. The Young Turks of London's fashion schools demand more – as, indeed, do many young women who share their cultural standards. It is rare that they feel exploited or demeaned by clothes which seem to others to be designed expressly to make them appear ugly, awkward and vulgar. They buy magazines such as London's *Dazed and Confused*, *Numero* in Paris, New York's *Paper* and *Surface*, which is produced in San Francisco but, like all magazines today, sold internationally, because they like the way their editorial content keeps up with the wilder shores of designer thinking – something impossible with more mainstream titles which need to represent the traditional elements in fashion, who may well have the huge advertising budgets without which most magazines cannot survive, but are usually well behind what is happening at the cutting edge.

And what is happening at the cutting edge of fashion as the twenty-first century begins is something new and exciting. The fashion show has not merely become an end in itself. With less and less commercial application to dress, it has begun to assume the status of an artistic event, an amalgam of theatre and art, which stands independent of everything else. We have all accepted its divorce from the clothes we will eventually buy; we now realize that its extravagances and grotesqueries are something much more central to twenty-first century fashion than the attention-grabbing, publicity-seeking exercises they were often previously considered. Certainly, fashion shows are making a statement – sometimes in the rawest and crudest of terms, sometimes in the most ethereal and romantic – but it is rarely a statement limited solely to fashion.

The runways of many currently influential young designers in London tell us much more than what they feel about fashion. They are used as an art gallery is used, to show us things which alter our perceptions of self, taste, sexuality and morals. In fact, many fashion shows have more in common creatively with current art movements than they do with glamorous high-fashion design. Clearly, in his keenness to shake us out of our

25

28

27

fashion complacency, Alexander McQueen is closer to the thinking of the artists Jake and Dinos Chapman than he is to a traditional couturier such as Valentino. There are greater similarities of approach between Hussein Chalayan and Mona Hatoum than between the designer and a member of the old guard, such as Karl Lagerfeld. As is perhaps to be expected, the radical realignments which unite all the arts are almost the province of the young and questioning, rather than the old and established.

As the runway shows of young designers have less to do with commercial lines, they increasingly assume the status of a vernissage because what they are predicating is more a form of art than fashion. The item on the catwalk is often to be seen as a one-off work of art, especially at couture level, never to be made a second time. In fact, it is possible to argue that much that is shown on the runways is viewed as the pure art of fashion – meant to stimulate, excite and disquiet more than to be worn. And such 'art–fashion' is projected as a fantasy not only on runways but also in photographs, frequently styled by the designer himself. Nick Knight and Juergen Teller, working closely with the designer whose clothes they are photographing, have created images much closer to art than to commercial fashion projection. And, like the presentations on the runways, the work of many young photographers and stylists creates a form of victim chic as women are stripped of high-fashion gloss and shown in an uncompromisingly dirty realist way, redolent of backwoods America, trailer trash, drugs and self-abasement, or presented as part of an unreal, heightened fantasy which frequently robs them of character, personality or even humanity, by turning them into exotic, extraordinary parodies of a dream-world of femininity.

Fashion is moving back into the cultural mainstream, increasingly seen as an adjunct to art as couture was in the early Fifties. Just as Cocteau was proud to be a friend of Dior, and Dalí was pleased to work with Schiaparelli, it is now possible to mention McQueen in the same breath as Damien Hirst without the comparison sounding risible. Both come from a shared cultural background which has created attitudes often hard for older or more traditionally educated people to comprehend. Whereas a designer like Yves Saint Laurent cut his cultural teeth on the works of writers such as André Malraux and Blaise Cendrars, a man like McQueen had his cultural standards formed by films and popular culture. And it is significant that the culture underpinning current avant-garde fashion fantasies is cinematic and televisual rather than literary. When Lagerfeld looks for stimulation he turns to books, while McQueen checks out his videos. Whereas the former's inspiration is classical, the latter's is vernacular.

Much of the fantasy of modern designers, especially those found in London, is meant to shock, in just the same way that artists currently set out to shock – and, in fact, as much art has done over the centuries. Cultural links go back a long way. Without making impossible claims, it isn't too difficult to see that what is currently happening in the London art and fashion scene echoes and restates obsessions which link to Swift and Hogarth in the eighteenth century, just as there are links between Jean Paul Gaultier's approach and those of Rabelais five centuries ago. Equally as clearly, when Hussein Chalayan sends out young female models with their genitalia exposed, he is behaving precisely in line with the thinking of the madams who ran the child bordellos in Victorian London, fin-de-siècle Paris and turn-of-the-century San Francisco. What has happened in fashion is that fantasy has become the new reality, often far ahead of the tenets controlling current commercial fashion and making a personal statement more than projecting a view of how women will be dressed in future. Fashion's avant-garde has never been so far ahead as it is today. Exactly like avant-garde art, equally as far ahead of what the majority find acceptable, it is in danger of leaving behind the millions of women who expect designers, photographers and fashion editors to tell them what to wear. Increasingly, designers prefer to use their catwalks to tell us how to think. It is surely only a question of time before the great modern art collections begin to include examples of the work of fashion designers as proof of current artistic thought. Then the rupture between clothes to be worn and clothes to be seen will be complete.

FETISHISM AND THE SHAPED BODY

1   (Opener)
Wolford, 1996,
photo Helmut
Newton

2   (Previous page)
Krizia bustier,
1992, photo
G. Gastel

3   (Previous page)
Thierry Mugler
evening dress,
1998

4   Ankle piece by
Shaun Leane
for Alexander
McQueen, shoes
by Manolo
Blahnik, 1997,
photo Sean Ellis

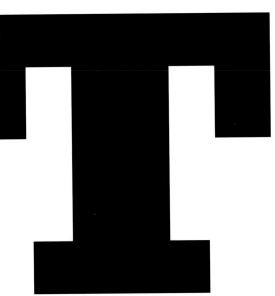

There is nothing in the world that cannot be fetishized. All that is required is an irrational reverence for it, either by an individual or a group of like-minded people. Fetishism was originally linked with sexual disorder, but in modern parlance it has come to mean any non-rational, over-heated desire for a specific object. Clearly, fashion being the irrational imposition of the new on an audience willing to accept it, fetishism and fashion don't merely go hand in hand: they grow from each other. Fashion is energized and changed by the 'must-have' syndrome which is a perfect example of the workings of fetishism. Designers know this; so do advertising agencies and magazine editors. And they've all known for a long time. As early as the Fifties, Nancy White, editor of American *Vogue*, made clear the real purpose of fashion magazines when she told a sales conference, 'The more fashion we can put on the backs of American women at whatever prices they can afford, the better for all of us.'

Exploited in the right way on catwalks, in shops and on advertising and editorial pages, no item is so unpromising that it cannot be sold as this moment's 'must-have'. Even the catastrophically mistimed and mismanaged Grunge fashion approach – the most spectacular fashion failure since Yves Saint Laurent's ill-fated Forties revival in 1971 – had its devotees, albeit briefly. No matter how meretricious, there are few things in fashion which can't be presented in a way that makes them sell. Why else do women join waiting lists for fetishized objects such as Gucci shoes or Prada bags? Why do they bribe, threaten and cajole in order to possess a fashion object so absolutely 'now' that it is dead by the next season – and pay a great deal of

money in order to buy into fashion's eternal rhythm of obsolescence?

Fashion has always made people obsessive, and the quicker it changes, the greater the desire to be part of it. We, of course, have better things to do than become slavish followers of fashion. We are sufficiently educated to see behind the hype and remain rational in our assessment of any new trend. So runs the myth. In actuality, fashion in the last two decades of the twentieth century has exerted a grip on people with an intensity not seen since Louis XIV's Versailles – or, at least, the upper-class world of the rich and indolent in Edwardian times. 'Fashion victim' has become a pejorative term, but it describes nothing more than the over-enthusiasm for the new which has always held the fashionable in thrall.

Diversity is what energizes modern fashion and fetishism increasingly concentrates on accessories more than total looks. The reason is that, since the Eighties, the name on an object has been the thing that makes it talismanic. Label freaks, who were less concerned with how something made them look, and more interested in what the designer's name said about them, were a phenomenon of that decade of high financial and social expectations, a time when money and its power had ceased to be a privilege of the few and seemed the birthright of the many. Recession cut that particular form of self-deception down to size, but it left a residual desire to have something which provided a high-fashion profile. It was still 'cool' to flaunt labels once considered exclusive, from the rip-off of the interlocking Cs of a 'Chanel' T-shirt made in Kowloon to the ubiquitous Polo or CK logos on items of dress with

similarly doubtful provenance. When the trend hit rock-bottom with the unemployed lining up for benefit sporting a chic logo, it was obvious that the time had come to find new and preferably more obscure objects of desire, and to keep them more exclusive by making them more expensive.

Gaultier and Moschino were the first to see the new opening, in the early Eighties, when they realized that the identifiable accessory was the thing that would make their names famous. They were aware that only a handful of people could afford their clothes. Hadn't Moschino made his name with slogans blatantly critical of a fashion system which increasingly sold goods not on their merit but on their price? Cleverly, he sold the clothes bearing the slogan for as high a price as those of any of his fellow designers in a double-standard double-take, the irony of which was largely ignored. By doing so, he made them into fetishistic objects in themselves, but it was with named belts that he and Gaultier hit a goldmine. A leather belt with the name of the designer cut out of steel or brass became a status symbol for the young and hip and, by becoming so, started a new line in fetishism. Everybody wanted a belt, bag or a piece of jewellery which proclaimed its credentials – and the wearer's. Whereas previously exclusivity had been the goal, with cachet being achieved simply because the majority were unaware of what the Louis Vuitton 'LV' pattern signified, now fetishism took label mania to new heights. The quilted Chanel bag with gold chains was copied everywhere, as was the company's most successful piece of jewellery, a simple pearl earring set in diamanté which, for several years, was the fashion editor's badge of authority –

6

rather as her Manolo Blahnik stilettos and Prada handbag are at the beginning of the new millennium.

Fetishism roared across the fashion spectrum in the Eighties and Nineties as new 'must-haves' were introduced, ruthlessly promoted with advertising campaigns costing millions, supplied in artificially small numbers to key retail outlets and, inevitably, precipitating a demand which far outweighed the production output. As fashion leaders have always known, success comes when demand cannot be met. This is what makes the Prada bag – cheaply produced in plastic with a small metal name tag – so desirable that it becomes a truly fetishistic object, especially for those with no possibility of obtaining it until it has become outmoded. This happens at a point which requires careful commercial judgement by designer and manufacturer, who must know when to move on, just before the unauthorized 'rip-offs' begin to be hawked by street traders in the major cities of the world, at a fraction of the cost of the original and, to untrained eyes, often virtually indistinguishable from it.

Of course, fetishistic objects would not make money if they were all kept in artificially short supply. There must be something for the fetishist to actually buy. The answer to that problem was discovered in the Eighties, the halcyon decade for sharp trading practices, and has since proved even more valuable than the goose that laid the golden eggs. Perfume provides the best and biggest example of fetishism for our times. Like designer labels, which took a new turn with fresh approaches to marketing, perfume as the object of compulsive buying was not new. Its sales figures had always been good, especially when it was linked with the name of a grand couturier. The perfume houses of Chanel and Dior made fortunes in the Fifties and Sixties. Ready-to-wear designers like Halston got in on the act in the Seventies, but true fetishism only really came to the perfume market with the promotion of the designer as personality

and champion of all areas of sophisticated life – and that was an Eighties phenomenon.

The very act of putting on perfume has become a form of fetishism, a rite of passage to womanhood. There are very few women in the Western world who do not wear perfume and, as manufacturers know, the secret of sales buoyancy lies with creating a special bond between perfume and buyer so that she finds one she likes, adopts it as 'her' scent and regularly replaces it with the same brand. But, if most women don't naturally change their perfume, they must be lured into buying new brands. This is achieved by two forms of advertising: campaigns using top models and photographers, and publicity surrounding the name of the eponymous designer. It is not by accident that perfume houses not linked with a designer's name, many of which had flourished for several decades, were dramatically reduced in numbers during the Eighties and were virtually nonexistent in the Nineties. Their anonymity gave no scope for exploitation in the way a high-profile name like that of Ralph Lauren, whose product stood for a way of life and an attitude of mind, or Calvin Klein, whose perfume advertising became synonymous with youth, were able to do, as an affordable part of a package which even fetishized an attitude to life. In the modern world, the successful perfumes are those bearing the name of an internationally famous designer, whose status is based on the power of his position in the fashion arena.

When a perfume is bought, it has been chosen for many other reasons than merely its smell. Some of the most powerful compulsions are largely subliminal. Bottle design and packaging are crucial. So are advertising campaigns. But the most fundamental is the designer name and the fashion approach related to it. Karl Lagerfeld's fragrances never attained the charisma of those with the Chanel label. It is hardly surprising. No female figure in the twentieth century has been more

hyped than she has. The Chanel suit, buttons, camellia and two-tone shoes are still potent fashion talismans, enduring and able to assimilate many variations without losing their integrity. Nothing designed by Lagerfeld under his own name ever reached that immutability.

Christian Lacroix has failed to become one of the couturiers with a strong perfume loyalty, even though his name is known worldwide. The reason is that the name alone is not enough. It must be linked with a clear mental perception of a fashion approach. In fact, Lacroix has an exceedingly strong and individualistic sense of fashion, but, in the main streets of the world, women do not have a clear mental picture of the kind of woman for which Lacroix's name stands.

Publicity is what creates fetishistic overtones in perfume names. It is not surprising that many of the best-selling fragrances bear the names of American designers, whose advertising budgets are so large that they enable them to command prime space in any of the media, from glossy magazine back covers to billboards and television advertising spots. When a women says 'I always wear *Chanel No.5*', as millions do, she has fetishized her perfume on the back of the name of an internationally successful designer. But, in perfume, as in fashion generally, new wine is increasingly often poured into old bottles. Alexander McQueen at Givenchy and John Galliano at Dior are prime examples of strong new names joining houses with strong old names which have been highly successful in perfume sales. In fact, there are plenty of people in the fashion world who believe that both men are employed by Bernard Arnault, chairman of LVMH (the conglomerate which owns both the houses of Givenchy and Dior), merely to ensure the publicity which keeps the fetishistic process alive. It is perhaps too early to assess the long-term impact of Galliano and McQueen, but, at this stage, it seems that both men make more impact on the broad public, as opposed to the fashion cognoscenti, with their private

7

8

10   Ann
      Demeulemeester,
      1997–8

11   Goths in London,
      1980, photo
      Derek Ridgers

12   Elspeth Gibson
      black dress,
      1998, photo
      Tim Richmond

11

10

lives, public utterances and personal commentaries than with their clothes. Most women would find it difficult to conjure up an image of a typical Givenchy or Dior creation, but few would fail to have a personal image of the men themselves. And it could well be that perfume sales will be secured in the future by fetishizing the image of the individual designer – as has long been the case with Coco Chanel. Certainly, both men have the strength of character for such an approach, and Galliano has the added advantage of an appearance uniquely recognizable, even in its many different manifestations.

It isn't merely personalities that are a colourful element of fashion as the new millennium begins. The clothes created by men such as Galliano and McQueen are complex, rich in references and, indeed, richly nuanced on many levels. Even so, they have not been able to oust the fashionable woman's most persistent fetish, for the colour black. Its power for men as well as women is well catalogued and stretches back to Elizabethan times. Its associations with authority, power and death have made it an awe-inspiring colour. Its associations with elegance and grandeur have made it the colour of sophistication. Its associations with satanism, sadomasochism and perversion have helped to make it sexy in an unorthodox way. The fact that it flatters face, figure and jewellery means that it has always had its place in the world of high fashion. It is found in portraits by Velázquez, Sargent and Boldini from the seventeenth to the nineteenth centuries. It figured prominently in the wardrobe of every society woman at the turn of the century. The 'little black dress' became a cliché in the stylish world of the upper classes in the Thirties, although there is no historic evidence that it was invented by Chanel, as is frequently claimed. In fact, it was a standard item of dress long before she created her version of it – and remained so well into the Fifties, when the concept of a 'wardrobe' for the different seasons and social calendars ceased to have a meaning and was replaced by the ubiquity of 'clothes'.

But, for all its long history, black was, until the Eighties, merely one of the colours in the wardrobe of a woman of fashion. It suddenly took centre stage as a result of the Japanese 'invasion' of Paris in 1981, although it had already become an integral part of the dress codes of art students, influenced by the Goths, whose chalk-white faces, deep purple eyeshadow and black lipstick

were far too serious to be seen with any other, more flippant, colour except, occasionally, blood red or papal purple. But none of this would have been sufficient to make black the longest-running fetish in modern fashion history if it hadn't caught the imagination of the industry itself. In fact, it spread like wildfire, at all levels. Designers wore black; fashion journalists wore black; students wore black; secretaries and computer programmers wore black. The new Eighties' woman, working in a hi-tech world which demanded not only the fact but also the appearance of efficiency, took to it in the form of the business suit – not only inevitably black but also trousered. The only exceptions were the grey or black-and-white checks of the Armani suit which, certainly in the upper echelons of commercial life, became a potent fashion but did nothing to dent the supremacy of black in middle and lower management.

The reason is to be found in the industry itself. Didn't even Giorgio Armani wear black more often than not? Certainly, most of his staff did. Gianni Versace was rarely seen in anything else. It was Karl Lagerfeld's favourite colour and Dolce & Gabbana made it their trademark. Black had such a stranglehold on fashion that, no matter how much colour was shown on a designer's runway, it was inevitably watched by an audience dressed entirely in black. No matter how brilliantly matched their colours were, buyers always asked designers the same question: 'Does it come in black?' Black became ubiquitous for all age groups and in all walks of life. Exactly why this happened is complicated by the fact that the semiotics of black changed during the Eighties and Nineties. Having begun as a strong statement of the intellectual probity of the new dress approaches introduced by the Japanese, and for most fashion followers given its accolade by Rei Kawakubo's cryptic remark that she worked with eight shades of the colour, it took on many different social references. Meant, perhaps, to be as all-embracing as a school uniform and as classless as a man's suit, black clothing was claimed to exert a sort of levelling influence on fashion, bringing a kind of democracy to the scene conjured by endless rails of apparently identical clothes in shops at every level.

Fashion journalists led the industry's approach with paeans to the fact that, in busy lives, an all-black wardrobe simplified choice and made dress decisions easier. Less frequently mentioned, they were

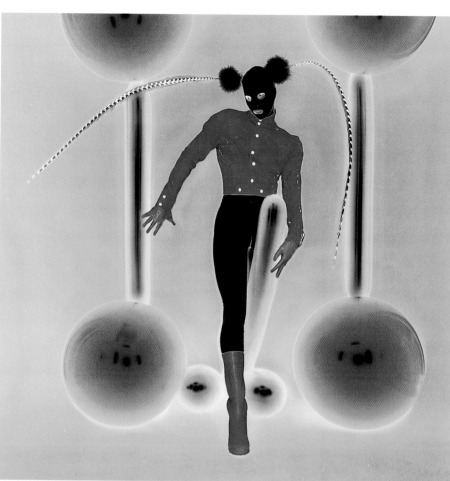

14

15

also grateful for the fact that black is the most flattering of colours, bringing a svelte quality even to neglected figures in a way in which no other colour can. But, the real reason why black held sway with so many for so long was that it made psychological bonding much easier – as fetish objects always have. It signified conformity and cohesion; it gave strength, simply from the huge numbers who wore it. Even at the end of the Nineties, it was possible to watch passengers alighting from commuter trains in New York, London, Paris and Tokyo, and count not just a preponderance but an overwhelming majority of women wearing black trouser suits, either by designers such as Ann Demeulemeester or Helmut Lang or chain-store versions of designer lines. The black trouser suit is the first example of a fetish for the millions.

The power of black is fading slowly, but it will not die. It links fashion with what most people see as the raunchy quality of much that is shown on top designer's runways. Black is, per se, the colour of power. When it exchanges wool and chiffon for leather and latex it adds to that power an erotic, even satanic, feeling of excitement. In the Eighties, PVC and rubber came out of the specialist closet of the S&M club and took their place on fashion's front line, following a trail blazed by black leather. 'Kinkiness' became one of fashion's new ways of having fun, while literally taking everything up to, and including, couture into the realm of fetishism. What had begun as mildly fetishistic in the form of women wearing men's black suits – a type of fantasy that stretched back to Marlene Dietrich in the Thirties – became something stronger when it was realized that many men found women dressed that way

as sexy as women wearing diaphanous negligées or
tight corsets and high heels. When the suit was in fine
leather, often with metal or diamanté studs, the power
of the effect was magnified. A new fetishism was born.
   But the old fetishism was coming up quickly from
behind. The image of Diana Rigg as Emma Peel in
The Avengers wearing an aggressive black catsuit,
complete with zips and studs, had lost none of its
power since its inception in the Sixties. At that time
it had been a classic, and blatant, example of a male
fetish. Most would have predicted that the look would
always remain at that point of retarded development
but, in fact, within twenty years, it was to become
mainstream fashion in the hands of certain designers.
These included Claude Montana, whose early Eighties'
leather collections were legendary in the power they
conferred on women; Thierry Mugler, whose mixtures of
leather and hi-tech hardwear created a semi-space age
dominatrix; Azzedine Alaïa, who took not only leather
and PVC but also jersey into the realm of high-camp
fetishism and, by his brilliance at winding it around
the body, managed to make the formerly utilitarian zip
into one of the great erotic devices of body-conscious
dress. All three designers broke down taboos and
made it possible for fashion statements to use aspects
of sexuality normally considered so perverse and
subversive as to be kept hidden. Now, anything
was possible in a fashion show.
   It isn't entirely easy to pinpoint why this movement took
hold in the early Eighties with such dramatic and speedy
effect. There are obvious social explanations: it was a
time when women in the West felt more socially and
economically empowered than they had before.
Economic independence – always more powerful in
changing our attitudes than the normally cited liberators
such as the Pill or abortion, and without the social and
religious stigma – enabled them to buy what they
wanted, when they wanted. More women in the age
group twenty to thirty-five (a crucial one for fashion)
were financially independent and, most importantly,
had bought into the belief that they were the hunters,
the predators and the choosers. Even more importantly,
they wanted to have bodies which reflected their power
and efficiency – bodies as machines fit enough to
enable them live the modern life. They dieted, they
jogged, they worked out. They wanted clothes which
highlighted young, toned flesh.
   They had their heroine, their modern Emma Peel,
in Madonna. Whether or not they liked her music
– although most did, responding to its confidence
– they realized (maybe subconsciously) that her attitudes
to sexuality were entirely those of the young, modern

19 Thierry Mugler,
    'Harley Davidson'
    bustier with leather
    shorts, 1992, photo
    Patrice Stable

20 Issey Miyake, 1980,
    photo Peter Knapp

20

woman. In fact, it is possible to make a convincing case that, with each new video, Madonna empowered women and weakened the already slackening power-hold on them which even young men frequently still considered a right of their sex. And there were other heroines. The importance of the supermodels was considerable. They helped make women body-conscious because designers were encouraged to exploit the potential of their perfect proportions by creating clothes which highlighted and revealed their anatomies more blatantly than they had previously. Whereas Yves Saint Laurent had removed bras in the Seventies but had covered the breasts with diaphanous blouses, Gianni Versace – and virtually every other designer – exposed breasts, stomachs and buttocks in the Eighties. It was disastrous for fashion because it was an approach which simply couldn't translate to the high street, it made fashion into performance art and opened the door to 'reality' in the form of the understated fashion of firms such as The Gap, Banana Republic, J. Crew and all the other, mainly American, manufacturers who saw the yawning credibility gap between designer fashion and reality, and stepped smartly in to fill it.

But it was very good for publicity. As newspapers grew in size, introduced colour printing and embarked on circulation wars, fashion became a prime tool for editors. When they decided that fashion editors should file daily news reports from the collections, they shifted a vital journalistic balance. A fashion editor reporting from Milan or New York could not make the final choice of picture for the next day's edition. It became the province of the picture desk watched over by the news desk – men who had no interest in fashion but were keen to outdo the opposition on the newsstands. It didn't take long for designers such as Versace, Gaultier and Westwood to see what sexual directness on the runway did in terms of publicity. Sexual blatancy became fashion's new game as it provided publicity opportunities previously not dreamed of. News desks weren't interested in whether a designer was good or bad; they saw it as no part of their job to help preserve the integrity of an industry. They were too excited by the possibilities legitimized by high fashion coverage to have a soft-porn input on their normally staid pages. Designers increasingly took the opportunity the newspapers sanctioned, and created clothes which fulfiled a multitude of fantasies, an indulgence they could afford as soaring profits from perfumes and licensed products, stimulated by the raunchy front-page runway shots, made all things possible and freed them from the compulsion to make clothes that would actually sell.

Chains, leather thongs, trousers zipped front and back: the runways were awash with the paraphernalia of twilight sexual worlds as women dressed in leather and rubber fantasy outfits stormed along them, gratifying every fetish known to man. Punk dog collars reappeared. Black leather biker's outfits were seen yet again. Thierry Mugler went a stage further and, in a J.G. Ballard *Crash* scenario, made bustiers based on the dashboards of Harley Davidson motorbikes.

In fact, the bustier was the fetishist garment – along with its close rival the corset – for much of the Eighties and Nineties, at least on the catwalks. Projecting the breasts as an erogenous zone was nothing new. Building a carapace for them in a way that made women look part of the insect world – predatory but ultimately vulnerable

21 The Corset, 1962,
photo Jeanloup
Sieff

22 Body sculpture by
Claude Lalaune for
Yves Saint Laurent,
1969, photo Manuel
Litran

23 Issey Miyake,
Rattan body, 1981,
photo Tsutomu
Wakatsuki

22

23

– was. It had begun with Yves Saint Laurent's moulded golden breastplate created by the sculptor Claude Lalaune, which he first showed in 1969; had been continued in Issey Miyake's early Eighties' experiments with polystyrene bustiers, constructed from a moulding of a female torso, along with his cane tops reminiscent of samurai armour; and had been softened into an adaptation of an eighteenth-century corset top by Vivienne Westwood. The movement reached a publicity apotheosis in 1987 when Madonna wore Gaultier's laced-up corset for public performances. It was still very much alive in the early Nineties when Alaïa produced red leather corsets with matching handbags in the same shape, and created the ultimate in fetishistic synergy with a corset made from imitation leopard skin.

The last two decades of the twentieth century were frustrating for fur fetishists because they were dominated by imitation furs but, until the last three years of the century, no designer dared to show real fur in their collections. The politically correct forces refused to countenance the slaughter of any creature for the vanities of fashion, a situation that was changed almost single-handedly by Anna Wintour, editor-in-chief of American *Vogue*, who not only began to accept advertisements from furriers, followed by very gentle editorial coverage – a real fur lining here, a fur collar there – but, finally, put her appearance where her convictions were, and began to wear chinchilla jackets. Anti-fur campaigners waged an aggressive war of attrition against her, but they could not alter the fact that the fashion climate had changed. It was as if a sluicegate had been opened, as fur poured back onto the runways of Paris, New York and Milan, with designers such as Tom Ford at Gucci and John Galliano at Dior taking the opportunity to work openly with it for the first time in their careers as rich customers stood in line for what had always in the past been the wealthy woman's indulgence and socially acceptable fetish. Only London stood against the tide, not only for social and moral reasons but also because its fashion designers

were not in tune with the high-luxury status dress produced in the other fashion capitals.

Rubber, leather, uniforms, fur – it would seem that all the fetishist areas are well covered by designers at the beginning of the twenty-first century. Frequently, the tone is ironic, the approach – certainly in the hands of the masters of sophistication such as Mugler and Gaultier – as much parody as anything else. Amazingly beautiful clothes were produced in the Nineties, including Gaultier's eighteenth-century caprices and, what will perhaps be seen as the archetypal end of millennium statement about this fashion approach, Thierry Mugler's 1998 couture evening dress consisting of two gold nipple rings from which flowed a diaphanous evening dress in black chiffon – and such approaches are sure to continue in the new millennium. It has already been proved that this particular area of fetishistic involvement can move beyond Westwood's pantomime fig leaves and transfer prints of rampant phalluses into the true realm of high-fashion clothes where shock tactics give way to the beauty of perfect craftsmanship.

What this whole movement is about has become clear. In the Nineties, fashion moved towards a new body consciousness not seen since Christian Dior's superb tailoring and magnificent evening gowns of the early Fifties. Appropriately enough, the movement reached its apotheosis with John Galliano when he was appointed design director at the House of Dior in 1997. He pulled together the various disparate strands which had for some time been a part of fashion without actually giving it coherence. He took the obsession with the voluptuous female which had interested many designers since the mid-Eighties, especially in Paris, and removed the raunchy quality. His romantically atavistic vision of the glamour of past decades gave late Nineties' femininity a softer – but no less sexy – silhouette, wrapped in the exotic trappings of the turn of the century, including fringes, capes, filigree embroidery and huge, theatrical evening coats based on those of

24

pre-World War I couturier Paul Poiret. Crudeness and vulgarity were banished, but at no cost to extreme sexuality, as he took the Edwardian influence which had first inspired Christian Dior and, with a tactful reticence and respect for the ethos of the house, made it suitable for the late twentieth-century woman by producing clothes which were feminine in a modern sense, with curves that followed the lines of the body.

Galliano was the last of the great fetishizers in twentieth-century fashion. Taking innerwear and making it outerwear, he produced brilliantly bias-cut satin slips – often leopard-printed – and, bordering them with lace or broderie anglaise, gave late Nineties' women a fashion look so in tune with an age which produced stars of the calibre of Gwyneth Paltrow, Nicole Kidman and Minnie Driver that it exerted a huge influence across fashion at all levels. The slip dress became a fashion standard not only because it was an oblique answer to earlier more blatantly sexual looks, but also because it didn't carry with it overtones of wealth. Any factory producing slips and petticoats could make a slip dress, even for very little money. That is why it was such a success, but the major reason was that Galliano, regularly and wrongly accused of being unrealistic and lacking commercial sense, had finally given women a way of dressing sexily, but not overtly or crudely so. His younger compatriot, Stella McCartney, at Chloé, shared many of his characteristics. Her lingerie dresses, with a figure-conscious cut, had a youthful verve and 'street' quality which gave them a very different personality, bringing together the 'Glam Rock chick' fun of Versace, the acid-cool cut of McQueen and McCartney's own credibility as a party girl, friend of top models and general mover and shaker on the scene.

What the slip dress did was to go a long way towards healing the rupture between a designer's show and what was bought in the shops. It was a rupture at its most extreme in Europe. As fashion shows in Paris – and, to a lesser extent, Milan – had become more extravagant and driven by fantasy, dresses were created to the highest and most costly levels for ready-to-wear as well as couture shows. Luxury had itself

became a fetish. Some of the most beautiful examples of the couturier's imagination and the supreme skills of his workroom floated down the runway towards the ultimate nemesis: to be photographed, with infinite pains and attention to artistic standards, appearing on a magazine page printed to the highest level of precision – and never to be seen again. In the French couture market there are no more than three hundred regular customers. If a couture outfit is ordered by three of them it is, in this rarified world, considered a bestseller. By far the majority of these monuments to dressmaking as an art are simply too expensive for even rich women to contemplate, and so they remain glorious, but sterile, examples of fashion's frequent flight from reality.

As ultimate wearability is no longer the cast-iron *sine qua non* it was in the Fifties, when Paris couture boasted upwards of two thousand women on its books, couturiers in the Nineties have gone for the grand gesture and have, with the exception of Yves Saint Laurent, given up any pretence that day wear is as important as evening wear. Out of a show of around seventy couture outfits, he still sends out at least twenty-five tailored suits or afternoon outfits of dress and jacket. Other, younger, designers often send out none, concentrating on ballgowns and sexy evening looks instead. They do so not entirely in self-indulgence and not only because the magazines tend to choose to photograph them instead of day wear but, because, stripped of their expensive beading and embroidery, they can be sold as wedding dresses – one of the staples of any French couture house today.

At the beginning of the new century, perhaps the most surprising thing in fashion is how many fashion houses still produce couture collections. In January 1999 the Chambre Syndicale de la Couture Parisienne – the controlling body of French fashion – listed fifteen full members, seven invited members, including Gaultier, Mugler and 'second-generation' designers such as Josephus Thimister, Ocimar Versolato and Dominique Sirop, and three associate members – Valentino, Versace and Valentin Yudashkin – all of whom show twice a year, presenting collections of at least fifty

28 Dolce & Gabbana,
1999, photo
Steven Klein

garments. Is it all a gloriously arrogant extravagance or is there an actual point?

To reach anything like a coherent answer, Paris must be measured against the other fashion capitals, none of which has any couture houses in the French manner. Each has its distinct personality, part popular myth, part reality. American fashion designers see their role as a practical one. They judge their success not only on artistic grounds, but also by taking into account how many units of clothing are produced and sold each season. In a market essentially geared to mass sales, there is little room for fantasy. Although New York designers such as Anna Sui and Betsey Johnson bow to the fetish market in many of their collections – something they can do because their businesses are relatively small and their target audience specialist – the people who drive American fashion forward and sell widely across the continent (Ralph Lauren, Donna Karan and Calvin Klein) leave the fetishist market to catalogue sales and limit themselves to cargo pants, cashmere sweaters and trouser suits.

Milanese designers do much the same, conscious that they produce the best manufactured ready-to-wear in the world, whether at the luxury mass-market level of Maxmara, or the top designer label such as that of Giorgio Armani, who dominated world fashion in the Eighties, lost some of his supremacy in the Nineties but begins the new century reinstated as a powerful leader of Italian ready-to-wear. Sophistication, top-quality fabrication and high-quality workmanship are what the world expects from the 'Made in Italy' label. It does not look to Milan for fantasy. Dolce & Gabbana, however, produce both fantasy and fetish on their runway as they continue to explore their obsession with the aspects of mind which distinguish Sicily from the rest of Italy, creating sexually specific collections overlaid with a nostalgic romanticism. Satin corsets, suspender belts, fishnet stockings and a great deal of marabou trimming are glamorous, sexy and, being largely unsaleable, rarely go into production. But what Dolce & Gabbana actually sell to their customers are a limited number of hand-painted dresses and vast quantities of crisp trouser suits. Like most Italian manufacturers, they are content to create clothes for fetishism in the mind of the beholder, while knowing what their customers actually buy.

This does not mean that D&G are not innovators who exert a true influence on international fashion. In fact, their attitudes are exploited at all levels of ready-to-wear but, no matter how many times commentators evoke the earthy magnetism of Italian actresses such as Anna Magnani and Silvana Mangano when describing the

29

pair's fashion shows, always high on raunchiness and
fetishistic looks, Dolce & Gabbana exert the greatest
influence – and make their money – by producing
young hip clothes, with black as their top-selling colour,
backed by powerful advertising campaigns which make
men and women feel sexy before they have even tried
on anything from the collections.

Much the same is true of the house of Versace,
whose eponymous designer was murdered in 1997.
Since then, the firm has been led by his sister,
Donatella, the woman whom insiders thought was
the source of much of the fetishistic element that was
so prominent in Gianni Versace's collections in the
Nineties. Certainly, she has continued the ethos of
the firm, creating fashion of a high fetishist content in
shape and fabric but gently easing away the raunchy
insouciance that characterized earlier Versace style,
epitomized by his remark, 'I don't believe in good taste'.
It is a claim that those who saw only his runway shows
might be inclined to believe but, then as now, the true
Versace is found in the boutiques around the world,
with their rails of perfectly crafted silk dresses, often
heavily beaded, hanging next to impeccably tailored
suits. The firm of Versace is, after all, Italian and
behind all the hype of sexuality and high-camp fetishism
stands the perfectionism for which the country's fashion
is renowned.

Like New York, Milan has a simple fashion personality.
The products of both cities are remarkably homogeneous.
Such is not the case in London. There is no such thing
as a 'London Look'. It is a city of fiercely independent
designer outlooks, which is why it is the only fashion
city which can rival the creativity of Paris. Inconsistent,
frequently incoherent, often outrageous, rarely
commercially viable, London fashion since the early
Eighties has been full of stops and starts, shocks and

31 Alexander
McQueen for
Givenchy *haute
couture*, 1998,
photo Robert
Wyatt

32 (Overleaf)
Alexander
McQueen, *Dazed
and Confused*,
1998, photo
Nick Knight

33 (Overleaf)
Alexander
McQueen, *Dazed
and Confused*,
1998, photo
Nick Knight

predictabilities, critical acclaims and financial failures. London stands in relation to other fashion cities rather as *The Simpsons* and *Southpark* do *vis-à-vis* Middle American values and political correctness. Subversive, a necessary corrective to complacent attitudes, London has produced a huge amount of new talent in the last twenty years, much of it stronger than that appearing elsewhere, and some of it in the world leadership class. The influence of Vivienne Westwood alone is justification enough for London to be placed in the vanguard of fashion originality. She has been an *agent provocateur* on behalf of the byways of sexuality ever since her proto-punk days in the Seventies when she sold T-shirts bearing pictures of seminude cowboys (confiscated by the police as obscene) and bondage trousers. She carried her attitudes forward into the Eighties through her experiments with bustles, brassieres and the whole concept of the woman constrained, if not actually manacled, by the sexual force of her clothes. The designer who most directly and fearlessly hooked into the world of S&M, bondage and sexual power-play, Westwood is a creative paradox. She is excited by the romance of history and is endlessly attracted to periods when women seemed to have control over their sexuality. Her heroines are women of the calibre of Elizabeth I, Nell Gwynne and the Gaiety Girls. Although her grasp of the true historic meaning of such figures is at best tenuous, she has used her emotional response to what she sees them standing for – a liberated woman syndrome probably more imaginary than actual – as a template on which to hang her fantasies of female power: the jutting breasts, the tightly corseted waists, the bustles and high platform shoes which most others see as proof of female subservience. For all the confusion of her historic knowledge, Westwood has created something unique in fashion. In her great days in the mid-Eighties she could truly be claimed as the emotional earth mother of London fashion before it

began to look to Paris and the rest of the world for creative sustenance of a more reliable kind. The fact that London designers have since made such an impact on international fashion should not cloud the truth: Vivienne Westwood was the designer who offered them the possibility of being outrageous, on which many subsequent careers have been founded.

It is arguable that no other city in the world could have produced a man such as Alexander McQueen, undoubtedly the greatest force to appear in world fashion since John Galliano, with whom – initially at least – he was constantly and erroneously compared and contrasted, although it was perfectly clear that both men had separate visions and their own uniquely personal fashion approaches. Even if the comparisons had not been creatively maladroit, they would have been inappropriate, in that Galliano had a ten-year head start on McQueen and, already at thirty-five, was an established figure when the younger man presented his first collection in 1995. Entitled 'Highland Rape', its shock tactics – blood trickling down models' legs and staining their disarrayed lace dresses, eyes apparently bruised, dishevelled hair – had never previously been used in a fashion show. It made a powerful statement of future intent by a designer determined to lose no opportunity to gain publicity by outrage. This was, after all, the man who called his 1992 graduation show 'Jack the Ripper Stalking his Victims'; the man who quickly followed Westwood, Mugler and even Galliano into the fetishist world; the man who early on knew that his vision was not only powerful but also unique; the man determined to become known, by any means.

McQueen's approach to fashion notoriety was carefully judged. Violence was a new concept on the catwalk, although fashion had, through the Nineties, flirted with it increasingly on the pages of the new breed of style magazine, such as *Dazed and Confused* and established titles such as *The Face*. They frequently

featured fashion shoots which were not just violent but grizzly, giving the impression that the models had been caught up in scenes of urban violence, made convincing by backgrounds from London's Docklands to the Hispanic areas of Los Angeles. They were obviously an influence on McQueen's emerging talents, just as they were eager to feature his versions of the violence they promulgated. In September 1998, the link was made clear when McQueen guest-edited issue 46 of *Dazed and Confused*, an examination of the concept of beauty in the light of physical disability. It became the biggest selling issue that the magazine had enjoyed since its inception.

By the standards of London fashion, McQueen presents a paradox. Keen to keep his integrity, determined not to weaken or dilute his vision, he is, nevertheless, commercially motivated in a way that Westwood and Galliano were not when they were at the same point in their careers. In interviews, he has claimed that he wishes to sell as much as he can, adding, 'I have to make a living out of what I do.' In fact, behind the easy crowd-pullers, such as his bumster pants, inspired by the view of labourers digging holes in the streets of London, McQueen's training in Savile Row has given him a rigour not always found in other contenders for his title of King of London's Avant-Garde. His clothes are impressively well-made, something to which London's designers in the past have given scant attention. His presentations, which are spectacular, newsworthy and conceived to cause the maximum alarm and outrage in order to achieve the fullest news coverage, never overshadow the quality of the clothes, which are as dramatic and uncompromising as the man. But they are also frequently beautiful, delicate and totally in tune with a modern and very gentle concept of femininity which hints at another man – a person of supreme sensitivity in the mould of Dior, Balenciaga and the truly great couturiers of the past

34   John Galliano for
     Dior, 1998, photo
     Nick Knight

century. It is one of several paradoxes in his work. When, with experience, he has resolved them and presents a unified fashion persona, Alexander McQueen could well develop into a seminal and far-reaching influence in the decades to come. Creatively much more complex – and even convoluted – than Westwood, he has within him the artistic sensitivity to do what most other designers have singularly failed to achieve: that is, to bring about an amalgam of fetishistic intensity with an understanding and respect for femininity as seen in real, rather than fantasy, women.

This is the last bastion. The crude stridency of much fetishism and body consciousness in dress which have characterized outré fashion in the last two decades has been valuable, as well as amusing. No one can seriously doubt the genius of men such as Mugler and Montana. It would be ludicrous not to acknowledge the strength and wit of Gaultier's balanced and mature approach to sexuality in dress which means that, beneath the initial shock, a logical and indeed wearable item is almost always found.

Vivienne Westwood's originality and courage have shone forth with a steady light. Like her male counterparts she has illuminated some of the murkier corners of sexuality and found in them scope for wit, irreverence and, occasionally, bad taste. In this, she is at one with Gaultier. Both exemplify what Diana Vreeland meant when she said that she had no objection to bad taste, it was no taste which she could not accept. In Gaultier's case the rules were broken by a knowing insider who had been trained in the traditions of *haute couture*. Much of the impact of Westwood originally stemmed from fashion gaucherie: it is important to recall that, almost uniquely in the field of world-class designers, she started her successful climb in fashion as an amateur, almost totally untrained. It makes her achievements even more monumental to note that she attended art school for less than a year before leaving to become a teacher. But, for all their variety of approaches, none of the designers attracted to the structural, visual and emotional possibilities of fetish fashion – a huge area as yet barely touched – has managed to produce a fashion statement that women would actually want to wear. From their isolated and rarified position vis-à-vis real life, designers are inclined to forget that the nuances of normal society are still remarkably restrictive when it comes to sexual clothing.

Fetishistic dress has still not crossed that great divide between fantasy and high-street actuality. Most of the marvellously inventive ways in which it has been used by designers in the past twenty years have died on the runway, or upon the magazine page, as we have already pointed out. But such a potentially fertile field must be revisited with different attitudes so that it can enrich and enliven a fashion scene grown stale with repetition. We have had the trailblazers – they have outraged and amused us. It is now time for a second wave of designers who will look at fetishism in a more controlled and calm way; who will resist the temptation to become crudely overexcited or who will look at this whole area of future fashion development and ask what there is in its marvels which can be adapted to the needs of women. In a word, raunchiness must give way to realism in order to open up the twenty-first century. Paradoxically, the way to realism in this field is almost certainly through romanticism – always a valuable, tempering force in fashion sexuality.

There are signs showing how the future might be in the work of Galliano at Dior, and especially in his couture collections for the house. Erroneously criticized for their impracticality and lack of realism, they have shown that Galliano – like his close contender, Gaultier – knows than modern couture must be a forcing house for new ideas. In the last seasons of the century he has, in what seems a giant paradox, taken fashion back to the days of Edwardian beauties with S-shaped figures, bending and undulating like swans, *belles poitrines* highlighted by brilliantly complex, figure-hugging cuts; and derrières thrown into sharp relief by long, clinging skirts ending in fish-tail trains, the movement of which was, for many Edwardian men, the height of erotic excitement as glamorous women swished them from side to side as they stepped, provocatively and slowly, across a room.

Galliano is not solely looking back, as some designers seem to be. His last couture collection of the Nineties contained a strong element of future shock, using PVC, industrial fastenings and fantasy space-age trappings, all of which were generally misunderstood but will influence the high street in the next few years more decisively than the work of most other designers. What he did was nothing so simplistic as 'twenty-first century' fashion. It was something much more subtle: it took and identified the futurist looks hinted at in the past twenty years and gave them a forward-looking credibility. He is, in fact, doing what his mentor, Christian Dior, did when he first presented the New Look. He is taking the past, deconstructing it and re-coordinating it to create a future. His approach, subtle and bold at the same time, makes clear that eroticism, even in its extreme form of fetishism, can grow up. When fashion designers realize that, the new fashion millennium can be said to have actually begun.

FORESEEING THE FUTURE

Fashion is the eternal relay race, with the baton of new ideas passed from one generation to the next. The results aren't always predictable. Just as in athletics the baton can be dropped, so a true sprinter can race ahead achieving goals that were previously unimaginable. In the fashion olympiad, however, the race never ends. The baton is always changing hands, and the track stretches to infinity.

Fashion design is a practical craft. What it can achieve is circumscribed by lifestyle, current moralities, technical methods and, above all, the limits of the human body and its range of movement. Because of these limitations, fashion often spends more time looking backwards than forwards. The roots of much modern fashion lie in rediscovering, recreating and recycling the past. The fashion industry in the second half of the twentieth century seemed to have been more interested in plagiarizing and plundering past eras than in attempting to solve current – and, more importantly, future – problems. Like architecture, it is far too often consumed by longings for a romantic historical past. As Rei Kawakubo of Comme des Garçons has said, 'From the point of view of finding possibilities, architecture and clothes-making share many potentials.'

Innovation in fashion is rare; a radical change in direction is even more so. Fads and fetishes, incandescent but brief, are all that can be expected in most decades. In this century, the one truly dramatic change in women's fashion occurred in the Forties when ordinary women began to wear trousers – something previously inconceivable, even in bohemian circles (except as part of a specific working uniform). Other inventions, however, have changed the course of

5   Madeleine Vionnet
    dress, 1934,
    photo Cecil
    Beaton

6   Madeleine Vionnet
    dress, 1931,
    photo George
    Hoyningen-Huene

fashion to a certain degree in the twentieth century – Madeleine Vionnet's bias cut is the perfect example. And there have been many adjustments in attitude, such as Chanel's adaptations of male dress for women and the historic borrowings of Vivienne Westwood. Rather than denigrate these designers, such examples point to the sheer difficulty of being original in fashion. Not only does most of the industry – not to mention the majority of customers – not welcome innovation, but designers frequently do not know how to produce it. Fashion of the past fifty years has exhibited little more than stylistic change as designers have followed repetitively certain lines and created individual fashion statements within an existing matrix.

There is one great exception. If anyone can be distinguished for inventing twentieth-century fashion for women, it is Madeleine Vionnet. She set fashion on a new path, deviating from the time-honoured tradition of disguising figure flaws – a demeaning approach to femininity that is summarized by fashion historian James Laver's definition of 'the shifting erogenous zone'. The idea that the female body is a collection of parts on display for the benefit of the male gaze is essentially a masculine fantasy of sexuality to which women have played for most of the past millennium.

6

Vionnet's philosophy of dress was simple: she believed that flattering clothes must complement the body, while following its movement. As a result, she evolved the bias cut, the first major step on the path to body-conscious clothing. It is because of Vionnet that women have gained the confidence to accept their bodies, instead of constraining them with boned bras and corsets or enhancing them – as in Dior's New Look – with horsehair hip pads.

The most fervent follower of the Vionnet approach to dress is the Paris-based couturier Azzedine Alaïa, born in Tunisia. He collects original Vionnet dresses and studies them to fully understand this particularly complex couturier whose clothes hang so perfectly and in so relaxed a form that it is hard to realize how technically sophisticated they are. The same could be said of Alaïa's clothes. Using many of Vionnet's techniques, especially her stitching and seaming, he creates clothes which appear constraining because they are tight and hug the body closely – so closely, in fact, that when Alaïa first emerged on the international fashion scene in the early Eighties, journalists quickly dubbed him the 'King of Cling'. It was apt to a point, but it tended to ignore the painstaking – and even scholarly – research behind Alaïa's apparently slick and sexy approach.

A perfectionist like Vionnet, Alaïa did not rely solely on knowing his mentor's approaches. He experimented during long hours of fittings, cutting each garment personally and trying each piece on the model many times over, adjusting and correcting as he went, refusing to stop until he was convinced he had honed the possibilities down to the one solution that worked better than all the others. No item was considered finished until it looked so natural on the body that it seemed like a second skin. Yet Alaïa's clothes are among the most complex of this century, engineered to perfection and produced to the standards of *haute couture*. Even though Alaïa has never promoted himself as anything more than a designer of practical, wearable dress for a certain type of woman, his work – in both concept and execution – can be compared to that of the great technicians of the century: not only Vionnet, but also Balenciaga, Charles James, Norman Norell and Roberto Capucci.

The women who wore Alaïa in the Eighties were newly enfranchised by the Seventies' emphasis on the importance of bodily fitness in modern fashion. Toned, trimmed, even muscular, the Alaïa woman was empowered by her physical health and vitality and wanted clothes that, instead of disguising imperfections, exposed her perfect frame in the most flattering way. Supermodels like Naomi Campbell, followed by movie stars and entertainers famed for their sexuality – women such as Brigitte Nielsen, Raquel Welch and Tina Turner – soon established a rapport with the designer. Turner's relentless, upbeat energy made her a perfect Alaïa model.

Alaïa's fashion reflects a philosophy of how women should look. Unlike most designers, who are always keen to capitalize on the new and move in fresh directions, Alaïa follows his own dictates and cares little about what other designers are doing. After briefly studying sculpture in Tunis, he arrived in Paris in 1957, but he did not become known to the fashion world for another twenty-three years. During that time, although often so poor that he could not afford quality fabric, he experimented as an artist. He worked as a dressmaker and even as a housekeeper for aristocratic patrons who supported him in return for the clothes he made to supplement their designer wardrobes. These patrons, the Marquise de Mazan in the late Fifties and the Comtesse Nicole de Blégiers in the early Sixties, played a vital role in Alaïa's career, by relieving him from the endless pressures to create that weigh so heavily on successful designers. Others also exerted an influence on Alaïa's psyche. He spent five unhappy days working with Christian Dior when he first came to Paris, and a more productive time with Guy Laroche. Alaïa's seminal experience, however, was working with Thierry Mugler in the Seventies.

7

9

Mugler is one of the most original and accomplished designers to have appeared in Paris in the past forty years. In fact, it is his example as much as Vionnet's to which Alaïa is indebted for the strength of his fashion vision. Many would claim that Mugler has always been ahead of the field technically. But, for most, his technical brilliance is overshadowed by a unique and, for a considerable number of women, shockingly non-politically correct sensibility that his supporters claim has cost him his true place in the hierarchy of Paris fashion. It is Mugler who first conceived the idea of body-conscious clothes and power dressing. His place in fashion history is assured, if for no other reason than the enormous influence of his hi-tech fantasy fashion on high-street dressing in the Eighties. Mugler's fuse was long and slow-burning, but it led directly to the wide shoulders, tightly pinched waists and body-hugging fashions of the decade – a fact sometimes forgotten by Alaïa's supporters. Both men wielded crucial influence on fashion in the Eighties, as did the creator of the most aggressive of all feminine silhouettes: Claude Montana.

Despised by feminists, who completely ignored the sensual and voluptuous aspects of his approach to female sexuality, Montana claimed as long ago as the Seventies that the two couturiers who had most influenced him were women, both of whom worked in Paris between the wars: Madeleine Vionnet and Madame Grès. Both women believed that the only valid fashion was that which remained simple and enhanced the contours of the female body. For all the apparent exuberance of his designs, Montana could be said to be a true disciple in that his clothes, like those of Mugler and Alaïa, were created to enhance the feminine figure. The silhouette he conceived, based on archetypes of masculinity such as bikers, storm troopers, American football players and samurai warriors, is characterized by padded, exaggerated shoulders; a small, tightly constrained waist – its narrowness frequently emphasized by a stiffened peplum; and hugely oversized collars. Montana's chosen material was leather, and he used it to powerful effect: one borrowed but not improved upon by many other designers, including Gianni Versace and Donna Karan, who have been much more influenced by this essentially Parisian movement than they might acknowledge.

The Montana shape of the Eighties became an archetype, then a cliché and, finally, in cruder hands than his, it assumed a vulgarity totally lacking in his original. Montana, in short, was a visionary who foresaw how sex and fashion could come together in a statement of irresistible power for millions of women. The matrix was male, the effect Amazonian. To call Montana's silhouette 'space-age' is to demean it by over-simplification. To think of it in terms of Futurism, Constructivism or any of the other art movements of this century does nothing to clarify the source of its power.

Montana's approach to female dress requires a sure hand and an impeccable sense of judgement. Despite its exaggerated features, Montana's fashion statement in the Eighties was never overblown – a testament to his creative skills, artistic finesse and ruthless self-control. It is unfortunate that the look he introduced, along

12

with Mugler and Alaïa, eventually became devalued by imitations, but it remains one of the strongest, most valid and universal movements to have appeared in fashion in the last twenty years.

The power look exerted considerable and immediate influence, one so pervasive that it couldn't last. The second major Eighties' movement hailed from Japan and in many ways marked a reaction to this approach to fashion and femininity. It has had a subtler but possibly broader impact on women's dress than any fashion statement of the past fifty years, although the fashion industry, and women in general, have been slow to embrace it.

The Japanese presence in Europe goes back to 1965, when Kenzo Takada arrived in Paris at the age of twenty-six, followed a year later by Issey Miyake, who became design assistant to Guy Laroche and then moved to Givenchy. Miyake followed his French experience with a year in New York working with Geoffrey Beene before returning to Japan in 1970. Like Kenzo and Hanae Mori, who became a member of the Chambre Syndicale de la Couture Parisienne in 1977, Miyake showed in Paris from that date. These three designers have become known as the first wave of what Europe xenophobically chooses to call the Japanese invasion.

Of the three, Hanae Mori was the one who adapted most readily to the standards and attitudes of Western fashion. Kenzo blazed a more independent trail. His Jungle Jap label, founded in 1970, exerted a wide influence on fashion in the following decade, arguably equal to that of Yves Saint Laurent at the time, although it did not last as long. Colour was what made Kenzo such a force: strong, primary colour mixed in patterns that took their inspiration from Africa, Asia, Native American art and costume and American popular culture. The mix – eclectic, rich and bursting with youthful exuberance – was taken up by the Italian firms Fiorucci and Benetton and every high-street boutique

from London and New York to Tokyo itself. Kenzo absorbed and disseminated broader cultural and ethnic influences than any previous fashion designer. His practice reflects the decade when fashion knew no limits; when designers and customers felt no compulsion to conform; when the Sixties' youth movement continued to affect fashion profoundly at all levels with its gloriously eclectic mix of everything and anything that seemed attractive at the moment. If the Seventies was the period when rigid taste was finally routed, Kenzo was surely one of its great instruments of change.

The fashion baton passed from Kenzo's confident hand to Issey Miyake, who was both more profoundly and more overtly Japanese. Miyake stood at the threshold of Japanese fashion, looking back to what Kenzo had achieved and forward to what was to come. It would be hard to overestimate his power in the late Seventies and Eighties, just as it would be impossible to dismiss the strength of his vision, which has kept him at the forefront of fashion's avant-garde for more than twenty years.

These Japanese designers share a characteristic compulsion to question, experiment and innovate. Their search for new paradigms has had valuable, far-reaching repercussions throughout the world of fashion. Miyake is well aware that he stands as a fulcrum between East and West; he knows that, even more so than Kenzo, he brought the two different aesthetics together to produce a Japanese style meaningful in the West. It is no criticism of Kenzo to claim Miyake as the father of modern Japanese fashion – certainly, if it were not for Kenzo's crucial influence, his countrymen might never have taken the leap and decided to show in Paris.

Miyake can be claimed as a visionary – but one who is entirely practical, who accepts fashion as a hybrid of commerce and art. He has followed his own path, never entirely allowing himself to be seduced by outright commercialism yet not failing to accept fashion's most

15

powerful imperative, which is to be profitable or go out of business. He has tempered a radical, and even didactic, tendency, common in many Japanese designers, with an understanding of the different attitudes to dress found in the West, without losing the strong personality of the East. Like other Japanese designers, he believes that fluidity and versatility characterize modern clothing. Not for him clothes forming a tightly jewelled and structured carapace that traps the woman inside. Not for him the bustier, bustle or padded hips so popular with designers who look to a European courtly past for inspiration. Instead, Miyake thinks freedom, giving women 'wind-coats', for example, that billow and fall back into shape; that can be wrapped around the body like a goosefeather quilt; and that can make the wearer the creator, allowing her, rather than the designer, to compress or expand the garment as she likes.

In 1988 Miyake began work on what seems to be a fashion approach so unique that it could well prove to be his historic memorial. He began to examine the possibility of pleats as the most comprehensive and accommodating approach to dress for the end of the twentieth century. In 1993 Miyake's 'Pleats Please' line became the focus of his prodigious creativity. No aesthetic breakthrough happens in a vacuum. Miyake's came via the Delphos dresses of Fortuny – made of finely pleated silk so malleable that a dress could be rolled into a tiny ball that could be held in the palm of a hand – and the fluid garments that characterize the radical approach of his mentor, Geoffrey Beene, and from whom he learned the importance of subtlety of cut and truth to fabric as the basis of the simplicity which both men feel brings modernity in fashion. Miyake then learned from Laroche and Givenchy the French approach to cut and style. Using his experience, he went on to create his unique approach to fashion. Miyake's pleats are malleable – to a point; they are also fluid. But what makes them exciting and new is their bounce – their ability to move not only with the body but also in counter rhythm to it. They are possibly the first examples of almost-animated dress, garments that flow in harmony with the features and movement of their wearers but with a flair of their own. Women have found the way they flatter, while accommodating a wide range of body types, highly attractive – between their launch in March 1993 and March 1997, 680,000 Pleats Please outfits were sold.

In October 1999, Miyake decided to step down as designer of his own-name line, handing over to his long-time collaborator, Naoki Takizawa. But this does not mean that Miyake is no longer involved in experiments

16

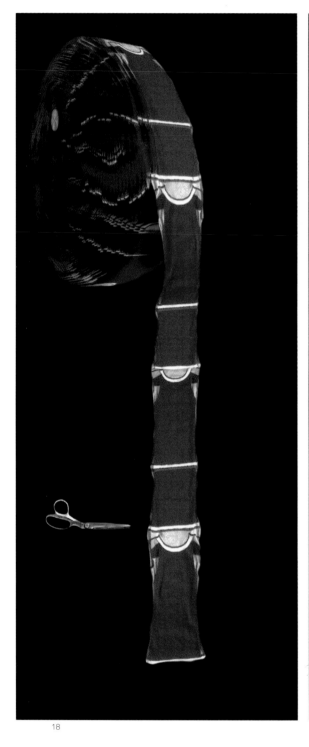
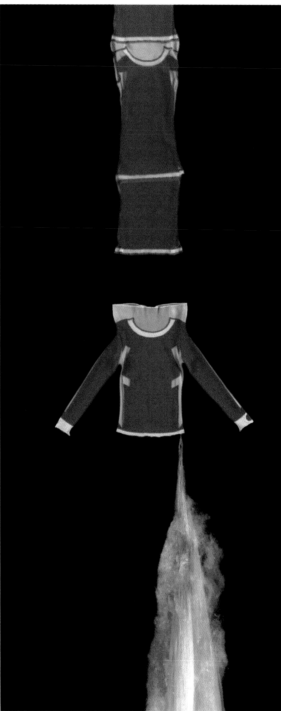

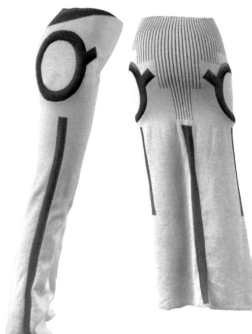

18 Issey Miyake,
'Eskimo' A-POC,
1999–2000

which question the basis of fashion which, in his view, is fabric – the raw material of creativity. He now devotes his energies to his revolutionary new concept A-POC (A Piece of Cloth) which moves fashion forward as an interactive craft in which all can participate. With A-POC, the wishes of the designer are a beginning, not an end. Each customer is able to create a garment which uniquely reflects her wishes. In a fundamental way, Miyake is giving back to the customer a freedom and control she had in the days of dressmakers, but which was swept away by the demands of mass-production. As the 'General Motors' banality of almost identical design suggestions from multinational fashion organizations threatens to stifle all originality in dress, many see Miyake's A-POC as a much needed breath of oxygen for a patient, if not actually dying, then certainly in need of serious resuscitation for the twenty-first century.

Unfortunately, in most places outside Japan, Miyake's revolutionary contribution to future fashion goes unmarked. His techniques are perhaps too subtle and complex to lend themselves to adaptation by mass-market manufacturers. Or maybe his vision is too advanced to be appreciated by the majority. Although his name is known (mainly through his perfumes) and respected (especially within the fashion industry), his sales are still largely to an élite, although his distinctive approach to fabric is more instantly recognizable than that of many designers. It is tempting to see Miyake as the artistic genius of our fashion age, a misunderstood trailblazer for the future. Yet he is more accurately a precursor and liberator whose strengths will be built on by the future leaders of fashion. Whether the Miyake disciples come from the East or the West remains to be seen, but Miyake stands as a seminal figure at the turn of the new century. Although his creativity shows no sign of waning, he has already left enough challenging ideas to inspire several generations of designers in the twenty-first century.

Like Kenzo, Miyake expresses a distinct *joie de vivre*, but with a more intellectual approach. His synthesis of Western and Eastern sensibilities was represented by his 1979 exhibition, 'East Meets West', at the International Design Conference in Aspen, Colorado, that was promoted not as fashion but as art and toured some of the West's most important museums and galleries, as did several other exhibitions of his work, including 'Bodyworks' (1983), seen in Tokyo, Los Angeles and San Francisco.

Since then, Japanese designers have become an established facet of Western fashion. All of them approach their work with a strong, nationalistic frame of mind. Most produce fashion of a timeless beauty and exactitude that transcends the West's frequently sexist, cynical and manipulative attitudes. Their clothes are often characterized by a youthful delicacy – even a diffidence – that makes them seem vulnerable. Yet nothing could be further from the truth. Japanese design may give the illusion of ephemerality, but in reality it is not only durable but also proof against most of the vagaries of fashion change. It would be easy to relegate it to a fashion wasteland – interesting but non-commercial – if it did not have such power.

It is possible to see the work of Rei Kawakubo, creator of the Comme des Garçons label, as the only valid creative force in fashion today. She founded Comme des Garçons in Tokyo in 1969 and began showing there in 1975, the year in which she opened her first boutique. She showed her first collection in Paris six years later, again, in 1981 – the year in which Yohji Yamamoto also presented in the French capital. Despite Kenzo, Mori and Miyake, the West was ill-prepared for this creative onslaught from the East. To eyes used to clothing created within a matrix of good taste barely altered over fifty years (and that is how retrograde most high fashion was in Paris in 1981) the Japanese aesthetic was an outrage. Deliberately ugly and tasteless as it seemed, there was nevertheless something too frightening about its dynamic for it to be dismissed according to the effete and privileged standards of Western high fashion. The challenge had to be addressed.

What was it about the new wave of Japanese design that seemed not only frightening but also destructive to Western eyes? It was nothing less than the total deconstruction of the Western approach to fashion. Kawakubo and Yamamoto literally tore Western dressmaking traditions apart at the seams and reassembled them, creating garments that recalled the tatterdemalion clothes of the vagrant and the torn, misaligned and ill-fitting dress of the mendicant. No wonder Paris – and, indeed, the whole of Western fashion – gasped and stared wide-eyed in horror. These were not clothes to be shrugged off and dismissed as an aberration. They had – for all their alien strangeness – an incontrovertible quality and strength. All but the most ostrich-like observers knew that things had changed and fashion would never be quite the same again. Two hundred years of culture had been undermined, ruptured and reassessed.

From the beginning, Yamamoto was the more accommodating of the two. He seemed more at ease compromising with Western fashion ideals, better able to assimilate Paris-based fashion culture. Kawakubo

19 Comme des
    Garçons, photo
    Craig McDean

20 (Overleaf)
    Comme des
    Garçons, 'Body
    Meets Dress;
    Dress Meets
    Body',
    1997, photo
    Paolo Roversi

21 (Overleaf)
    Comme des
    Garçons, 1998–9,
    photo Craig
    McDean

appeared to work in the kamikaze tradition – she was determined to make an impact at any cost. Her austere approach, based on the eloquence of fabric as an integral part of life, brought a reassessment of clothes design. Cotton and coarse wool were hand-printed, beaten, reshaped, defibred and distressed. In Comme des Garçons' fashions, fabric was the animating force, as it had been with the work of Madeleine Vionnet. Classic *haute couture* line, as defined by the traditions of Western dressmaking, lost its meaning and was replaced by a new form of line equally as rigorous and demanding. It took the West over ten years to realize that this line was as strong as that which it aimed to displace.

Kawakubo had appropriated clothes to serve her personal compulsion to uncover the new and express the essential spirit of her time. Her integrity and radical self-examination reflected an ideology that was unique in Paris in the early Eighties but traditional in Japan, the source of most of Kawakubo's apparently revolutionary but, in fact, remarkably logical ideas. Her work is better understood in the context of architectural developments of the last twenty years than by comparison with Western fashion of that period. Crucial to her way of thinking was the Pompidou Centre, designed by Renzo Piano and Richard Rogers between 1971 and 1977. The project was an updated expression of Le Corbusier's dictum that a house is a 'machine for living in'. The architects exposed the structure of the Pompidou building in a deliberate attempt to make the viewer realize that the mechanical and engineering aspects of architecture are worthy of consideration, need not be hidden from view and, indeed, are an integral part of the beauty and aesthetic power of the building.

This is precisely the approach taken by Rei Kawakubo in her early days in Paris, when she exposed seams, left items unfinished and turned fabrics inside out. She believed that articulating the structure was not only the point of a garment, but also the mark of a designer's skill. The effect of this thinking on her early collections was dramatic. It was hailed as a form of radicalism never before seen in dress, but it is also possible to see Kawakubo's approach in a less flattering light. Just as the Pompidou Centre can be considered an attempt by the French government to regain the artistic centre stage it had lost in the Sixties, so Kawakubo's intentions were equally political: to proclaim a new order with the Japanese aesthetic at its head. It isn't easy to rationalize the concept of exposing the mechanics of clothing – aesthetically, socially or historically. It is, however, easy to dismiss it as a superficial modernist flourish, a bravura performance.

23

24

What she released was something new in fashion, something that had a much greater influence on dress than anything deriving from traditional French high-fashion sources. By exposing the inner layers of a garment, Rei Kawakubo brought into the public domain the intimacies of dress. Things normally only felt by the skin were seen in full view. In the hands of less subtle designers, underwear became outerwear – with varied degrees of delicacy and crudeness. Change in fashion frequently assumes unpredictable forms. A designer's aesthetic is appropriated – often subconsciously – and subjected to different mental processes. The corset mania that gripped Jean Paul Gaultier, Vivienne Westwood and a host of less skilled designers was part of the thinking of Rei Kawakubo in the early Eighties, when she was deconstructing and reassembling clothing to produce what she saw as a modern form of female sexuality.

Since those days, Kawakubo has continued her experiments regardless of the public's lack of understanding, the occasional derision and the general bewilderment that greets much that she proposes. Never attracted to the populist path, she feigns indifference to the frequently hostile reception her collections receive. Determined to challenge conformity, she takes a totally approach uncompromising, so much so that early Commes des Garçons garments – sometimes with three sleeves or only a fraction of a collar – required diagrams explaining how to put them on. But it must be remembered that many of her collections over the past twenty years have articulated a feeling of the moment; many have been beautiful; all have been technically advanced and every garment she has created has presented a challenge to conventional fashion thinking.

If she is not so controversial as she once was, Rei Kawakubo is no tamed spirit. Witness her 1997 'Body Meets Dress; Dress Meets Body' collection, which was greeted with almost universal bafflement. In it, she distorted the female shape by padding it at various points so that the wearer frequently seemed to be suffering from a form of elephantiasis. People who had forgotten the sixteenth-century stomacher or the nineteenth-century bustle considered Kawakubo's experiments a joke in very bad taste. The collection raised questions that will eventually need to be answered in the West – about garments and their relationship to the body, the concept of beauty and the tyranny of line. In her initial salvo, however, it seems unlikely that Kawakubo was looking back for historical references. As occurs so often in her oeuvre, the genesis was architecture, initially the geodesic domes of Buckminster Fuller, the American architect and engineer

who used to astound and discomfort his colleagues by asking them how much their buildings weighed – a radical concept that would have been understood by Kawakubo. But, in fact, the deepest influence on her thinking – and surely the inspiration for 'Body Meets Dress; Dress Meets Body' – is the architecture of modern Japan as seen in the work of Masaharu Takasaki (specifically, the Crystal Light Building); Eisaku Ushida and his Scottish partner, Kathryn Findlay (their Soft and Hairy House inspired by the work of Dalí); and, above all, Tadao Ando. All have eschewed the linearity associated with architecture, just as Kawakubo has rejected the conventional approach to line in fashion.

Her compatriot, Yohji Yamamoto, early on assumed a pioneering position that was similar in philosophy, although in no serious way did it parallel Kawakubo's approaches, despite the fact that commentators tend to speak of them in one voice. Like her, he works as an explorer, delving into the nature of Western and Japanese clothing conventions to uncover a meaningful synthesis of both. Even more so than Rei Kawakubo, Yohji Yamamoto is essentially modern, a man who has viewed with perplexity the exercises in fashion atavism that have overrun both Paris and London in the past ten years. Yamamoto looks back only in order to move forward. His imagination does not dwell on visions of the more sumptuous creations in the history of Western fashion. If it is possible for a designer to speak with a neutral voice – classless, accentless and ageless – then that is what Yamamoto has attempted to do in twenty years of viewing Occidental clothing conventions through an uncompromisingly Oriental eye. He has examined Paris couture from the viewpoint of Japanese tradition.

Like Kawakubo, Yamamoto chose to work predominantly in black – or its opposite, white – because they are neutral, carry little emotional historical baggage and remove the problem inherent in all fashion – preconceived assumptions about what dress can and should achieve, not only for the wearer but also for the viewer. In an era when exposure of the body has moved from titillation to vulgarity to cliché, Yamamoto's approach might seem almost prudish in its modesty. However, it would be wrong to assume that because Yamamoto's clothes rarely expose the flesh that they are the work of a man indifferent to the sexual power – and, indeed, importance – of clothes that reveal the nuances, if not the reality, of the body. Garments by Yamamoto rely for their allure on the interplay of movement between flesh and fabric, and this interplay testifies to his skill in projecting a concept of female sexuality that is neither totally Western nor entirely Japanese: it is a sexuality diametrically opposed to both Western raunchiness

27

and the modesty and self-effacement that seem to characterize traditional Japanese attitudes.

The man who says, 'If fashion is clothes, then it is not indispensable. But if fashion is a way of looking at our daily lives, then it is very important indeed', is not likely to be susceptible to compromise. But Yamamoto is probably the designer most open to influences, and he uses his design studio to foster a continuing dialogue between his own assumptions and those of others. His collections are a form of work in progress. It often takes several of them to clarify a new idea – and, unlike many Western designers, he never merely makes dress statements but always proposes new ideas, perspectives and parameters. The label in his clothing frequently states, 'There is nothing so boring as a neat and tidy look.' Yamamoto likes the 'messiness' of high creativity but fears the possibility of losing control. Could that be why black, the traditional colour of the samurai, is still his favourite colour?

28

The impact of Kawakubo, Yamamoto and the many strong Japanese designers who have followed them to Paris, such as Junya Watanabe – whose studied delicacy and economy show a great indebtedness to the Comme des Garçons ethic – has been considerable and continues. It is in many ways proof of their avant-garde thinking that they are still not entirely assimilated into fashion's mainstream. Western tradewinds do not, to any great extent, blow their way. Some of these designers would be in serious financial difficulties without their other clothing lines – often less radical and controversial than their Paris counterparts – that sell so well in Japan. Their influence, nevertheless, will be a major force in world fashion in the twenty-first century, just as their radical reassessment of clothes and the body is already seen in the experimental work of young designers like the Paris-based American Jeremy Scott and even tangentially in the attitudes of Viktor & Rolf.

The intellectual high ground of fashion shifted perceptively, if briefly, in the late Eighties and early Nineties away from the Japanese to a group of Belgian designers who became known as the Antwerp Six. Dirk Bikkembergs, Ann Demeulemeester, Martin Margiela, Walter Van Beirendonck, Dries Van Noten and Dirk Van Saene address the questions of deconstruction and minimalism with an entirely European sensibility. Despite the generic title given to them when they first became a

29

32

31

feature of the international fashion world, and the fact that they exhibited together at the British Designers' Show in London for several seasons in the Eighties, they have subsequently taken different routes.

By far the most radical and, many would contend, the most original thinker is Martin Margiela, whose uncompromising approach to communication has frequently left the fashion world feeling baffled, if not short-changed. Margiela initiated the concept of recycling (some might say cannibalizing) items of dress as part of his own statement. It might be a sleeve removed from a man's shirt to create a blouse, a sweater made from military-issue socks, a pair of jeans incorporated into a skirt or headscarves tied around the body as aprons or tops. A former assistant to Jean Paul Gaultier, Margiela has been seen as a leader of what has been dubbed *la mode destroy* because of his early attraction to slashing and fraying garments. In fact, he is a fashion conservationist who dislikes the transitory approach to modern fashion and the speed with which ideas are taken up and then discarded. The object of his recycling is simple: he believes that clothes should continue to have a life, in one form or another, until they literally fall apart. His fashions, like the surroundings in which he works, are masterpieces of bricolage – tactile, evocative and negating everything the runways and salons of traditional French couturiers stand for.

Margiela's presentations are as uncompromising as his clothes. In 1989, he placed an advertisement in the free newspaper *Paris Boum Boum*, inviting people to his show in a basement disco. The next season he showed on wasteground in a poor area of the 20th arrondissement in Paris, and the local children joined in the show. In 1991, the invitation to his show was a handwritten telephone number that connected the caller to an answering machine giving the location and time of the presentation. Later that year, he showed in a metro station that had not been used since 1939. Most recently, he has removed both models and catwalk and shown his clothes on video screens or even suspended on hangers held by white-coated 'assistants'. It is perhaps not surprising that many members of the press become impatient with Margiela's approach, seeing it either as a bad joke or an insult to their professionalism.

It is neither. But it is a challenge to preconceived ideas of modern fashion and how it should be presented. Margiela's approach raises the question of whether he is an artist *manqué* posing as a fashion designer, or a fashion designer determined to treat fashion with the same intellectual rigour accorded to other artistic

34

35

efforts. The jury is still out, but it need not waste time enquiring as to whether Margiela is a great designer, or a commercial one. His line created for Hermès is the epitome of luxury: relaxed and unassertive, it is shown with a total lack of 'tricks' in the Hermès flagship shop on the Rue Faubourg St Honoré by women who are neither professional models nor all young. The effect is totally convincing.

Margiela stands with Demeulemeester and Van Noten as the major figures in Belgian fashion, but Bikkembergs and Van Beirendonck also have their place, especially for their radical and challenging approach to menswear. Van Beirendonck's second line, aptly named Wild and Lethal Trash, is aimed at both sexes, although he firmly denies the concept of unisex. Sex is, nevertheless, the driving force behind W&LT, and it is of a highly specialist kind, as could be expected from the man who named his first collection (presented in 1982) 'Sado' in homage to the work of the British artist, Allen Jones. Condemned as near pornography by many, W&LT has a serious following among the young of Europe and all who are interested in S&M.

Dirk Bikkembergs's approach is more tempered but, like Margiela, he takes an uncompromising intellectual view of fashion. He shares Margiela's belief that how the clothes are presented is a seminal part of a collection and has held fashion shows in such 'un-chic' environments as the Gare du Nord in Paris and the old sewers in an attempt to find a setting that fits his clothes. Like Van Beirendonck, he works on sartorial principles which reflect a unified approach to dressing both sexes, but eschews the use of the word unisex, preferring his simple but impeccably cut clothes to say what needs to be said. It is this lack of compromise, seen at its most complete in Demeulemeester's work, which ensures respect for the Belgians – a respect likely to continue with the 'second generation' Antwerp-trained designers, Josephus Thimister and Véronique Branquinho, whose clothes produce a strong statement in the Belgian tradition of robust practicality and sophisticated style.

As the new century begins, it is the Japanese and Belgians who appear to have laid the sturdiest foundations for the future, but it remains to be seen how long it will take for their radicalism to win out over the romantic historicism promoted by many of the most powerful and influential designers currently working in Paris. Perhaps the new century should move forward with designers considering the laconic statement by one of fashion's earliest minimalists, Geoffrey Beene, who once said, 'Simplicity is what chic and style are about … The road to simplicity is very complex.'

FASHION, PROTEST AND THE WAR FROM WITHIN

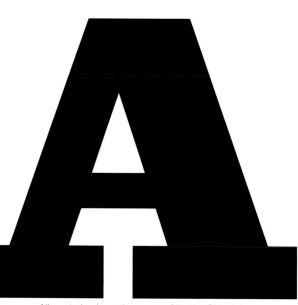

All centuries bear the scars of battle. Skirmishes – ideological as well as actual – are part of the history of humanity. It is not just territorial and geographical but also emotional, social and intellectual territories mankind has fought to annex. The sound of warfare is not limited to the swish of the slashing sword or the boom of the exploding cannon. The echo of Martin Luther nailing his credo to the door of the Wittenberg church in 1517 has followed us through history. It is as much the noise of battle as are the grinding tanks, droning aircraft or the tramp of the soldiers' marching feet.

This century has seen ideological protest flourish to an extent far greater than in other centuries. Wars of will have flared and raged in virtually every corner of the globe as people have followed the dictates of their conscience with as much bravery and courage as any shown by the uniformed soldier. The battles have been fought over basic human rights and on behalf of the dispossessed. The skirmishes pit the liberal against the autocrat; the democrat against the dictator; women against men; youth and ethnic groups against the Establishment, which is almost always determined to fight to retain the status quo, no matter how ultimately untenable it is.

When, on 21 August 1968, Czech radio signalled the collapse of Prague to the Russians by abruptly ceasing to play *Má Vlast* by Bedřich Smetana, very few fashionable people in the West were deeply concerned. When the police barricades had gone up in Saint Germain three months earlier, nobody in the gilded halls of the Paris couturiers felt that a student demonstration in solidarity with blue-collar workers could be of any interest to them. Both were wrong, but it was a mistake

most people in the fashionable world at that time would have made. It seemed preposterous that battles in the streets could actually influence fashion, but if members of the couture Establishment had spent less time preening their egos and thinking of their glorious past; if they had not assumed their world was safe, set in the rich amber of time; if they had had sufficient curiosity, let alone vision, to pull back the heavy silk drapes of their cocooned existence, they could have seen the future.

The Sixties often get a bad name because they have become indelibly linked with the fatuity of Swinging London, but they were a period of great political and social unrest. It was a time when the young took on the rest of society in what seemed a hopelessly uneven struggle. In fact, it was a battle they could not lose, because they were at the forefront of a sociopolitical movement that was already pervasive in the West. It had to do with the breakdown of old hierarchies, traditional formalities and obsolete attitudes. The battleground was America, the most exciting, frightening and challenging place a young person could live in the Sixties. The protest centre of the globe, it was there that many crucial battles were fought for the rest of the world. One by one people stood up to be counted, from Timothy Leary, who advocated the use of LSD to his students in 1963; to Betty Friedan, whose book *The Feminine Mystique* (1963) was to be incredibly influential for at least a generation; to Rachel Carson, whose *Silent Spring* (1962) was the first book to point out the dangers of pesticides; to Ralph Nader who, in *Unsafe at Any Speed* (1965), took on Detroit and the powerful automobile industry over the issue of car safety; to the anonymous black civil rights marchers in Alabama who

refused to disperse when ordered to do so by state troopers wielding high-pressure hoses. Chanting the single word 'Freedom', the marchers pushed forward in a scene that presaged social protest over the next thirty years.

It was an age when the young found themselves in serious conflict with their parents over just about everything. A new culture was emerging, one with youth at its centre, and the old culture could do nothing about it but start running scared. Why were the established forces at such a disadvantage? They lacked a driving force, a single unifying element that cut across social classes, religious differences and levels of education. They lacked pop music – the 'missing link' that, with its provocative lyrics and charismatic counterculture figures, inspired young people globally to believe that the fact that they were at variance with their parents and authority in general was the strength which would enable them to alter society. For them, Jimi Hendrix made more sense than the whole of the House of Representatives.

Nevertheless, it was a decade when young Americans witnessed for the first time a president – John F. Kennedy – who engaged their attention and respect, and a black religious leader – Martin Luther King, Jr – who was determined to stand up and be counted. In the same decade both men were gunned down and the world learned of the atrocities committed in Cambodia and Vietnam. Faced with these events, the young had every right to reject the old order as rotten and not in any sense reflective of their beliefs. But, for every young person who joined the freedom fighters in the South or adopted an antiwar stance, there were at least two who protested by rejecting the society that had produced

5   Françoise Hardy,
1969, photo
Reg Lancaster

6   'The War is Over!',
Central Park,
New York, 1975,
photo Dagmar

such atrocities. They retreated into their own personal nirvanas, isolated from the world by a self-absorbed obsession with drugs, music and the most liberated approach to sex that the young had ever openly dared to practise.

It was axiomatic that those involved in the struggle, as well as those who walked away from it, were opposed to the materialism that increasingly underpinned and drove American society. They were disinclined to buy into the formula that individuals work in order to become consumers, thereby bettering themselves, improving their quality of life and promoting the common good. Clearly, fashion plays an integral role in such a consumer society. It was the easiest thing for protesters to turn their backs on, and the most obvious. Those who have given up a certain food for ideological reasons can demonstrate the fact only by telling others, but if they opt out of a dress system their appearance immediately conveys the fact. Bra-burning was an overtly symbolic act. Women who removed their bras for ideological reasons didn't need to shout it from the rooftops. The proof of their gesture was visible; there was no need for words.

The semiotics of this approach were fundamental to fashion. Not only did the 'no-bra' movement repudiate male attitudes to female sexuality, it dismissed the whole ethos of high fashion, which was predicated on the assumption that women dress in order to win the approval of men. Conversely, at almost the same time, the complex symbolism of male gay dress codes was emerging, aimed at gaining the attention and approbation of other men. A handkerchief of a certain colour, or a particular way of attaching car keys to a belt became shorthand for a whole map of sexual preferences. This was not a language that begged for universal understanding. It was aimed at insiders and, unlike hippie dress, for example, was for a long time unknown to those outside that world. But most dress codes spoke clearly enough of the protest their wearers were making.

The Rastafarian's dreadlocks and colourful knitted head coverings or the sleekly urban dress of the black militants conveyed an inescapable message, just as the combat jacket and Che Guevara beret were totems of ideological disaffection. Not since the Sans-Culottes and Incroyables in revolutionary France had clothing been used so specifically to proclaim attitudes and allegiances.

These were newsworthy extremes of fashion protest, but there was an equally important ground swell to be found in women's fashion, which largely changed attitudes without resorting to political brouhaha or protest. Yet women's wholesale rejection of high fashion in the Sixties was highly political, nothing less than a remapping of what femininity might be in the future. Status dressing of the kind that had kept couture at the forefront of fashion for a hundred years was rightly seen as a comment on the status of the male who paid for such clothes – because, as was pointed out at the time, no woman who had earned enough money to buy her own couture clothes would dream of spending it in such a way. The expression 'status wives' would not be heard for another twenty years, but by the mid-Sixties the concept was discredited even if the nomenclature was wanting.

This was a major protest – so much so that it might even be called a revolution. It was not overt or aggressive enough to be called a rebellion, but it signified a fundamental shift in female attitudes. Clothing is never devoid of status. It proclaims, therefore it is. It would be wrong to imagine that status was removed from female dress by the rejection of couture. What changed was the nature of the status. Clothes that proclaimed the wealth of a woman's husband lost their appeal. Clothes that communicated the status of a woman as a healthy, independent, participatory member of society filled the gap. The age of sexual desirability in fashion had slipped away. The leadership no longer automatically belonged

to the woman over thirty. Youth took over fashion as it was doing in other fields and brought with it a new form of status: that of dressing down to please oneself rather than dressing up to please others.

This was not something new in fashion. Rich women had always enjoyed opportunities to relax the often stringent dress codes of the past, but they did so in their boudoirs, away from the need for display. In the twentieth century the *dégagé* approach involved sportswear, which was not dress for sport but informal yet smart dress for occasions when a woman's clothes did not need to signify her social position. Normally, a woman wore sportswear in her home or when relaxing with others of her class. It was frequently the only acceptable way to dress in the country.

Sportswear is generally considered the invention of Seventh Avenue, the head and heart of American ready-to-wear fashion, which first became a recognizable entity in the Thirties. In fact, sportswear was not invented but evolved in response to the need for a more flexible clothing approach than that found in Paris. It was essentially modern in its emphasis on practicality and its rejection of traditional status fashion. The American designer Elizabeth Hawes summed up this movement in *Fashion is Spinach*, her 1938 bestseller written to debunk the mysteries of fashion, when she claimed that fashion 'has become a complete anachronism in modern life. One good laugh and the deformed thief would vanish into the past.' Her prediction had a delayed fuse. It took another twenty-five years for that to happen.

These were clothes a woman could dress in herself without soliciting help from maid, husband or sister. As such, they were the breakthrough in twentieth-century fashion, modernizing women's attitudes as much as their appearance. The relaxed dress codes of the Sixties, which loosened up and softened female dress, followed this tradition. Even so, for many women dressing informally didn't mean appearing unladylike. The formal

7   Betsey Johnson
     for Paraphernalia,
     1966, photo David
     Montgomery

8   Betsey Johnson
     and her daughter,
     1996, photo
     Charles Harris

hats and gloves – white cotton for summer, dark leather for winter – had gone but a well-groomed appearance was still *de rigueur*. The Sixties began to change this custom as different criteria for taste began to emerge in initially tentative movements. While high fashion – that is, Paris fashion – continued to be predicated on the assumption that the well-dressed woman was the ladylike woman, in the streets the rules were frequently flouted. Satin hot pants, platform soles and ankle straps, denim jackets and diamanté glitter do not a traditional lady make – and that was part of their attraction. Entire wardrobes took over the role previously assigned to millinery and became amusing, witty or outrageous in a way not seen since the Surrealist touches found in Elsa Schiaparelli's couture collections in the Thirties. Hair, the wilder and woollier the better, became a focal point of a woman's personality, even more than her make-up, which could be rainbow-coloured and even include black lipstick.

For those women not ready for complete subversion, there were other, more subtle trends that demonstrated one's rebellion against high fashion. Eclecticism beckoned them down the gypsy road of recycling. A whole new world of second-hand clothing stretched alluringly ahead, promising endless possibilities for theatricality, originality and role play. Women could now adapt and redefine their personality as well as their appearance without any reference to official fashion diktats and at a fraction of the cost of mainstream fashion. Flea markets, thrift shops, charity sales, granny's attic and church fundraising events all became the happy hunting ground for women looking for clothes with personality – or which, at the very least, could be put together to reflect their personalities. Laura Ashley capitalized on this mood and, later, it influenced Lagerfeld's exercises in high-camp fancy dress for the Chloé label and even Ralph Lauren's homesteader's wife look in the late Seventies.

For most of the Seventies everyone had fun being as individualistic as personal courage allowed. Eclectic, and sometimes amazingly inventive, dress combinations emerged, breaking decades-old rules about mixing patterns, fabrics and colours. A free-for-all promiscuity became the norm, to be quickly copied by commercial designers. Protest was annexed by the very industry being protested against – as all successful fashion protests are. But the modern ragbag look had already made an important, lasting breakthrough. Women now had an alternative to the carefully edited proposals of chainstores or boutiques. Further, the looks created by designers would never exert the same authority again. Far from being the sole arbiters of brief fads,

high-fashion houses merely proposed, or, if they were very lucky, originated fads, as in the case of Westwood's mini-crini in the Eighties – although photographed and talked about, rarely worn beyond the narrow confines of London's clubland – or Versace's sharp oranges, mauves, pinks and pale greens in the Nineties. To all intents, fashion dictatorship had been shunted onto the sidelines. Grand couturiers, irrelevant to most women for all fashion purposes, were promoted as celebrities, but their collections were seen increasingly as fantasies whose sole purpose was to generate publicity for the many accessories and non-couture items sold under their names.

Having tasted freedom, women would never go back. The designers who meant something to them now were people like Betsey Johnson of New York, in many respects a loose cannon who has proved to be a persistent, although minor, star. As early as the mid-Sixties, she had picked up the vibes of the young and hip and, by the Seventies, her designs for Alley Cat were a cunning mix of New York funkiness and post-Carnaby Street cool. Her clothes were highly successful commercially and prompted one American commentator to claim that wearing a Johnson dress was 'like putting on a good mood'. Nevertheless, the newly emancipated fashionable woman was by no means always convinced. She realized that traditional designer codes had roped women into timorous conformity with rules of taste that were closely linked to a largely meaningless class system. The source for change was now the young woman, often still in her twenties, who, refusing to look back, was rejecting rules that had held her mother in thrall.

Designers propose, consumers dispose. The last twenty-five years of the twentieth century witnessed a tidal wave of ideas at all levels of fashion as designers desperately attempted to engage the hearts and minds of women to the extent that their predecessors had. Designers have now become both as fecund and as unfocused as nature. With a biblical sense of plenty, they spill their creative seed with extravagant largesse twice a year and then must leave it to the public to decide what, if anything, comes to fruition. But today's public is very different to the one that dress designers of the past had to please. With no structure and very few rules to guide them, modern designers have found themselves faced with millions of women echoing Andy Warhol's comment, 'I like boring things' – by which they mean clothes that fit a life, rather than impose on it. For most women the theatricality of high fashion is entertaining – and even, perhaps, moving – but inconceivable to wear.

7

9   Rudi Gernreich,
1971, photo
William Claxton

It wasn't just hippies, punks, Mary Poppins housewives, New Romantics and New Agers who saw no relevance in high fashion. Fashion insiders felt the same way. It was as a direct result of the decadent downward spiral of French *haute couture* that other fashion capitals grew in strength. The growth of simplicity and the 'back to basics' approach of American and Italian designers in the late Seventies and early Eighties was a powerful indictment of French fashion leaders for ignoring the realities of modern living as experienced by the majority of women.

This was more than protest, more than rebellion. It was revolution. It took sportswear and placed it at the head of the creative chain, a position it had never held before but was to maintain for the rest of the century. Creative vigour produces creative heroes, and the measure of the strength of this alternative approach to fashion is not only how quickly it ceased to be viewed as alternative but also how rapidly its major practitioners became world stars. This happened not as a result of aggressive publicity but because women approved of this approach and said, 'Yes, this is what we want. Give us more.'

The role of the creator of women's clothing changed during this revolution. No longer a purveyor of the extraordinary, as the couturier had been, the designer elevated ordinary clothing to a level of designer excellence it had never reached in previous decades, when mass-produced, ready-to-wear clothing was thought to lack the luxury and elegance of the products of the couturier's salon. In fact, the job description and title had changed. Designer was the word preferred by the new-wave creators. They eschewed 'couturier' as elitist and old-fashioned.

This was the dream, although it was rarely spoken: to create fashion that would impact on millions, not hundreds. Only one nation could create this impetus. American designers took the tired and sagging French flag of fashion and transformed it into the razzmatazz of the Stars and Stripes – and they did so in a remarkably short time. Women were ready for the prestige of a designer label that announced not primarily that they were rich (although American designer clothes were never cheap, even when designated sportswear) but that they were modern. This meant being young, hip and cool, with contemporary taste and a style lexicon indicating a relaxed, no-fuss assurance and status that had nothing to do with the rich and indigestible confections of couture. Modern fashion put a transatlantic gloss on attitudes that wealthy Americans had begun to borrow from European aristocracy as long ago as the Thirties, when Fred Astaire was a regular visitor to Wilton House, home of the ancient Salisbury family, and Gloria Swanson married a French marquis.

The designer who most successfully led fashion's initial protest against Paris was Perry Ellis, although the whole American movement which approached fashion as a form of industrial design was probably begun by Rudi Gernreich, the California-based Austrian who began a long and varied design career in the Fifties. Having studied dancing, he was aware of the practicalities of movement and made ease and flexibility the basis of his fashion designs, which were often little more than variations on leotards or body stockings. 'Pared-down' and 'minimal' are now clichés in the vocabulary of fashion but they were perfectly appropriate to Gernreich's body-conscious, spiritually free clothes of the Sixties and Seventies. The designer received bad press for his notorious topless bathing costume of 1964 and his view that a woman's breasts should be exposed – not in the blatant Playboy manner but with the finesse shown by Yves Saint Laurent, a designer with whom Gernreich had much in common. A radical thinker and uncompromising originator, he can lay claim to be the father of much modern American fashion. Certainly, he was far in advance of André Courrèges, Paco Rabanne and even Pierre Cardin, who had all tried briefly and unsuccessfully to modernize French fashion in the Sixties.

Gernreich's approach began to bear fruit in the Seventies with the new wave of American designers, a New York school whose creative impact rivalled its equivalent in the fine arts. The Rothkos, Motherwells and Pollocks exhibited in the world's art galleries in the Fifties and Sixties electrified viewers with their modernity. Their fashion equivalents did the same. A garment was no longer the basis for decorative additions. It was complete in itself: minimal, functional and devoid of anecdotal extras. Its beauty was in its crafting, the quality of its material and the fact that it functioned exactly in the same way as the beauty of an industrial machine. The greatest and most productive revolution in fashion had taken design back to its basic essentials. A suit by Calvin Klein had more in common with a Greek chiton than with most of what was being created in Paris.

Paradoxically, the man who was to bring New York fashion thinking to the apotheosis of international refinement was a foreigner to the American way of life, but not to the design principles that informed U.S. fashion. Giorgio Armani came from the country that understands design better than any other and from a city whose linearity assumes an almost Surrealist perfection. Just as Diana Vreeland once said that it was important to be born in Paris – which was true of her generation of fashion followers – so Giorgio Armani could claim that Milan is essential to his international fashion approach. It is the city where southern Italian fantasy and northern Italian practicality collide, creating uniquely assured and universal design.

The argument as to who can lay claim to be the greatest fashion designer of the last decades of the twentieth century will continue well into the twenty-first. There are many contenders, but in assessing which designers exerted the greatest influence on the way

10 Giorgio Armani,
1997, photo
Paolo Roversi

women – and, indeed, men – dressed only three of them are found to be worthy of serious consideration: Yves Saint Laurent, Ralph Lauren and Giorgio Armani. All three are distinguished by their determination to break old hegemonies and improve fashion not only for the élite but for all. It is easy to forget the scope of their protest. Yves Saint Laurent literally recast the form of female dress for the second half of the twentieth century. Ralph Lauren developed the concept of the luxury of minimalism. Giorgio Armani gave women's dress an ease and elegance that was based on the logic of their lifestyle.

In a sense, all three have become victims of their skills. They so completely understood what was required in modern dress that their revolutionary approaches have been entirely integrated into the mainstream. Although many fashion historians become overexcited by localized – even parochial – social protests like punk or shortlived fads like grunge, it is important to remember that Saint Laurent, Lauren and Armani created the bricks from which the huge modern ready-to-wear edifice was constructed, and they did so by running counter to the mainstream. Their importance cannot be overstated.

Saint Laurent, Lauren and Armani are almost universally recognized names thanks to large publicity budgets and extremely efficient press offices. But that is not what makes them the most influential designers of the second half of the twentieth century. Saint Laurent, Lauren and Armani are not even always the most interesting or stimulating designers showing in any one season. Many would put John Galliano, Jean Paul Gaultier and Dolce & Gabbana ahead on that score. Nevertheless, the fact remains that even now, as the twenty-first century begins, more women in the world wear clothes consistently inspired by Saint Laurent, Lauren and Armani than by any other designers of the past twenty years.

What binds together this triumvirate of such disparate talents is a similar approach to women, a belief that fashion must always be subservient to style, and an undeviating modernity. All three are totally opposed to the nostalgia and revivalism that dominate much of fashion at the end of the century; if they quarry any past, it is their own individual past. They look for no new approaches, no new stimuli. Their design attitudes are as unchanging as a novelist's style. They use them to answer new questions created by changed attitudes to sex, the workplace and the role of women, just as designers do in the automobile and industrial design fields. As Bill Kaiserman, a minor but consistent New York minimalist, has said, 'There are just a few shapes that are acceptable.' He might have added that only a few fabrics and even colours are possible in a streamlined and efficient design approach, although Saint Laurent's assured and powerful colour palette must be excepted from the rule.

The protest against Paris has deepened and broadened in the past ten years to include the cult of street style for young and, in some cases, even pre-teen fashion followers. Children of the Seventies (which Tom Wolfe dubbed the 'Me Decade') watched their elder brothers and sisters go ethnic and then adopt the uniforms of terrorist chic. They saw countercultures come and go. They understood how *Saturday Night Fever* articulated the times for so many people that, in terms of fashion culture, it became the most important film of the decade. And, in the Eighties and Nineties, they evolved their own form of elitism based on group thinking that made them the most conformist young people since the pre-World War II era.

What they all wanted was the totemic power of casual sport dress, heightened to an almost fetishistic degree. The baseball cap, white T-shirt, jeans and trainers of the moment were cult objects subject to minutely calculated dress rules and changes in taste so subtle (yet so significant to the insiders) that many observers were totally ignorant of the sartorial upheavals happening below the surface of mainstream fashion. In fact, it has been claimed – probably correctly – that in the Eighties and Nineties nobody over the age of eighteen could begin to understand the movements taking place in street style. And how could they be expected to? These movements originated in the school playground or on the bus and were subject to little influence from anyone outside teenage circles apart from the pop stars and sportsmen whose lives, attitude and 'product' were used as the commercial basis for youth culture.

Many of the most powerful 'outsider' influences in what was, in effect, youth's protest against organized fashion went unremarked and even unnamed by much of mainstream fashion. Even commentators tended to discover the new names just too late, after trends had moved on. Europeans found particular difficulty understanding a movement that so frequently was generated and energized by cultural and ethnic movements in America. In fact, one could claim that all youth fashion in the last years of the twentieth century has been American youth fashion – but, unlike trends in the past, this one is not campus-led. The impetus comes from inner-city streets and is almost exclusively Latino, Afro-Caribbean and even Asian in spirit, although it is eagerly embraced by Caucasian American kids and spread to the world.

These are clothes that fall outside the parameters of fashion at all levels. As a fashion statement, they are often tired and overfamiliar. What matters is the way in which the items of dress are put together, how they are arranged to give one item prominence now, and another later. Nothing is created; instead, everything is styled. As such, elements of dress are arranged, rather as flowers are, in accordance with rarely stated visual rules. The object is to achieve a teenage insistence on conformity. Just who decrees that baggy shorts and reversed baseball caps will be worn by all boys aged ten to fifteen, from anywhere in the world, is impossible

11   Carhartt, 1999,
      photos Orion Best

12   High-street
      clothes, 1998,
      photo Donald
      Christie

13   (Overleaf)
      Stüssy,
      1999, photos
      Juergen Teller

to pinpoint but teenage looks are much more likely
to emerge obliquely, from cartoon characters or jokey
drawings, than the sketch pads of fashion designers.
The result is a gritty, uneasy look hacked out between
style and function. Youth fashion is not primarily
conveyed to the public via fashion magazines or trendy
style publications, which, by their nature, are always a
step behind. Its conduit and showcase, after the streets
themselves, is MTV, which began broadcasting in 1981
and immediately attracted stars such as Madonna, Cyndi
Lauper and Annie Lennox. MTV became the best
medium ever for pop music, which, unlike any other
music in the world, depends for its initial effect almost
as much on appearance as on sound. It has also had
a huge, worldwide impact on young fashion, an impact
which shows no sign of diminishing. In fact, pop videos
reach more people than any fashion magazine could
hope to. Their impact is global.

It was only a year after MTV began broadcasting that
arguably the most universally popular street-fashion
label of the Nineties was founded. Stüssy began as a
surfing-based company in 1982 but moved into clothing
three years later. The California-based firm, along with
other clothing cult names such as Mossimo and
Quicksilver, both of whom have boutiques in Europe,
has consistently gauged the tenor of the streets to
produce a series of looks that instantly captured the
imagination of teenagers as well as their twenty- and
even thirty-something brothers and sisters. The firm's
clothing became the look, whether it was based on
workwear or the preppy or surfing lifestyle. Stüssy is
now a world-class label and its turnover is in excess
of $20 million per year – a success achieved through
the recognition that status-conscious kids in clubs and
on the streets allow fashion fads to race like wildfire
through their ranks, as the Acid House low-slung jeans
and hooded tops of the Eighties did in London and
designer Ben Davis's baggy, 'coarse clothing' did in
San Francisco before being taken up across America.

Ben Davis and the workwear boom has proved to be
one of the most interesting of the Nineties anti-fashion
protests, along with the Michigan-based company
Carhartt, which was founded in 1889 to provide blue-
collar workers with durable clothing and suddenly found
its products adopted as fashion statements in the late
Eighties. The firm's 'chain-gang' blue jackets became
a craze in 1989 after they were worn on MTV by the
gangster rappers NWA (Niggers With Attitude). As the
New York Times pointed out in 1992, the firm's blanket-
lined jackets were an essential garment for urban crack
dealers, who were out in all weathers. Sales of Carhartt
workwear reached $90 million in 1990, bolstered by the

11

13

UNITED COLORS
OF BENETTON.

14

14 Benetton
    advertisement,
    1992, photo
    Oliviero Toscani

15 (Overleaf)
    Benetton
    advertisement,
    1989, photo
    Oliviero Toscani

16 (Overleaf)
    Benetton
    advertisement,
    1992, photo
    Oliviero Toscani

fact that the clothing was regularly seen in many music videos. When the Tommy Boy record label gave away a Carhartt jacket in a special promotion, it seemed an obvious choice: this was one of the coolest items of clothing on the streets.

Cult fashion has become one of the most important, and lucrative, offshoots of North American culture. The brief history of the streetwear firm Cross Colours illustrates the advantages and disadvantages of serving this market. Founded in Los Angeles in 1990, it racked up sales of over $15 million within a year and became ubiquitous wear for black hip hop celebrities. According to the *Los Angeles Times*, the firm took orders worth $40 million at a 1992 menswear exhibition in Las Vegas. Soon, however, Cross Colours became a victim of its own success: fashion bootleggers so successfully copied its distinctive green, yellow, red and black colour combination which was based on traditional African kente cloth that the company went out of business in 1994.

'No Fear' T-shirts; 'Co-Ed Naked Attitude' T-shirts; Kangol caps – the worlds of college, school and street produce instant fads. Some of these, like 'No Fear', founded in 1990 at the University of New Hampshire, have nationwide influence; others, like Kangol, spread throughout the world, riding on the popularity of hip hop music. In the late Eighties, rappers such as Run DMC and LL Cool J were rarely seen without their Kangol headgear, and the fad continued into the Nineties. This is a volatile and fast-moving fashion world where, if a manufacturer reacts quickly enough, considerable profits are possible. Keeping informed is essential. In 1992 a marketing firm called Pop Eye was set up in Laguna Beach, California, to provide videos of the latest street fashions for clothing companies who need a quick information feedline. It has been claimed that, after MTV, this firm is the most efficient processor of youth culture in the Nineties, and its clients include Nike, Speedo and

Reebok. Pop Eye cameras appear regularly on street and campus, at rock shows and clubs, capturing the new ways in which the young dress and then speeding the information back to clients.

MTV is the barometer of the times as far as young fashion is concerned and it is watched by everybody in the fashion world who hopes to capitalize on this lucrative but risky market, even if they are already clients of Pop Eye. Upmarket firms are especially anxious to appeal to youth, and many look to the phenomenal success of companies such as Benetton, Esprit and Fiorucci from the past as well as The Gap and J Crew, whose great surges occurred in the late Eighties and the Nineties.

Benetton, founded in 1965, was set up as a new form of manufacture in that the clothes were made by independent contractors and then brought together for dyeing, labelling and shipping at the Benetton headquarters in Treviso, northern Italy. It was to become one of the most successful labels in the world thanks to its bold marketing, strong fashion image and the fact that, in terms of price and attitude, it went against the prevailing ethos of Italian high fashion and eschewed high status. Benetton clothes stand for equality and have always been advertised as universally accessible – both literally (there are over one thousand Benetton outlets across the world) and ideologically. In fact, it is the Benetton advertising campaigns rather than the clothes that excite passions. The clothes are characterized by simplicity, excellent colour and a level of taste understood as easily by the young as by more sophisticated customers. Under the creative guidance of photographer Oliviero Toscani, Benetton advertising campaigns have broken most taboos, outraged sensibilities, and been accused of being corrupt and in bad taste, but they have never ceased to excite interest as well as adverse comment. The ads present shocking, hyper-realistic tableaux – not in order to sell clothes but

to change attitudes, almost as if their intention is, by aggressively questioning our tacit assumptions, to make us worthy of the Benetton label – a new twist, indeed, in fashion protest. Such harsh and shocking images, the most notorious being the deathbed scene of an Aids victim and the symbolic black and white horses mating, reflect vital contemporary issues and are so calculatingly confrontational that their result is often counter-productive to their assumed purpose: to annex the worlds of sport and casual wear for a permanent yuppie lifestyle into which we are all expected to buy.

Benetton is clearly ideologically sound, although they have a swaggering determination to shock – often at any cost. The San Francisco-based firm Esprit projects a similarly idealistic, anti-high-fashion attitude, which is perhaps expected of a firm originally known as the Plain Jane Dress Company. Founded in 1968, only three years after Benetton, Esprit has enjoyed the same high level of commercial success, and for much the same reason. Both firms identified their markets very early and then, having gained a loyal customer following, led them where they wanted them to go. Esprit set out to capitalize on the healthy outdoor lifestyle of the West Coast, which is based on sport, fitness and a rejection of 'fancy' dressing. Esprit's great selling point (never made explicit in its advertising) was that its clothes made it easy for everybody to look alike – an essential psychological force with young customers. When in the Nineties the firm took its obsession with healthy outdoor living to the next level by creating the 'ecollection', clothing manufactured to environmentally friendly standards, it could be said that Esprit had conquered the minds as well as the hearts of a sizeable portion of the young market.

This quintessentially American approach linked the Nineties to the protests and ideological intensities of co-eds and draft dodgers in the Sixties and Seventies. But it did more than that: it harked back to a nostalgic

UNITED COLORS
OF BENETTON.

15

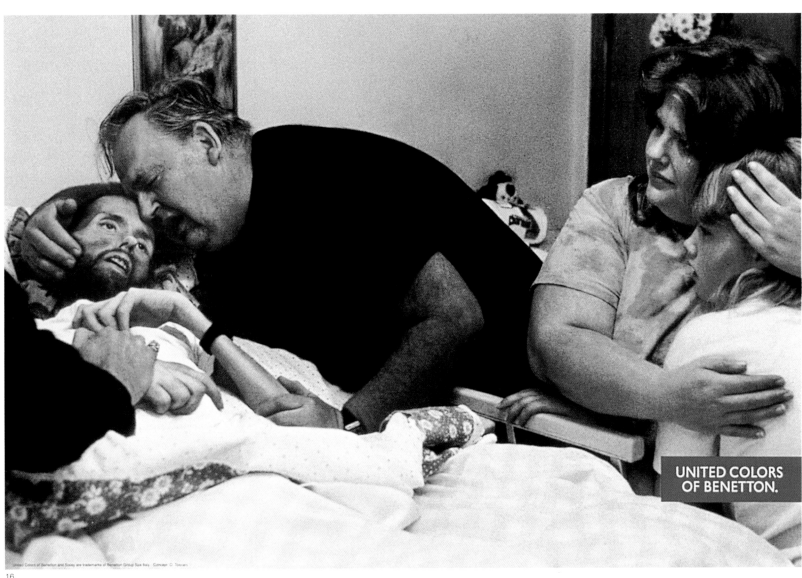

UNITED COLORS
OF BENETTON.

17 Esprit,
    'ecollection', 1992

18 L.L. Bean, 1994
    and 1997

19 Kim Basinger in
    Gap, 1989, photo
    Herb Ritts

20 Gap, 1999, photo
    David Sims

18

17

vision of the backwoods American and appealed to the
urban couch potato who dreamed of the great outdoors.
Esprit was in a direct emotional line with the world of
L.L. Bean, a New England-based mail-order firm
supplying a Thoreau-esque idyll of camping and fishing
equipment, casual outdoor clothes, and the excitement
that comes from receiving a parcel and anticipating the
adventure of mountains and prairies. It is a world of
make-believe so popular that by the Eighties L.L. Bean,
founded in 1912, had become a mainstream member of
the retail fashion world, catering to a remarkably wide
range of Americans who had in common country-style
taste and a belief that clothing status had nothing to do
with frills but a great deal to do with fitness of purpose.

If, as can be argued, firms such as Benetton and Esprit
have wielded fashion influence by deliberately standing
apart from fashion, if they have clothed attitudes to life
as much as ways of life, then it must be agreed that the
most influential of the anti-fashion mass-market firms is
surely the Gap. Named after 'the generation gap', it has
been more successful in filling it than any manufacturer
or designer in the fashion world. Gap clothing is worn by
teenagers and octogenarians; Gap Kids caters to infants
and children, and even now, the firm's designers could
well be working on a Gap Geriatric line, so determined
is the company to provide its brand of clothing for all
age groups and lifestyles. The sartorial equivalent of
the Catholic Church or even the Communist party, its
egalitarianism is equalled by its chic. There is no fashion
content and that is the secret of Gap's worldwide
following. Changes to its basic range of well-cut T-shirts,
jeans and cotton sweaters are slight; colour ranges are
controlled and narrow; everything about The Gap is
non-statement, non-status and confident. The firm
allows itself a little more leeway in its Banana Republic
label and its Old Navy line, but nothing one might call
ebullience. Old Navy is promoted by the *grande dame*
of U.S. idiosyncratic fashion wisdom, Carrie Donovan,
who has become something of a cult figure through her
television appearances advertising the line. Like many
highly successful mass-manufacturers, the Gap has
always believed in strongly focused and narrowly
targeted advertising campaigns that use 'real' people
with whom the buyer can identify. Its 'Individuals of Style'
campaign was as distinctive and aspirational as that
great landmark in American advertising, the Blackglama
'What Becomes a Legend Most' campaign to promote
the wearing of mink.

Across the board, from Calvin Klein and Ralph Lauren
to the giants of sports style, the fashion business in the
U.S. is dominated by powerful, persistent and extremely
costly advertising campaigns. The most successful have

19

21 Tommy Hilfiger,
    1993 and 1999,
    photos Dan Lecca
    and Peter Arnell

22 Tommy Hilfiger,
    1999, photo
    Peter Arnell

been those mounted by fashion entrepreneur Tommy Hilfiger, whose firm, founded in 1969, became a phenomenon of the Nineties. Although Hilfiger products almost entirely lack new fashion ideas, in the youth market this is not necessarily a disadvantage. Originality is much less important than identifiable token stylistic gestures – young fashion followers not only read labels as if they were messages from a sartorial god, they also expect colours, shapes and design features to be easily spotted on a dark night. Hilfiger's focused approach does not disappoint them, but it is doubtful that he would have turned a modest career into a millionaire label without his advertising campaigns.

Hilfiger was almost unknown until he launched his first major advertising campaign in 1986 and his name joined the handful of designers recognized worldwide. His totem red, white and blue jackets are worn by middle-aged dads on trips to the shopping mall, while their teenage sons wear the rugby shirt in the same colours – the shirt made famous by Snoop Doggy Dogg on an appearance on 'Saturday Night Live' in 1994. By then Hilfiger's advertising had been so successful that he hardly needed the exposure. His chutzpah is evident in his 1986 slogan: 'The 4 Great American Designers for Men Are: R_ L_, P_ E_, C_ K_, T_ H_. ' Nobody asked why his name should be placed alongside that of Ralph Lauren, Perry Ellis and Calvin Klein. Instead, most people rushed out to find – and buy into – it. A legend had been created.

Cynics say that advertising could only wield such power in the U.S., where all publicity is seen as ultimately good, but they aren't entirely correct. The history of grunge – the pale and sickly son of punk – presents a contrasting and cautionary tale, proving that what is promoted is much less significant than when it is done. In fashion, it is not only size but also timing that matters. It is the tempo of the times that decides what will succeed and what will fail. And successes and

failures are never as straightforward as they initially appear, which is why those who dismiss the popularity of advertising campaigns by Benetton or Hilfiger as a fluke, or as something easily achieved, are wrong. No amount of advertising, no matter how imaginative or outrageous, will have an effect if the image – and the image of the product that it represents – fails to strike a chord with the public or the fashion world. Grunge failed with both.

With hindsight it is easy to imagine how close grunge could have come to succeeding. Developed in the early Nineties, it could be seen as a valid answer to fashion's despondency at its disastrous sales figures after the high-spending, flamboyant Eighties fashion scene, the mood of which was expressed in Michael Douglas's comment in the film *Wall Street* (1987) when he boldly claimed 'Greed is Good!' After the Eighties, Grunge seemed more in line with the serious and grim mood of the early Nineties. It even reflected the cultural mood of anarchy at the centre of much of what was new in the art world, from Damien Hirst's shark in formaldehyde to Quentin Tarantino's explosively violent film *Reservoir Dogs* (1992) and the urban horrors revealed in Brett Easton Ellis's novel *American Psycho* (1991). If this wasn't the moment for grunge, when would be?

Grunge was fashion's damage-control exercise, an attempt to claw back some of the ground lost since the mid-Eighties. It was based – somewhat loosely – on an alternative music scene that began in Seattle. Grunge was hard rock reassessing Seventies' heavy metal, a self-mocking, beer- and heroin-inspired reflection of the hopelessness of being young, homeless and uncool. Even the word grunge was originally a wry comment on how a guitar could sound when played by less than competent hands. Then the desolate scene changed when the group Nirvana achieved a platinum disc and the grunge sound was played by every local radio station across America. The film *Singles* (1992),

24

starring Matt Dillon, became grunge's theme movie. Grunge groups sprang up like mushrooms, all clad in the same kind of dress: flannel shirts, combat boots or Converse shoes and the obligatory ripped jeans, aptly described as the 'uniform of suburban burnouts everywhere'. Like circling sharks, fashion designers, who felt that because they were young they had to be hip, homed in and grunge fashion was born on a wave of euphoria. If Nirvana's album *Nevermind* (1991) had sold eight million copies worldwide, they reasoned, there had to be a market for dress that reflected the mood.

So, briefly, grunge became fashion's equivalent to the French Revolution. Urban bohemianism thrived, riding on the back of promotional tours like the 1991 Lollapalooza Festival, an ensemble of arts and music featuring groups such as Pearl Jam and Soundgarden. Marc Jacobs introduced the look at Perry Ellis; he was followed by fellow New York designers Anna Sui and Christian Francis Roth. American *Vogue* dipped a nervous toe in to feel the waters with a grunge story shot by Steven Meisel and styled by Grace Coddington. It was notable that the men in the shoot had a much more extreme look than the women. The movement's signature Doc Martens and Converse boots were featured but, bizarrely, for a look based on urban unemployment, so were upmarket labels like J. Crew, Banana Republic, Calvin Klein (featured with a $750 dress) and, most ludicrous of all,

the Irish fashion fantast Lainey Keogh with a cashmere sweater at $1400.

Grunge was a commercial disaster. It is generally held in New York that it was Marc Jacobs's grunge collection that forced the demise of the Perry Ellis company. Interestingly, the fashion industry itself, led by senior journalists, rewarded Jacobs with the 1992 Fashion Designers of America Womenswear Designer of the Year Award. The last laugh on the essentially patronizing attempt to jump on a bandwagon came from the *New York Times*, which perpetrated what has become known as The Great Grunge Hoax in November 1992. Fed totally invented information by a record company employee in Seattle, the newspaper did not check the source and duly published the 'street cred' terms for items of grunge dress – such as 'wack slacks' for ripped jeans – and behaviour – such as 'lame strain' for someone lacking cool. The British magazine *Sky* was similarly caught.

There Grunge should have ended. But Calvin Klein's use of Kate Moss, the archetypal 'grunge girl', for his advertisements led to a longer reign of heroin chic, which was photographed for upmarket style magazines by female photographers such as Pamela Hanson and Ellen von Unwerth. Meanwhile, whole grunge collections were put on sale across America by stores desperate to move them at any price.

When entering a helicopter, bow down.

26 Diesel
    advertisements:
    (top) photo David
    LaChapelle, 1995;
    (bottom)
    photo Henrik
    Halvarsson, 1996

27 Nike
    advertisement,
    1999, photo
    Frederika Helwig

27

    Attempting to take on the character of alternative
fashion movements is clearly dangerous for mainstream
fashion. The distance between the two must be
respected and maintained. Diesel was founded in
provincial northern Italy in 1978 in two rooms with twenty
sewing machines and one telephone – as unpromising
a debut as can be imagined. By 1985, it was selling
200,000 pairs of jeans. Ten years later it was selling
five million pairs, there were Diesel shops in major
world cities and the annual turnover had shot up from
an initial $5 million to $350 million. It was a triumph not
only for confidence and skill but also for conviction.
Whereas designers tried to exploit grunge in the hope
of making quick profits by pandering to hyped fad, firms
such as Diesel – and it is by no means unique – base
their achievements on distancing themselves from
fashion's mainstream and using the fact that they are
not part of the fashion system as their major strength.
    Firms like this look beyond the crazes and brief
but intense movements that characterize the youth-
dominated market so that they can observe the thinking
behind them. They realize that certain sources of
inspiration, although not eternal, can certainly be revisited
many times over. These include Western wear, industrial
clothing, workwear and sports gear. In many respects,
they can be claimed as the true wellsprings of modern
fashion because they reflect the moods and aspirations
of a considerable proportion of the world's young fashion
followers. Underlying them all is the world's love affair
with Americana. Diesel's label reads, 'Diesel: Jeans and
Workwear', linking the firm's upmarket leisure wear with
the Klondike, Lonesome Cowboys and the whole
mythology of the Wild West. Its advertising campaign
of 1991 was based on the slogan 'Successful Living',
which is in the same sporting spirit as Nike's 'Just Do It'.
Positive, yet slightly aggressive and challenging, the
slogan enfranchises the Diesel jeans wearer, making
him or her feel fitter to take their place in society. As the
twenty-first century begins, it is this approach to dress,
rather than the élite appeal of Paris fashion, that appears
to be leading the field in the continuing, intense and
endlessly fascinating fashion race.

DESIGNERS' BIOGRAPHIES

ALAÏA, Azzedine
b.Tunis, Tunisia, c.1940
Education: École des Beaux-Arts, Tunis
Career: Assistant dressmaker in Tunis. Moved to Paris in 1957.
Worked briefly for Christian Dior and Guy Laroche. Worked
for Thierry Mugler, 1957–9. Launched own line of custom
clothing in 1960. Launched ready-to-wear line in 1980

ALBINI, Walter
b.Busto Arsizio, Italy, 1941; d.Milan, 1983
Education: Instituto State di Belle Arte e Moda, Turin, 1959–60
Career: Fashion illustrator, Paris and Milan, 1961–4; freelance
designer for Bastile, Callaghan, Krizia etc, 1964–83; opened
own fashion house in 1965

ARMANI, Giorgio
b.Piacenza, Italy, 1934
Education: Studied medicine at University of Bologna, 1952–3
Career: Window display artist for La Rinascente stores,
1954, Rinascente menswear buyer, 1954–60; designer for
Nino Cerruti, 1960–70; freelance designer, 1970–5; Armani
menswear collection, 1974; womenswear, 1975; Emporio
Armani, 1981

ASHLEY, Laura
b.Dowlais, Wales, 1925; d.Coventry, England, 1985
Career: Ashley-Mountney Prints Ltd, founded with husband,
Bernard, 1954; Laura Ashley Ltd, 1968; 185 retail outlets by
1985

BALENCIAGA, Cristóbal
b.Guetaria, Spain, 1895; d.Javea, 1972
Career: Founded fashion house, Barcelona, 1922 and
Madrid, 1932; Paris house, 1937; war years spent in Spain;
closed Paris house, 1968; retired to Madrid

BEENE, Geoffrey
b.Haynesville, Louisiana, 1927
Education: Studied medicine at Tulane University, New
Orleans, 1943–6; studied fashion at Traphagen School, New
York, 1947–8; Chambre Syndicale d'Haute Couture and
Académie Julien, Paris, 1948
Career: Display assistant at I. Magnin, Los Angeles, 1946;
apprentice tailor at Molyneaux, Paris, 1948–50; designer for
Teal Traina, New York, 1958–63; Geoffrey Beene Inc.
founded, 1963

BENETTON
Italian casualwear firm, founded in Treviso, Italy in 1965
by Giuiana, Luciano, Gilberto and Carlo Benetton. First
Benetton outlet opened in Belluno, Italy in 1968. European
expansion began in 1978; New York, 1979

BERARDI, Antonio
b.Grantham, England, 1968
Education: Central St Martins College of Art & Design, 1990–4
Career: Final year collection bought by Liberty and A La
Mode; February 1996 took part in New Generation, a show
sponsored by Marks & Spencer; December 1996 signed
production contract with Italian firm, Givuesse; February
1999 first show in Milan as part of Italian Fashion Week;
Nominated for Best New Designer for VH1 Awards, 1997;
Nominated for Avant-Garde Designer for VH1 Awards, 1999

BIKKEMBERGS, Dirk
b.Flamersheim, Germany, 1962
Education: Royal Academy of Arts, Antwerp
Career: Freelance designer, 1982–7; Dirk Bikkembergs-
Homme Co., 1985; first menswear collection, 1988; first
womenswear line, 1993

BLAHNIK, Manolo
b.Santa Cruz, Canary Islands, 1943
Education: University of Geneva, 1960–5; art school, Paris,
1965–70
Career: First collection for Ossie Clark and Zapata Boutique,
London, 1972; opened shop in London, 1973, then in New
York and Hong Kong; has designed shoes for Jean Muir,
Perry Ellis, Calvin Klein, John Galliano and Antonio Berardi

BYBLOS
Founded in 1973 as a division of Genny SpA; independent
company formed c.1983; Designers include Versace
1975–6 and Guy Paulin; principal designers from 1981,
Alan Cleaver and Keith Varty; Collections include Byblos
Uomo 1983, Byblos USA and Options Donna, 1985

CARDIN, Pierre
b.San Andrea da Barbara, Italy, 1922
Education: Studied architecture, Saint Etienne, France
Career: Bookkeeper and tailor's cutter, Vichy, 1936–40;
Manby men's tailor, Vichy, 1939; served in Red Cross during
World War II; design assistant for Madam Paquin and Elsa
Schiaparelli, 1945–6; head of workrooms, Christian Dior,
1946–50; founder director of Pierre Cardin fashion house,
Paris from 1950; first collection 1951; ready-to-wear
collection 1959

CHALAYAN, Hussein
b.Nicosia, Cyprus, 1970
Education: Central St Martins College of Art & Design,
London, 1989–93; final year collection featured in windows
of Browns boutique, London
Career: Launched own label, 1994; winner of first Absolut
Vodka, Absolute Creation Award, 1995; exhibitions of work
include *Style, Music and Media*, Barbican Art Gallery,
London, 1996; *The Cutting Edge*, Victoria & Albert Museum,
London 1997; *Colette*, Paris, 1998, Kyoto Museum, New
York and Vienna, 1999; British Fashion Awards Designer of
the Year, 1999

CHANEL, Gabrielle (Coco)
b.Saumur, France, 1883; d.Paris, 1971
Education: Convents, Aubazine (1895–1900); Moulins, 1900–2
Career: Clerk, Moulins, 1902–4; café-concert singer,
1905–8; established millinery and women's fashion house
in Paris, 1913; fashion shops in Deauville, 1913, Biarritz,
1916; *Chanel No.5* perfume marketed from 1921; stage
costume designer, 1912–37 and film costume designer,
1931–62

CLARK, Ossie
b.Oswaldtwistle, England, 1942; d.London, 1996
Education: Manchester College of Art, 1957–61; Royal
College of Art, 1961–5
Career: Freelance designer, Quorum, London and Henri
Bendel, New York, 1964–74, also Mendes, French ready-
to-wear company; designer, Quorum, 1965–74; designer,
Radley, 1968 and 1983; Bath Museum of Costume, Dress
of the Year Award, 1969

CONRAN, Jasper
b.London, 1959
Education: Bryanston School, Dorset; Parson's School of
Design, New York, 1975–7
Career: Worked for Fiorucci, New York, 1977, then ICI and
Courtaulds, London; design consultant, Wallis Fashion
Group, 1977; first womenswear collection, 1978; menswear
shown from 1988; also theatre designer; British Fashion
Council Designer of the Year Award, 1986

COURRÈGES, André
b.Pau, France, 1923
Education: Studied engineering at École des Ponts et
Chaussées, then fashion in Pau and Paris
Career: Cutter, Cristóbal Balenciaga, Paris, 1945–62;
independent fashion designer, Paris, 1960–6; founded
fashion house, Paris, 1961–5; first *haute couture* collection,
1965; Couture Future ready-to-wear, 1969; first perfume
Empreinte, 1971; men's ready-to-wear, 1973; produced
collection with Heab-Charles de Castelbajac, 1994–5

DEMEULEMEESTER, Ann
b.Kortrijk, Belgium, 1959
Education: Royal Academy of Fine Arts, Antwerp, 1978–81
Career: First collection of women's ready-to-wear, 1981;
freelance designer for international ready-to-wear collections,
1981–7; founded BVBA '32' company, with husband, 1985

DIESEL
Founded by Renzo Rosso (b.Padua, Italy, 1955)
Education: Marconi Technical Institute, Padua, 1970–5
Career: Production Assistant, Moltex, 1976; founded Diesel,
with Adriano Goldschmied, 1978; sole ownership of firm,
1985; annual sales $5 million in 1985, $350 million in 1995

DIOR, Christian
b.Granville, France, 1905; d.Montecatini, Italy, 1957
Education: Studied political science at École des Sciences
Politiques, Paris, 1920–5
Career: Art dealer, 1928–31; freelance designer, 1934–7;
assistant designer, Piguet, 1937–9; designer, Lelong, 1941–6;
Maison Dior opened, 1947; perfumes include *Miss Dior*, 1947

DOLCE & GABBANA
Domenico Dolce: b.Palermo, Italy, 1958; **Stefano** Gabbana:
b.Milan, 1962
Career: Opened fashion consulting studio, 1982; first major
women's collection, 1985; knitwear, 1987; menswear
collection, 1990; D&G diffusion line, 1994

ESPRIT
Founded in 1968. Originally called the Plain Jane Dress
Company, name changed to Esprit de Corp in 1970; world
sales $1 billion in 1977–8; annual production in excess of
60 million garments and accessories; Ecollection, using
organic fabrics and ecologically sound production methods,
1992; Esprit Kids, Footwear and Accessories, 1990

FATH, Jacques
b.Maisons-Laffitte, France, 1912; d.Paris, 1954
Education: Studied bookkeeping and law, Commercial
Institute, Vincennes, France
Career: Bookkeeper, then trader at the Paris Bourse,
1930–2; first collection, 1937; ready-to-wear for Joseph
Halpert, 1948; formed own company in America, 1951;
ready-to-wear collection in Paris, 1954; Neiman Marcus
Award, 1949; business sold, 1957

GALLIANO, John
b.Gibraltar, Spain, 1960
Education: Studied design at Central St Martins College
of Art & Design, London
Career: Graduation collection sold to Brown's boutique,
London; freelance designer, established John Galliano
fashion house, London, 1984; moved to Paris, 1990; chief
designer, Hubert de Givenchy, 1996; designer-in-chief,
Christian Dior, 1997; British Fashion Council Designer of the
Year Award, 1987; Bath Costume Museum Dress of the Year
Award, 1987

THE GAP
Founded 1969
Originally a store selling Levis jeans, the firm expanded and
diversified during the Seventies, including opening further
retail stores; own label items launched in 1983, the year in
which the Gap bought the Banana Republic label; Gap Kids,
1985; Old Navy Clothing Company shops opened in 1994

GAULTIER, Jean Paul
b.Arcueil, France, 1952
Education: École Communale, College d'Enseignement and
Lycée d'Arcueil, to 1969
Career: Design assistant, Pierre Cardin, 1972–4; also
worked for Esterel and Patou; designer, Cardin United States
Collection, 1974–5; Majago, Paris, 1976–8; founder, Jean
Paul Gaultier SA, 1978; menswear line, 1984; Junior
Gaultier line, 1987; licences include perfumes, 1991, and
jeans, 1992; Fashion Oscar Award, Paris, 1987

GERNREICH, Rudi
b.Vienna, Austria, 1922; d.Los Angeles, 1985
Education: Studied at Los Angeles City College, 1938–41;
Los Angeles Art Center School, 1941–2
Career: Costume designer, Leslie Horton Co. 1942–8;
freelance clothing designer, Los Angeles and New York,
1948–51; designer, William Bass Inc., 1951–9; founder, GR
Designs, Los Angeles, 1960–4; designer, Rudi Gernreich
Inc., 1964–8

GIBB, Bill
b.Fraserburgh, Scotland, 1943; d.London, 1988
Education: Central St Martins College of Art & Design,
London, 1962–6; Royal College of Art, London, 1966–8
Career: Founded Alice Paul boutique, 1967–9; freelance
designer for Baccarat, 1969–72; Bill Gibb Fashion Group,
1972–88; *Vogue* Designer of the Year, 1970; ITV Best
Fashion Show Award, London 1979

GIGLI, Romeo
b.Castel Bolognese, Italy, 1949
Education: Studied architecture. Travelled internationally for
ten years
Career: First collection for Quickstep by Luciano Papini;
handknits, 1972; designer, Dimitri Couture, 1978; Romeo
Gigli label from 1981; designer Romeo Gigli for Zama sport,
1984; designer then consultant, Callaghan for Zama sport;
signature perfume, 1991

GIVENCHY, Hubert de
b.Beauvais, France, 1927
Education: Studied at the College Felix-Fauré, Beauvais and
Montalembert; École Nationale Supérieure des Beaux Arts,
Paris; Faculty of Law, University of Paris
Career: Worked in Paris for Lucien Lelong, 1945–6; Pignet,
1946–8; Jacques Fath, 1948–9, Schiaparelli, 1949–51;
established Maison Givenchy, 1952; president, Société
Givenchy Couture and Société des Parfums, Givenchy, from
1954; perfumes include *De*, 1957; *Givenchy III*, 1970;
Ysatis, 1984

GUCCI
Founded as saddlery shop by Guccio Gucci (1881–1953) in
Florence, Italy in 1906; developed as retailer of accessories,
1923; subsequently became Società Anonima Guccio
Gucci, 1939 and opened many Gucci shops worldwide;
Aldo Gucci head of firm from 1960s; Maurizio Gucci
becomes president of Gucci shops, 1989; design/creative
directors: Dawn Mello, 1990–1; Richard Lambertson,
1989–92; Tom Ford, 1994 to present

HALSTON
b.Des Moines, Iowa, 1932; d.San Francisco, 1990
Education: Studied at Indiana University, Bloomington, and
Art Institute of Chicago to 1953
Career: Freelance milliner, Chicago, 1952–3; window dresser,
Chicago, 1954–7; designer and hats division manager, Lilly
Daché, New York, 1958–9; millinery and clothing designer,
Bergdorf Goodman, New York, 1959–68; founder and
designer, Halston Ltd, couture, New York, 1962–73; with
Henry Pollack Inc., established Halston International, 1970;
Halston Originals with Ben Shaw, 1972; company has been
owned by Halston Borghese Inc. since 1992

HILFIGER, Tommy
b.Elmira, New York, 1952
Career: Owner and designer, People's Places, New York
until 1979; founder, designer and vice-chairman, Tommy
Hilfiger Corporation, New York; company floated on Stock
Exchange, 1992

JACOBS, Marc
b.New York, 1964
Education: Graduated from Parsons School of Design,
New York, 1984
Career: Designer, Sketchbook label for Ruben Thomas Inc.,
New York, 1984–5; managed own firm, 1986–8; named vice-
president for womenswear, Perry Ellis, 1988; head designer,
Perry Ellis, New York, 1989–93; Marc Jacobs, 1994 to present

JOHNSON, Betsey
b.Weathersfield, Connecticut, 1942
Education: Studied at Pratt Institute, Brooklyn, New York,
1960–1; Syracuse University, New York, 1964
Career: Guest editor, *Mademoiselle*, New York, 1964–5;
designer, Paraphernalia boutiques, New York, 1965–9;
designer, Alvin Duskin Co., San Francisco, 1970 and for
Butterick patterns, New York, 1971 and 1975; head designer,
BJ Vines, 1978; owner, Betsey Johnson Stores, 1979

KARAN, Donna
b.Forest Hills, New York, 1948
Education: Studied at Parsons School of Design, New York
Career: Assistant designer, Anne Klein & Co., and Addenda
Co., New York, 1967–8; designer, Anne Klein, 1968–71;
launched Anne Klein II diffusion line, 1982; designer, Donna
Karan New York (DKNY), 1985; menswear collection, 1991;
founded Donna Karan Beauty Co., perfume and cosmetic
division, New York, 1992; DKNY Kids, 1992

KAWAKUBO, Rei
b.Tokyo, Japan, 1942
Education: Graduated in fine arts, Keio University, Tokyo, 1964
Career: Worked in advertising department, Asahi Kasei
textile firm, 1964–6; freelance designer, 1967–9; founder-
designer, Comme des Garçons, 1969; firm incorporated,
1973; menswear line Homme introduced, 1978; awarded
Chevalier de L'Ordre des Arts et des Lettres, Paris, 1993

KENZO
b.Kyoto, Japan, 1940
Education: Studied at the Bunka College of Fashion, Tokyo
Career: Designer for Sanai department store; pattern
designer, *Soen* magazine, Tokyo, 1960–4; freelance
designer, Paris, from 1965; designer for Pisanti; established
Jungle Jap boutique in Paris, 1970; launched both Kenzo
Jeans and Kenzo Jungle in 1986; childrenswear, 1987;
womenswear, 1988; *Kenzo* perfume, 1988; costume
designer for opera and film director; awarded Bath Museum
of Costume Dress of the Year Award, 1976 and 1977;
Chevalier de L'Ordre des Arts et des Lettres, Paris, 1984

KLEIN, Calvin
b.New York, 1942
Education: Studied at Fashion Institute of Technology, New York, 1959–62
Career: Assistant designer, Dan Millstein, New York, 1962–4; freelance designer, New York, 1964–8; Calvin Klein Co., formed in partnership with Barry Schwartz, 1968; company reorganized, 1991; perfumes include *Obsession*, 1985 and *Eternity*, 1988

LACROIX, Christian
b.Arles, France, 1951
Education: Studied art history at Paul Valéry University, Montpellier and museum studies at the Sorbonne, Paris, 1973–6
Career: Freelance fashion sketcher, 1976–8; assistant at Hermès, Paris, 1978–80; designer and Artistic Director, house of Patou, 1981–7; opened own couture and ready-to-wear house, 1987; Christian Lacroix *haute couture* and Boutique salons established in Paris, 1987; *C'est la Vie!* perfume launched, 1990; designed costumes for American Ballet Theater's *Gaieté Parisienne*, New York, 1988

LAGERFELD, Karl
b.Hamburg, Germany, 1938
Career: Design assistant at Balmain, 1955–8; art director, Patou, 1958–63; freelance designer for Chloé, Krizia, Ballantyne, Timwear, Charles Jourdan, Valentino, Fendi, Cadette and Max Mara, from 1964; director of collections and ready-to-wear, Chanel, from 1983; Karl Lagerfeld and KL ready-to-wear firms established in Paris and Germany, 1984; perfumes include *Lagerfeld*, 1975; *KL for Women*, 1983 and *KL for Men*, 1984; also photographer and stage designer

LANG, Helmut
b.Vienna, Austria, 1956
Career: Established own fashion studio in Vienna, 1977; developed ready-to-wear collections, 1984–6; moved several times between Paris and Vienna, 1988–93; Professor of Fashion Masterclass, Vienna, since 1993

LAUREN, Ralph
b.New York, 1939
Education: Studied business science, City College of New York, late 1950s
Career: Part-time sales assistant, Alexanders Stores, New York, 1956–7; assistant menswear buyer, Allied Stores, New York, 1958–61; salesman, Bloomingdale's and Brooks Brothers, New York, 1962; road salesman in New England for A. Rivetz neckwear manufacturer, Boston, c.1964–6; designer, Polo Neckwear division, Beau Brummel, New York, 1967; founder, designer and chairman, Polo Fashions, New York, from 1968; perfumes include *Polo*, *Lauren*, 1978 and *Safari*, 1990

LÉGER, Hervé
b.Bapaume, France, 1957
Education: Studied Arts Plastiques in Paris until 1975
Career: Designed hats for Venus et Neptune, Pablo Delia, Dick Brandsma, 1975–7; assistant for Tan Giudicelli, couture and ready-to-wear, 1977–80; assistant to Karl Lagerfeld at Fendi, Rome, 1980–2; designer, Chanel, 1982–3; designer for Cadette, Milan, 1983–5; founded own company, MCH Diffusion, 1985; partnership with Mumm, 1992; first ready-to-wear collection for Hervé Léger SA, 1993; designed theatre costumes, Milan, 1992 and Opéra de Paris, 1994

McCARDELL, Claire
b.Frederick, Maryland, 1905; d.New York, 1958
Education: Attended Hood College, Maryland, 1923–5, and Parsons School of Design, New York and Paris, 1926–9
Career: Fashion model; knitwear designer, Robert Turk, Inc., New York, 1929–31; designer Hattie Carnegie, New York 1938–40; designer, Claire McCardell for Townley Frocks, New York, 1940–58

McCARTNEY, Stella
b.London, 1971
Career: Central St Martins College of Art & Design, London, 1991–5
Career: In 1986, aged fifteen, worked with Christian Lacroix on his 'Premier Couture' collection; assistant to Betty Jackson and fashion assistant on British *Vogue*; after college worked with Edward Sexton, a Savile Row tailor before being appointed designer-in-chief at Chloé; awarded *Elle* British Designer of the Year, 1999

MACDONALD, Julien
b.Merthyr Tydfil, Wales, 1972
Education: University of Brighton, 1991–4; Royal College of Art, London, 1994–6
Career: Worked with Japanese designer Koji Tatsuno and Alexander McQueen while still a student; won knitwear competition organized by Karl Lagerfeld and became knitwear designer at Chanel while still at the Royal College; launched own label in 1997

McQUEEN, Alexander
b.London, 1969
Education: Central St Martins College of Art & Design, London, 1990–2
Career: Left school at sixteen; worked as a cutter in Savile Row and for the costumier Angels & Bermans; aged twenty travelled to Tokyo to work with Koji Tatsuno; worked with Romeo Gigli in Milan before completing his MA at Central St Martins College of Art & Design; student graduate collection in 1992; Designer of the Year Award, 1996 and 1997; appointed design director of Givenchy in November 1996, producing his first collection in January 1997; awards include *Elle* British Designer of the Year, 1997 and International Designer of the Year, 1998; CFDA Night of the Stars, 1998; McQueen has designed fifteen collections for his own label

MANDELLI, Mariuccia
b.Bergamo, Italy, 1933
Career: Worked as a teacher, Milan, 1952–4; designer and founder, with Flora Dolci, of Krizia firm, Milan, from 1954; Kriziamaglia knitwear, 1966; Kriziababy range, 1968

MARGIELA, Martin
b.Louvain, Belgium, 1957
Education: Royal Academy of Fine Arts, Antwerp, 1977–80
Career: Freelance designer, Milan, 1980–1; freelance fashion stylist, Antwerp, 1982–5; design assistant to Jean Paul Gaultier, 1985–7; showed first major collection under own label in Paris, 1988; knitwear line manufactured by Miss Deanna SpA, Italy, 1992

MISSONI
Ottavio Missoni b.Dubrovnik, Croatia, 1921
Rosita Missoni b.Golasecca, Italy, 1931
Career: Italian knitwear and fashion house founded in Gallarate, Italy, 1953; first collection produced for Rinascente Stores, 1954; Missoni label introduced, 1958; first Paris showing, 1967

MIYAKE, Issey
b.Hiroshima, Japan, 1938
Education: Studied at Tama Art University, Tokyo, 1959–63; École de la Chambre Syndicale de la Couture Parisienne, 1965
Career: Design assistant, Guy Laroche, 1966–8, and Givenchy, 1968–9; designer, Geoffrey Beene, New York, 1969–70; established Miyake Design Studio in Tokyo, 1970; director, Issey Miyake International; perfumes include *L'Eau d'Issey*, 1993 and *L'Eau d'Issey pour Homme*, 1995; theatre designer from 1980

MIZRAHI, Isaac
b.New York, 1961
Education: Graduated from Parsons School of Design, New York, 1982
Career: Assistant designer, Perry Ellis, New York, 1982–3; womenswear designer, Jeffrey Banks, New York, 1984; designer, Calvin Klein, New York, 1985–7; formed own company, 1987; closed fashion house, 1998

MONTANA, Claude
b.Paris, France, 1949
Education: Studied chemistry and law
Career: Freelance jewellery designer, London, 1971–2; designer, Michelle Costas, Paris, 1973; assistant designer, 1973, and head designer, 1974, MacDouglas Leathers, Paris; freelance designer, Complice, 1975; founded own company, 1979; designer in charge of *haute couture*, Lanvin, 1989–92; continues ready-to-wear collections under own name

MOSCHINO, Franco
b.Abbiategrasso, Italy, 1950; d.Lake Annone, 1994
Education: Studied fine art, Accademia delle Belle Arti, Milan, 1968–71
Career: Freelance designer and illustrator, Milan, 1969–70; sketcher for Versace, 1971–7; designer for Italian company Cadette, 1977–82; founded own company Moonshadow, 1983; launched Moschino COUTURE!, 1983; CHEAP & CHIC, 1988; UOMO, 1986 and CHEAP & CHIC UOMO, 1991

MUGLER, Thierry
b.Strasbourg, France, 1948
Education: Studied at the Lycée Fustel de Conlange, 1960–5 and at the School of Fine Arts, Strasbourg, 1966–7
Career: Dancer, Opéra de Rhin, Strasbourg, 1965–6; assistant designer, Gudule boutique, Paris, 1966–7; designer, André Peters, London, 1968–9; freelance designer, Milan, Paris, 1970–3; created Café de Paris fashion collection, Paris, 1973; founder, Thierry Mugler, 1974, owner from 1986; professional photographer from 1967

OZBEK, Rifat
b.Istanbul, Turkey, 1953
Education: Studied architecture at Liverpool University, 1970–2; studied fashion design at Central St Martins College of Art & Design, London, 1974–7
Career: Worked with Walter Albini for Trell, Milan, 1978–80; designer for Monsoon, London, 1980–4; established own firm, Ozbek, 1984; Future Ozbek established, 1987; New Age collection, 1989

PRADA
Luxury leather goods company founded by Mario Prada and his brother in 1913; taken over by granddaughter Miuccia Bianchi Prada in 1978; studied political science; studied mime at Piccolo Teatro di Milano; worked briefly for the Communist party

PUCCI, Emilio
b.Naples, Italy, 1914; d.Florence, 1992
Education: Educated at the University of Milan, 1933–5; University of Georgia, 1935–6; Reed College, Portland, Oregon, 1936–7; University of Florence, 1941; bomber pilot in Italian Air Force, 1938–42
Career: Women's skiwear designer, 1948; freelance fashion designer, 1949; president, Emilio Pucci, Florence and New York, 1950; vice-president for design and merchandising, Formfit International, 1960s

QUANT, Mary
b.London, 1934
Education: Studied art and design at Goldsmith's College of Art, London, 1952–5
Career: Fashion designer, from 1955; established Bazaar boutique and Alexander's restaurant, London, 1955; founder and director, Mary Quant Ginger Group wholesale design and manufacturing firm, 1963, and Mary Quant Ltd, 1963; designed for JC Penney, Puritan Fashions, Alligator Rainwear, Kangol, Dupont Europe, Staffordshire Potteries; member of the Design Council, London, from 1971

RABANNE, Paco
b.San Sebastián, Spain, 1934
Education: Studied architecture at L'Ecole Nationale des Beaux-Arts, Paris, 1952–5
Career: Presented first *haute couture* collection, 12 Experimental Dresses, Paris, 1964; other lines introduced included men's ready-to-wear, 1983; women's ready-to-wear, 1990; leather goods, 1991; perfumes include *Paco Rabanne pour Homme*, 1973

RHODES, Zandra
b.Chatham, England, 1940
Education: Studied textile design, Medway College of Art, 1959–61, and Royal College of Art, 1961–4
Career: Established dressmaking firm with Sylvia Ayton, London, 1964, and textile design studio with Alexander McIntyre, 1965; partner and designer, Fulham Clothes Shop, 1967–8; freelance designer, 1968–75; director, Zandra Rhodes UK Ltd, and Zandra Rhodes Shops Ltd, from 1975; awards include English Fashion Designer of the Year Award, 1972; Royal Designer for Industry, Royal Society of Arts, 1977

SAINT LAURENT, Yves
b.Oran, Algeria, 1936
Education: Studied at L'Ecole de la Chambre Syndicale de la Couture, 1954
Career: Independent clothing stylist, Paris, 1953–4; designer and partner, 1954–7, chief designer, Dior, Paris, 1957–60; founder and designer, Yves Saint Laurent Paris, from 1962; Rive Gauche ready-to-wear line introduced, 1966; perfumes include *Y*, *Rive Gauche*, *Opium* and *Paris*; film and theatre designer from 1959

SANDER, Jil
b.Wesselburen, Germany, 1943
Education: Graduated from Krefeld School of Textiles, 1963; foreign exchange student, University of Los Angeles, 1963–4
Career: Fashion journalist, McCall's, Los Angeles and for *Contanze* and *Petra* magazines, Hamburg, 1964–8; freelance clothing designer, 1968–73; opened first Jil Sander boutique, Hamburg, 1968; founded Jil Sander Moden, Hamburg, 1969; first women's collection, 1973; perfumes include *Woman Pure* and *Man Pure*; awards include the Fil D'Or, 1980–5

SCOTT, Jeremy
b.Missouri, 1973
Education: Pratt Institute, New York
Career: Internship with Marc Jacobs, moved to Paris in 1995 to set up his own company; appointed jeans and accessories adviser to Trussardi in 1998

SITBON, Martine
b.Casablanca, Morocco, 1952
Education: Graduated from Studio Bercot, Paris, 1974
Career: Fashion consultant and freelance designer, 1974–84; own name collection launched, 1984; ready-to-wear designer at Chloé, 1987–96

SMITH, Paul
b.Nottingham, England, 1946
Career: Opened first menswear shop, 1970; opened shop in Covent Garden, London, 1979; New York store, 1987; Tokyo store, 1991; introduced women's line, 1993; achieved cult status in Japan in the Nineties; British Design for Industry Award, 1991; Commander of the British Empire, 1994; flagship London shop opened in Notting Hill, 1998

SORELLE FONTANA
Founded in Rome, Italy by sisters Zoe (1911–78), Micol (1913–) and Giovanna (1915–) Fontana
Opened Fontana studio in Palazzo Orsini, Rome, 1943, designing and producing gowns for the aristocracy and many film stars; participated in first catwalk presentation of Italian Alta Moda, Florence, 1951; designed first ready-to-wear collection, 1960; incorporated as Sorelle Fontana Alta Moda SrL by Micol Fontana, Rome, 1985; designed costumes for many films

SUI, Anna
b.Dearborn Heights, Michigan, 1955
Education: Parsons School of Design, New York, c.1973–5
Career: Stylist for photographer Steven Meisel and for junior sportswear firms in New York, 1970s to 1981; sportswear designer, Simultanee, New York, 1981; also designed own line, from 1980; formed own company, New York, 1983; first runway show, 1991; menswear line added, 1992

VALENTINO
b.Voghera, Italy, 1932
Education: Studied French and fashion design, Accademia dell'Arte, Milan, to 1948; Chambre Syndicale de la Couture, 1949–51
Career: Assistant designer, Jean Dessès, 1950–5, and Guy Laroche, 1956–8; assistant to Princess Irene Galitzine, 1959; business established, Rome, 1960; showed first ready-to-wear collection, 1962; Valentino Piu, interior décor, textile and gift company established, 1973; signature perfume launched, 1978

VAN BEIRENDONCK, Walter
b.Brecht, Belgium, 1957
Education: Royal Academy of Fine Arts, Antwerp, 1975–80
Career: Exhibits at the British Designer Show, London, 1987 as one of 'The Antwerp Six'; first Wild & Lethal Trash collection, 1993, first Paris show, January 1995; first line launched, January 1999; Walter Van Beirendonck, 1996; Erotic Design, Design Museum, London, 1997; Visions of the Body, Kyoto, 1999

VERSACE, Donatella
b.Reggio Calabria, Italy, 1955
Education: Studied Modern Languages, University of Florence, 1975–8, during which time she began to work alongside her brother, Gianni. Began designing Versus line independently in 1993; became designer-in-chief of the firm of Versace in 1997, on the death of her brother. Appointed Millenium Visiting Professor at Central St Martins College of Art & Design, London, 2000

VERSACE, Gianni
b.Reggio Calabria, Italy, 1946; d. Miami, Florida, 1997
Education: Studied architecture, Calabria, 1964–7
Career: Designer and buyer in Paris and London for his mother's dressmaking studio, 1968–72; freelance designer, Callaghan, Complice, Genny, Milan, 1972–7; formed own company, Milan, 1978; signature perfume launched, 1981; theatrical costume designer for La Scala and Bejart Ballet, from 1982; awards include Council of Fashion Designers of America International Award, 1993

VIONNET, Madeleine
b.Aubervilliers, France, 1876; d.Paris, 1975
Career: Dressmaker's apprentice, Aubervilliers, 1883–93; dressmaker, House of Vincent, Paris, 1893–5; cutter, then head of workroom, Kate Reilly, London, 1895–1900; designer, Doucet, 1905–11; designer, Maison Vionnet, 1912–14 and 1919–39

WESTWOOD, Vivienne
b.Glossop, England, 1941
Education: Studied one term at Harrow Art School, then trained as a teacher
Career: Teaching, before working as a designer, from c.1971; with partner Malcolm McLaren, proprietor of boutique variously named Let It Rock, 1971, Too Fast to Live, Too Young to Die, 1972, Sex, 1974, Seditionaries, 1977, and World's End, from 1980; first showed under own name, 1982; professor of fashion, Academy of Applied Arts, Vienna, 1989–91; British Designer of the Year Award, 1990 and 1991; Order of the British Empire, 1992

YAMAMOTO, Yohji
b.Yokohama, Japan, 1943
Education: Graduated in law, Keio University, 1966; studied at Bunka College of Fashion, Tokyo, 1966–8; won Soen and Endu prizes; earned scholarship to Paris, 1968; studied fashion, 1968–70
Career: Designer, custom clothing, Tokyo, from 1970; formed ready-to-wear company, 1972; showed first collection, Tokyo, 1976; Yohji Yamamoto design studio established, Tokyo, 1988

ZORAN
b.Banat, Yugoslavia, 1947
Education: Studied architecture at University of Belgrade
Career: worked variously in New York, including salesman at Balmain boutique, accessory designer for Scott Barrie, salesman and designer for Julio, 1971–6; freelance designer in New York, from 1976; first collection shown, 1977; showroom established in Washington, DC, 1982; also maintains studio in Milan

BIBLIOGRAPHY

Agins, Teri, *The End of Fashion*, New York, 1999

Alfonsi, Maria-Vittoria, *Leaders in Fashion: I Grandi Personaggi della Moda*, Bologna, 1983

Amies, Hardy, *Just So Far*, London, 1954

Amies, Hardy, *Still Here*, London, 1984

Anketell, Michael, *Heavenly Bodies*, Dallas, 1999

Antonio – 60,70,80, London, 1995

Aragno, Bonizza Giordani, *Moda Italia: Creativity and Technology in the Italian Fashion System*, Milan, 1988

Aragno, Bonizza Giordani, *Callaghan 1966: The Birth of Italian Pret-à-porter*, Milan, 1997

Ash, Juliet and Wilson, Elizabeth, *Chic Thrills: A Fashion Reader*, London, 1992

Babitz, Eve, *Fiorucci: The Book*, Milan, 1980

Bailey, David and Harrison, Martin, *Shots of Style*, London, 1985

Baillen, Claude, *Chanel Solitaire*, London, 1973

Barthes, Roland, *The Fashion System*, New York, 1983

Bassman, Lillian, *Photographs by Lillian Bassman*, New York, 1997

Baudot, François, *Alaïa*, London, 1996

Baudot, François, *Chanel*, London, 1996

Baudot, François, *Christian Lacroix*, London, 1996

Baudot, François, *Yohji Yamamoto*, London, 1997

Baudot, François, *Thierry Mugler*, London, 1998

Baudot, François, *A Century of Fashion*, London, 1999

Bauret, Gabriel, *Alexey Brodovitch*, New York, 1999

Beaton, Cecil, *The Glass of Fashion*, London, 1954

Beaton, Cecil, *The Face of the World*, London, 1957

Belussi, Florence, *Benetton: Information Technology in Production and Distribution*, Brighton, 1987

Bénaïm, Laurence, *Issey Miyake*, London, 1997

Bergé, Pierre, *Yves Saint Laurent*, London, 1996

Bocca, Nicoletta, *Moda Poesia e Progetto*, Milan, 1990

Brampton, Sally, *Helen Storey: Ten Years*, London, 1994

Broughton, Frank (ed.), *Time Out Interviews, 1968–1998*, London, 1998

Brubach, Holly, *A Dedicated Follower of Fashion*, New York, 1999

Buiazzi, Graziella, *La Moda Italiana: Dell'Antimoda Allo Stilisto*, Milan, 1987

Capucci, Roberto, *L'Arte Nelle Moda*, Milan, 1990

Carter, Ernestine, *Magic Names of Fashion*, London, 1980

Carter, Ernestine, *The Changing World of Fashion*, London, 1997

Casadio, Mariuccia, *Missoni*, London, 1997

Casadio, Mariuccia, *Moschino*, London, 1997

Casadio, Mariuccia, *Emilio Pucci*, London, 1998

Casadio, Mariuccia, *Versace*, London, 1998

Cassini, Oleg, *In My Own Fashion*, New York, 1987

Cassini, Oleg, *A Thousand Days of Magic*, New York, 1995

Castle, Charles, *Model-Girl*, London, 1977

Cawthorne, Nigel, *The New Look: The Dior Revolution*, London, 1997

Chanel: Ouverture Pour La Mode à Marseilles, Marseilles, 1989

Chapsal, Madeleine, *Sonia Rykiel*, Paris, 1985

Chapsal, Madeleine, *L'Elegance de Années 50; Photographie par Henry Clarke*, Paris, 1986

Charles-Roux, Edmonde, *Chanel and Her World*, London, 1981

Charles-Roux, Edmonde, *Chanel*, London, 1989

Chase, Edna Woolman, *Always in Vogue*, New York, 1954

Chenoune, Farid, *Jean-Paul Gaultier*, London, 1996

Coleman, Elizabeth Ann, *The Genius of Charles James*, New York, 1982

Coleridge, Nicholas, *The Fashion Conspiracy*, London, 1988

Combray, Richard de, *Armani*, Milan, 1982

Combray, Richard de and Quintaville, Arturo Carlo, *Giorgio Armani*, Milan, 1982

Cullerton, Brenda, *Geoffrey Beene*, New York, 1995

Dahl-Wolfe, Louise, *A Photographer's Scrapbook*, New York, 1984

Daria, Irene, *The Fashion Cycle*, New York, 1990

Davis, Fred, *Fashion, Culture and Identity*, Chicago, 1992

De le Haye, Amy and Tobin, Shelley, *Chanel: The Couturier at Work*, London, 1994

De Marly, Diana, *The History of Haute Couture 1850–1950*, London, 1980

Delbourg-Delphis, Marylève, *La Mode pour la Vie*, Paris, 1983

Delpais, Delbourg, *Le Chic et la Mode*, Paris, 1982

Derycke, Luc and Van de Veire, Sandra, *Belgian Fashion Design*, Amsterdam, 1999

Deslandres, Yvonne, *Histoire de la Mode au XX Siècle*, Paris, 1986

Diamonstein, Barbaralee, *Fashion: The Inside Story*, New York, 1985

Dictionnaire de la mode au XX siècle, Paris, 1996

Dior, Christian, *Dior By Dior*, London, 1957

Dolce & Gabbana, *Wildness*, Milan, 1997

Dorfles, Gillo, *Moda and Modi*, Milan, 1979

Dupire, Beatrice, and Sy, Hady, *Yves Saint Laurent: Forty Years of Creation*, New York, 1998

Duras, Marguerite, *Yves Saint Laurent: Images of Design*, Munich, 1988

Edelman, Amy Holman, *The Little Black Dress*, New York, 1997

Encyclopédie de la Mode, Tielt, late 1980s

Encyclopédie de la Mode au XX siècle, Paris, 1994

Esten, John, *Man Ray – Bazaar Years*, Milan, 1988

Evans, Caroline and Thornton, Minna, *Women and Fashion: A New Look*, London, 1989

Ewing, William A., *Blumenfeld: A Fetish for Beauty*, London, 1996

Fairbrother, Trevor, *Herb Ritts' Work*, New York, 1996

Fairchild, John, *The Fashionable Savages*, New York, 1965

Fairchild, John, *Chic Savages*, New York, 1989

The Fashion Book, London, 1998

Felix, Zdenek, *Helmut Newton: Selections From His Photographic Works*, Munich, 1993

Féraud, Louis, *Louis Féraud*, Paris, 1985

Ferragamo, Salvatore, *Shoemaker of Dreams*, London, 1957

Finlayson, Iain, *Denim: An American Legend*, Norwich, 1990

Fox, Patty, *Star Style: Hollywood Legends as Fashion Icons*, Santa Monica, 1995

Fraser, Kennedy, *The Fashionable Mind, Reflections on Fashion 1970–1981*, New York, 1981

Fraser, Kennedy, *On the Edge: Images from 100 Years of Vogue*, New York, 1992

Gaines, Steven, *Simply Halston: The Untold Story*, New York, 1991

Gaines, Steven and Churcher, Sharon, *Obsession: The Lives and Times of Calvin Klein*, New York, 1994

Gan, Stephen, *Visionaire's Fashion 2000: Designers at the Turn of the Millennium*, New York, 1997

Gan, Stephen, *Visionaire's Fashion 2001*, New York, 1999

Garland, Madge, *Fashion: A Picture Guide to It's Creators and Creations*, London, 1962

Garner, Philippe and Mellor, David, *Cecil Beaton*, London, 1994

Gaultier, Jean Paul, *À Nous Deux la Mode*, Paris, 1990

Giacomoni, Stefano, *The Italian Look Reflected*, Milan, 1984

Gibbs, David (ed.), *Nova 1965–1975*, London, 1993

Giordani, Aragno B., *Forty Years of Italian Fashion*, Florence, 1983

Giroud, Françoise, *Christian Dior*, London, 1987

Giroud, Françoise, *Dior*, Paris, New York and London, 1987

Givry, Valerie de, *Art and Mode*, Paris, 1998

Godfrey, John (ed.), *A Decade of i-Deas, The Encyclopedia of the 1980s*, London, 1990

Golbin, Pamela, *Créateurs des Modes*, Paris, 1999

Grand, France, *Comme des Garçons*, London, 1998

Gross, Michael, *Model*, New York, 1995

Grumbach, Didier, *Histoires de la Mode*, Paris, 1994

Grundberg, Andy, *Brodovitch*, New York, 1989

Guillaume, Valérie, *Jacques Fath*, Paris, 1993

Guillaume, Valérie, *Courrèges*, London, 1998

Hall-Duncan, Nancy, *The History of Fashion Photography*, New York, 1979

Halliday, Leonard, *The Fashion Makers*, London, 1966

Handley, Susannah, *Nylon: The Manmade Fashion Revolution*, London, 1999

Harris, Alice, *The White T*, New York, 1996

Harrison, Martin, *Appearances*, London, 1991

Harrison, Martin, *Norman Parkinson Photographs 1935–1990*, London and New York, 1995

Harrison, Martin, *Patrick Demarchelier, Exposing Elegance*, New York, 1997

Hawes, Elizabeth, *Fashion is Spinach*, New York, 1938

Hawes, Elizabeth, *Why is a Dress?*, New York, 1942

Head, Edith, *The Dress Doctor*, Boston, 1959

Healy, Robin, *Balenciaga: Masterpieces of Fashion Design*, Melbourne, 1992

Hebdige, Dick, *Subculture, The Meaning of Style*, London, 1979

Henry Clarke, Paris, 1996

Hilfiger, Tommy, *All American: A Style Book*, New York, 1997

Hilfiger, Tommy and de Curtis, Anthony, *Rock Style*, New York, 1999

Holborn, Mark, *Issey Miyake*, Cologne, 1995

Hollander, Anne, *Sex and Suits*, New York, 1994

Hollander, Anne, *Feeding the Eye*, New York, 1999

Howell, Georgina, *Sultans of Style: 30 Years of Fashion and Passion 1960–1990*, London, 1990

Howell, Georgina, *In Vogue: 75 Years of Style*, London, 1991

Howell, Georgina, *In Vogue*, London, 1992

Hulanicki, Barbara, *From A to Biba*, London, 1983

In Black and White: Dress from the 1920s to Today (exh. cat.), Ohio State University, Columbus, 1992

Italian Fashion: The Origins of High Fashion and Knitwear, Milan, 1987

Johnston, Lorraine, *The Fashion Year Vol.III*, London, 1985

Join-Dieterle, Catharine, *Le Dessin Sous Toutes ses Coutures*, Paris, 1995

Jones, Dylan, *Paul Smith: True Brit*, London, 1996

Jones, Mablen, *Getting It On: The Clothing of Rock 'n' Roll*, New York, 1987

Jones, Terry, *Catching the Moment*, London, 1997

Jouve, Marie-Andrée, *Balenciaga*, London, 1997

Jouve, Marie-Andrée and Demorneaux, Jaqueline, *Balenciaga*, Paris, 1988

Kamitsis, Lydia, *Paco Rabanne: A Feeling for Research*, Paris, 1996

Kamitsis, Lydia, *Paco Rabanne*, London, 1999

Kay, Hilary, *Rock and Roll Memorabilia*, New York, 1992

Kazmaier, Martin, *Sixty Years of Photography*, Munich, 1991

Keenan, Brigid, *Dior in Vogue*, London, 1981

Kennedy, Shirley, *Pucci: A Renaissance in Fashion*, New York, 1991

Kingswell, Tamsin, *Red or Dead*, London, 1998

Klein, William, *In and Out of Fashion*, New York, 1994

Knight, Nick, *Nicknight*, Munich, 1994

Koda, Harold, *Three Women: Madeleine Vionnet, Claire McCardell and Rei Kawakubo*, New York, 1987

Kohle, Yohannan and Nolf, Nancy, *Claire McCardell: Redefining Modernism*, New York, 1998

König, Rene, *À La Mode*, New York, 1973

LaChapelle, David, *Lachapelle Land*, New York, 1996

LaChapelle, David, *Hotel Lachapelle*, New York, 1999

Lagerfeld, Karl, *Photographer*, Cologne, 1990

Lambert, Eleanor, *World of Fashion: People, Places, Resources*, New York, 1976

Lang, Jack, *Thierry Mugler, Photographer*, Paris, 1988

Latour, Anny, *Kings of Fashion*, London, 1958

Lawford, Valentine, *Horst, His Work and His World*, New York, 1984

Laymarie, Jean, *Chanel*, Geneva, 1987

Lebenthal, Joel, *Radical Rags: Fashions of the Sixties*, New York, 1990

Lee, Sarah Tomerlin (ed.), *American Fashion*, New York, 1975

Levin, Phyllis Lee, *The Wheels of Fashion*, New York, 1965

Lévy, Bernard-Henri, *Yves Saint Laurent Par Yves Saint Laurent*, Paris, 1986

Liaut, Jean-Noël, *Cover Girls and Supermodels 1945–1965*, New York, 1996

Liberman, Alexander, *Irving Penn: Passage, A Work Record*, New York, 1991

Liebovitz, Annie, *Photographs 1970–1990*, New York, 1991

Lindbergh, Peter, *Selected Work 1996–1998*, Paris, 1998

Livingston, Kathryn E., *Patrick Demarchelier: Fashion Photography*, Boston, 1989

Looking at Fashion: Biennale di Firenze, Florence, 1996

Lopez, Antonio, *Antonio's Girls*, London, 1982

Lovatt-Smith, Lisa, *Fashion Images de Mode, No.1*, Göttingen, 1996

Lovatt-Smith, Lisa, *Fashion Images de Mode, No.2*, Göttingen, 1997

Lovatt-Smith, Lisa, *Fashion Images de Mode, No.3*, Göttingen, 1998

Lovatt-Smith, Lisa, *Fashion Images de Mode, No.4*, Göttingen, 1999

Lyman, Ruth, *Paris Fashion: The Great Designers and Their Creations*, London, 1972

McCardell, Claire, *What Shall I Wear? The What, Where, When and How Much of Fashion*, New York, 1956

McCrum, Elizabeth, *Fabric and Form: Irish Fashion Since 1950*, Belfast, 1996

McDermott, Catherine, *Street Style: British Design in the 1980s*, London, 1987

McDowell, Colin, *The Directory of Twentieth-Century Fashion*, London, 1984

McDowell, Colin, *Shoes, Fashion and Fantasy*, London, 1989

McDowell, Colin, *Dressed to Kill: Sex, Power and Clothes*, London, 1992

McDowell, Colin, *Hats: Status, Style, Glamour*, London, 1992

McDowell, Colin, *The Designer Scam*, London, 1994

McDowell, Colin, *Forties' Fashion and the New Look*, London, 1997

McDowell, Colin, *Galliano: Romantic, Realist, Revolutionary*, London, 1997

McDowell, Colin, *Jean Paul Gaultier*, London, 2000

McDowell, Colin, *Manolo Blahnik*, London and New York, 2000

McGill, Leonard, *Disco Dressing*, New Jersey, 1980

McKnight, Gerald, *Gucci: A House Divided*, New York, 1987

McRobbie, Angela, *Zoot Suits and Secondhand Dresses*, London, 1989

McRobbie, Angela, *British Fashion Design: Rag Trade of Image Industry*, London, 1998

Mackrell, Alice, *Coco Chanel*, London, 1992

Madsen, Axel, *Living for Design: The Yves Saint Laurent Story*, New York, 1979

Malossi, Giannino, *Liberi Tutti: 20 Anni di Moda Spettacolo*, Milan, 1987

Malossi, Giannino, *The Style Engine*, Milan and New York, 1998

Malossi, Giannino (ed.), *Material Man: Masculinity, Sexuality, Style*, New York, 2000

Martin, Richard, *Fashion and Surrealism*, New York, 1987

Martin, Richard, *Beene: 30 Years*, New York, 1993

Martin, Richard, *Contemporary Fashion*, Detroit, 1995

Martin, Richard, *This is a Pair of Levi Jeans: The Official History of the Levis Brand*, San Francisco, 1995

Martin, Richard, *Charles James*, London, 1997

Martin, Richard, *Gianni Versace*, New York, 1997

Martin, Richard, *Versace*, London, 1997

Martin, Richard, *Cubism and Fashion*, New York, 1998

Martin, Richard and Koda, Harold, *Giorgio Armani*, New York, 1990

Martin, Richard and Koda, Harold, *Giorgio Armani: Images of Man*, New York, 1990

Martin, Richard and Koda, Harold, *Infra-Apparel*, New York, 1993

Martin, Richard and Koda, Harold, *Orientalism: Visions of the East in Western Dress*, New York, 1994

Martin, Richard and Koda, Harold, *Haute Couture*, New York, 1995

Mauries, Patrick, *David Seidner*, Munich and London, 1989

Mauries, Patrick, *Pieces of Pattern: Lacroix By Lacroix*, London, 1992

Mauries, Patrick, *Christian Lacroix: The Diary of a Collection*, London, 1996

Maywald, Willy, *Willy Maywald et la Mode*, Paris, 1986

Mendes, Valerie, *Pierre Cardin: Past, Present, Future*, London, 1990

Mendes, Valerie, *Black in Fashion*, London, 1999

Milbank, Caroline Rennolds, *Couture: The Great Designers*, New York, 1985

Milbank, Caroline Rennolds, *New York Fashion: The Evolution of American Style*, New York, 1989

Miller, Lesley, *Cristobal Balenciaga*, London, 1993

Mirabella, Grace, *Geoffrey Beene Unbound*, New York, 1994

Miyake, Issey, *East Meets West*, Tokyo, 1978

Miyake, Issey, *Body Works*, Tokyo, 1983

Miyake, Issey, *Photographs by Irving Penn*, New York, 1988

Miyake, Issey, *Pleats Please*, Tokyo, 1990

Miyake, Issey, *Making Things*, Paris, 1999

Moffitt, Peggy and Claxton, William, *The Rudi Gernreich Book*, New York, 1991

Mohrt, Françoise, *The Givenchy Style*, Paris, 1998

Mohrt, Françoise, *Hubert de Givenchy*, Paris, 1998

Montgomery, M.R., *In Search of L.L. Bean*, Boston, 1984

Moor, Jonathon, *Perry Ellis*, New York, 1988

Morris, Bernadine, *Scaasi: A Cut Above*, New York, 1996

Morris, Bernadine, *Valentino*, London, 1996

Morris, Bernadine and Walz, Barbara, *The Fashion Makers*, New York, 1978

Moschino, Franco, *X Anni di Kaos 1983–1993*, Milan, 1993

Mugler, Thierry, *Fashion Fetish Fantasy*, London, 1998

Mulassano, Adriana, *The Who's Who of Italian Fashion*, Florence, 1979

Mulassano, Adriana, *Moda e Modi*, Milan, 1980

Mulvagh, Jane, *Vogue History of Twentieth-Century Fashion*, London, 1988

Mulvagh, Jane, *Vivienne Westwood, An Unfashionable Life*, London, 1998

Newton, Helmut, *Pages from the Glossies: Facsimiles 1956–1998*, Zürich, 1998

Nickerson, Camilla and Wakefield, Neville, *Fashion*, Zürich, 1996

Oldham, Todd, *Without Boundaries*, New York, 1997

Orban, Christine, *Emanuel Ungaro*, London, 1999

Packer, William, *Fashion Drawing in Vogue*, London, 1983

Parkinson, Norman, *Lifework*, London, 1983

Pelle, Marie-Paule and Mauries, Patrick, *Valentino: Thirty Years of Magic*, New York, 1991

Perier, Anne-Marie, *Elle: 1945–1995 Nos Cinquante Premieres Années*, Paris, 1995

Piaggi, Anna, *Karl Lagerfeld: A Fashion Journal*, London, 1986

Piaggi, Anna, *Anna Piaggi's Fashion Algebra*, London, 1998

Pochna, Marie-France, *Christian Dior*, London, 1987

Pochna, Marie-France, *Nina Ricci*, Paris, 1992

Pochna, Marie-France, *Dior*, London, 1996

Polan, Brenda, *The Fashion Year Vol.1*, London, 1983

Polhemus, Ted, *Diesel*, London, 1998

Polhemus, Ted and Procter, Lynn, *Fashion and Anti-Fashion*, London, 1978

Pringle, Colombe, *Roger Vivier*, London, 1999

Provoyeur, Pierre, *Vivier*, Paris, 1991

Quant, Mary, *Quant by Quant*, London, 1966

Quick, Harriet, *Catwalking: A History of the Fashion Model*, London, 1997

Quirico, Tiziana, *Krizia*, Milan, 1995

Relang, Regina, *30 Anni di Moda*, Milan, 1983

Rhodes, Zandra, *The Art of Zandra Rhodes*, London, 1984

Rinaldi, Paolo, *Walter Albini: Style in Fashion*, Milan, 1998

Robert Altman's Pret-à-Porter, London, 1995

Robertson, Grace, *Photojournalist of the Fifties*, London, 1989

Roshco, Bernard, *The Rag Race*, New York, 1963

Ross, Andrew, *No Sweat: Fashion, Free Trade and the Rights of Garment Workers*, London, 1997

Rossellini, Isabella (ed.), *10 Years of Dolce & Gabbana*, Milan, 1996

Rosso, Renzi, *Forty: Diesel*, Milan, 1996

Rous, Henrietta, *The Ossie Clark Diaries*, London and Zürich, 1998

Sainderichin, Ginette, *Kenzo*, London, 1999

Schiaparelli, Elsa, *Shocking Life*, London, 1954

Schnurnberger, Lynn, *Let There Be Clothes*, New York, 1991

Sebag-Montefiore, Hugh, *Kings on the Catwalk*, London, 1992

Sebba, Anne, *Laura Ashley, A Life by Design*, London, 1990

Senneville, Elisabeth de, *Elisabeth de Senneville: Un Mode Hors/Mode*, Paris, 1994

Sieff, Jeanloup, *Jeanloup Sieff, Forty Years of Photography*, Paris, 1990

Silmon, Pedro, *The Bikini*, London, 1986

Sischy, Ingrid, *Donna Karan*, London, 1998

Sloane, Eunice, *Illustrating Fashion*, New York, 1977

Sneakers: Size Isn't Everything, London, 1998

Snow, Carmel, *The World of Carmel Snow*, New York, 1962

Soli, Pia, *Il Genio Antipatico*, Venice, 1984

Sozzani, Carla and Masucci, Anna, *Walter Albini*, Milan, 1990

Sozzani, Franca, *Black Book*, Paris, 1998

Sozzani, Franca, *Dolce & Gabbana*, London, 1999

Steele, Valerie, *Women of Fashion*, New York, 1991

Steele, Valerie and Major, John S., *China Chic: East Meets West*, New York, 1999

Stegemeyer, Anne, *Who's Who in Fashion?*, New York, 1980

Strute, Karl, and Doelkin, Theodor, *Who's Who in Fashion*, Zürich, 1982

Sudjic, Deyan, *Rei Kawakubo and Comme des Garçons*, London, 1990

Takamura, Zeshu, *Roots of Street Style*, Tokyo, 1997

Talley, André Leon, *Valentino*, Milan, 1982

Tournier, Michel, *Azzedine Alaïa*, Munich, 1998

Trachtenberg, Jeffrey A., *Ralph Lauren: The Man Behind the Mystique*, New York, 1988

Tucker, Andrew, *The London Fashion Book*, London, 1998

Tucker, Andrew, *Dries Van Noten*, London, 1999

Turner, Lowri, *Gianni Versace: Fashion's Last Emperor*, London, 1997

Turner, Peter, *American Images. Photography 1945–80*, London, 1985

Valentino, *Trent'Anni di Maglia*, Milan, 1991

Vent'Anni di Vogue Italia 1964–1984, Milan, 1984

Vercelloni, Isa Tutino (ed.), *Missonologia: The World of Missoni*, Milan, 1995

Vercelloni, Isa and Lucchini, Flavio, *Milan Fashion*, Milan, 1975

Vergani, Guido, *The Sala Bianca: The Birth of Italian Fashion*, Milan, 1992

Versace, Gianni, *Versace: Signatures*, New York, 1992

Versace, Gianni, *Designs*, New York, 1994

Versace, Gianni, *Men Without Ties*, New York, 1994

Versace, Gianni, *Do Not Disturb*, New York, 1996

Versace, Gianni, *Rock and Royalty*, New York, 1996

Versace, Gianni, *The Art of Being You*, New York, 1997

Versace, Gianni, *The Naked and the Dressed: 20 Years of Versace by Avedon*, New York, 1998

Viramontes, *Drawings*, Tokyo, 1988

Vogue: 1964–1994, Milan, 1995

Vraiment Faux (exh. cat.), Fondation Cartier Pour l'Art Contemporain, Paris, 1988

Vreeland, Diana, *Allure*, New York, 1980

Vreeland, Diana, *Yves Saint Laurent*, New York, 1983

Vreeland, Diana, *Immoderate Style*, New York, 1993

Vreeland Fashion Jewellery (Sotheby's New York sale catalogue), New York, 1987

The Warhol Look (exh. cat.), Whitney Museum, New York, 1997

Watson, Linda, *Vogue Twentieth-Century Fashion*, London, 1999

Westerbeck, Colin, *Irving Penn, A Career in Photography*, New York, 1998

White, Emily, *The Fashion Year Vol.2*, London, 1984

White, Nancy, *Style in Motion: Munkacsi Photographs*, New York, 1963

White, Palmer, *Schiaparelli*, New York, 1986

White, Palmer, *The Master Touch of Lesage*, Paris, 1987

Wilcox, Claire and Mendes, Valerie, *Modern Fashion in Detail*, London, 1991

Williams, Beryl, *Young Faces in Fashion*, Philadelphia, 1956

Williams, Val, *Look at Me, Fashion & Photography in Britain, 1960s to the Present*, London, 1998

Wilson, Elizabeth, and Taylor, Lou, *Through the Looking Glass*, London, 1989

Wintour, Anna, *The Idealizing Vision*, New York, 1991

Wozencroft, Jon, *The Graphic Language of Neville Brody*, London, 1988

Zahm, Volker, *Art Fashion*, Göttingen, 1994

Zito, Adele, *Italian Fashion: The Protagonists*, Milan, 1993

CHRONOLOGY

1945

World War II – European hostilities cease
Atom bombs dropped on Hiroshima and Nagasaki force
a Japanese surrender
French *Elle* founded by Hélène Gordon-Lazareff
Conditions for membership of La Chambre Syndicale de la
Couture Parisienne published

1946

Louis Réard creates the bikini – named after the South
Pacific atoll on which the atom bomb was tested
Bettina becomes Jacques Fath's model and 'the most
photographed face in France'
Estée Lauder founds cosmetic firm
Carven's *Ma Griffe* perfume launched
Production of the Vespa scooter begins
Rita Hayworth stars in Charles Vidor's film *Gilda*
King Vidor's film *Duel in the Sun*
Jean Cocteau's film *La Belle et la bête*

1947

The Marshall Plan for European economic recovery launched
Christian Dior launches the 'New Look'
Tennessee Williams, *A Streetcar Named Desire*

1948

Christian Dior signs contract with Prestige in New York to
produce their own brand of nylon stockings
First Wranglers jeans for women launched
Adidas splits into two separate companies: Adidas and Ruda
(name changed to Puma in 1949)
Doctor Alfred C. Kinsey publishes *Sexual Behaviour in the
Human Male* ('The Kinsey Report')
Nina Ricci's *L'Air du Temps* perfume launched
Mahatma Gandhi assassinated

1949

The doe-eyed make-up look created by Etienne Aubrey
Orlon introduced
George Orwell, *Nineteen Eighty-Four*
Mies van der Rohe, Farnsworth House, Plano, Illinois

1950

U.S. forces invade Korea
Senator McCarthy's anti-Communist witchhunt begins in U.S.
Charles M. Schultz's *Peanuts* comic strip debuts
Bette Davis and Marilyn Monroe star in *All About Eve*
Emilio Pucci photographed wearing his own design ski
clothes by Toni Frissell
Pucci opens his own couture house
Nino Cerruti starts producing clothes using his family firm's
fabric

1951

Cosmetic company Orlane created
Dacron launched by Du Pont
J.D. Salinger's novel *The Catcher in the Rye* introduces
Holden Caulfield, teenage cult hero
I Love Lucy, starring Lucille Ball, begins its long run on U.S.
television
Festival of Britain, London

1952

Coronation of Queen Elizabeth II
Gian Battista Giorgini presents Italian fashion to world press
in the Pitti Palace, Florence
Gaby Aghiou founds Chloé fashion house
Salvatore Ferragamo introduces stiletto heels
Hubert de Givenchy opens his own fashion house

1953

Jacqueline Lee Bouvier marries John F. Kennedy
Ottavio and Rosita Missoni found their knitwear company
First man's polyester suit
Hardy Amies granted the Royal Warrant as dressmaker to
the Queen
Marilyn Monroe stars in *Gentlemen Prefer Blondes*

1954

Coco Chanel makes her comeback
Jacques Fath dies
Audrey Hepburn stars in *Sabrina*, costumes by Edith Head
The Barefoot Contessa starring Ava Gardner, costumes by
Fontana Sorelle of Rome
General Motors produce their 50 millionth private car
James Baldwin, *Go Tell it on the Mountain*
Françoise Sagan, *Bonjour tristesse*
Marlon Brando stars in Elia Kazan's film *On the Waterfront*

1955

Dior's A-line introduced
Mary Quant opens Bazaar on King's Road, London
Claire McCardell featured on the cover of *Time* magazine
John Fairchild becomes head of *WWD*'s Paris bureau
George Demenstral invents Velcro
Playboy magazine introduces the nude centrefold
Jack O'Neill invents the wet suit
Elvis Presley's first contract with RCA records
Vladimir Nabokov, *Lolita*
James Dean stars in *Rebel without a Cause* and *East of Eden*
The film *Blackboard Jungle* makes Bill Hailey's *Rock Around
the Clock* a hit
James Dean dies in a car crash

1956

Grace Kelly marries Prince Rainier II of Monaco
Balenciaga introduces the chemise, christened 'The Sack' in
America
Brigitte Bardot stars in Roger Vadim's film *And God Created
Woman*
Marilyn Monroe stars in *Bus Stop*, sponsored by Lee Jeans
Elvis Presley releases *Blue Suede Shoes* and *Heartbreak Hotel*
Allen Ginsburg, *Howl and Other Poems*
Transatlantic telephone service introduced
Frank Lloyd Wright, Guggenheim Museum, New York

1957

U.S.S.R. launches Sputnik satellite
National Guardsmen called in to enforce racial integration at
Little Rock, Arkansas
Christian Dior dies
Audrey Hepburn stars in *Funny Face*, costumes by Givenchy
Mariuccia Mandelli's first Krizia collection
Elvis Presley inducted into U.S. army
The musical *West Side Story* opens in New York
Jack Kerouac, *On the Road*

1958

Commercial jets begin transatlantic flights
Yves Saint Laurent's Trapeze dress
Claire McCardell dies
Bri-Nylon introduced by British Nylon Spinners
First Italian Trade Commission fashion show held in America
Vincente Minnelli's film *Gigi*, costumes designed by Cecil
Beaton
Simone de Beauvoir, *The Second Sex*
Hit singles: *Good Golly, Miss Molly* (Little Richard); *Tom
Dooley* (The Kingston Trio) and *All I Have to Do is Dream*
(The Everly Brothers)

1959

Fidel Castro liberates Cuba
Valentino opens his salon in Rome
Lycra introduced by Du Pont
Hollywood costume designer Adrian dies
Buddy Holly dies in plane crash
William Burroughs, *Naked Lunch*
Jack Lemmon, Tony Curtis and Marilyn Monroe star in Billy
Wilder's film *Some Like it Hot*
Alec Issigonis designs the Mini car
Mattel introduce the Barbie doll

1960

The contraceptive pill introduced
John F. Kennedy becomes President of the United States
Jackie Kennedy chooses Oleg Cassini as her official
dressmaker
Pierre Cardin's first menswear collection
Doc Martens (invented in 1945) produced under licence
in U.K. by R. Griggs and Co.
Invention of hairspray
Anita Ekberg stars in Federico Fellini's film *La Dolce Vita*
Alfred Hitchcock's film *Psycho*
Chubby Checker releases *The Twist*
Brian Hyland releases *Itsy Bitsy, Teenie Weenie, Yellow
Polka-dot Bikini*
Andy Warhol's comic strip painting, *Dick Tracy*

1961

Berlin wall erected
Nelson Mandela arrested (released 1990)
Yves Saint Laurent opens his own fashion house
Armani joins Cerruti as menswear designer
Dr Scholl exercise sandals invented
'Young Contemporaries' exhibition, London introduces
Pop Art
Amnesty International founded

1962

Marilyn Monroe dies
John Glenn becomes the first man in space
Telstar, the first communications satellite, launched
Peter O'Toole stars in David Lean's film *Laurence of Arabia*
Jeanne Moreau stars in François Truffaut's film *Jules et Jim*
Andy Warhol opens The Factory on 47th Street, New York
Bridget Riley's first solo exhibition

1963

Martin Luther King makes his 'I Have a Dream' speech
in Washington
John F. Kennedy makes his 'Ich bin ein Berliner' speech
at the Berlin Wall
John F. Kennedy assassinated in Dallas, Texas
Diana Vreeland becomes editor-in-chief of U.S. *Vogue*
Helen Gurley Brown launches *Cosmopolitan* magazine
Mary Quant creates Ginger Group, her mass-market line
The Beatles' world tour begins
Bob Dylan releases *Blowing in the Wind*

1964

U.S. Civil Rights Act passed
Biba mail order launched
Rudi Gernreich designs topless swimsuit
Audrey Hepburn stars in *My Fair Lady*, costumes designed
by Cecil Beaton
First Pirelli calendar, designed by Derek Birdsall, photographed
by Harri Peccinotti
The Rolling Stones' first U.S. appearance on the Ed Sullivan
Show
Nancy Sinatra releases *These Boots Were Made for Walking*

1965

U.S. take offensive in Vietnam War
Black nationalist leader, Malcolm X, assassinated
Race riots in Watts, Los Angeles
Paco Rabanne introduces plastic disc dresses
Benetton founded
Karl Birkenstock invents eponymous sandals
TGI Fridays – New York's first singles bar – opens
Julie Christie stars in *Darling*
The Who release *My Generation*

1966

The Cultural Revolution begins in China
Masters & Johnson publish *Human Sexual Response*
'Swinging London' coined by *Time* magazine
Yves Saint Laurent's 'Le Smoking'
Yves Saint Laurent launches Rive Gauche ready-to-wear line
Pierre Cardin's Cosmonaut collection
Twiggy's first modelling contract
The Kinks release *Dedicated Follower of Fashion*
Frank Zappa and The Mothers of Invention release debut
album *Freak Out* – rock's first double album
Star Trek television series first aired

1967

Che Guevera killed in Bolivia
Six Days War between Israel and Arab nations
Polo Ralph Lauren founded
Elio Fiorucci opens first boutique
Faye Dunaway and Warren Beatty star in *Bonnie and Clyde*
Catherine Deneuve stars in Luis Buñuel's film *Belle de Jour*
The Beatles release *Sgt. Pepper's Lonely Hearts Club Band*
Monterey Pop Festival, starring Jimi Hendrix, begins the
Summer of Love in San Francisco
Rolling Stone magazine launched

1968

Student riots in Paris
Czechoslovakia overrun by Russian forces
Martin Luther King murdered
Richard Nixon becomes President of the United States
Robert Kennedy murdered
Yves Saint Laurent introduces the jump suit
Jacqueline Kennedy chooses a Valentino dress for her
wedding to Aristotle Onassis
Paraphernalia boutique opens on Lexington Avenue,
New York
Clinique make-up range launched
The 'Clyde' suede sneaker introduced by Puma
Jane Fonda stars in *Barbarella*
Roman Polanski's film *Rosemary's Baby*
Stanley Kubrick's film *2001: A Space Odyssey*
The musical *Hair* opens in New York
Naomi Sims is the first black woman to appear on the cover
of *Life* magazine

1969

Neil Armstrong, U.S. astronaut, walks on the moon
British troops sent to Northern Ireland in an attempt
to restore order in the province
Comme des Garçons label introduced
Silver collection by André Courrèges
Biba Kensington High Street store opened
The Woodstock Music and Arts Fair, known simply
as 'Woodstock'
Hand-held blow-dryers come onto the general market
Peter Fonda and Dennis Hopper star in *Easy Rider*
Federico Fellini's film *Satyricon*
First presentation by Gilbert and George
Gay riot, The Stonewall Bar, New York

1970

10,000 women march in New York for equal rights, including
free abortion on demand
Germaine Greer, *The Female Eunuch*
National Guard kill four students at Kent State University, Ohio
Paul Smith opens his first shop in Nottingham
Kenzo opens his own shop
British *Vogue* name Bill Gibb Designer of the Year
Borg introduce fake furs
Hot pants appear
Robert Altman's film *MASH*
Jimi Hendrix and Janis Joplin die of drug overdoses

1971

Coco Chanel dies
Thierry Mugler presents his first collection, under the label
'Café de Paris'
Diana Vreeland dismissed as editor of U.S. *Vogue*
Let It Rock boutique opened by Vivienne Westwood
(renamed Sex in 1974)
Yves Saint Laurent's *Rive Gauche* perfume launched
Maybelline introduces *Great Lash* mascara
The Coty Fashion Critics' Award given to Levi Strauss
Friends of the Earth founded in Britain
Andy Warhol creates the cover for the Rolling Stones' *Sticky
Fingers* album
The Doors release *LA Woman*
Stanley Kubrick's film *A Clockwork Orange*
Gordon Parks's film *Shaft*

1972

President Nixon visits China
Watergate scandal
Cristóbal Balenciaga dies
Norman Norell dies
Diana Vreeland appointed Special Consultant at the
Costume Institute of the Metropolitan Museum of Art
Dior's *Diorella* perfume launched
W issued as a broadsheet
The Alternative Miss World competition initiated by Andrew
Logan
Francis Ford Coppola's film *The Godfather*
Bernardo Bertolucci's film *Last Tango in Paris*
Liza Minnelli stars in Bob Fosse's film *Cabaret*
David Bowie releases *Ziggy Stardust*

1973

Formal Peace Treaty withdraws U.S. military personnel from
Vietnam
International oil crisis
Yves Saint Laurent's Peasant Look
American designers – Renta, Halston, Perry Ellis and Calvin
Klein – invited by Chambre Syndicale to show in Versailles
'Inventive Paris Clothes 1909–39' exhibition at the
Metropolitan Museum of Art
Madeleine Vionnet dies
Timberland company founded
T-shirt mania begins
Erica Jong, *Fear of Flying*
Betty Friedan, *The Feminine Mystique*
Jane Fonda's Work-Out Programme released
Jørn Utzon's Sydney Opera House opens

1974

President Nixon resigns
Gianfranco Ferré shows first collection under his own name
Elsa Peretti starts designing jewellery for Tiffany
Alain Wertheimer buys Chanel
Beverly Johnson becomes U.S. *Vogue*'s first black cover girl
Elizabeth Arden launches Visible Difference skin cream

1975

Giorgio Armani founds his own company
Stephen Spielberg's film *Jaws*
Malcolm McLaren launches The Sex Pistols
Bob Marley single *Natty Dread* makes dreadlocks a cult
Dolly Parton has three separate singles at Number 1 in the
American hit parade

1976

First Concorde flight across the Atlantic
Yves Saint Laurent's Russian collection
Yves Saint Laurent's Chinese collection
Calvin Klein launches jeans line
New Balance 320 trainers appear
Mainbocher dies
Derek Jarman's film *Sebastiane*
Renzo Piano and Richard Rogers, Pompidou Centre, Paris,
First Body Shop opens in Brighton
Shere Hite's *The Hite Report* published

1977

Studio 54 opens in New York
Elvis Presley dies
Zandra Rhodes's Conceptual Chic collection
Yves Saint Laurent's *Opium* perfume launched
John Travolta stars in *Saturday Night Fever*
David Lynch's film *Eraserhead*
Never Mind the Bollocks, Here's the Sex Pistols album
released
Iggy Pop releases *Lust for Life*

1978

First in vitro baby born
First own-name collection by Versace
Karl Lagerfeld's first collection for Fendi
Missoni designs exhibited at the Whitney Museum, New York
Betsey Johnson founds her own company
Charles James dies
John Travolta and Olivia Newton-John star in *Grease*
Brooke Shields stars in Louis Malle's film *Pretty Baby*
Dallas begins on U.S. television
Greenpeace founded

1979

Margaret Thatcher becomes first female British Prime Minister
Katharine Hamnett founds her own company
Miuccia Prada takes over family luggage company founded
in 1913
Estée Lauder Prescriptives range launched
Cecil Beaton dies
Norman Hartnell dies
Franc Roddam's film *Quadrophenia*
Blondie releases *Heart of Glass*
Village People release *YMCA*

1980

Ronald Reagan becomes President of the United States
John Lennon murdered
Fifteen-year-old Brooke Shields stars in a Calvin Klein jeans
commercial directed by Richard Avedon
i-D magazine launched
Richard Gere stars in *American Gigolo*, costumes designed
by Giorgio Armani
Jack Nicholson stars in Stanley Kubrick's film *The Shining*
CNN television network opens
First Apple computer marketed
Major Picasso retrospective exhibition held at the Museum
of Modern Art, New York

1981

New York Times runs the first article on the AIDS epidemic
MTV launched
Rei Kawakubo and Yohji Yamamoto invited to show in Paris
by the Chambre Syndicale
Hollywood costume designer Edith Head dies
The Face magazine launched
Harrison Ford stars in *Raiders of the Lost Ark*
Dynasty begins on U.S. television
Boy George forms Culture Club

1982

Giorgio Armani appears on the cover of *Time* magazine
Christian Lacroix's first couture collection for Patou
Pierre Balmain dies
Nike introduces 'Air force' basketball shoes
Steven Spielberg's film *ET the Extra-Terrestrial*
Peter Greenaway's film *The Draughtsman's Contract*
Ridley Scott's film *Bladerunner*

1983

Launch of the compact disc
Sally Ride becomes the world's first female astronaut
Karl Lagerfeld becomes artistic director at Chanel
Yves Saint Laurent exhibition held at the Metropolitan
Museum of Art, New York – the first show devoted to
a living designer
Franco Moschino's first collection
Walter Albini dies
Swatch watches – 'fashion that ticks' – launched
Beauty Without Cruelty founded
Umberto Eco, *The Name of the Rose*
Mickey Rourke and Matt Dillon star in Francis Ford
Coppola's film *Rumble Fish*
Madonna releases her first single, *Holiday*

1984

Bernard Arnault acquires Dior as part of his LVMH Moët
Hennessy Louis Vuitton conglomerate
Donna Karan's first collection under her own name
John Galliano graduates from Central St Martins College
of Art & Design
Katharine Hamnett confronts Margaret Thatcher wearing
her '58% Don't Want Pershing' T-shirt
Tina Brown relaunches *Vanity Fair* magazine
Michael Jordan first endorses Nike running shoes
Carl Lewis wins four gold medals wearing Nike at the
Los Angeles Olympics
Harrison Ford stars in *Indiana Jones and the Temple of Doom*
Michael Jackson releases *Thriller*
Bruce Springsteen releases *Born in the USA*
Frankie Goes to Hollywood release *Relax*
Turner prize inaugurated, Tate Gallery, London

1985

Perestroika begins under President Gorbachev
Dolce & Gabbana's first collection launched
Tommy Hilfiger founds his own company
Jean Paul Gaultier introduces skirts for men
Laura Ashley dies
Rudi Gernreich dies
Dior's *Poison* perfume launched
British and U.S. editions of *Elle* launched
Leigh Bowery opens Taboo club
Bret Easton Ellis, *Less Than Zero*
Meryl Streep and Robert Redford star in *Out of Africa*
Ecstasy drug made illegal in U.S.
Rock Hudson dies of AIDS

1986

Explosion at Chernobyl nuclear power plant
Live Aid founded by Bob Geldof
Ralph Lauren's flagship store, the Rhinelander building
in New York, opens
Perry Ellis dies
Arena magazine launched
Tama Janavitz, *Slaves of New York*
Alex Cox's film *Sid and Nancy*
Spike Lee's film *She's Gotta Have It*
David Lynch's film *Blue Velvet*
Run DMC release *My Adidas*
Seattle-based group Nirvana formed
Richard Rogers, Lloyds Building, London

1987

'Black Monday' (19 October 1987): Dow Jones industrial
average drops 508 points
'Irangate' inquiry into U.S. arms sales to Iran
Romeo Gigli's first collection under his own name launched
Christian Lacroix shows his pouf skirt
Paco Rabanne launches Concentré Actif Restructurant
– the world's first anti-wrinkle cream for men
Sale of the Duchess of Windsor's jewels in Geneva
Oliver Stone's film *Wall Street*
Rock group Guns 'n' Roses formed
U2 releases *The Joshua Tree*
Ice-T releases first album, *Rhyme Pays*
Prozac goes on sale
Andy Warhol dies
Fred Astaire dies
I.M. Pei creates the Louvre pyramid in Paris

1988

Christian Lacroix appears on the cover of *Time* magazine
Moschino CHEAP & CHIC range launched
Bill Gibb dies
Nike's 'Just Do It' slogan coined
Givenchy acquired by LVMH
Anna Wintour appointed editor-in-chief of U.S. *Vogue*
Suzy Menkes appointed fashion editor of the *International
Herald Tribune*
Lear's, the first U.S. magazine aimed at women over forty, is
launched
Tank Girl comic strip first appears in *Deadline* magazine

1989

The Berlin Wall is dismantled
Student protest in Tiananmen Square, Beijing
Gianfranco Ferré appointed designer-in-chief at Dior
Atelier Versace couture line created
Diana Vreeland dies
Fashion illustrator Erté dies
First episode of *Baywatch* screened on U.S. television
The Simpsons first screened on U.S. television
Courtney Love forms rock group, Hole

1990

The internet becomes generally available
Allure magazine first published
Halston dies
Norman Parkinson dies
Camille Paglia, *Sexual Personae*
Naomi Wolf, *The Beauty Myth*
Pedro Almodóvar's film *Tie Me Up! Tie Me Down!*
Twin Peaks television series first screened
Will Smith stars in television sitcom *The Fresh Prince of Bel Air*

1991

Civil war begins in Yugoslavia
Anna Sui's first collection
Dazed and Confused magazine founded by the
photographer Rankin
Visionaire magazine launched
Bret Easton Ellis, *American Psycho*
River Phoenix and Keanu Reeves star in Gus Van Sant's film
My Own Private Idaho
John Singleton's film *Boyz N the Hood*
Madonna begins her *Blonde Ambition* tour
Alcoa, the Pittsburgh aluminium company, allows casual
dress for office workers
Basketball legend Magic Johnson tests positive for AIDS
Damien Hirst, *The Physical Impossibility of Death in the
Mind of Someone Living*: a tiger shark in a glass tank of
formaldehyde

1992

McDonald's opens a branch in Beijing
Alexander McQueen graduates from Central St Martins
College of Art & Design
Jean Paul Gaultier introduces Gaultier jeans
Marky Mark models for Calvin Klein underwear adverts
Liz Tilberis appointed editor of *Harper's Bazaar*
Tina Brown appointed editor of the *New Yorker*
Susan Faludi, *Backlash*
Quentin Tarantino's film *Reservoir Dogs*
K.D. Lang releases *Ingenue*
Madonna releases her *Sex* book, photographed by
Steven Meisel
Euro Disney opens outside Paris

1993

First CD-ROM released
Marc Jacobs's Grunge collection for Perry Ellis results in the
firm closing its womenswear line
Alexander McQueen introduces Bumsters
Patrick Cox introduces Wannabe loafers
W relaunched as magazine
Madame Grès dies, her death is not made public until
thirteen months later
Toni Morrison wins the Nobel Prize for Literature
The X Files first broadcast on U.S. television
Beavis and Butt-head television show launched
Ice-T releases *Cop Killer*
Rachel Whiteread wins Turner Prize for 'House'

1994

Jackie Kennedy Onassis dies
Franco Moschino dies
Tom Ford becomes design director at Gucci
Issey Miyake creates Pleats Please line
Yves Saint Laurent wins case against Ralph Lauren for
plagiarism
Todd Oldham appointed consultant for Escada
U.S. debut of the Wonderbra
In Style magazine launched
Oliver Stone's film *Natural Born Killers*
Robert Altman's film *Prêt-à-Porter*
Quentin Tarantino's film *Pulp Fiction*
Rapper Snoop Doggy Dogg wears clothes by Tommy Hilfiger
on the television show *Saturday Night Live* and starts a craze

1995

'Not guilty' verdict in the O.J. Simpson murder trial
Giorgio Gucci murdered
Jean Muir dies
Oscar de la Renta takes over Balmain couture
Levi Strauss launch their internet site
Drag artist Ru Paul becomes 'spokesmodel' for MAC
cosmetics
Isaac Mizrahi's film *Unzipped*
Bill Gates, *The Road Ahead*
Alice Silverstone stars in *Clueless*
Nicole Kidman stars in Gus Van Sant's film *To Die For*
Damien Hirst wins the Turner Prize

1996

Galliano and McQueen respectively appointed as design
chiefs at Dior and Givenchy
Ossie Clark murdered
'Il tempo e la moda' at Florence Biennale, known in English
as 'Looking at Fashion'
Ewan McGregor stars in Danny Boyle's film *Trainspotting*
John F. Kennedy Jr marries Carolyn Bessette

1997

Diana, Princess of Wales, killed in car crash in Paris
Gianni Versace murdered in Miami
Jean Paul Gaultier's first couture collection
Marc Jacobs appointed designer at Louis Vuitton
Michael Kors appointed designer at Celine
Nicolas Ghesquiere appointed designer at Balenciaga
Christie's, New York hold a sale of dresses owned by Diana,
Princess of Wales
Sotheby's, New York hold a sale of the contents of the Duke
and Duchess of Windsor's Paris home
Sensation exhibition at the Royal Academy of Arts, London
Frank Gehry, Guggenheim Museum, Bilbao
Richard Meier, Getty Center, Los Angeles
Dolly the sheep cloned

1998

President Clinton impeached over the Monica Lewinsky affair
Isaac Mizrahi closes his fashion house
Alber Elbaz appointed ready-to-wear designer at Yves Saint
Laurent
Peter Speliopoulus appointed designer at Cerruti
Gilles Dufour appointed ready-to-wear designer at Balmain
Narcisso Rodriquez appointed ready-to-wear designer at
Loewe
Ralph Lauren pays $13 million to restore 'Old Glory',
the American flag
Roger Vivier dies

1999

Liz Tilberis dies
Kenzo retires
Issey Miyake hands over the design of his firm but continues
to work with A-POC (A Piece of Cloth)
Prada and LVMH buy Fendi
Amsterdam court upholds Gucci's independence of LVMH
Gucci buys controlling share of Yves Saint Laurent
Christie's, New York hold a sale of the belongings of Marilyn
Monroe
John F. Kennedy Jr and Carolyn Bessette killed in a plane
crash

2000

Israeli troops withdraw from Lebanon
John Gielgud dies
Report by the British Medical Association claims that thin
models in the media contribute to the rise in eating disorders

ACKNOWLEDGEMENTS   Illustration Acknowledgements

Figures refer to page numbers:
Advertising Archives, London: 207; A&C Anthology/© Mats Gustafson: 166; A&C Anthology/© Glen Luchford: 153, 232; A&C Anthology/© Steven Meisel: 235; A&C Anthology/© Luis Sanchis: 363; A&C Anthology/© Inez van Lamsweerde & Vinoodh Matadin: 157, 229, 448; photo John Akehurst: 193, 413, 453(t); courtesy Paolo Rinaldi, Milan: 127, 258; courtesy Paolo Rinaldi, Milan/Chris von Wangenheim: 259; © All Action: 97; © All Action/Alan Davidson: 90; © All Action/Dave Hogan: 86; © All Action/Pat Arnal: 87, 108–09, 111, 138, 307; *Arena Homme Plus*/Nathaniel Goldberg: 246; courtesy Giorgio Armani: 260(ml); courtesy Giorgio Armani/Aldo Fallai: 260(l), 260(r), 260(fr); courtesy Giorgio Armani/Peter Lindbergh: 260(fl), 260(mr), 260(t), 261(l); courtesy Giorgio Armani/Paolo Roversi: 472; courtesy Giorgio Armani/Ellen von Unwerth: 261(r); courtesy Laura Ashley: 292 Balenciaga Archives, Paris. All rights reserved: 28; © David Bailey: 321; © Gian Paolo Barbieri: 104; Katy Barker Agency/Guido Mocafico: 395(t); Katy Barker Agency/Tom Munro: 154; Katy Barker Agency/Terry Richardson: 182, 216; L.L. Bean, Inc.: 482(tr); courtesy Geoffrey Beene Inc.: 273(bl); United Colors of Benetton/Oliviero Toscani: 478, 480, 481; courtesy Antonio Berardi: 382(r); courtesy Antonio Berardi/© Dan Lecca: 382(bl); courtesy Antonio Berardi/Chris Moore: 382(tl); courtesy Dirk Bikkembergs/Michel Comte: 356, 357; courtesy Pattie Boyd: 294; courtesy Véronique Branquinho/© Houbrechts-Daniels: 459; Paul Caranicas, New York, courtesy Gallery Bartsch & Chariau/Antonio Lopez: 131(m), 168, 169; courtesy Carhartt/Orion Best: 474; photo Jean-François Carly: 147, 353, 362; courtesy Hussein Chalayan/Andreas Kokkino: 386(bl); courtesy Hussein Chalayan/Chris Moore: 386(t); courtesy Chanel: 395(b); Chanel Archives/Karl Lagerfeld: 102; courtesy Comme des Garçons/Craig McDean: 447; courtesy Comme des Garçons/Paolo Roversi: 446; photo Michel Comte: 352; The Condé Nast Publications Inc., New York/courtesy *Vogue* © 1954: 24; The Condé Nast Publications Inc., New York/courtesy *Vogue* © 1945/René Bouché: 162; The Condé Nast Publications Inc., New York/courtesy *Vogue*/© William Klein: 56; The Condé Nast Publications Inc., New York/courtesy *Vogue* © 1984/Tony McGee: 378; The Condé Nast Publications Inc., New York/courtesy *Vogue* © 1954/Roger Prigent: 22; The Condé Nast Publications Inc., New York/courtesy *Vogue* © 1954/Karen Radkai: 203; The Condé Nast Publications Inc., New York/courtesy *Vogue* © 1976/Bob Richardson: 253; The Condé Nast Publications Inc., New York/courtesy *Vogue* © 1954/Richard Rutledge: 32; The Condé Nast Publications Inc., New York/courtesy *Vogue* © 1974/Francesco Scavullo: 131(tl); The Condé Nast Publications Inc., New York/courtesy *Vogue* © 1974/Francesco Scavullo: 273(t) The Condé Nast Publications Inc., New York/courtesy *Vogue* © 1967/Alexis Waldeck: 252; The Condé Nast Publications Inc., New York/courtesy *Vogue* © 1969/Alexis Waldeck: 272; The Condé Nast Publications Ltd/© *Vogue*/Clive Arrowsmith: 293, 303; The Condé Nast Publications Ltd/© *Vogue*/Alex Chatelain: 257, 381; The Condé Nast Publications Ltd/© *Vogue* 1948/Clifford Coffin: 9; The Condé Nast Publications Ltd/© *Vogue* 1946/Clifford Coffin: 21; The Condé Nast Publications Ltd/© *Vogue*/Corinne Day: 183; The Condé Nast Publications Ltd/© *Vogue*/Anthony Denny: 118; The Condé Nast Publications Ltd/© *Vogue*/Norman Eales: 369; The Condé Nast Publications Ltd/©

Vogue/Charles Harris: 469; The Condé Nast Publications Ltd/© *Vogue*/Nick Knight: 142, 249, 275; The Condé Nast Publications Ltd/© *Vogue*/Barry Lategan: 130, 219, 301, 329; The Condé Nast Publications Ltd/© *Vogue*/David Montgomery: 274, 284, 296, 468; The Condé Nast Publications Ltd/© *Vogue*/Harri Peccinotti: 295; The Condé Nast Publications Ltd/© *Vogue*/Bob Richardson: 173(bl); The Condé Nast Publications Ltd/© *Vogue*/Paolo Roversi: 306; The Condé Nast Publications Ltd/© *Vogue*/Lothar Schmidt: 302; The Condé Nast Publications Ltd/© *Vogue*/Lord Snowdon: 82–3, 95(t); The Condé Nast Publications Ltd/© *Vogue*/Tyen: 332; The Condé Nast Publications Ltd/© *Vogue*/Tim Walker: 192, 411, 461; The Condé Nast Publications Ltd/© *Vogue*/Albert Watson: 380(ml); courtesy Jasper Conran/Tessa Traeger: 276; Corbis: 52(bl), 52(tr), 53; Corbis/Library of Congress/Arthur Siegel: 63; Corbis/Studio Patellani/Federico Patellani: 89; Corbis/John Springer: 75; Dagmar, New York and Tuscon: 368, 376(b), 467; courtesy Ann Demeulemeester: 348(br), 354(bl), 398(bl); courtesy Ann Demeulemeester/Chris Moore: 453(m); courtesy Demont Photo Management/William Claxton © 1999: 470; courtesy Diesel/Henrik Halvarsson: 490(b); courtesy Diesel/David LaChapelle: 490(t); courtesy Christian Dior: 10, 13, 164, 310; photo Sean Ellis: 106, 146–7, 236, 237, 393, 400, 429; photo Jerome Esch: 240–1, 247, 304–05, 308, 347(t), 425, 450–1, 452, 454; courtesy Esprit: 482(l); courtesy *The Face*: 211, 214(b); Michèle Filomeno/Javier Vallhonrat: 342; © Micol Fontana Foundation, Rome: 33, 34, 35, 68; Frank Magazine/Cometti: 267(br); Frank Magazine/Satoshi Saikusa: 277, 320, 333; Frank Magazine/Terry Richardson: 384–5; courtesy Gap/David Sims: 483; courtesy Gap/Herb Ritts: 482(br); courtesy Ghost: 348(bl); courtesy Romeo Gigli: 330; courtesy Givenchy/© Bruno Pellerin: 358, 359; photo Nan Goldin: 181; courtesy Howard Greenberg Gallery, New York/© Lillian Bassman: 14; courtesy Gucci/Hasue: 267(tl); courtesy Gucci/Luis Sanchis: 266; courtesy Gucci/Mario Testino: 228, 349, 268–9; courtesy Tommy Hilfiger/Peter Arnell: 484(m), 485; courtesy Tommy Hilfiger/Dan Lecca: 484(t), 484(b); courtesy Barbara Hulanicki: 290(br); courtesy Barbara Hulanicki: 291; Hulton Getty: 15, 31, 42, 44–5, 52(tl), 361, 366; Hulton Getty/Steve Eason: 462; Hulton Getty/Bert Hardy: 365; Hulton Getty/Reg Lancaster: 466; Hulton Getty/Michael Lawn: 78; courtesy Lauren Hutton: 128; courtesy *i-D* Magazine: 209; courtesy *i-D* Magazine/Marc Lebon: 180; courtesy *i-D* Magazine/Carter Smith: 210; courtesy *i-D* Magazine/Juergen Teller: 214(t); courtesy *i-D* Magazine/Travis: 215; courtesy Donna Karan/Peter Lindbergh: 271; courtesy Steven Klein Studio, New York: 414–15; © William Klein: 57, 125; photo Peter Knapp: 41, 51, 119(tl), 196, 199, 201, 283, 285, 322, 402–03, 404, 407, 436; courtesy Peter Knapp: 200(b); courtesy Peter Knapp: 200(t); photo Nick Knight: 137, 151(b), 178, 179, 184, 208, 212–13, 220, 312, 313, 343, 396, 397, 420, 421, 423, 449(tl); Kobal Collection: 38(tl); Kobal Collection/Clarence Sinclair Bull: 250(t); Kobal Collection/Bud Fraker: 39, 69, 71; Kobal Collection/Laszlo Willinger: 251; courtesy Krizia, Milan: 328; courtesy Krizia, Milan/G. Castel: 390; courtesy Krizia, Milan/Patrick Demarchelier: 245, 263; courtesy Christian Lacroix/© Alain-Charles Beau: 99; Christian Lacroix/Guy Marineau: 98, 344 (1st row left), (4th row left), (5th row right); photo Barry Lategan: 120, 121, 135, 279, 289, 323, 324–5, 426, 437; courtesy Polo Ralph Lauren/Bruce Weber: 81, 270, 297; Ellison Lee/Mikael Jansson: 149, 262, 346, 488–9; Ellison Lee/Tim Richmond: 399; courtesy Alexander

Liberman/Grigsby: 202(bl); Lighthouse Artists Management, Paris/Peter Lindberg: 221, 432, 433; courtesy Svetlana Lloyd: 11, 124; courtesy Svetlana Lloyd/Michel Molinare: 114; courtesy Svetlana Lloyd/Roy Round: 394; Camilla Lowther Management/Lee Jenkins: 316–17; Camilla Lowther Management/Perry Ogden: 341, 345, 348(tr), 463; Camilla Lowther Management/Christophe Rihet: 187, 453(br); © Craig McDean, New York: 158, 227, 231(tl), 444–5; courtesy Donna McDonna: 371(tr); photo Niall McInerney: 311, 314, 315, 326, 327, 331, 347(b), 380(tm), 380(br), 383, 387, 391, 416; © Frances McLaughlin-Gill, New York: 16, 17, 115, 117, 204, 205; Magnum Photos/© Ferdinando Scianna: 233; courtesy Steen Sundland Studio: 338; courtesy Martin Margiela/© Ronald Stoops: 455(m); courtesy Martin Margiela/© Tatsuya Kitayama: 455(tr); courtesy Martin Margiela/© Jean-Claude Coutasse: 456–7; © Duane Michals, New York: 254, 255; © Miyake Design Studio: 442–3; © Miyake Design Studio 1988/Tsutomu Wakatsuki: 409; Issey Miyake/Philippe Brazil: 440(tl); Issey Miyake/Kazumi Kurigami: 441; Issey Miyake/Noriaki Yokosuka: 438; © Ministère de la Culture, France (AFDPP)/Photo Studio Harcourt: 47; © Ministère de la Culture, France (AFDPP) France/Sam Lévin: 58–9; courtesy Claude Montana: 434, 435; photo Sarah Moon: 172; © Chris Moore: 410; courtesy Moschino: 195; courtesy Moschino/Arnaldo Castoldi: 226; courtesy Thierry Mugler: 234; © Jeremy Murch: 21; courtesy Nike/Frederika Helwig: 491; L'Officiel/Claude Guegan: 336; photo Terry O'Neill: 60, 64–5, 72, 73, 122, 123(mr), 123(r), 129, 132–3, 144, 287, 290(tl), 370, 371(ml), 375, 377; PA News Photo Library/Neil Munns: 151(t); courtesy Gladys Perint Palmer: 167; Photofest: 38(m), 38(bl), 43, 62(b), 70; © Photographische Sammlung/SK Stiftung Kultur – August Sander Archiv, Cologne 355; photo Platon: 77, 105, 439; courtesy Emilio Pucci SRL: 37; courtesy Emilio Pucci SRL/Toni Frissell: 36; courtesy Mary Quant: 50(l), 50(mr), 50(r); courtesy Mary Quant/David Bailey: 50(m); courtesy Mary Quant/William Claxton: 50(ml); Rex Features: 61, 250(br); Rex Features/Peter Brooker: 152(mr); Rex Features/Camera 5: 38(bmr); Rex Features/Hamai: 66, 67, 74 Rex Features/Dave Lewis: 152(ml); Rex Features/Frank Monaco: 54–5; Rex Features/Ezio Praturlon: 38(br); Rex Features/David Redfern: 62(tl), 62(r); Rex Features/Sipa: 48–9; Rex Features/Sipa/Olympia: 152(tr); Rex Features/Sipa/Sichov: 103; Rex Features/Sipa/Tabak/Sunshine: 152(bl); photo Bettina Rheims: 143, 405 photo Derek Ridgers: 372, 373, 374, 376(t), 379, 398(tr); courtesy Herb Ritts Studio: 231(br); photo Paolo Roversi: 110, 190, 191, 222, 224, 309, 339, 427, 449(r); courtesy Jil Sander/David Sims: 278, 280, 281, 354(br); Yves Saint Laurent Archives: 101, 298, 299, 340; Yves Saint Laurent Archives/Pierre Boulat: 94; Yves Saint Larent Archives/Guy Bourdin: 300; Yves Saint Laurent Archives/Jean-Paul Cadé: 337; © Francesco Scavullo: 96; Marina Schinz, New York/© Erwin Blumenfeld Estate: 171; Scoop (Paris Match)/Manuel Litran: 409(t); photo Jeanloup Sieff: 23, 46, 92, 93, 119(br), 197, 206, 288, 408; photo David Sims: 145, 150, 155, 188, 223; Smile Management/Mario Sorrenti: 113; courtesy of Sotheby's London/© Cecil Beaton Archive: 20, 79, 430; photo Patrice Stable: 406; courtesy Staley-Wise Gallery, New York/Genevieve Naylor: 25; courtesy Staley-Wise Gallery, New York/Louise Dahl-Wolfe Estate: 27, 123(ml); Streeters Ltd/Miles Aldridge: 148, 185, 319, 350–1; Streeters Ltd/Marcus Tomlinson: 239, 242, 412; Streeters Ltd/Marcus Tomlinson/Stylist Soraya Dayani: 186, 218; courtesy Stüssy/Juergen Teller: 476, 477; Sygma/© Grazia

Neri: 84–5; photo Mario Testino (Arena Homme Plus, Spring/Summer 1999 edition)/Stylist Carine Roitfeld: 159; photo Mario Testino (Visionaire No.18 'The Fashion Issue'), published September 1996/Fashion Yves Saint Laurent/Stylist Carine Roitfeld: 238; courtesy Josephus Thimister/© Erin Morin: 458(t); courtesy Josephus Thimister/© Frédérique Dumoulin (Java): 458(b); courtesy Christine Tidmarsh/Mike de Dulmen, Paris: 18, 19; photo Deborah Turbeville: 173(tr); courtesy of Valentino Archives: 95(bl), 165; courtesy Walter Van Beirendonck/Jean-Baptiste Mondino: 401(t); courtesy Walter Van Beirendonck/Ronald Stoops: 401(br); courtesy Van Cleef & Arpels/© All rights reserved: 123(l); courtesy Dries Van Noten: 334, 335; courtesy Versace Archives/D. Ordway: 140–1; courtesy Versace Archives/Richard Avedon: 225, 264, 265, 417; courtesy Albert Watson Photography Inc.: 100; © Bruce Weber: 175, 176, 177; © Wolford/Helmut Newton: 389; photo Robert Wyatt: 418; Z Photographic/Donald Christie: 465, 475, 486, 487; Z Photographic/Martina Hoogland Ivanow: 243; Z Photographic/Juergen Teller: 189, 230; courtesy Zoran srl/John Moe: 256

Author's Acknowledgements

For Laurie Purden

This book was first conceived by Richard Schlagman and developed in conversations with David Jenkins, whose enthusiasm for the project equalled mine. In the long gestation and writing time, David moved on from Phaidon but the role of encourager and comforter which such a large project requires was taken on with great involvement by Tamasin Doe and later by Vivian Constantinopoulos. But it is to Cleia Smith that I owe the greatest editorial debt. Admirably rational in her judgement and patient in her determination to make the book as good as it possibly could be, she was firm and fair in her rejections as well as her acceptances. Never heavy-handed, she steered the project to its complex conclusion with tact and humour. Thanks must also go to Fabien Baron, who art directed the book; to Joseph Logan, who designed it; and to Alex Myers and Philippa Thomson who carried out the picture research. Philippa's sharp eye is seen in the merest flick through this book. As a picture editor, she was resourceful, intelligent and able to solve problems long before they reached me. That being said, there was one disappointment. I regret that, despite long negotiations with Helmut Newton, with tactful help from his London agent, Tiggy Mackonohie, we were unable to obtain two pictures I very much wished to use. I apologize to readers for this omission.

I would like to thank Audrey Cooke and Christina Motley for vital help with preparing the manuscript, but my real debt is to Sarah Halliwell who not only typed, but did sterling work in organizing the manuscript. Finally, as always with a book of this nature, I would like to acknowledge the assistance I have received from designers, fashion houses and PR organizers who often provided information at very short notice with great efficiency.

Phaidon Press Limited
Regent's Wharf
All Saints Street
London N1 9PA

First published 2000

© 2000 Phaidon Press Limited

ISBN 0 7148 3897 7

A CIP catalogue record for this book is available from the British Library

Printed in Hong Kong

Designed by Baron & Baron, Inc.